Radford's Artistic Homes

1908

A Schiffer Classic

Home of the Radford Publications: The Radford Building, 1827-29-31-33 Prairie Avenue, Chicago, Illinois.

Schiffer Publishing Ltd
4880 Lower Valley Road, Atglen, PA 19310 USA

Foreword by Tina Skinner

Library of Congress Control Number: 2001093351

Revised layout by Bonnie M. Hensley
Revised cover designed by Bruce M. Waters

ISBN: 0-7643-1455-6
Printed in China

Published by Schiffer Publishing Ltd.
4880 Lower Valley Road
Atglen, PA 19310
Phone: (610) 593-1777; Fax: (610) 593-2002
E-mail: Schifferbk@aol.com
Please visit our web site catalog at **www.schifferbooks.com**
We are always looking for people to write books on new and related subjects. If you have an idea for a book please contact us at the above address.

This book may be purchased from the publisher.
Include $3.95 for shipping.
Please try your bookstore first.
You may write for a free catalog.

In Europe, Schiffer books are distributed by
Bushwood Books
6 Marksbury Ave.
Kew Gardens
Surrey TW9 4JF England
Phone: 44 (0) 20 8392-8585; Fax: 44 (0) 20 8392-9876
E-mail: Bushwd@aol.com
Free postage in the U.K., Europe; air mail at cost.

More Schiffer Titles

www.schifferbooks.com

Outdoor Wood Works
With Complete Plans for Ten Projects
Tina Skinner

A collection of ideas for improving the environment around the house. Hundreds of ideas are presented in full-color photographs. Permanent outdoor fixtures like benches and gazebos make the environs more comfortable, while flower boxes, retaining walls, and other accents add beauty. Ten complete project plans, from a simple screen around a utility box to an outdoor storage shed, are included.

Size: 8 1/2" x 11" | 146 color photos | 160 pp.
ISBN: 0-7643-0446-1 | hard cover | $19.95

Great Kitchen Designs
A Visual Feast of Ideas and Resources
Tina Skinner

370 full-color pictures of hundreds of beautiful kitchens to help you create your own unique cooking/dining/entertaining environment. All the elements of beautiful kitchens—flooring, cabinetry, windows, walls, lighting, appliances, surrounds, backsplashes and more—are pictured and discussed. Includes a special chapter on the small kitchen, plus a resource guide listing designers and manufacturers. An invaluable resource for anyone planning to remodel an old kitchen or build a new one and a great reference book for kitchen design professionals.

Size: 8 1/2" x 11" | 370 color photos | 176 pp.
ISBN: 0-7643-1211-1 | soft cover | $29.95

Garden Projects for the Backyard Carpenter
Tina Skinner

Thirty great project ideas! Illustrations and step-by-step instructions make it easy to create over 30 projects: decks and shade shelters, gazebos, work and storage areas, decorative arbors, planter boxes and garden borders, benches and a swing, a picnic table, doghouses, and a bluebird nesting box.

Size: 8 1/2" x 11" | 438 photos | 112 pp.
ISBN: 0-7643-1234-0 | soft cover | $19.95

Creative Patios
Tina Skinner

This collection of beautiful photographs will help you choose a patio style suitable for your home, speak your contractor's language, furnish and organize outdoor areas, create containers and border areas for dynamic gardens and landscaping displays, and develop outdoor sanctuaries with artfully placed planter boxes, shrubs, and privacy screens. Includes step-by-step instructions for installing a paver patio.

Size: 8 1/2" x 11" | 310 photos | 192 pp.
Resource Guide
ISBN: 0-7643- 1278-2 | soft cover | $29.95

The Virginia House
A Home for Three Hundred Years
Anne M. Faulconer

Illustrated with over 200 color photographs, this survey of Tidewater Virginia homes from 1640 to 1830 shows tiny cottages and great plantation houses set in formal gardens with an emphasis on small dwellings which are affordable, full of history, and suitable for 20th century life. Floor plans and details enable the reader to build his own Virginia dream house or renovate to project a genteel Virginian image.

Size: 8 1/2" x 11" | 200 color plates/50 b/w drawings (HABS)
Index | 192 pp.
ISBN: 0-7643-0598-0 | soft cover | $19.95

The Cape Cod House
Stanley Schuler

Designed for those who may wish to build their own Cape Cod home, here are many variations of the basic floor plan, plus 174 photos to show the nearly limitless possibilities this traditional style home offers. Examples range from tiny single style to double, triple, modified, and "modern" interpretations. The Cape Cod house is clearly adaptable to every taste and every budget.

Size: 8 1/2" x 11" | 174 photos | 144 pp.
Index
ISBN: 0-916838-63-3 | hard cover | $25.00

Saltbox and Cape Cod Houses
Revised and Expanded 2nd Edition
Stanley Schuler

Homes in traditional Saltbox and Cape Cod styles are being built all over America because the designs embody a practical and unassuming charm. Here are examples of old traditional styles and newer adaptations portrayed in over 270 color photos. The uncomplicated, sensible two-story floor plans of both of these New England types have endeared them to home builders since the 1600s, and with few adaptations they are perfectly suited to the modern tastes.

Size: 8 1/2" x 11" | 276 photos | 160 pp.
Index
ISBN: 0-7643-0998-6 | hard cover | $29.95

Yesterday's Structures: Today's Homes
Lucy D. Rosenfeld

56 innovative adaptations of old, abandoned structures into modern family homes, apartments, and condominiums are displayed in more than 290 images and plans. Among the structures restored to use are churches, schools, factories, barns, a light house, a giant gas tank, and even a missile silo. This fascinating text is divided between structures retrofitted for single family living and larger buildings adapted to multi-family use. The projects also range from commercial enterprises quickly completed to personal labors of love that have taken some twenty-five years of work.

Size: 8 1/2" x 11" | over 305 color photos | 176 pp.
ISBN: 0-7643-1014-3 | hard cover | $39.95

Old New England Homes
Revised and Expanded 2nd Edition
Stanley Schuler

Colonial, Georgian, Federal, and Victorian homes presented with an informative and readable text and 245 color photos. Various aspects and angles of the buildings are shown, in addition to the beautiful frontal views. Floor plans are given for many of the homes, making this new edition an important book for architects and potential home owners alike.

Size: 8 1/2" x 11" | 438 photos | 224 pp.
Index
ISBN: 0-7643-0995-1 | hard cover | $35.00

Architectural Details from Old New England Homes
Revised and Expanded 3rd Edition
Stanley Schuler

Over 350 color and black-and-white photographs show the various architectural styles of old New England homes with special attention to the details. A supporting text explains the history and significance of the style. Architectural drawings provide close-up views of fireplaces, doorways, windows, stairs, and cupboards built in the 17th, 18th, and 19th centuries.

Size: 8 1/2" x 11" | 350+ photos | 176 pp.
Index
ISBN: 0-7643-0981-1 | soft cover | $29.95

Design.	Page.	Price, Plans and Specifications.	Estimated Cost. From About.	To About.
7008	65	$15.00	$2,500.00	$2,750.00
7009	140	12.00	1,750.00	1,900.00
7010	29	12.00	2,075.00	2,225.00
7011	164	15.00	3,350.00	3,550.00
7012	36	12.00	1,650.00	1,850.00
7013	37	10.00	1,750.00	1,950.00
7014	20	12.00	1,700.00	1,850.00
7015	21	10.00	1,750.00	1,900.00
7017	103	15.00	2,050.00	2,200.00
7020	216	12.00	1,950.00	2,150.00
7022	80	15.00	3,100.00	3,350.00
7024	55	10.00	1,350.00	1,500.00
7025	237	12.00	1,225.00	1,400.00
7026	176	12.00	2,200.00	2,400.00
7031	249	12.00	2,100.00	2,300.00
7032	97	15.00	2,050.00	2,400.00
7033	248	12.00	1,950.00	2,200.00
7034	119	15.00	5,250.00	5,500.00
7036	72	15.00	2,175.00	2,375.00
7037	129	12.00	1,875.00	2,125.00
7039	201	15.00	1,950.00	2,200.00
7041	46	12.00	1,700.00	1,850.00
7042	236	12.00	1,850.00	2,050.00
7046	190	15.00	2,150.00	2,350.00
7048	131	15.00	2,400.00	2,600.00
7049	211	15.00	2,550.00	2,800.00
7050	152	12.00	1,950.00	2,150.00
7053	255	15.00	2,275.00	2,425.00
7054	28	15.00	2,775.00	2,925.00
7056	142	15.00	2,175.00	2,325.00
7058	228	12.00	1,450.00	1,600.00
7059	242	20.00	2,675.00	2,900.00
7060	155	15.00	1,700.00	1,900.00
7062	128	12.00	1,950.00	2,200.00
7065	143	15.00	2,700.00	2,950.00
7066	102	12.00	2,350.00	2,550.00
7068	118	12.00	2,150.00	2,325.00
7069	191	12.00	1,475.00	1,625.00
7070	200	12.00	1,700.00	1,850.00
7071	153	10.00	2,150.00	2,325.00
7072	130	15.00	2,150.00	2,350.00
7073	13	15.00	2,250.00	2,450.00
7075	243	15.00	3,550.00	3,750.00
7076	64	12.00	1,975.00	2,125.00
7077	229	12.00	2,175.00	2,325.00
7078	210	12.00	2,250.00	2,450.00
7079	12	12.00	2,350.00	2,600.00
7080	167	12.00	1,900.00	2,050.00
7082	254	15.00	2,450.00	2,700.00
7083	100	10.00	1,850.00	2,050.00
7084	47	12.00	1,900.00	2,100.00
7085	81	12.00	2,100.00	2,300.00
7086	101	12.00	1,150.00	1,300.00
7087	188	15.00	2,000.00	2,250.00
7088	179	10.00	1,550.00	1,700.00
7089	189	12.00	1,400.00	1,600.00
7090	177	12.00	2,250.00	2,350.00
7091	231	10.00	1,550.00	1,650.00
7092	73	15.00	2,150.00	2,350.00
7093	54	10.00	1,375.00	1,525.00
7094	154	12.00	1,850.00	2,100.00
7095	141	12.00	1,775.00	1,925.00
7096	165	12.00	2,175.00	2,325.00
7099	233	10.00	1,350.00	1,500.00
9001	86	20.00	4,175.00	4,460.00

Design.	Page.	Price, Plans and Specifications.	Estimated Cost. From About.	To About.
9002	183	$15.00	$2,750.00	$3,160.00
9003	148	15.00	2,300.00	2,600.00
9004	149	15.00	2,650.00	2,950.00
9005	171	15.00	2,500.00	2,750.00
9006	134	12.00	2,100.00	2,350.00
9007	35	15.00	3,200.00	3,600.00
9010	34	15.00	2,460.00	2,640.00
9011	158	15.00	2,450.00	2,800.00
9012	206	15.00	2,750.00	3,000.00
9013	159	15.00	3,250.00	3,560.00
9014	19	12.00	1,700.00	1,850.00
9015	184	12.00	1,650.00	1,930.00
9016	109	12.00	2,200.00	2,450.00
9019	108	12.00	2,150.00	2,300.00
9020	9	15.00	2,400.00	2,650.00
9021	196	12.00	1,800.00	2,160.00
9022	245	12.00	1,875.00	2,000.00
9024	11	15.00	2,460.00	2,650.00
9025	214	12.00	1,750.00	1,940.00
9028	110	15.00	2,600.00	2,775.00
9030	122	12.00	1,750.00	1,950.00
9031	62	10.00	1,500.00	1,650.00
9034	207	12.00	1,850.00	1,950.00
9035	244	10.00	1,650.00	1,875.00
9037	113	12.00	1,750.00	1,900.00
9038	197	15.00	2,050.00	2,200.00
9039	10	12.00	2,650.00	2,800.00
9040	204	12.00	2,050.00	2,340.00
9041	220	12.00	1,650.00	1,850.00
9043	43	12.00	1,800.00	1,950.00
9044	170	12.00	2,100.00	2,350.00
9045	146	10.00	1,700.00	1,950.00
9048	27	12.00	1,600.00	1,850.00
9049	111	12.00	1,730.00	1,950.00
9050	26	10.00	1,540.00	1,730.00
9051	185	12.00	1,850.00	2,160.00
9053	147	12.00	1,730.00	1,850.00
9054	160	12.00	1,700.00	1,950.00
9055	215	12.00	1,550.00	1,675.00
9056	161	12.00	1,450.00	1,750.00
9057	173	10.00	1,400.00	1,650.00
9059	256	12.00	2,000.00	2,250.00
9060	112	10.00	1,450.00	1,630.00
9061	125	12.00	1,750.00	1,975.00
9063	195	12.00	1,700.00	1,950.00
9064	87	12.00	2,650.00	3,050.00
9066	18	12.00	2,450.00	2,675.00
9067	182	15.00	2,150.00	2,300.00
9069	135	12.00	2,200.00	2,430.00
9071	251	12.00	2,250.00	2,460.00
9072	250	12.00	2,750.00	3,050.00
9073	257	12.00	1,950.00	2,100.00
9076	221	12.00	1,950.00	2,100.00
9077	63	12.00	1,650.00	1,930.00
9078	124	12.00	2,350.00	2,475.00
9079	90	10.00	1,275.00	1,500.00
9080	52	12.00	1,575.00	1,750.00
9081	91	10.00	750.00	950.00
9083	123	12.00	1,475.00	1,730.00
9084	205	10.00	1,450.00	1,650.00
9089	53	10.00	1,250.00	1,400.00
9092	172	10.00	1,550.00	1,725.00
9093	42	15.00	1,850.00	2,100.00
9094	194	12.00	1,850.00	2,175.00
9519	136	22.00	6,475.00	6,875.00
9515	137	26.00	3,150.00	3,550.00

INDEX

Foreword

American life was changing drastically at the start of the new century – in the early 1900s. The middle class exploded between 1900 and 1917. Apartment dwellers were able to buy homes for the first time and were moving to new housing developments in cities and suburbs, made more accessible by improved public transport and the growing presence of the automobile.

To meet the demand for new housing, companies sprang up to supply ready-made home kits and house blueprints. From catalogs and publications like *Radford's Artistic Homes*, potential home owners could choose their dream home and purchase plans or even complete house kits. The mail-order business reached its greatest popularity between 1910 and 1930, with an estimated 500,000 such homes produced between 1900 and 1939.

Magazines targeted toward housewives began to advertise home plans, selling blueprints or even "redi-cut" home kits. These kits were popular because they allowed new homeowners to buy their home in stages, a necessity since long-term mortgages were not available at this time. Major mail order companies jumped into the fray — Sears and Roebuck began selling house kits in 1908, and Montgomery Ward offered house plans in 1910, kits in 1918.

The Radford Architectural Company of Chicago stayed out of the kit business, advertising itself as the "Largest Architectural Establishment in the World." Radford is largely responsible for many of the homes, commercial buildings, and even barns built in the early years of this century. Drive down any older residential area in any major U.S. city, and you'll see examples of homes like those illustrated in this book.

Radford's target customer was an expanding middle class, with a patriarch who headed off to work every morning, and a matriarch who stayed home to run the house alone. Servants were becoming too expensive for the average household, and home design was scaling down to help overworked housewives. Fancy parlors and sitting rooms were being abandoned for "living rooms," and the servant's quarters were being dropped at the same time kitchens were scaled down to accommodate a single worker — mom.

This is the era of the bungalows – humble, single-story structures that cropped up by the thousands across the country. There are many examples of bungalows in this book, with creative variations that were marketed toward those willing to spend a little more for something really special. These houses are primarily two-story single family homes for those with upper-middle class means, though most of the designs still emphasize family over formal entertaining areas.

When this book first came out, in 1908, it was touted as the "largest single book of house designs ever published." Here are 252 renderings of homes deemed most desirable in the turn-of-the-century market. Radford's architects created "the newest and most up-to-date designs in modern homes" for this catalog. The floor plans and architectural renderings were published in hard cover book form, much like those published in Home Plans books on the market today, and for an additional fee of $10 or so, future homeowners could own the blueprints to their dream house. At the back of this book, Radford even offered consumers the chance to sketch out their own ideas on graph paper, with customized pencil drawings of floor plans and elevations to follow for a fee of $10.

The Great Depression dealt a deadly blow to domestic building in general. Housing starts fell 90 percent between 1925 and 1933, and by the time the country emerged from World War II, affordable mass-produced suburban tract houses were the norm, designed and financed by local entrepreneurs. Presumably, this marked the end of Radford Architectural Co., as well. Their legacy lives on, however, in these hundreds of home plans, documenting American architecture at the turn of the century.

—Tina Skinner

Radford's Artistic Homes

The Americans are a nation of home builders. A man's standing in any community is based largely on the kind of house he lives in. If it is his own home he enjoys an importance that does not attach to the man who pays rent. The instinct of home owning is as natural as the air we breathe. From the bird of the air who builds her nest in the spring to man, the king of all, it finds expression in various forms.

One may wonder, in glancing over the beautiful structures shown in this book, at the marvelous advance made in home architecture in recent years. It is not a difficult stretch of imagination between the makeshift habitations of the early days to the beautiful habitations of comfort and luxury shown in these pages, yet it has been a development slow and sure, keeping pace with the advancement of the race along all lines.

It will be noticed, in glancing over the pages of this book, that there is a wide diversity of design shown in the houses. This is done deliberately, as the taste in home architecture is as wide as that in any other field. There are houses for people of moderate means and there are others for the more wealthy. But in every case the design is made with reference to convenience and economy, and no pains or expense has been spared in their preparation.

We would have you know that every design shown is made by the best architects in the world, who have made a study of home architecture and that alone. So that what you see here represents the best that possibly could be secured. During the many months that it has been in preparation the volume has received the benefit of the most careful attention and many designs have been rejected to make place for others that were considered better. In a word, it is the best that could be secured.

Now, the purpose in presenting this book to the public at this time is to make more easy the problem of house building for the dweller in rural communities, in small towns and in cities, for there are designs here that will be found adapted to any community. In selecting the design of a house there are a number of factors that should be taken into consideration. The size of the lot, the possible slope of the ground and the surrounding buildings have much to do with the design. In other words, the artistic sense will direct the selection of a design that will be in harmony with the surroundings. These are things that should be considered at the outset, for the selection of the design indeed is the most important feature of the problem. Pick a design that assures plenty of room for the needs of the family, and even of its future needs. It will not be necessary to consider the matter of convenience, for the architects have

solved that problem for you in every case. Every house is planned from the inside and not from the outside; that is to say, the convenience of arrangement has been the first consideration, and we believe this fact will be appreciated by the wives and daughters.

Now, as to the location of the house, it should not be placed in the middle of the lot. To provide lawn room and a place for shrubbery and flower beds the house should be at one side or well back so that when the lawn decorations are placed the picture will be artistic and the grounds will seem to be really a part of the house. Often this point is overlooked and an otherwise stylish house is ruined by being out of harmony with the lot on which it sits.

A man who builds a home owes a duty not alone to his family and himself, but he is under a moral obligation to the community as well. What we mean by this statement is that no man has a moral right to build a house that will be unworthy of the community in which he lives or which, by its lack of style, will tend to depreciate the value of property in the neighborhood. In house building, as in all other things in which men engage, the purpose should be improvement and betterment. So we advocate only a house built from accurately drawn plans, a house with style.

As the house may be the habitation of the family for life, no greater calamity in a material way can befall the owner than to discover when the house is complete that it is faulty in arrangement or in appearance. This is apt to be the case with a house built without plans. On the other hand, it is a source of constant joy and satisfaction to live in a house that is properly constructed from accurately drawn plans and which is worthy of the neighborhood.

Let us impress upon your mind one vital thing. NEVER build a house without plans to work from. It is hardly necessary to tell you that no more foolish thing is ever done by a man than to try to build without plans or with rough pencil sketches that are just as bad. We could show you in our files thousands of letters from persons who have ordered plans after failing miserably in their efforts to build without accurate drawings. Here are some of the things that happen to the man who tries to build without plans: His house lacks style, that peculiarly pleasing aspect that is only possible in a house built from an accurate design. He wastes materials. He wastes the time of his workmen. He wastes nervous energy in worry over mistakes, and when the house is done, if it ever is, he has a monstrosity that people laugh at as they go along the street. This window will not be square and that floor will not be level, and worst of all, he himself will be dissatisfied with it.

Now, every design in this book is drawn with a faithful regard for mathematical accuracy, and there is no error to bother the builder. It is safe to say that the saving in materials that will result from building after any of these plans will more than pay the price of them. So be sure you start right—build only with accurately drawn plans.

We Illustrate in this Book

the perspective view and floor plans of over 250 low and medium-priced houses. In the preparation of this work great care has been exercised in the selection of original, practical and attractive house designs, such as seventy-five to ninety per cent of the people to-day wish to build. In drawing these plans special effort has been made to provide for the MOST ECONOMICAL CONSTRUCTION, thereby giving the home builder and contractor the benefit of the saving of many dollars; for in no case have we put any useless expense upon the building simply to carry out some pet idea. Every plan illustrated will show, by the complete working plans and specifications, that we give you designs that will work out to the best advantage and will give you the most for your money; besides every bit of space has been utilized to the best advantage.

$100.00 Plans for only $10.00

This department has for its foundation the best equipped architectural establishment ever maintained for the purpose of furnishing the public with complete working plans and specifications at the remarkably low price of only $7.00 to $15.00 per set. Every plan we illustrate has been designed by a licensed architect, who stands at the head of his profession in this particular class of work and has made a specialty of low and medium-priced houses. The price usually charged for this work is from $75.00 to $100.00.

What We Give You

The first question you will ask is, "What do we get in these complete working plans and specifications? Of what do they consist? Are they the cheap printed plans on tissue paper without details or specifications?" We do not blame you for wishing to know what you will get for your money.

Blue Printed Working Plans

The plans we send out are the regular blue printed plans, drawn one-quarter inch scale to the foot,.showing all the elevations, floor plans and necessary interior details. All of our plans are printed by electricity on an electric circular blue-printing machine, and we use the very best grade of electric blue-printing paper; every line and figure showing perfect and distinct.

Foundation and Cellar Plans

This sheet shows the shape and size of all the walls, piers, footings, posts, etc., and of what materials they are constructed; shows the location of all windows, doors, chimneys, ash-pits, partitions, and the like. The different wall sections are given, showing their construction and measurements from all the different points.

Floor Plans

These plans show the shape and size of all rooms, halls and closets; the location and size of all doors and windows; the position of all plumbing fixtures, gas lights, registers, pantry work, etc., and all the measurements that are necessary are given.

Elevations

A front, right, left and rear elevation are furnished with all the plans. These drawings are complete and accurate in every respect. They show the shape, size and location of all doors, windows, porches, cornices, towers, bays, and the like; in fact, give you an exact scale picture of the house as it should be at completion. Full wall sections are given, showing the construction from foundation to roof, the height of stories between the joists, height of plates, pitch of roof, etc.

Roof Plan

This plan is furnished where the roof construction is at all intricate. It shows the location of all hips, valleys, ridges, decks, etc. All the above drawings are made to scale one-quarter inch to the foot.

Details All necessary details of the interior work, such as door and window casings and trim, base, stools, picture moulding, doors, newel posts, balusters, rails, etc., accompany each set of plans. Part is shown in full size, while some of the larger work, such as stair construction, is drawn to a scale of one and one-half inch to the foot. These blue-prints are substantially and artistically bound in cloth and heavy water-proof paper, making a handsome and durable covering and protection for the plans.

Specifications The specifications are typewritten on Lakeside Bond Linen paper, and are bound in the same artistic manner as the plans, the same cloth and water-proof paper being used. They consist of twenty-two pages of closely typewritten matter, giving full instructions for carrying out the work. All necessary directions are given in the clearest and most explicit manner, so that there can be no possibility of a misunderstanding.

Basis of Contract The working plans and specifications we furnish can be made the basis of contract between the home builder and the contractor. This will prevent mistakes, which cost money, and they will prevent disputes which are unforeseen and never settled satisfactorily to both parties. When no plans are used the contractor is often obliged to do some work he did not figure on, and the home builder often does not get as much for his money as he expected, simply because there was no basis on which to work and upon which to base the contract.

No Misunderstanding Can Arise when a set of our plans and specifications is before the contractor and the home builder, showing the interior and exterior construction of the house as agreed upon in the contract. Many advantages may be claimed for the complete plans and specifications. They are time savers, and, therefore, money savers. Workmen will not have to wait for instructions when a set of plans is left on the job. They will prevent mistakes in cutting lumber, in placing door and window frames, and in many other places where the contractor is not on the work and the men have received only partial or indefinite instructions. They also give instructions for the working of all material to the best advantage.

Free Plans for Fire Insurance Adjustment You take every precaution to have your house covered by insurance; but do you make any provision for the adjustm nt of the loss, should you have a fire? There is not one man in ten thousand who will provide for this embarrassing situation. You can call to mind instances in your own locality where settlements have been delayed because the insurance companies wanted some proof which could not be furnished. They demand proof of loss before paying insurance money, and they are entitled to it. We have provided for this and have inaugurated the following plan, which cannot but meet with favor by whoever builds a house from our plans.

Immediately Upon Receipt of Information from you that your house has been destroyed by fire, either totally or partially, we will forward you, free of cost, a duplicate set of plans and specifications, and in addition we will furnish an affidavit giving the number of the design and the date when furnished, to be used for the adjustment of the insurance.

Without One Cent of Cost to You and without one particle of trouble. We keep a record of the number of the house design and the date it was furnished, so that, in time of

loss, all it will be necessary for you to do is to drop us a line and we will furnish the only reliable method of getting a speedy and satisfactory adjustment. This may be the means of saving you hundreds of dollars, besides much time and worry.

Our Liberal Prices

Many have marveled at our ability to furnish such excellent and complete working plans and specification at such low prices. We do not wonder at this, because we charge but $7.00 to $15.00 for a more complete set of working plans and specifications than you would receive if ordered in the ordinary manner, and when drawn especially for you, at a cost of from seventy-five to one hundred dollars. On account of our large business and unusual equipment, and owing to the fact that WE DIVIDE THE COST of these plans among so many, it is possible for us to sell them at these low prices. The margin of profit is very close, but it enables us to sell thousands of sets of plans, which save many times their cost to both the owner and the contractor in erecting even the smallest dwelling.

Our Guarantee

Perhaps there are many who feel that they are running some risk in ordering plans at a distance. We wish to assure our customers that there is no risk whatever. If, upon receipt of these plans, you do not find them exactly as represented, if you do not find them complete and accurate in every respect, if you do not find them as well prepared as those furnished by any architect in the country, or any that you have ever seen, we will refund your money upon the return of the plans from you in perfect condition. All of our plans are prepared by architects standing at the head of their profession, and the standard of their work is the very highest. We could not afford to make this guarantee if we were not positive that we were furnishing the best plans put out in this country, even though our price is not more than one-seventh to one-tenth of the price usually charged.

Bill of Material

We do not furnish a bill of material. We state this here particularly, as some people have an idea that a bill of material should accompany each set of plans and specifications. In the first place, our plans are gotten up in a very comprehensive manner, so that any carpenter can easily take off the bill of material without any difficulty. We realize that there are hardly two sections of the country where exactly the same kinds of materials are used, and, moreover, a bill which we might furnish would not be applicable in all sections of the country. We furnish plans and specifications for houses which are built as far north as the Hudson Bay and as far south as the Gulf of Mexico. They are built upon the Atlantic and Pacific Coasts. and you can also find them in Australia and South Africa. Each country and section of a country has its peculiarities as to sizes and qualities; therefore, it would be useless for us to make a list that would not be universal. Our houses, when completed, may look the same whether they are built in Canada or Florida, but the same materials will not be used, for the reason that the customs of the people and the climatic conditions will dictate the kind and amount of materials to be used in their construction.

Estimated Cost

It is impossible for anyone to estimate the cost of a building and have the figures hold good in all sections of the country. We do not claim to be able to do it. The estimated cost of the houses we illustrate is based on the most favorable conditions in all respects, and includes everything but the plumbing and heating. We are not familiar with your local conditions, and, should we claim to know the exact cost of a building in your locality, a child would know that our statement was false. We leave this matter in the hands of the reliable contractors. for they. and they alone. know your local conditions.

We Wish to be Frank With You and therefore make no statement that we cannot substantiate in every respect. If a plan in this book pleases you; if the arrangement of the rooms is satisfactory, and if the exterior is pleasing and attractive, then we make this elaim—that it can be built as eheaply as if any other architect designed it, and we believe cheaper.

We Have Studied Economy in construction, and our knowledge of all the material that goes into a house qualifies us to give you the best for your money. We give you a plan that pleases you, one that is attractive, and one where every foot of space is utilized at the least possible cost. Can any architect do more, even at seven to ten times the price we charge you for plans?

Reversing Plans We receive many requests from our patrons for plans exactly according to the designs illustrated, with the one exception of having them reversed or placed in the opposite direction. It is impossible for us to make this change and draw new plans, except at a cost of about eight times our regular price. We see no reason why our regular plans will not answer your purpose. Your carpenter can face the house exactly as you wish it, and the plans will work out as well facing in one direction as in another. We can, however, if you wish, and so instruct us, make you a reversed blue-print and furnish it at our regular price; but in that case all the figures and letters will be reversed, and, therefore, liable to cause as much confusion as if your carpenter reversed the plan himself while constructing the house.

We Would Advise however, in all cases where the plan is to be reversed, and there is the least doubt about the contractor not being able to work from the plans as we have them, that two sets of blue-prints be purchased, one regular and the other reversed, and in such cases we will furnish two sets of blue-prints and one set of specifications for only fifty per cent added to the regular cost, making the $10.00 plan cost only $15.00.

Immediate Delivery Guaranteed Our equipment and facilities are such that we can send out the same day we receive order the complete plans and specifications for any house we illustrate. Delivery is made by express whenever possible, otherwise plans and specifications are forwarded by mail.

PUBLISHED BY

The Radford Architectural Co.

1827-29-31-33 Prairie Ave., Chicago, Illinois

Design No. 9020

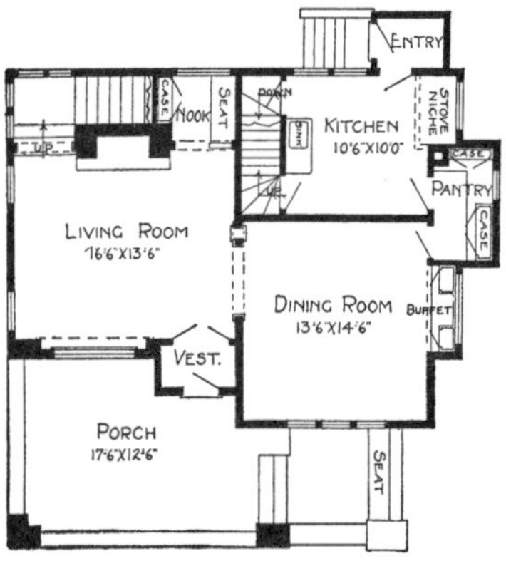

First Floor Plan.

The arrangement of this House is as follows:

FIRST FLOOR PLAN.

Living Room, 16 feet 6 inches by 13 feet 6 inches.
Dining Room, 13 feet 6 inches by 14 feet 6 inches.
Kitchen, 10 feet 6 inches by 10 feet.
Pantry and Front Porch.

SECOND FLOOR PLAN.

Bedroom, 12 feet by 13 feet.
Bedroom, 13 feet 6 inches by 14 feet 6 inches.
Bathroom, 10 feet 6 inches by 7 feet.
2 Closets.

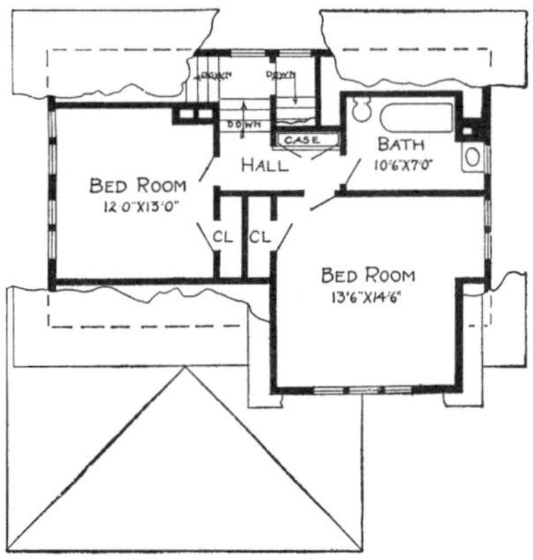

Second Floor Plan.

This Building is 36 feet 6 inches in width; 30 feet in length.

Price of Complete Working Plans and Specifications $15.00

The Blue Printed Working Plans for this House consist of basement plan; roof plan; first and second floor plans: front, right, left and rear elevations; wall sections and all necessary details.

The Typewritten Specifications contain all the necessary information for the proper construction of the House

Design No. 9039

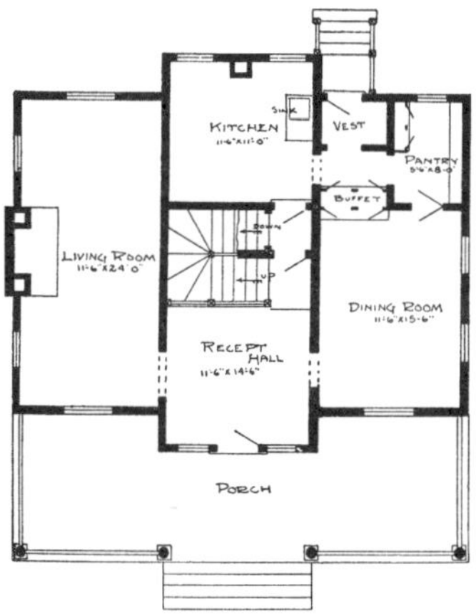

First Floor Plan.

The arrangement of this House is as follows:

FIRST FLOOR.

Reception Hall, 11 feet 6 inches by 14 feet 6 inches.
Living Room, 11 feet 6 inches by 24 feet.
Dining Room, 11 feet 6 inches by 15 feet 6 inches.
Kitchen, 11 feet 6 inches by 11 feet.
Pantry, Front and Rear Porches.

SECOND FLOOR.

Bedroom, 11 feet 6 inches by 14 feet.
Bedroom, 11 feet by 20 feet.
Sewing Room, 11 feet 6 inches by 6 feet 6 inches.
Bedroom, 11 feet 6 inches by 15 feet 6 inches.
Bathroom, 11 feet 6 inches by 8 feet.
4 Closets.

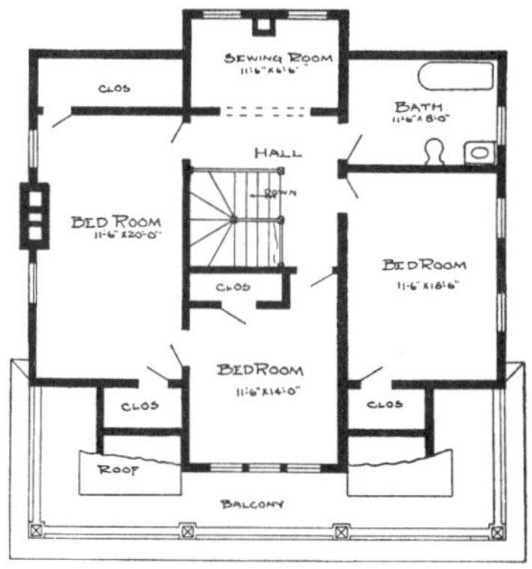

Second Floor Plan.

This Building is 37 feet in width; 31 feet 6 inches in length.

Price of Complete Working Plans and Specifications.................... $12.00

The Blue Printed Working Plans for this House consist of basement plan; roof plan; first and second floor plans; front, right, left and rear elevations; wall sections and all necessary details.

The Typewritten Specifications contain all the necessary information for the proper construction of the House.

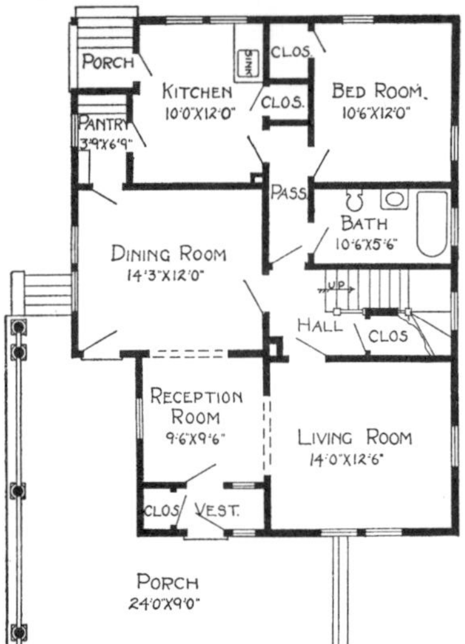

First Floor Plan.

Design No. 9024

The arrangement of this House is as follows:

FIRST FLOOR PLAN.

Reception Room, 9 feet 6 inches by 9 feet 6 inches.
Living Room, 14 feet by 12 feet 6 inches.
Dining Room, 14 feet 3 inches by 12 feet.
Kitchen, 10 feet by 12 feet.
Bedroom, 10 feet 6 inches by 12 feet.
Bathroom, 10 feet 6 inches by 5 feet 6 inches.
Pantry, Front and Rear Porches.

SECOND FLOOR PLAN.

Bedroom, 14 feet by 12 feet 6 inches.
Bedroom, 14 feet by 11 feet.
Store Room, 14 feet by 10 feet 6 inches.
8 Closets.

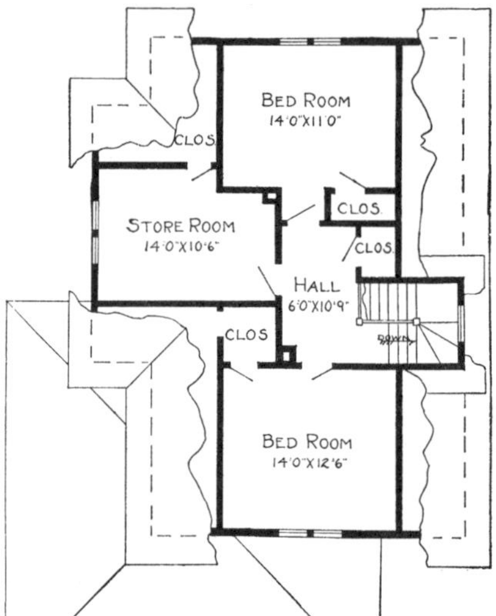

Second Floor Plan.

This Building is 30 feet in width; 39 feet in length.

Price of Complete Working Plans and Specifications $15.00

The Blue Printed Working Plans for this House consist of foundation plan, roof plan, first and second floor plans; front, right, left and rear elevations; wall sections and all necessary details.

The Typewritten Specifications contain all the necessary information for the proper construction of the House.

Design No. 7079

Size: Width, 28 feet; Length, 29 feet 6 inches, exclusiye of porches

PRICE

of Blue Prints, together with a complete set of typewritten specifications

ONLY TWELVE DOLLARS

We mail Plans and Specifications the same day order is received.

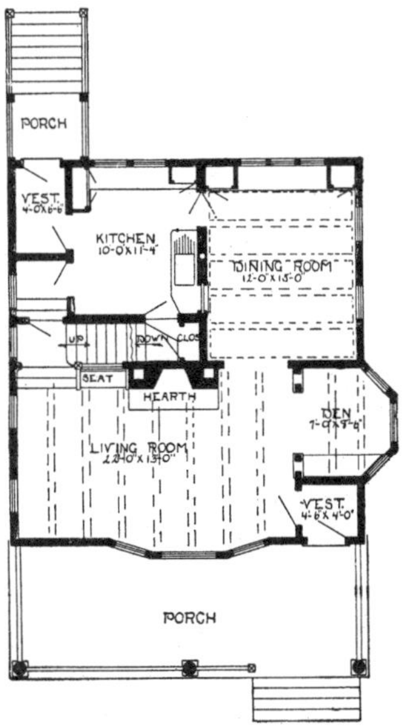

First Floor Plan

Blue prints consist of cellar and foundation plan; roof plan; first and second floor plans; front, rear, two side elevations; wall sections and all necessary interior details. Specifications consist of about twenty pages of typewritten matter.

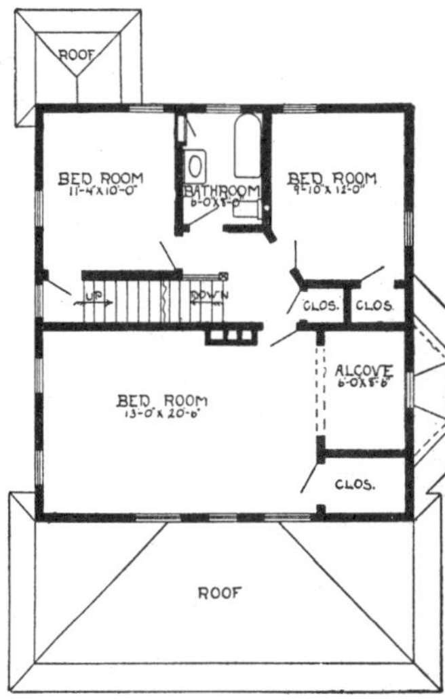

Second Floor Plan

Design No. 7073

Size: Width, 31 feet; length, 38 feet, exclusive of porches

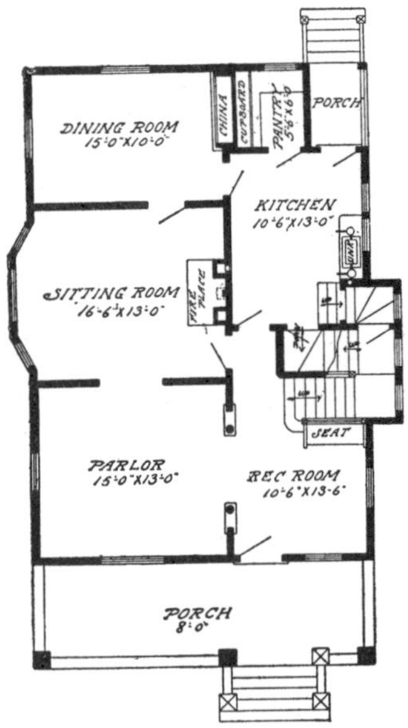

First Floor Plan.

Blue prints consist of cellar and foundation plan; roof plan; first and second floor plans; front, two side elevations; wall sections and all necessary interior details. Specifications consist of about twenty pages of typewritten matter.

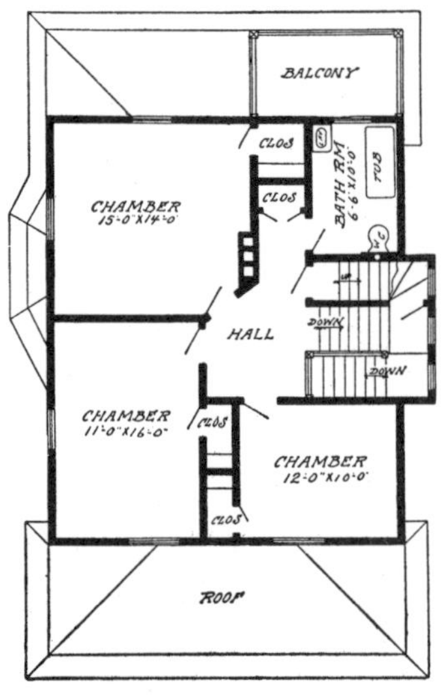

Second Floor Plan.

PRICE

of Blue Prints together with a complete set of typewritten specifications

ONLY FIFTEEN DOLLARS

We mail Plans and Specifications the same day order is received.

PRICE

of Blue Prints, together with a complete set of typewritten specifications is

ONLY TEN DOLLARS

We mail Plans and Specifications the same day order is received.

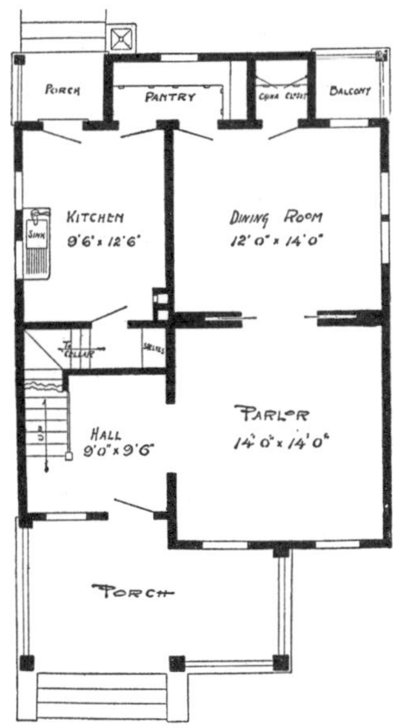

First Floor Plan

Design No. 95

Blue prints consist of cellar and foundation plan; first and second floor plans; front, rear, two side elevations; wall sections and all necessary interior details. Specifications consist of about twenty pages of typewritten matter.

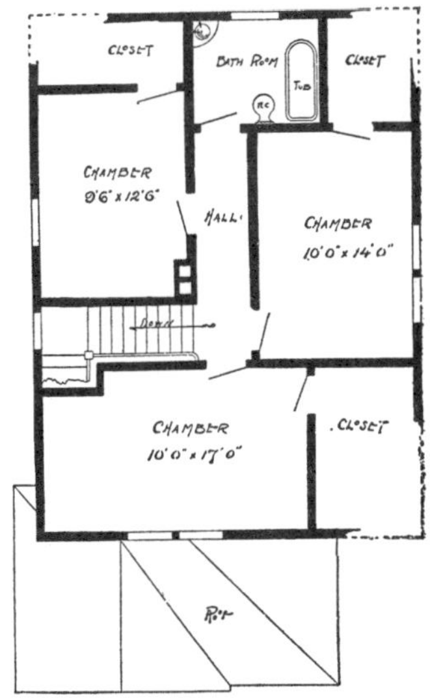

Second Floor Plan

Size: Width, 25 feet; length, 32 feet, exclusive of porches.

On account of our large business and unusual equipment, and owing to the fact that we divide the expense among so many, it is possible to sell at these low prices, give such excellent plans and immediate shipment.

The home builder will derive a great deal of satisfaction in watching the construction of his house if he has a set of complete working plans to examine as the work progresses.

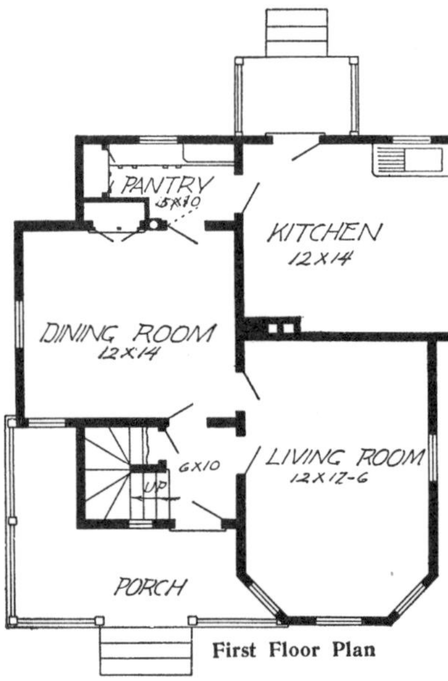

First Floor Plan

Design No. 2040

Blue prints consist of basement plan; roof plan; first and second floor plans; front, rear, two side elevations; wall sections and all necessary interior details. Specifications consist of about twenty pages of typewritten matter.

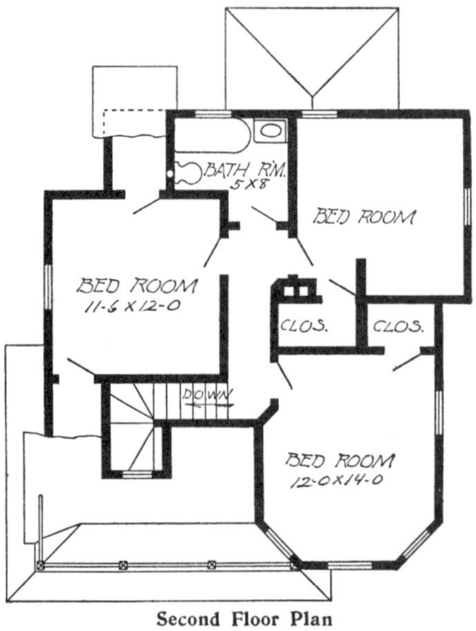

Second Floor Plan

PRICE

of Blue Prints, together with a complete set of typewritten specifications is

ONLY TWELVE DOLLARS

We mail Plans and Specifications the same day order is received.

SIZE: Width, 29 feet 6 inches; length, 31 feet exclusive of porches.

Perhaps there are many who feel that they are running some risk in ordering plans at a distance. We wish to assure our customers that there is no risk whatever.

If, upon receipt of plans, you do not find them exactly as we represent, if you do not find them complete and accurate in every respect, if you do not find them as well prepared as those furnished by any architect in the United States, or any one that you have ever seen, we will refund your money upon the return of the plans from you in perfect condition.

DESIGN NUMBER 6079

Size: width, 30 feet; length, 26 feet 6 inches, exclusive of porches

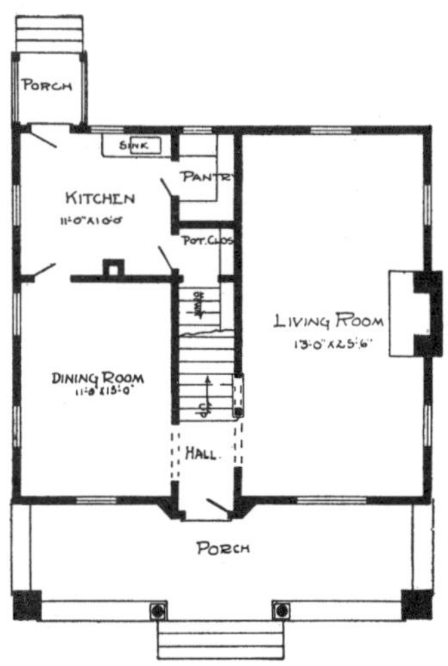

First Floor Plan

BLUE PRINTS consist of basement plan; roof plan; first and second floor plan; front, rear, two side elevations; wall sections and all necessary interior details. Specifications consist of about twenty pages of typewritten matter.

PRICE

of Blue Prints, together with a complete set of typewritten specifications

ONLY TEN DOLLARS

We mail plans and specifications the same day order is received.

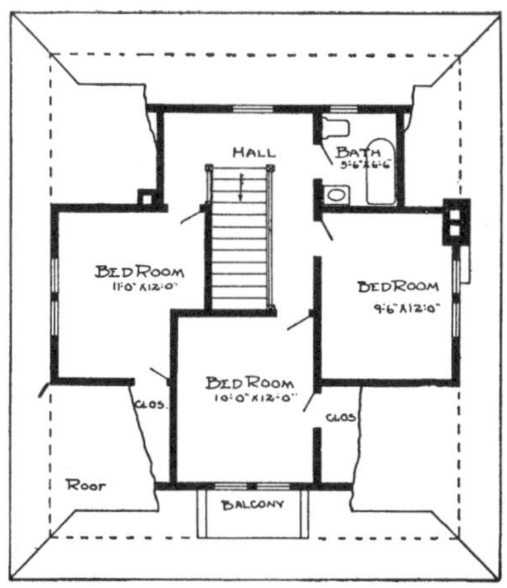

Second Floor Plan

DESIGN NUMBER 6077

Size: Width, 28 feet 6 inches; Length, 40 feet.

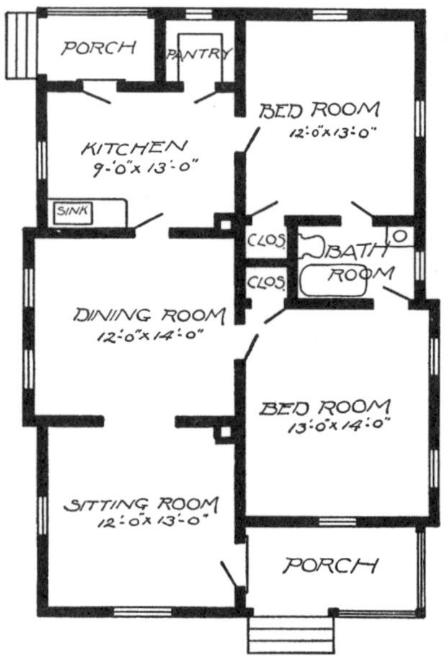

Floor Plan

BLUE PRINTS consist of foundation plan; roof plan; floor plan; front, rear, two side elevations; wall sections and all necessary interior details. Specifications consist of about fifteen pages of typewritten matter.

PRICE

of Blue Prints, together with a complete set of typewritten specifications

ONLY TEN DOLLARS

We mail plans and specifications the same day order is received.

Design No. 9066

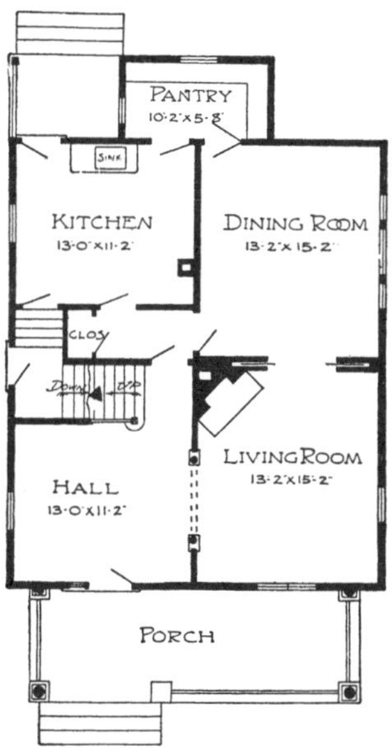

First Floor Plan.

The arrangement of this House is as follows:

FIRST FLOOR.

Reception Hall, 13 feet by 11 feea 2 inches.
Living Room, 13 feet 2 inches by 15 feet 2 inches.
Dining Room, 13 feet 2 inches by 15 feet 2 inches.
Kitchen, 13 feet by 11 feet 2 inches.
Pantry, Front and Rear Porches.

SECOND FLOOR.

Bedroom, 13 feet 2 inches by 10 feet 2 inches.
Bedroom, 13 feet 2 inches by 14 feet 2 inches.
Bedroom, 13 feet 2 inches by 14 feet 8 inches.
Bathroom, 8 feet 2 inches by 7 feet 8 inches.
7 Closets.

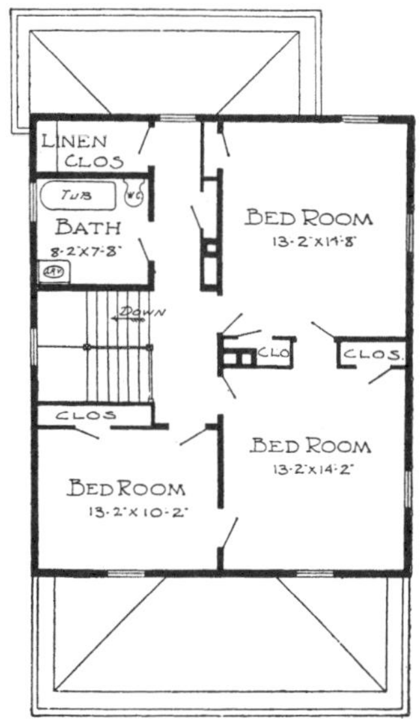

Second Floor Plan.

This Building is 37 feet 6 inches in width; 27 feet 6 inches in length.

Price of Complete Working Plans and Specifications.. $12.00

The Blue Printed Working Plans for this House consist of basement plan; first and second floor plans; front, right, left and rear elevations; wall sections and all necessary details.

The Typewritten Specifications contain all the necessary information for the proper construction of the House.

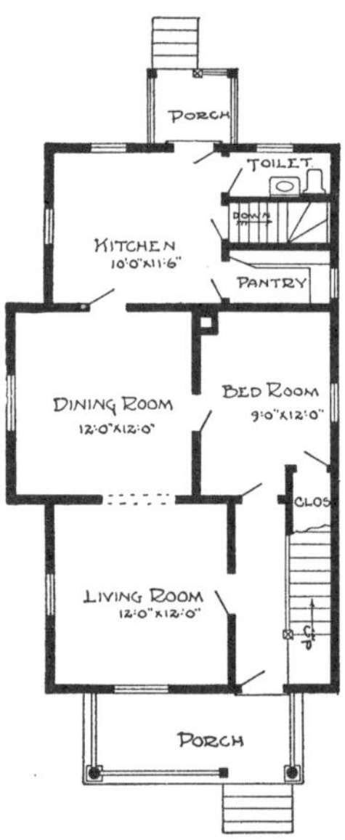

First Floor Plan.

Design No. 9014

The arrangement of this House is as follows:

FIRST FLOOR.

Reception Hall, 6 feet 6 inches by 12 feet.
Living Room, 12 feet by 12 feet.
Dining Room, 12 feet by 12 feet.
Kitchen, 10 feet by 11 feet 6 inches.
Lavatory, 3 feet by 7 feet.
Bedroom, 9 feet by 12 feet.
Pantry, Front and Rear Porches.

SECOND FLOOR.

Bedroom, 12 feet by 12 feet.
Bedroom, 12 feet by 10 feet.
Bedroom, 12 feet by 14 feet 6 inches.
7 Closets.

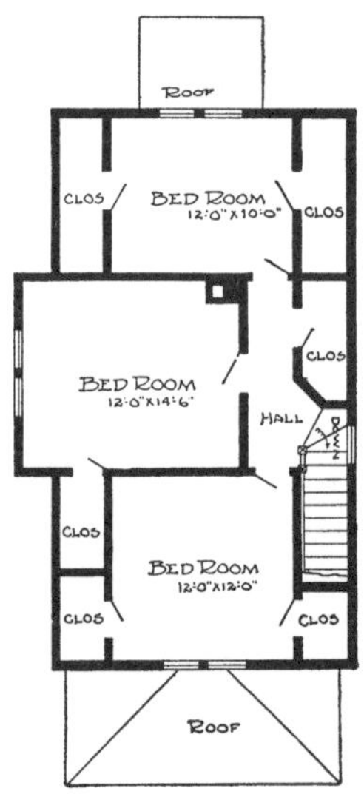

Second Floor Plan.

This Building is 22 fent 6 inches in width; 36 feet in length.

Price of Complete Working Plans and Specifications.. $12.00

The Blue Printed Working Plans for this House consist of basement plan; roof plan; first and second floor plans; front, right, left and rear elevations; wall sections and all necessary details.

The Typewritten Specifications contain all the necessary information for the proper construction of the House.

Design No. 7014

Size: Width, 25 feet 6 inches; Length, 27 feet 6 inches, exclusive of porches

PRICE

of Blue Prints, together with a complete set of typewritten specifications

ONLY TWELVE DOLLARS

We mail Plans and Specifications the same day order is received.

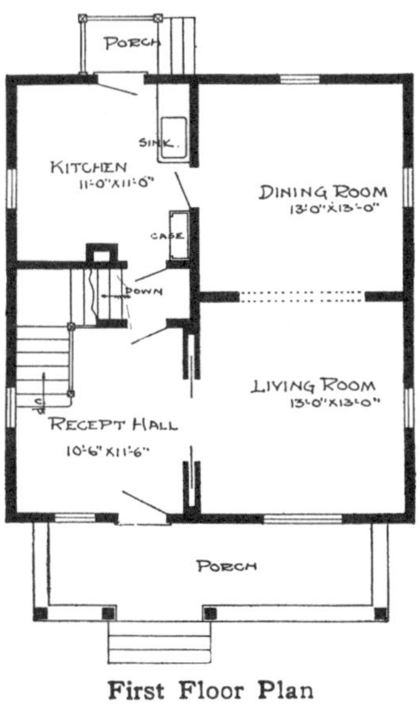

First Floor Plan

Blue prints consist of basement plan; roof plan; first and second floor plans; front, rear, two side elevations; wall sections and all necessary interior details. Specifications consist of about twenty pages of typewritten matter.

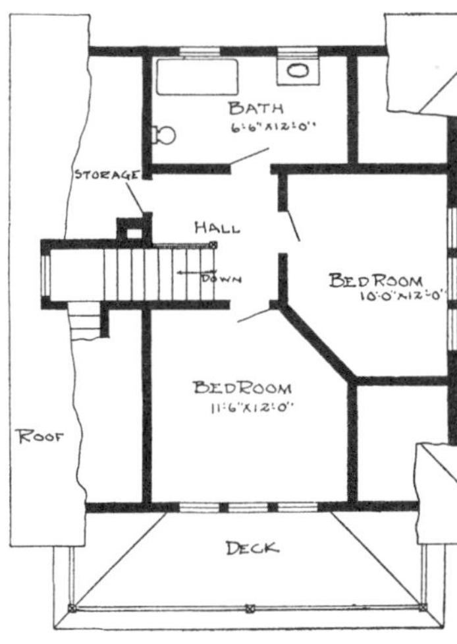

Second Floor Plan

Design No. 7015

Size: Width, 22 feet 6 inches; Length, 40 feet, exclusive of porches

Blue Prints consist of basement plan; floor plan; front, rear, two side elevations; wall sections and all necessary interior details. Specifiations consist of about fifteen pages of typewritten matter.

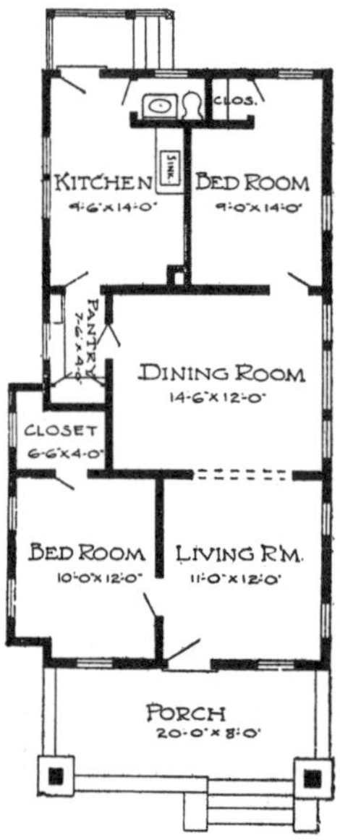

Floor Plan

PRICE

of Blue Prints, together with a complete set of typewritten specifications

ONLY TEN DOLLARS

We mail Plans and Specifications the same day order is received.

Design No. 2014

PRICE
of Blue Prints, together with a complete set of typewritten specifications is

ONLY TWELVE DOLLARS

We mail Plans and Specifications the same day order is received.

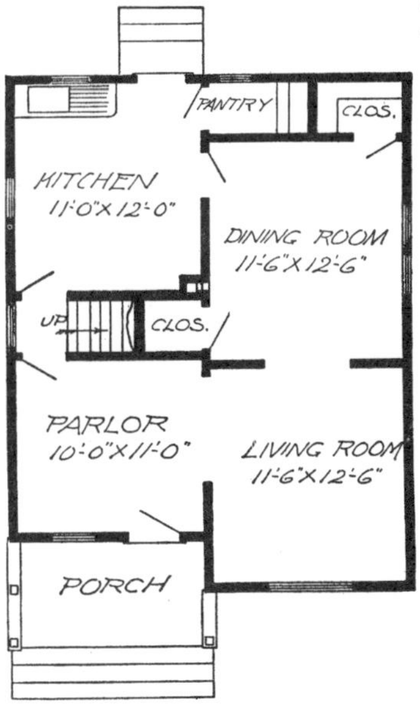

First Floor Plan

Blue prints consist of basement plan; first and second floor plans; front, rear, two side elevations; wall sections and all necessary interior details. Specifications consist of about twenty pages of typewritten matter.

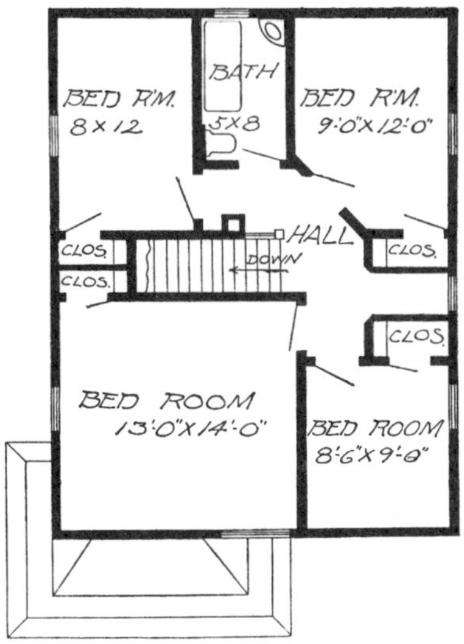

Second Floor Plan

SIZE: Width, 24 feet; length, 30 feet, exclusive of porch

When preparing to build a home, be sure to start right. You can start right only when you have a complete set of working plans and specifications, to be used as a guide for the workmen.

The estimated cost of the houses we illustrate is based on the most favorable conditions in all respects, and does not include plumbing and heating. Always consult your reliable contractors and material dealers. They know your local conditions.

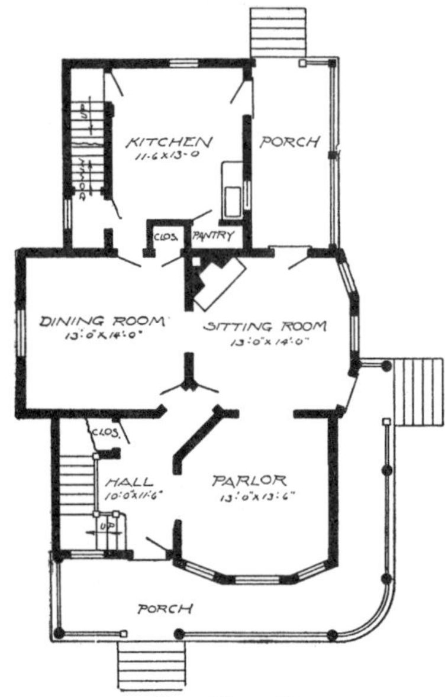

First Floor Plan

Design No. 517

Blue prints consist of cellar and foundation plan; roof plan; first and second floor plans; front, rear, two side elevations; wall sections and all necessary interior details. Specifications consist of about twenty pages of typewritten matter.

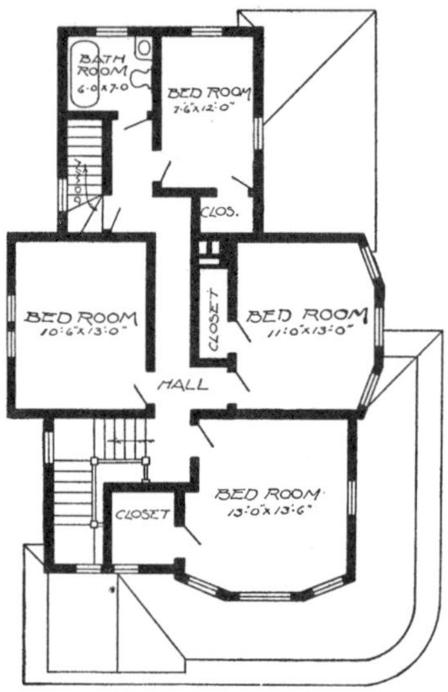

Second Floor Plan

PRICE

of Blue Prints, together with a complete set of typewritten specifications is

ONLY TWELVE DOLLARS

We mail Plans and Specifications the same day order is received.

Size: Width, 24 feet 6 inches; length, 44 feet, exclusive of porch.

The majority of the people build only one house in a life time, and therefore, it is the duty of every prospective builder to make his home as comfortable and attractive as possible.

This kind of a home costs no more to build than the ordinary structures usually seen in towns and villages, and the prospective builder can well afford to take a little time and investigate the latest designs.

DESIGN NUMBER 6021

Size: width, 28 feet, 6 inches; length, 28 feet, exclusive of porches

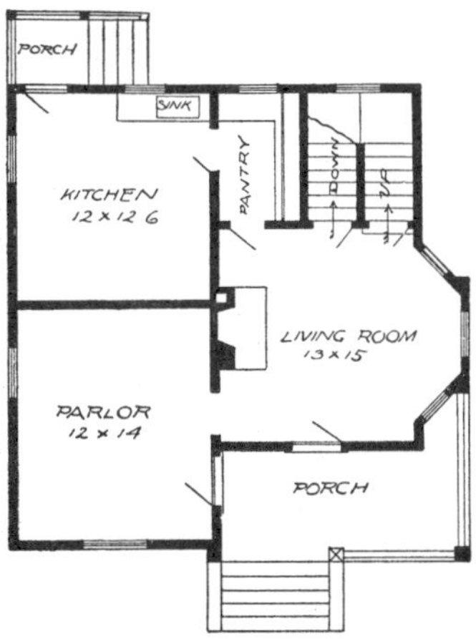

First Floor Plan

BLUE PRINTS consist of basement plan; roof plan; first and second floor plans; front, rear, two side elevations; wall sections and all necessary interior details. Specifications consist of about twenty pages of typewritten matter

PRICE

of Blue Prints, together with a complete set of typewritten specifications

ONLY TEN DOLLARS

We mail plans and specifications the same day order is received.

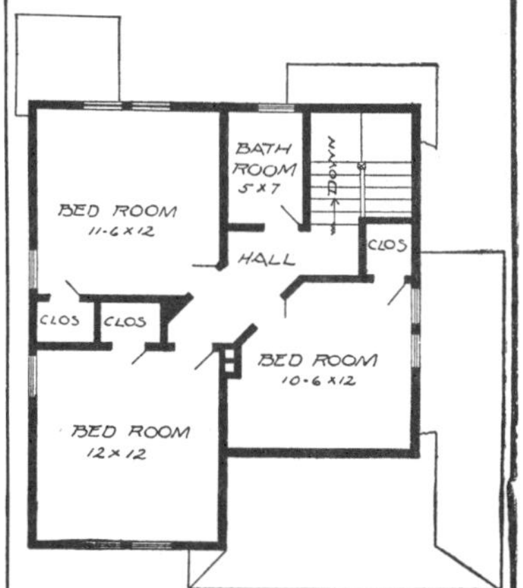

Second Floor Plan

DESIGN NUMBER 6008

Size: width, 28 feet 6 inches; length, 28 feet 6 inches, exclusive of porches

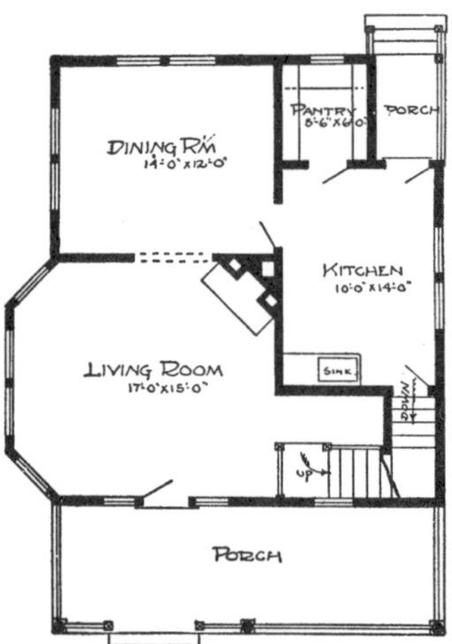

First Floor Plan

BLUE PRINTS consist of basement plan; first and second floor plan; front, rear, two side elevations; wall sections and all necessary interior details. Specifications consist of about twenty pages of typewritten matter.

PRICE

of Blue Prints, together with a complete set of typewritten specifications

ONLY TWELVE DOLLARS

We mail plans and specifications the same day order is received.

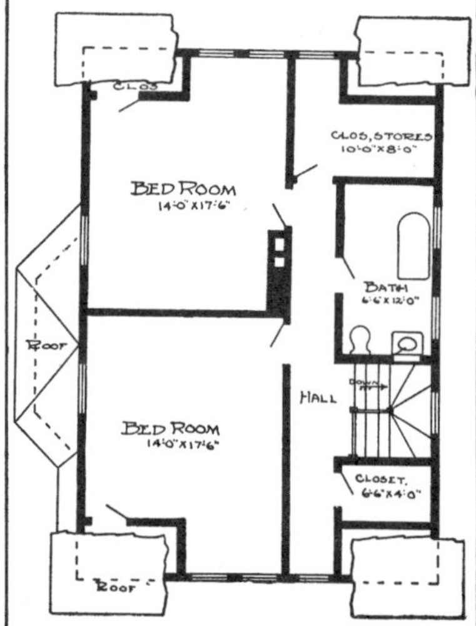

Second Floor Plan

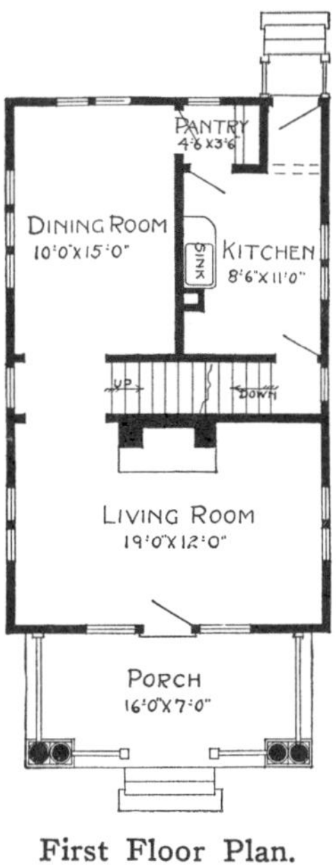

First Floor Plan.

Design No. 9050

The arrangement of this House is as follows:

FIRST FLOOR.

Living Room, 19 feet by 12 feet.
Dining Room, 10 feet by 15 feet.
Kitchen, 8 feet 6 inches by 11 feet.
Pantry and Front Porch.

SECOND FLOOR.

Bedroom, 14 feet by 12 feet.
Bedroom, 8 feet 6 inches by 12 feet.
Bathroom, 5 feet by 12 feet.
4 Closets.

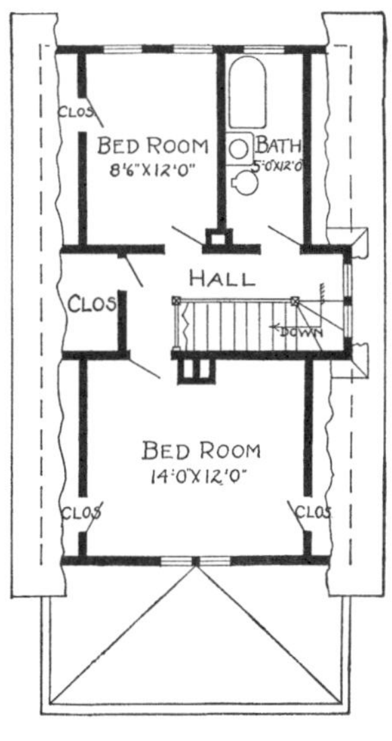

Second Floor Plan.

This Building is 20 feet in width; 32 feet in length.
Price of Complete Working Plans and Specifications.. $10.00
The Blue Printed Working Plans for this House consist of basement plan; first and second floor plans, front, right, left and rear elevations; wall sections and all necessary details.
The Typewritten Specifications contain all the necessary information for the proper construction of the House.

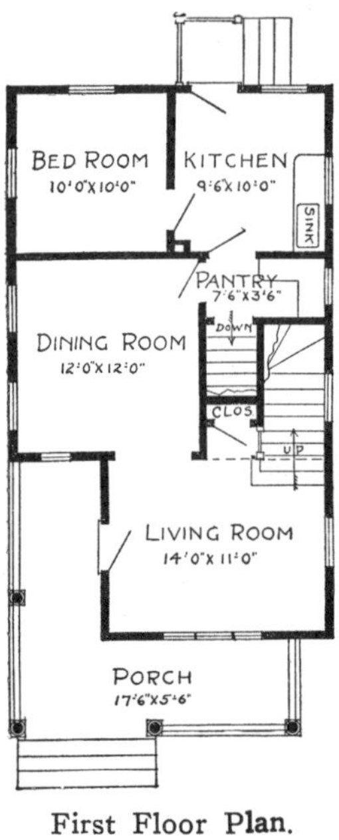

First Floor Plan.

Design No. 9048

The arrangement of this House is as follows:

FIRST FLOOR.

Living Room, 14 feet by 11 feet.
Dining Room, 12 feet by 12 feet.
Kitchen, 9 feet 6 inches by 10 feet.
Bedroom, 10 feet by 10 feet.
Pantry, Front and Rear Porches.

SECOND FLOOR.

Bedroom, 12 feet by 10 feet.
Bedroom, 12 feet by 9 feet 6 inches.
Bathroom, 6 feet 6 inches by 9 feet.
4 Closets.

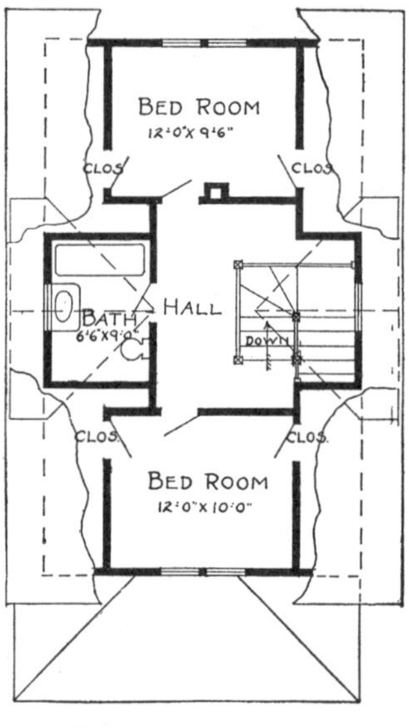

Second Floor Plan.

This Building is 21 feet in width; 34 feet 6 inches in length.

Price of Complete Working Plans and Specifications.. $12.00

The Blue Printed Working Plans for this House consist of basement plan, roof plan, first and second floor plans; front, right, left and rear elevations; wall sections and all necessary details.

The Typewritten Specifications contain all the necessary information for the proper construction of the House.

Design No. 7054

Size: Width, 38 feet; Length, 36 feet 6 inches, exclusive of porches

PRICE

of Blue Prints, together with a complete set of typewritten specifications.

ONLY FIFTEEN DOLLARS

We mail Plans and Specifications the same day order is received.

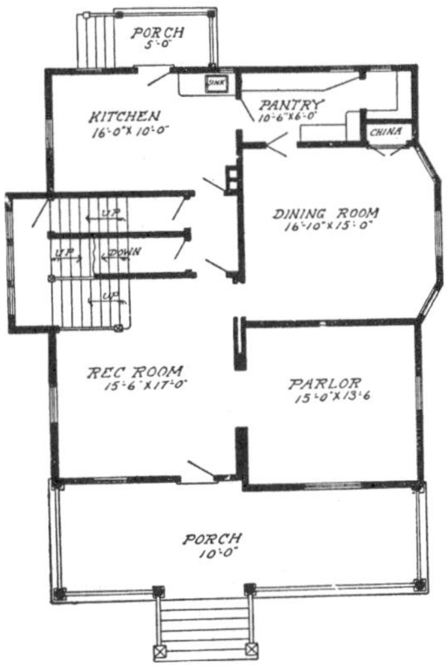

First Floor Plan

Blue prints consist of basement plan; roof plan; first and second floor plans; front, rear, two side elevations; wall sections and all necessary interior details. Specifications consist of about twenty pages of typewritten matter.

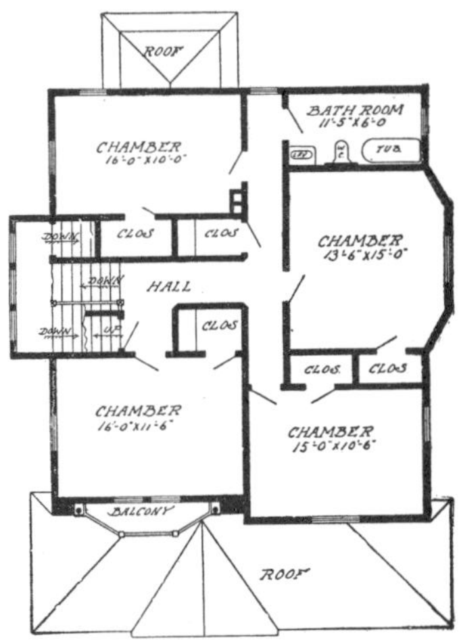

Second Floor Plan

Design No. 7010

Size: Width, 27 feet 6 inches; Length, 30 feet, exclusive of porches

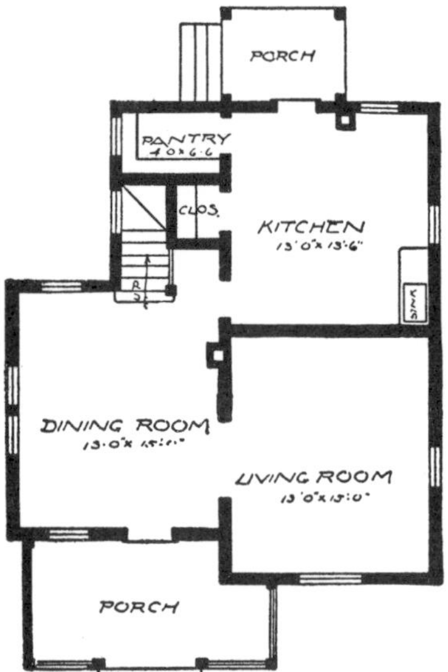

First Floor Plan

Blue prints consist of cellar and foundation plan; roof plan; first and second floor plans; front, rear, two side elevations; wall sections and all necessary interior details. Specifications consist of about twenty pages of typewritten matter.

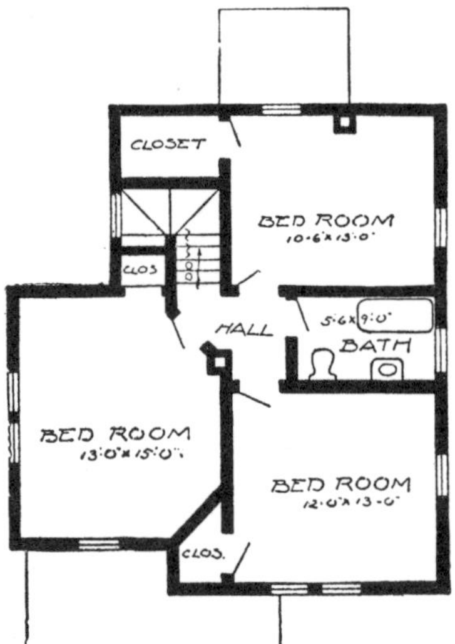

Second Floor Plan

PRICE

of Blue Prints, together with a complete set of typewritten specifications

ONLY TWELVE DOLLARS

We mail Plans and Specifications the same day order is received.

PRICE
of Blue Prints, together with a complete set of typewritten specifications is

ONLY
EIGHT
DOLLARS

We mail Plans and Specifications the same day order is received.

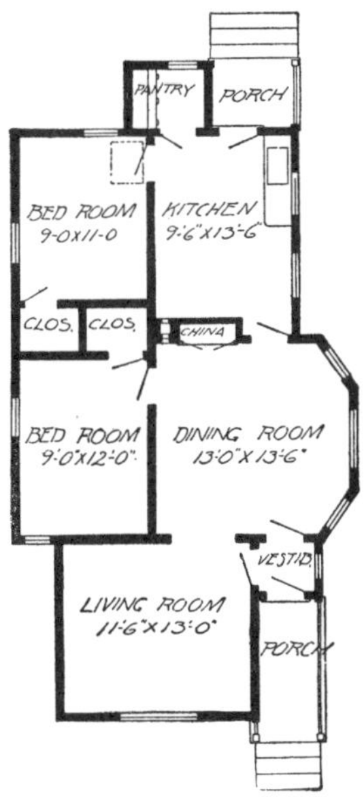

Floor Plan

Design No. 2016

Blue prints consist of foundation plan; roof plan; floor plan; front, rear, two side elevations; wall sections and all necessary interior details. Specifications consist of about fifteen pages of typewritten matter.

SIZE: Width, 24 feet; length, 44 feet 6 inches, exclusive of porch

All of the plans illustrated in this book have been prepared by licensed architects standing at the head of their profession, and the standard of their work is of the very highest.

We could not afford to make this guarantee if we were not positive that we were furnishing the best plans put out in this country, even though our price is not more than one-seventh to one-tenth the price usually charged.

Design No. 45

Blue prints consist of cellar and foundation plan; roof plan; floor plan; front, rear, two side elevations; wall sections and all necessary interior details. Specifications consist of about twenty pages of type-written matter.

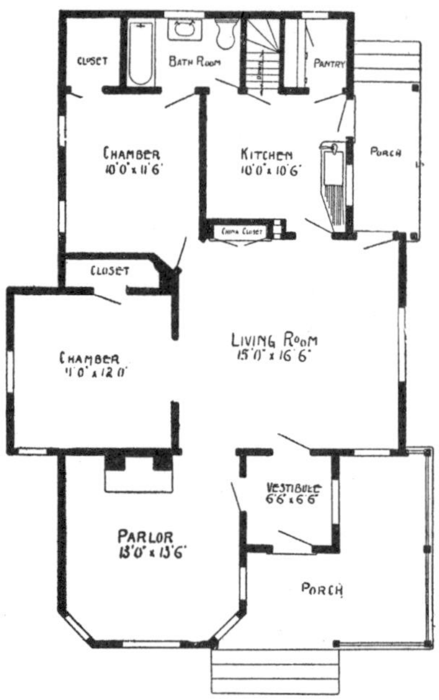

Floor Plan

PRICE

of Blue Prints, together with a complete set of typewritten specifications is

ONLY TEN DOLLARS

We mail Plans and Specifications the same day order is received.

Size: Width, 30 feet; length, 46 feot, exclusive of porches.

All of our plans ase printed by electricity on a circular blue printing machine. We use the very best grade of electric blue printing paper and take great care to have every line perfect and distinct.

We do not blame you for wishing to know what you will get for your money. The plans we send out are the regular blue printed plans, drawn one-quarter inch scale to the foot, showing all elevations, floor plans and necessary interior details.

DESIGN NUMBER 6053

Size: width, 35 feet; length, 23 feet, 6 inches exclusive of porches

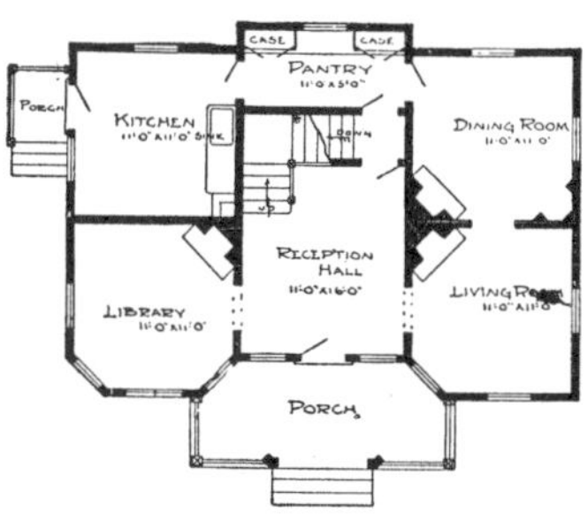

First Floor Plan

BLUE PRINTS consist of basement plan; roof plan; first and second floor plans; front, rear, two side elevations; wall sections and all necessary interior details. Specifications consist of about twenty pages of typewritten matter.

PRICE

of Blue Prints, together with a complete set of typewritten specifications.

ONLY TWELVE DOLLARS

We mail plans and specifications the same day order is received.

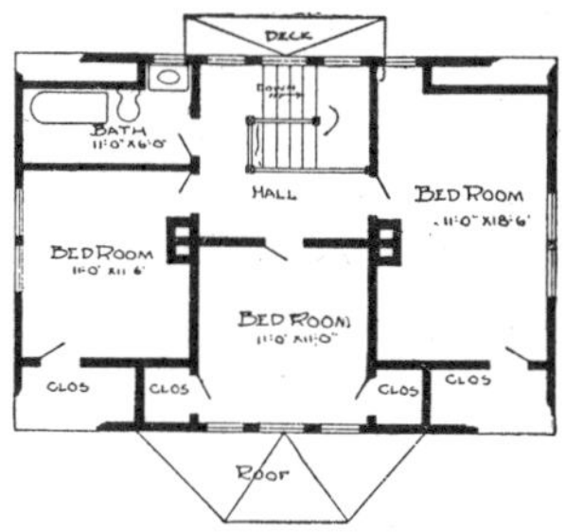

Second Floor Plan

DESIGN NUMBER 6059

Size: width, 39 feet; length, 25 feet 6 inches, exclusive of porch

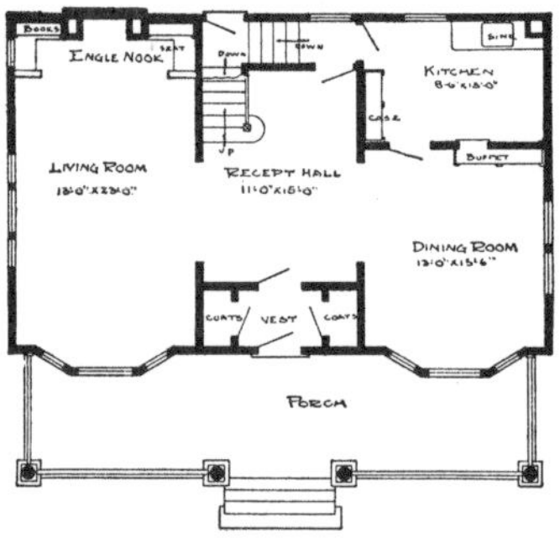

First Floor Plan

BLUE PRINTS consist of basement plan; roof plan; first and second floor plans; front, rear, two side elevations; wall sections and all necessary interior details. Specifications consist of about twenty pages of typewritten matter.

PRICE

of Blue Prints, together with a complete set of typewritten specifications

ONLY TWELVE DOLLARS

We mail plans and specifications the same day order is received.

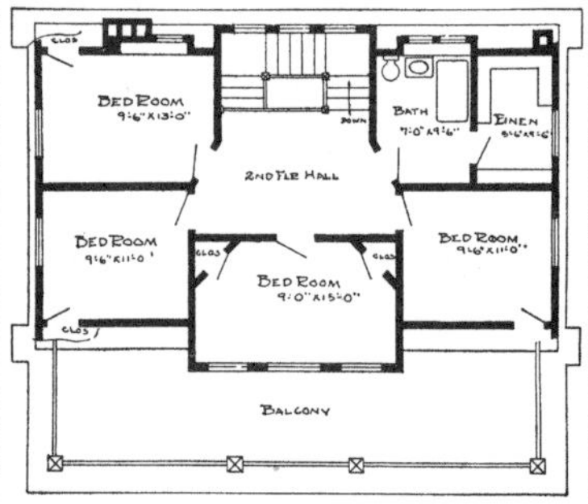

Second Floor Plan

Design No. 9010

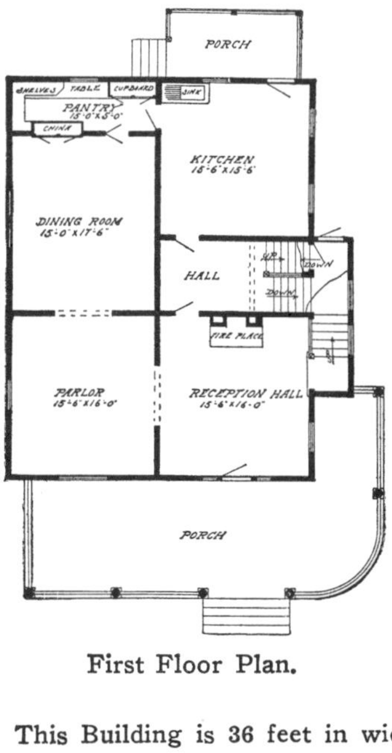

First Floor Plan.

The arrangement of this House is as follows:

FIRST FLOOR.

Reception Hall, 15 feet 6 inches by 16 feet.
Parlor, 15 feet 6 inches by 16 feet.
Dining Room, 15 feet by 17 feet 6 inches.
Kitchen, 15 feet 6 inches by 15 feet 6 inches.
Pantry, Front and Rear Porches.

SECOND FLOOR.

Bedroom, 14 feet 6 inches by 16 feet.
Bedroom, 16 feet by 16 feet.
Bedroom, 11 feet by 15 feet 6 inches.
Bedroom, 14 feet by 15 feet 6 inches.
Bathroom, 5 feet by 15 feet 6 inches.
4 Closets.

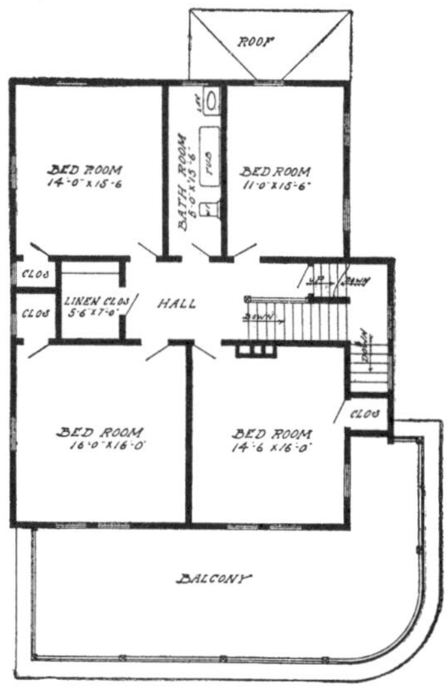

Second Floor Plan.

This Building is 36 feet in width; 40 feet 6 inches in length.

Price of Complete Working Plans and Specifications.. **$15.00**

The Blue Printed Working Plans for this House consist of basement plan; roof plan; first and second floor plans; front, right, left and rear elevations; wall sections and all necessary details.

The Typewritten Specifications contain all the necessary information for the proper construction of the House.

Design No. 9007

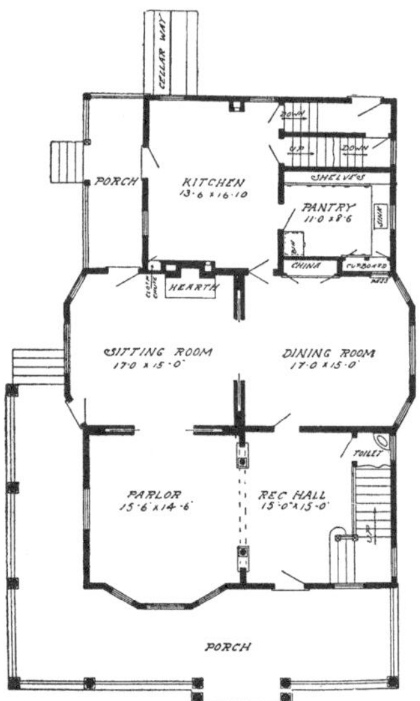

First Floor Plan.

The arrangement of this House is as follows:

FIRST FLOOR.

Reception Hall, 15 feet by 15 feet.
Parlor, 15 feet 6 inches by 14 feet 6 inches.
Living Room, 17 feet by 15 feet.
Dining Room, 17 feet by 15 feet.
Kitchen, 13 feet 6 inches by 16 feet 10 inches.
Pantry, Front and Rear Porches.

SECOND FLOOR.

Bedroom, 15 feet 6 inches by 15 feet.
Bedroom, 17 feet 6 inches by 13 feet.
Bedroom, 13 feet by 15 feet.
Sewing Room, 10 feet 6 inches by 10 feet 6 inches.
Servant's Room, 9 feet 6 inches by 8 feet.
Bathroom, 9 feet 6 inches by 7 feet 6 inches.
6 Closets.

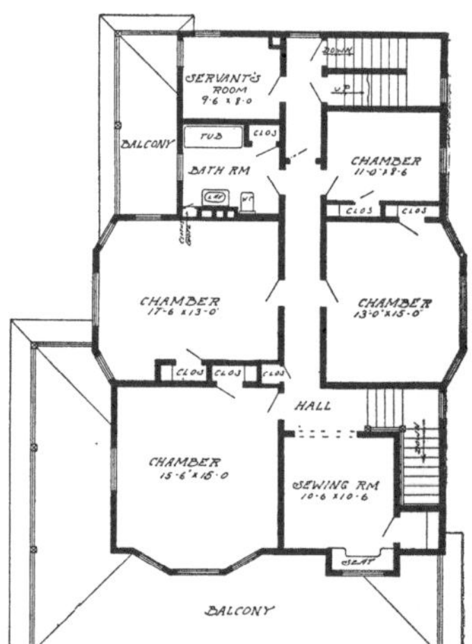

Second Floor Plan.

This Building is 36 feet in width; 51 feet in length.

Price of Complete Working Plans and Specifications.. $15.00

The Blue Printed Working Plans for this House consist of basement plan; roof plan; first and second floor plans; front, right, left and rear elevations; wall sections and all necessary details.

The Typewritten Specifications contain all the necessary information for the proper construction of the House

Design No. 7012

Size: Width, 18 feet; Length, 38 feet 6 inches, exclusive of porch

PRICE

of Blue Prints, together with a complete set of typewritten specifications

ONLY TWELVE DOLLARS

We mail Plans and Specifications the same day order is received.

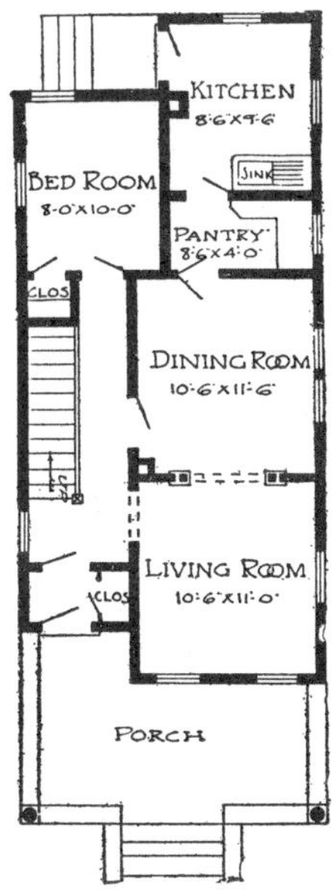

First Floor Plan

Blue prints consist of foundation plan; first and second floor plans; front, two side elevations; wall sections and all necessary interior details. Specifications consist of about fifteen pages of typewritten matter.

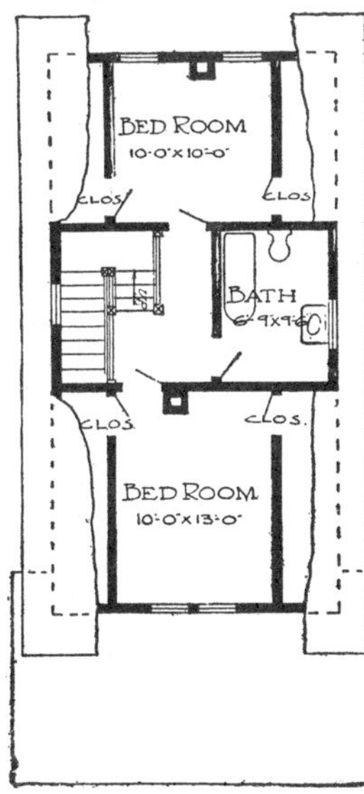

Second Floor Plan

Design No. 7013

Size: Width, 22 feet 6 inches; Length, 30 feet, exclusive of porches

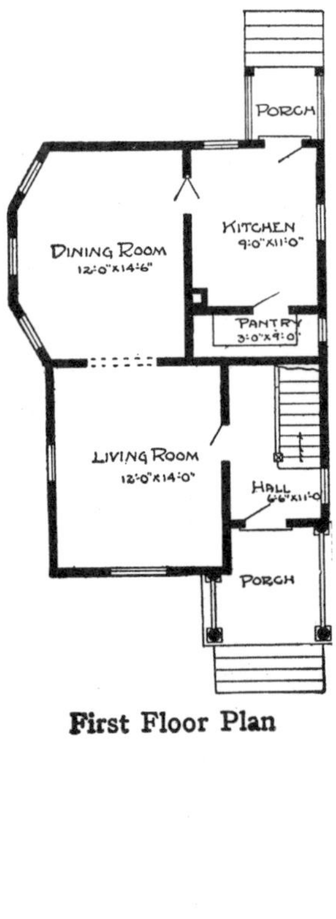

First Floor Plan

Blue prints consist of foundation plan; roof plan; first and second floor plan; front, rear, two side elevations; wall sections and all necessary interior details. Specifications consist of about twenty pages of typewritten matter.

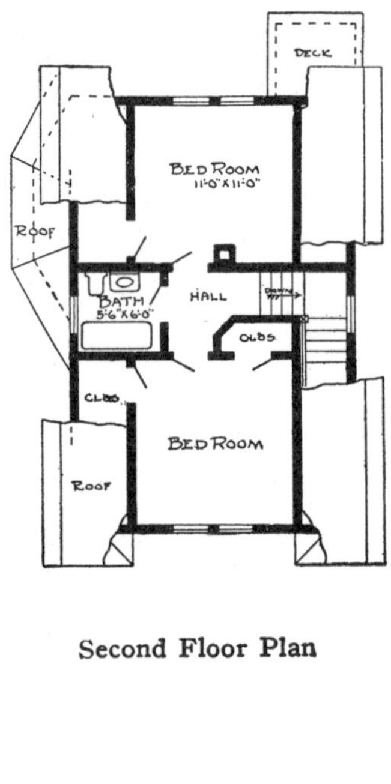

Second Floor Plan

PRICE

of Blue Prints, together with a complete set of typewritten specifications

ONLY TEN DOLLARS

We mail Plans and Specifications the same day order is received.

PRICE
of Blue Prints, together with a complete set of type-written specifications is

ONLY TEN DOLLARS

We mail Plans and Specifications the same day order is received

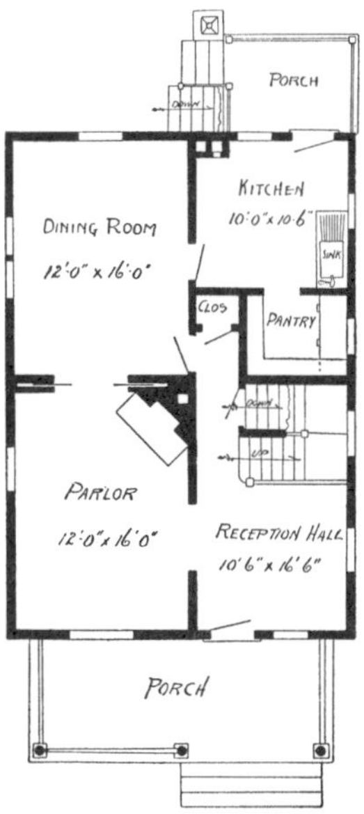

First Floor Plan

Design No. 160

Blue prints consist of cellar and foundation plan; first and second floor plan; front, two side elevations; wall sections and all necessary interior details. Specifications consist of about twenty pages of type-written matter.

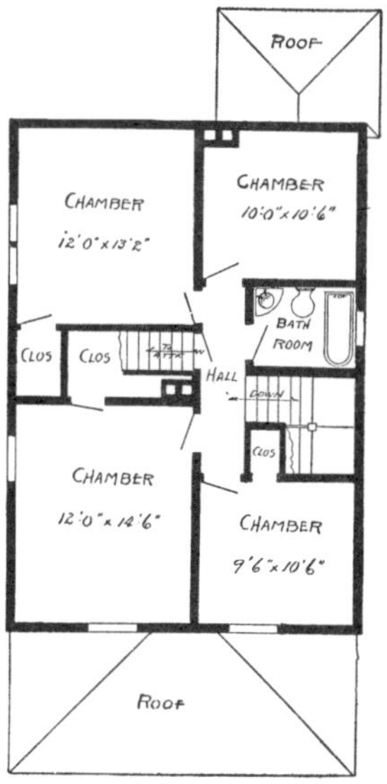

Second Floor Plan

Size: Width, 24 feet; length, 34 feet, exclusive of porches.

It is not uncommon to hear of disputes, and even lawsuits, between owners and contractors. It is usually occasioned by lack of plans and proper understanding. One party is probably as much in error as the other.

Don't proceed with the construction of your house until you get complete plans. Experienced contractors are the most particular in this respect, knowing the advantage and saving to both themselves and the home builder.

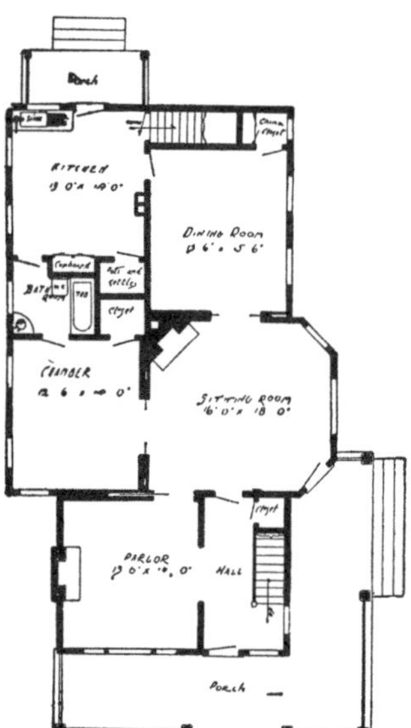

First Floor Plan

Design No. 19

Blue prints consist of cellar and foundation plan; first and second floor plans; front, rear, two side elevations; wall sections and all necessary interior details. Specifications consist of about twenty pages of typewritten matter.

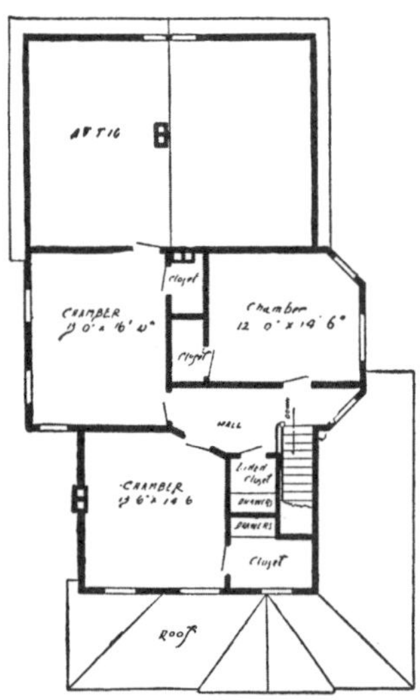

Second Floor Plan

PRICE

of Blue Prints, together with a com plete set of typewritten specifications is

ONLY TWELVE DOLLARS

We mail Plans and Specifications the same day order is received.

Size: Width, 32 feet; length, 52 feet, exclusive of porches.

The floor plans we furnish show the shape and size of all rooms, halls and closets; the locations and sizes of all doors and windows; the position of all plumbing fixtures, gas lights, registers, pantry work, etc., and all the measurements that are necessary are given.

All necessary details of interior work, such as door and window casings and trim, base, stools, picture moulding, doors, newel posts, balusters, rail,etc., accompany each set of plans. Part is shown in full size, while some of the larger work, such as stair construction, is drawn to a scale of one and one-half inch to the foot.

DESIGN NUMBER 6045

Size: Width, 29 feet; length, 45 feet, exclusive of porches

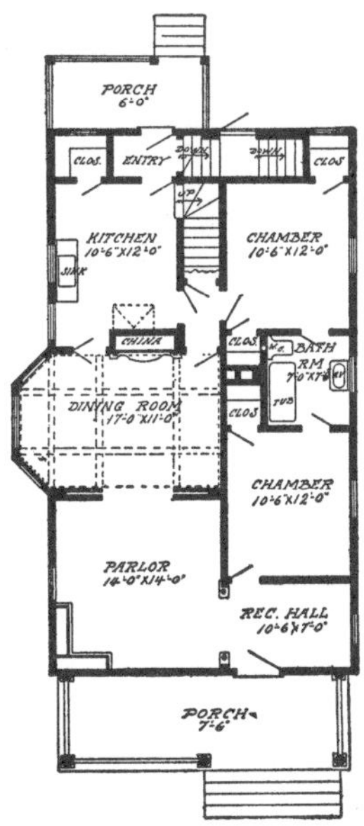

Floor Plan

BLUE PRINTS consist of basement plan; attic and roof plan; floor plan, front, rear, two side elevations; wall sections and all necessary interior details. Specifications consist of about fifteen pages of typewritten matter.

PRICE

of Blue Prints, together with a complete set of typewritten specifications

ONLY TEN DOLLARS

We mail plans and specifications the same day order is received.

D E S I G N   N U M B E R   6 0 0 2

Size: width, 24 feet; length, 31 feet, exclusive of porches

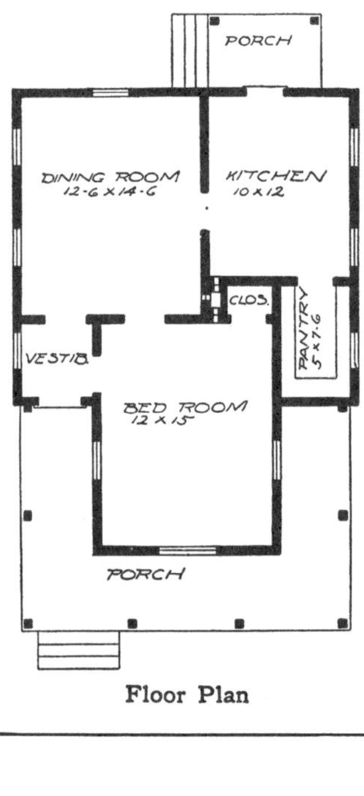

Floor Plan

BLUE PRINTS consist of foundation plan; roof plan; floor plan; front, rear, two side elevations; wall sections and all necessary interior details. Specifications consist of about fifteen pages of typewritten matter.

PRICE

of Blue Prints, together with a complete set of typewritten specifications

ONLY EIGHT DOLLARS

We mail plans and specifications the same day order is received.

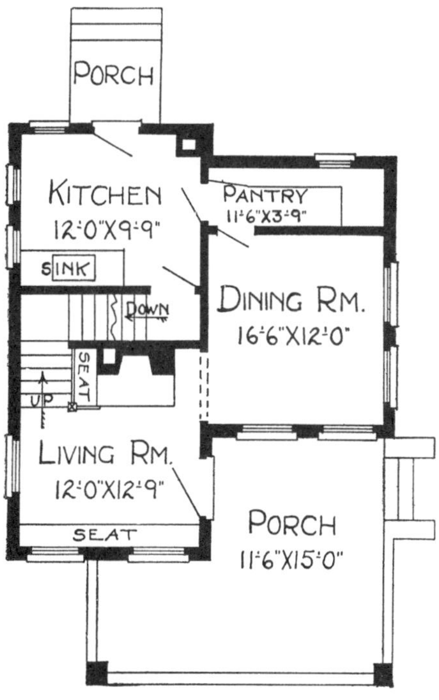

First Floor Plan.

Design No. 9093

The arrangement of this House is as follows:

FIRST FLOOR.

Living Room, 12 feet by 12 feet 9 inchec.

Dining Room, 16 feet 6 inches by 12 feet.

Kitchen, 12 feet by 9 feet 9 inches.

Pantry, Front and Rear Porches.

SECOND FLOOR.

Bedroom, 9 feet by 13 feet.

Bedroom, 8 feet 6 inches by 13 feet.

Bathroom, 10 feet 6 inches by 6 feet.

5 Closets.

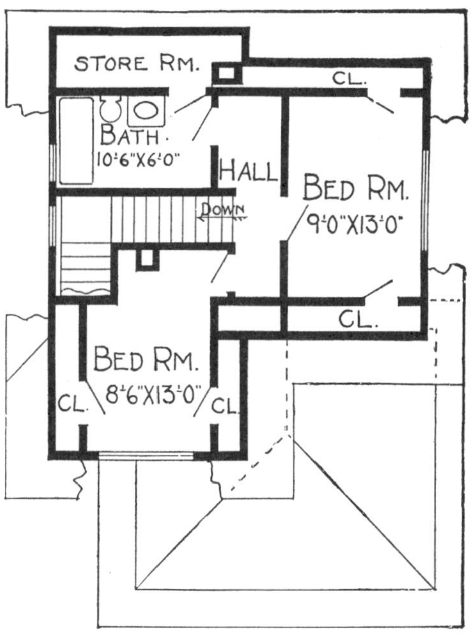

Second Floor Plan.

This Building is 25 feet 4 inches in width; 28 feet in length.

Price of Complete Working Plans and Specifications **$15.00**

The Blue Printed Working Plans for this House consist of basement plan; roof plan; first and second floor Plans; front, right, left and rear elevations; wall sections and all necessary details.

The Typewritten Specifications contain all the necessary information for the proper construction of the House.

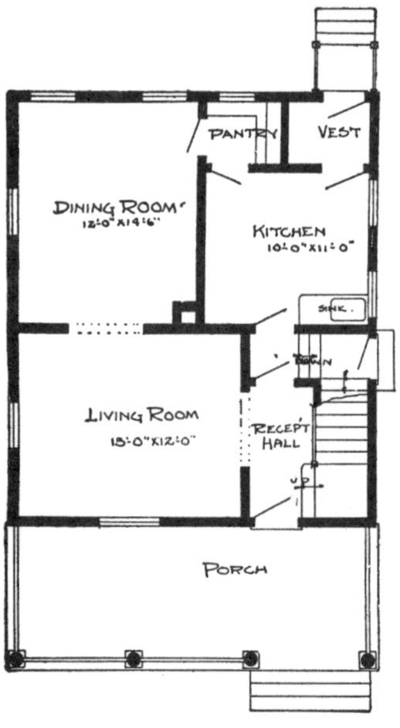

First Floor Plan.

Design No. 9043

The arrangement of this House is as follows:

FIRST FLOOR.

Reception Hall, 8 feet by 8 feet 6 inches.

Living Room, 15 feet by 12 feet.

Dining Room, 12 feet by 14 feet 6 inches.

Kitchen, 10 feet by 11 feet.

Pantry, Front and Rear Porches.

SECOND FLOOR.

Bedroom, 10 feet by 16 feet.

Bedroom, 8 feet 6 inches by 16 feet.

Bedroom, 9 feet by 10 feet.

Bathroom, 5 feet 6 inches by 7 feet.

4 Closets.

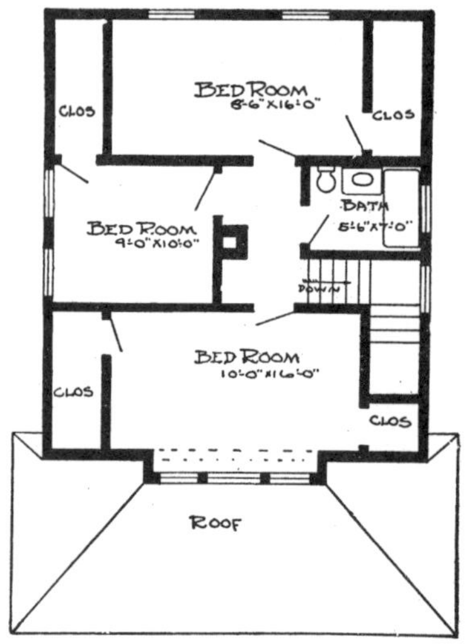

Second Floor Plan.

This Building is 24 feet 6 inches in wid2h; 28 feet in length.

Price of Complete Working Plans and Specifications...... .... $12.00

The Blue Printed Working Plans for this House consist of basement plan; roof plan; first and second floor plans; front, right, left and rear elevations; wall sections and all necessary details.

The Typewritten Specifications contain all the necessary information for the proper construction of the House.

Design No. 2009

Blue prints consist of cellar and foundation plan; first and second floor plans; front, rear, two side elevations; wall sections and all necessary interior details. Specifications consist of about twenty pages of typewritten matter.

PRICE
of Blue Prints, together with a complete set of typewritten specifications is

ONLY TWELVE DOLLARS

We mail Plans and Specifications the same day order is received.

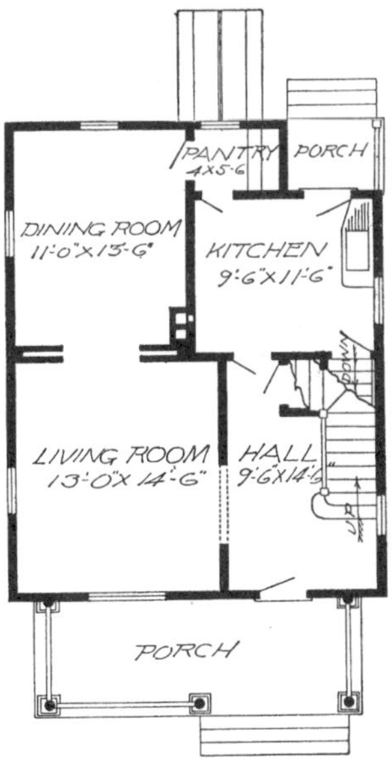

First Floor Plan

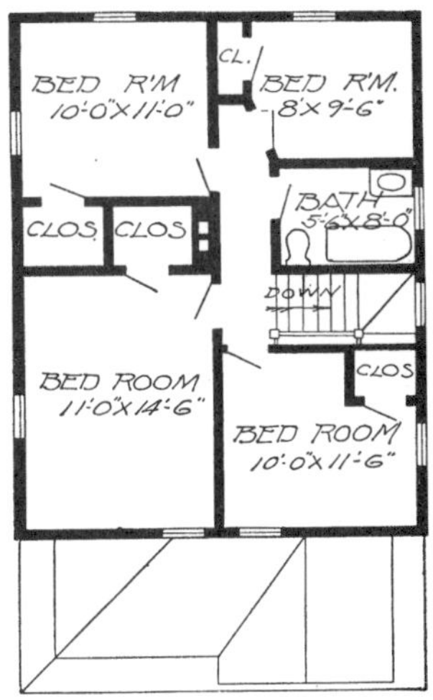

Second Floor Plan

SIZE: Width, 24 feet; length, 30 feet, exclusive of porch

The contractor is often obliged to do some work which he did not figure on, and the home builder often does not get as much as he expected, simply because complete plans and specifications are not used in the construction of the house.

We always advise ordering plans plenty of time in advance when you wish to build, for then you will have sufficient opportunity to get in all your bids. We are prepared to fill mail and telegraph orders the same day received.

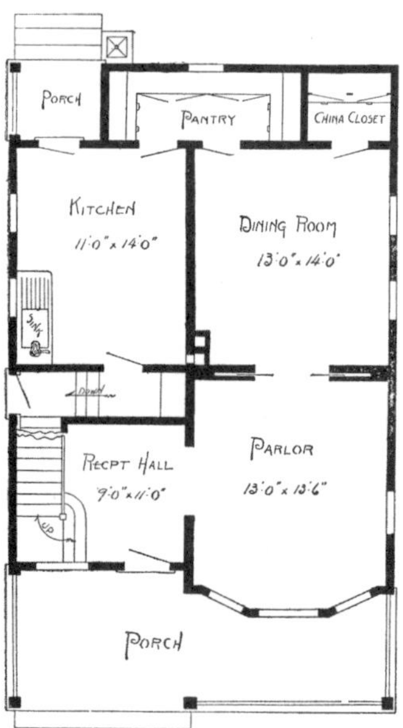

First Floor Plan

Design No. 150

Blue prints consist of cellar and foundation plan; roof plan; first and second floor plans; front, two side elevetions; wall sections and all necessary interior details. Specifications consist of about twenty pages of typewritten matter.

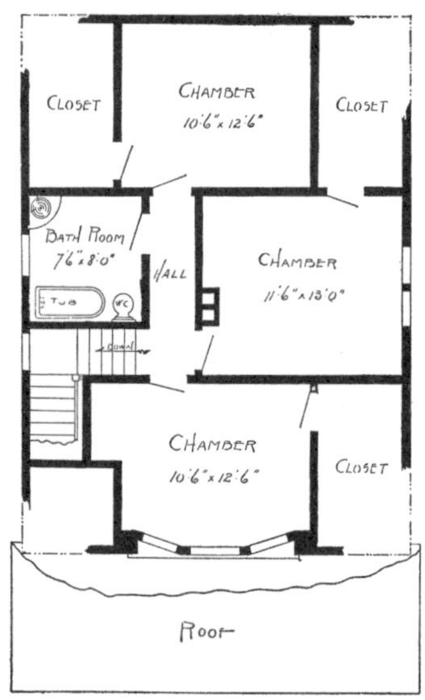

Second Floor Plan

PRICE

of Blue Prints, together with a complete set of typewritten specifications is

ONLY TEN DOLLARS

We mail Plans and Specifications the same day order is received

Size: Width, 25 feet, 6 inches; length, 36 feet, exclusive of porch.

Many have marveled at our ability to furnish such excellent and complete working plans and specifications at such low prices.

We do not wonder at this, because we charge but $5.00 for a more complete set of working plans and specifications than you would receive if ordered in the regular manner, and when drawn especially for you, at a cost of from fifty to seventy-five dollars.

Design No. 7041

Size: Width, 26 feet 6 inches; Length, 31 feet 6 inches, exclusive of porches

PRICE

of Blue Prints, together with a complete set of typewritten specifications

ONLY TWELVE DOLLARS

We mail Plans and Specifications **the same day order is received.**

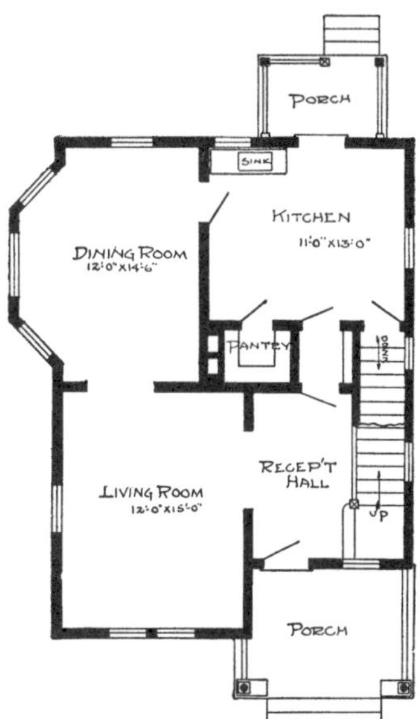

First Floor Plan

Blue prints consist of basement plan; roof plan; first and second floor plans; front, rear, two side elevations; wall sections and all necessary interior details. Specifications consist of about twenty pages of typewritten matter.

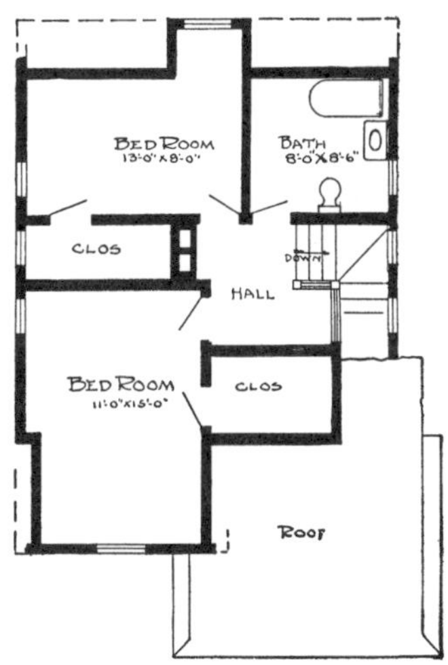

Second Floor Plan

Design No. 7084

Size: Width, 25 feet; Length, 26 feet 6 inches, exclusive of porches

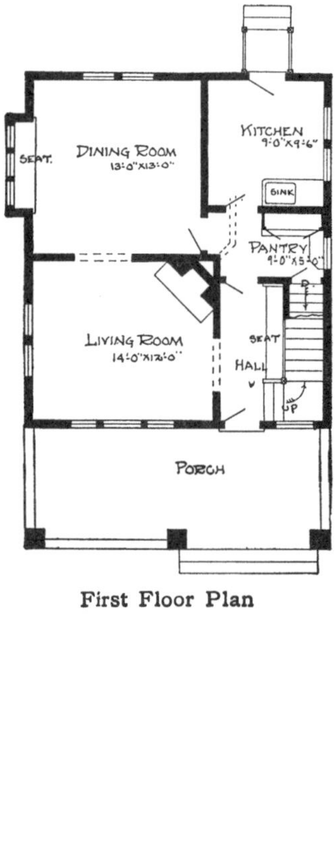

First Floor Plan

Blue prints consist of basement plan; first and second floor plans; front, rear, two side elevations; wall sections and all necessary interior details. Specifications consist of of about twenty pages of typewritten matter.

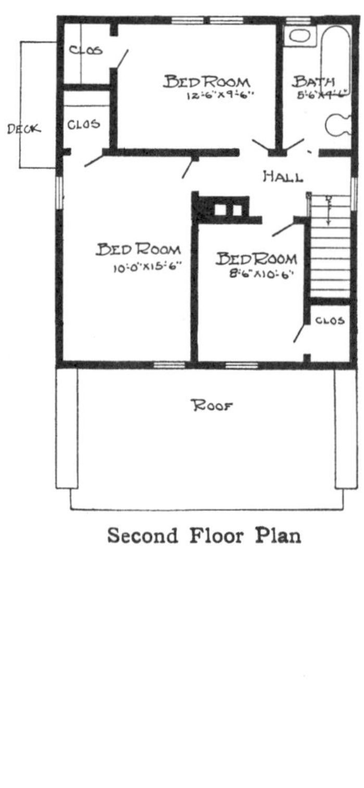

Second Floor Plan

PRICE

of Blue Prints, together with a complete set of typewritten specifications

ONLY TWLEVE DOLLARS

We mail Plans and Specifications the same day order is received.

DESIGN NUMBER 6060

Size: Width, 31 feet, 6 inches; length, 40 feet, 6 inches exclusive of porches

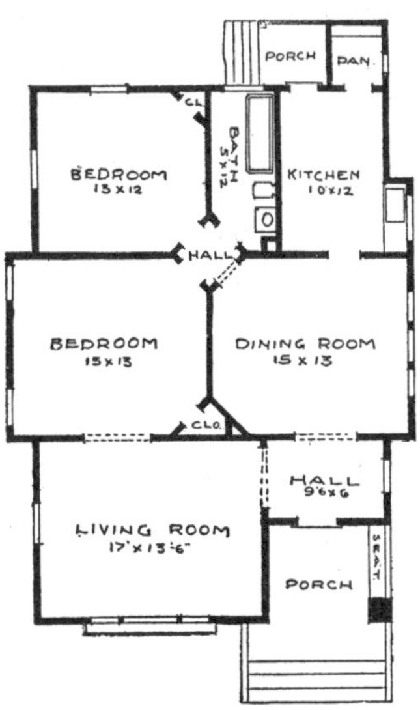

Floor Plan

BLUE PRINTS consist of foundation plan; floor plan; front, rear, two side elevations; wall sections and all necessary interior details. Specifications consist of about fifteen pages of typewritten matter.

PRICE

of Blue Prints, together with a complete set of typewritten specifications

ONLY TEN DOLLARS

We mail plans and specifications the same day order is received.

DESIGN NUMBER 6025

Size: width, 32 feet, 9 inches; length, 41 feet, 6 inches, exclusive of porches

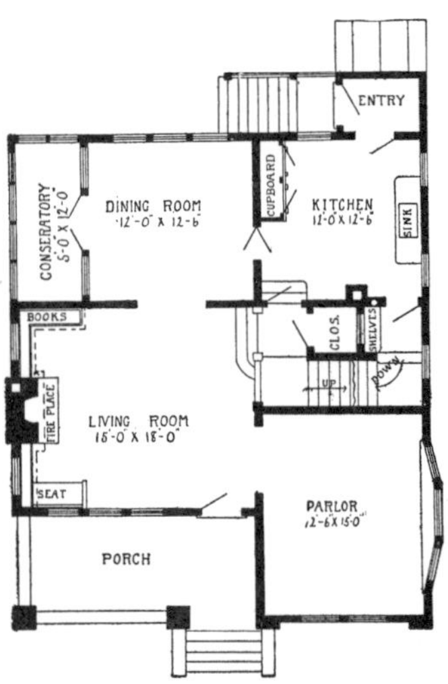

First Floor Plan

BLUE PRINTS consist of cellar and foundation plan; roof plan; first and second floor plans; front, rear, two side elevations; wall sections and all necessary interior details. Specifications consist of about twenty pages of typewritten matter.

PRICE

of Blue Prints, together with a complete set of typewritten specifications

ONLY FIFTEEN DOLLARS

We mail plans and specifications the same day order is received.

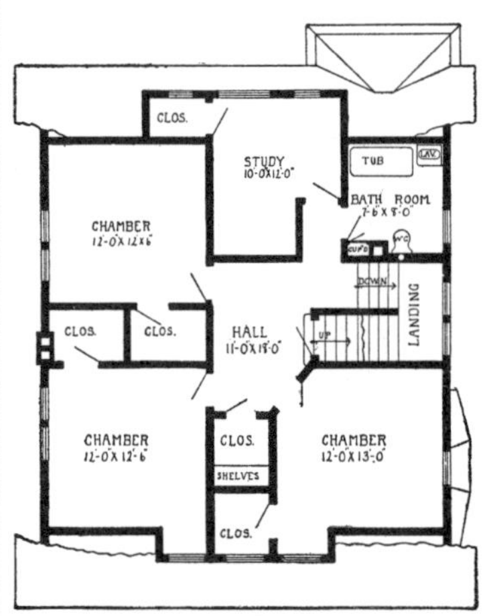

Second Floor Plan

DESIGN NUMBER 6074

Size: width, 20 feet; length, 38 feet, exclusive of porches

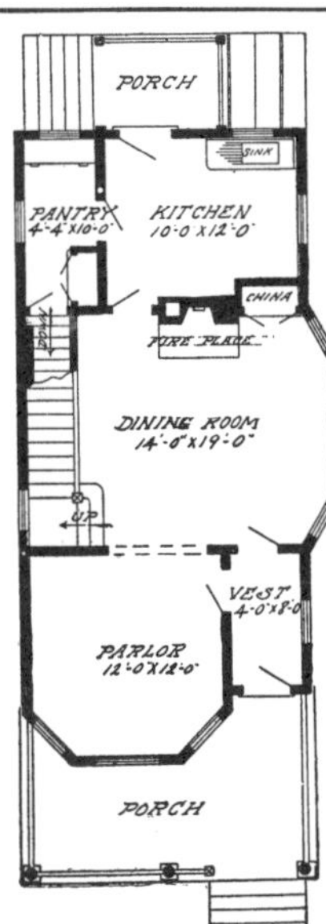

First Floor Plan

BLUE PRINTS consist of basement plan; first and second floor plans; front, rear, two side elevations; wall sections and all necessary interior details. Specifications consist of about twenty pages of typewritten matter.

PRICE

of Blue Prints, together with a complete set of typewritten specifications

ONLY TWELVE DOLLARS

We mail plans and specifications the same day order is received.

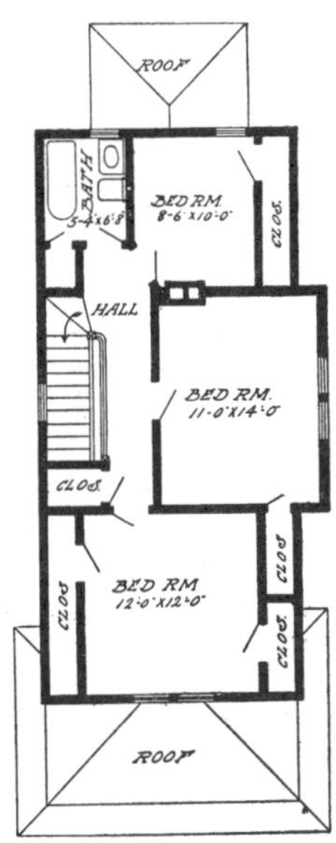

Second Floor Plan

DESIGN NUMBER 6054

Size: width, 21 feet; length, 28 feet, exclusive of porches

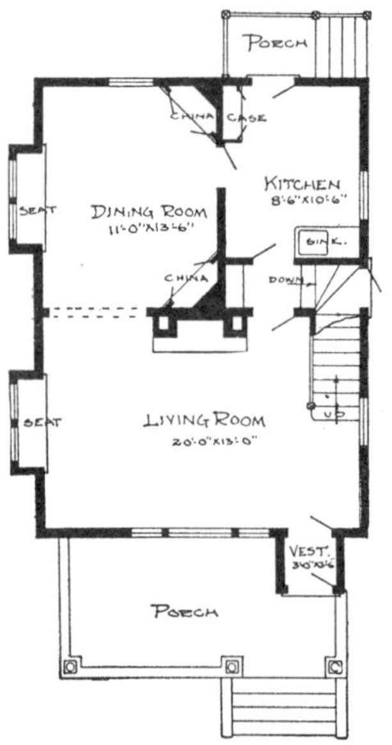

First Floor Plan

BLUE PRINTS consist of basement plan; first and second floor plans; front, rear, two side elevations; wall sections and all necessary interior details. Specifications consist of about twenty pages of typewritten matter.

PRICE

of Blue Prints, together with a complete set of typewritten specifications

ONLY TEN DOLLARS

We mail plans and specifications the same day order is received.

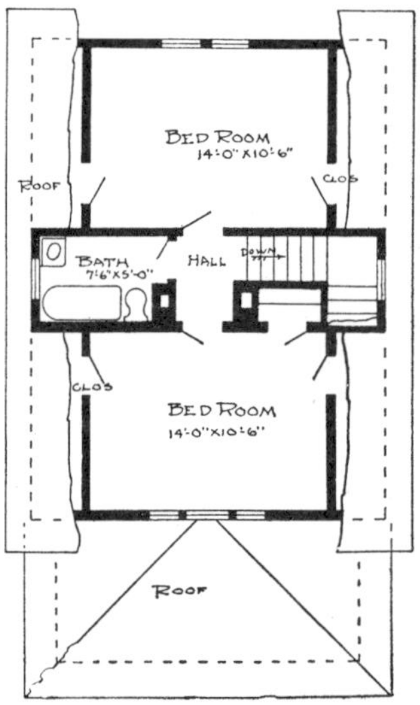

Second Floor Plan

Design No. 9080

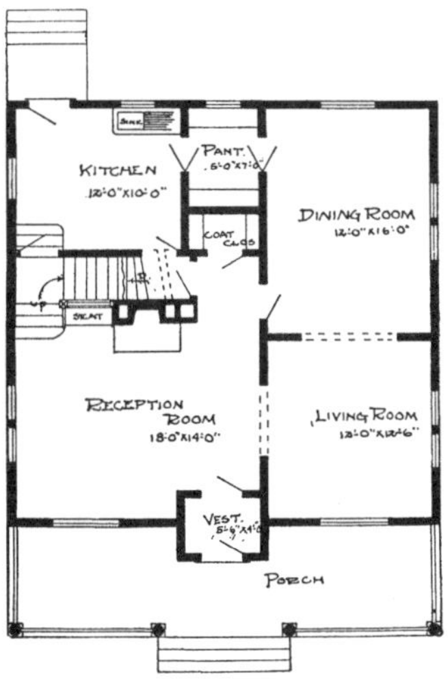

First Floor Plan.

The arrangement of this House is as follows:

FIRST FLOOR.

Reception Hall, 18 feet by 14 feet.
Living Room, 12 feet by 12 feet 6 inches.
Dining Room, 12 feet by 6 feet.
Kitchen, 12 feet by 10 feet.
Pantry and Front Porch.

SECOND FLOOR.

Bedroom, 12 feet by 9 feet 6 inches.
Bedroom, 12 feet by 16 feet 6 inches.
Bedroom, 12 feet by 10 feet.
Bathroom, 7 feet by 13 feet.
5 Closets.

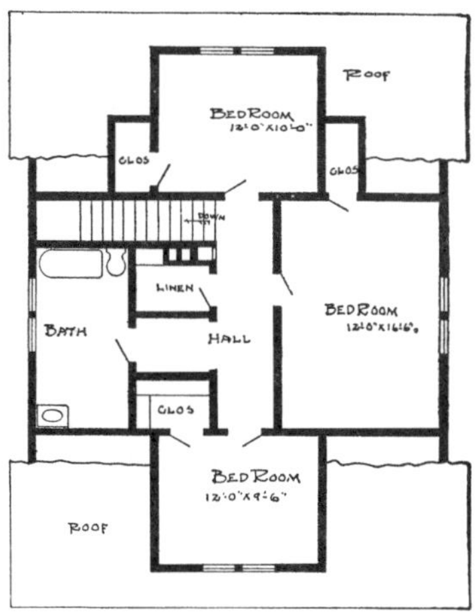

Second Floor Plan.

This Building is 31 feet 6 inches in width; 30 feet in length.

Price of Complete Working Plans and Specifications.. $12.00

The Blue Printed Working Plans for this House consist of basement plan; first and second floor plans; front. right, left and rear elevations; wall sections and all necessary details.

The Typewritten Specifications contain all the necessary information for the proper construction of the House.

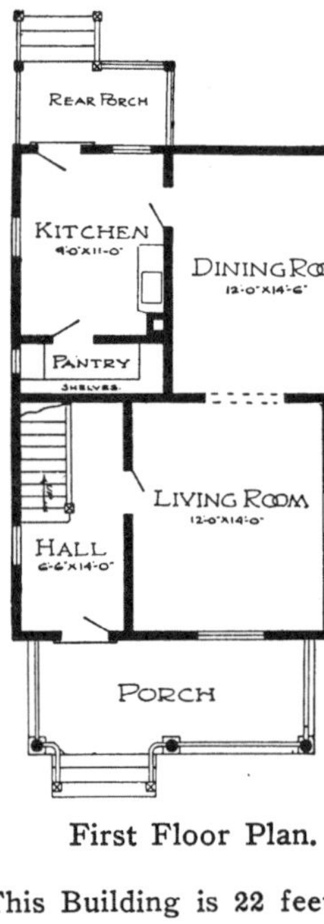

First Floor Plan.

Design No. 9089

The arrangement of this House is as follows:

FIRST FLOOR.

Reception Hall, 6 feet 6 inches by 14 feet.

Living Room, 12 feet by 14 feet.

Dining Room, 12 feet by 14 feet 6 inches.

Kitchen, 9 feet by 11 feet.

Pantry, Front and Rear Porches.

SECOND FLOOR.

Bedroom, 11 feet by 11 feet 6 inches.

Bedroom, 11 feet by 11 feet.

Bathroom, 6 feet by 5 feet 6 inches.

3 Closets.

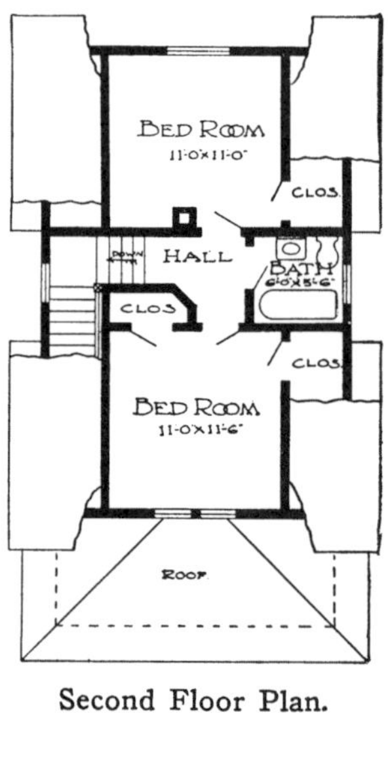

Second Floor Plan.

This Building is 22 feet 6 inches in width; 30 feet in length.

Price of Complete Working Plans and Specifications.. $10.00

The Blue Printed Working Plans for this House consist of basement plan; first and second floor plans, front, right, left and rear elevations; wall sections and all necessary details.

The Typewritten Specifications contain all the necessary information for the proper construction of the House.

Design No. 7093

Size: Width, 34 feet; Length, 28 feet 6 inches, exclusive of porch

PRICE

of Blue Prints, together with a complete set of typewritten specifications

ONLY TEN DOLLARS

We mail Plans and Specifications the same day order is received.

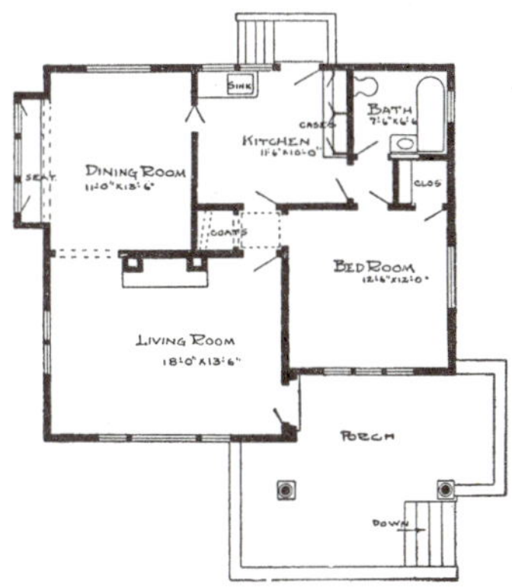

Floor Plan

Blue Prints consist of basement plan; roof plan; floor plan; front, rear, two side elevations; wall sections and all necessary interior details. Specifications consist of about fifteen pages of typewritten matter.

Design No. 7024

Size: Width, 29 feet; Length, 26 feet 6 inches, exclusive of porch

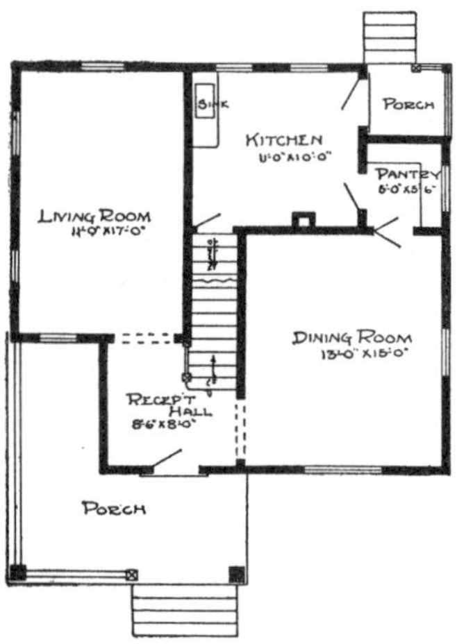

First Floor Plan

Blue prints consist of basement plan; first and second floor plans; front, rear, two side elevations; wall sections and all necessary interior details. Specifications consist of about twenty pages of typewritten matter.

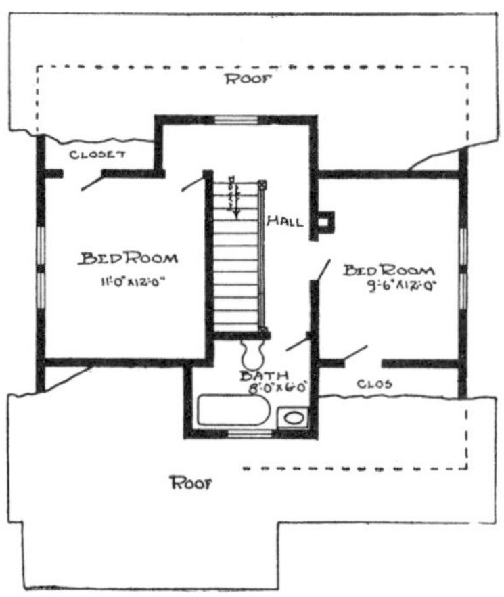

Second Floor Plan

PRICE

of Blue Prints, together with a complete set of typewritten specifications

ONLY TEN DOLLARS

We mail Plans and Specifications the same day order is received.

PRICE
of Blue Prints, together with a complete set of typewritten specifications is

ONLY TWELVE DOLLARS

We mail Plans and Specifications the same day order is received.

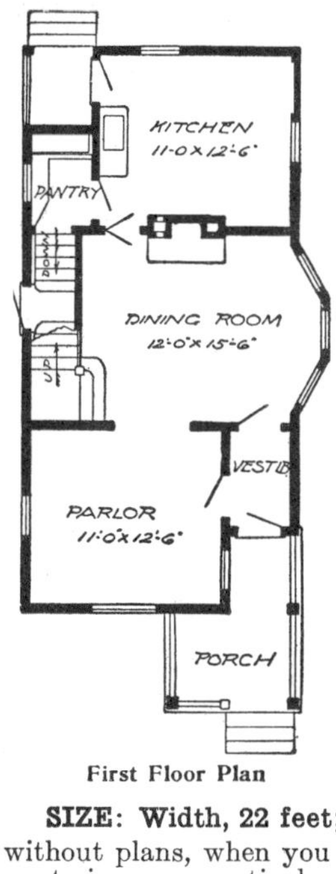

First Floor Plan

Design No. 2006

Blue prints consist of cellar and foundation plan; first and second floor plans; front, rear, two side elevations; wall sections and all necessary interior details. Specifications consist of about twenty pages of typewritten matter.

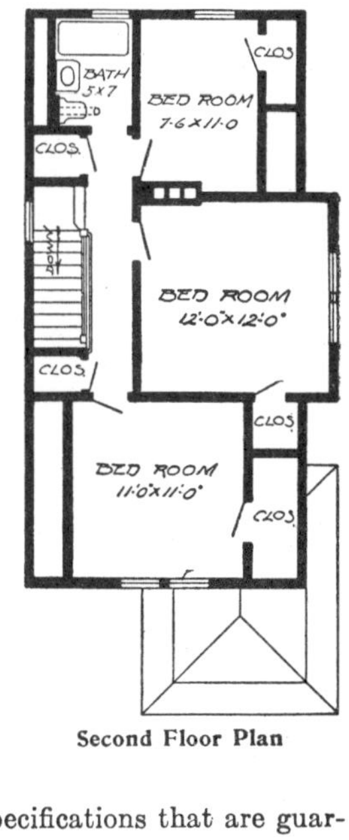

Second Floor Plan

SIZE: Width, 22 feet; length, 36 feet, exclusive of porch

Why attempt building without plans, when you can secure a complete set of plans and specifications that are guaranteed to be thoroughly accurate in every particular, at such low prices.

These working plans and specifications can be made the basis of contract between contractor and home builder. They will prevent mistakes which cost money, and they will prevent disputes, which are never settled satisfactorily to both parties.

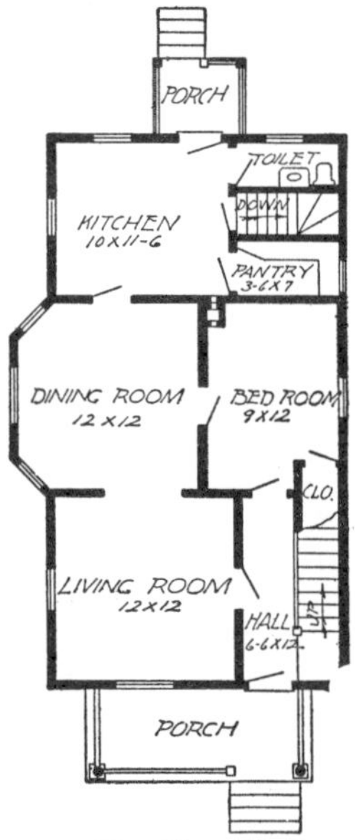

First Floor Plan

Design No. 2032

Blue prints consist of basement plan; roof plan; first and second floor plans; front, rear, two-side elevations; wall sections and all necessary interior details. Specifications consist of about twenty pages of typewritten matter.

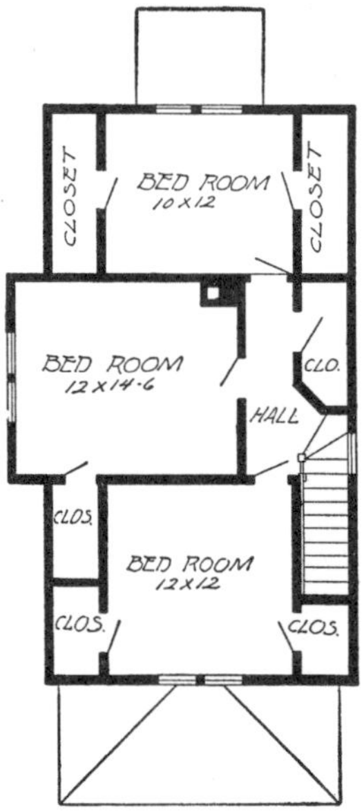

Second Floor Plan

PRICE

of Blue Prints, together with a complete set of typewritten specifications is

ONLY TWELVE DOLLARS

We mail Plans and Specifications the same day order is received.

SIZE: Width, 22 feet 6 inches; length, 36 feet exclusive of porches.

The houses we illustrate have been designed by licensed architects to meet the needs of the people and they have a reputation for being practical, attractive and artistic.

The prospective builder should not lose sight of the fact that some day it may be necessary or desirable to sell the bouse, and, if it is attractive and artistic, it can always be disposed of and at a profit to the owner.

DESIGN NUMBER 6031

Size: width, 25 feet, 6 inches; length, 36 feet, 6 inches, exclusive of porches

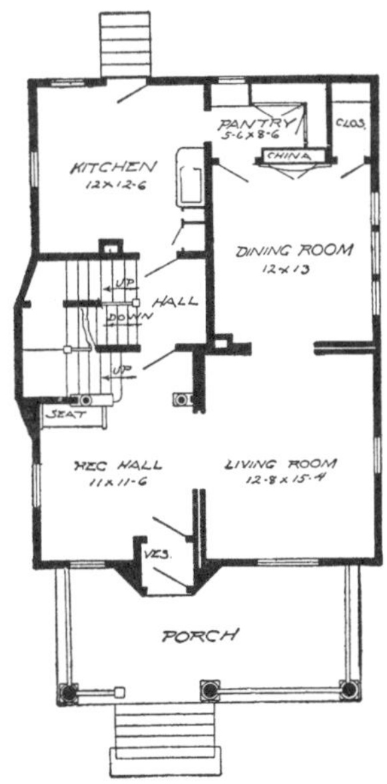

First Floor Plan

BLUE PRINTS consist of basement plan; roof plan; first and second floor plans; front, rear, two side elevations; wall sections and all necessary interior details. Specifications consist of about twenty pages of typewritten matter.

PRICE

of Blue Prints, together with a complete set of typewritten specifications

ONLY TWELVE DOLLARS

We mail plans and specifications the same day order is received.

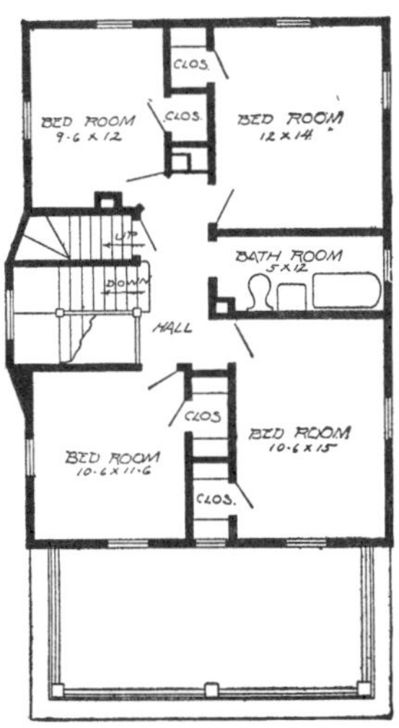

Second Floor Plan

DESIGN NUMBER 6088

Size: width, 24 feet, 6 inches; length, 32 feet, exclusive of porches

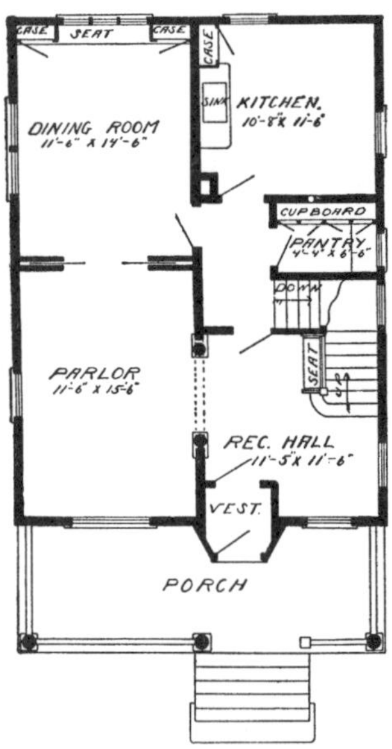

First Floor Plan

BLUE PRINTS consist of basement plan; first and second floor plans; front, rear two side elevations; wall sections and all necessary interior details. Specifications consist of about twenty pages of typewritten matter.

PRICE

of Blue Prints, together with a complete set of typewritten specifications

ONLY TEN DOLLARS

We mail plans and specifications the same day order is received.

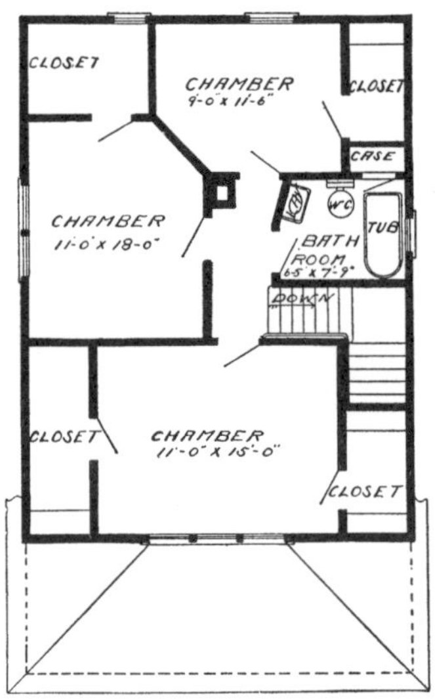

Second Floor Plan

DESIGN NUMBER 6035

Size: width, 26 feet 6 inches; length, 29 feet 6 inches, exclusive of porches

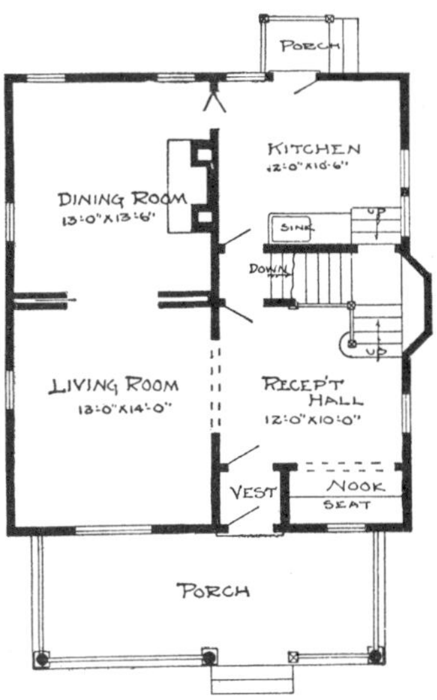

First Floor Plan

BLUE PRINTS consist of basement plan; roof plan; first and second floor plans; front, rear and two side elevations; wall sections and all necessary interior details. Specifications consist of about twenty pages of typewritten matter.

PRICE

of Blue Prints, together with a complete set of typewritten specifications

ONLY TWELVE DOLLARS

We mail plans and specifications the same day order is received.

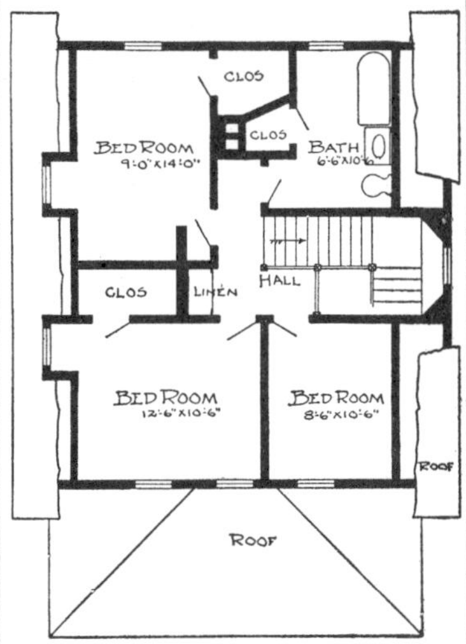

Second Floor Plan

DESIGN NUMBER 6069

Size: width, 28 feet 6 inches; length, 28 feet, exclusive of porches

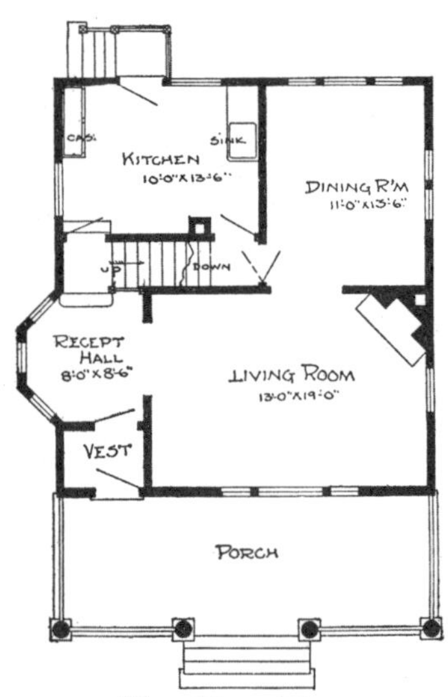

First Floor Plan

BLUE PRINTS consist of basement plan; roof plan; first and second floor plans; front, rear, and two side elevations; wall sections and all necessary interior details. Specifications consist of about twenty pages of typewritten matter.

PRICE

of Blue Prints, together with a complete set of typewritten specifications

ONLY TWELVE DOLLARS

We mall plans and specifications the same day order is reseived.

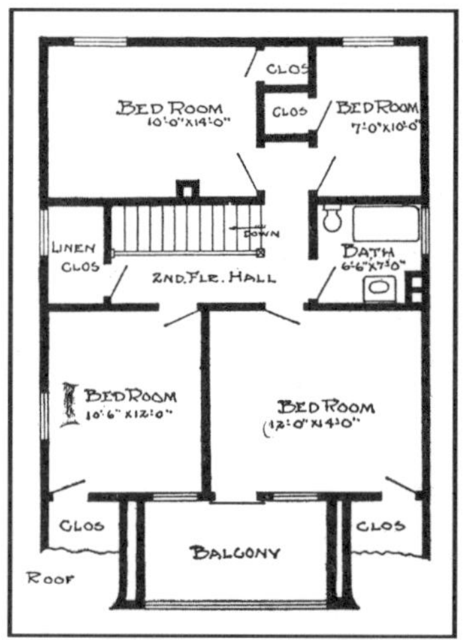

Second Floor Plan

Design No. 9031

The arrangement of this House is as follows:

Living Room, 16 feet by 12 feet.
Hall, 5 feet 6 inches by 7 feet.
Dining Room, 16 feet by 12 feet.
Kitchen, 11 feet by 10 feet 6 inches.
Bedroom, 11 feet by 11 feet 9 inches.
Bedroom, 12 feet by 12 feet.
Bathroom, 5 feet 6 inches by 7 feet 6 inches.
Pantry, Front and Rear Porches.
2 Closets.

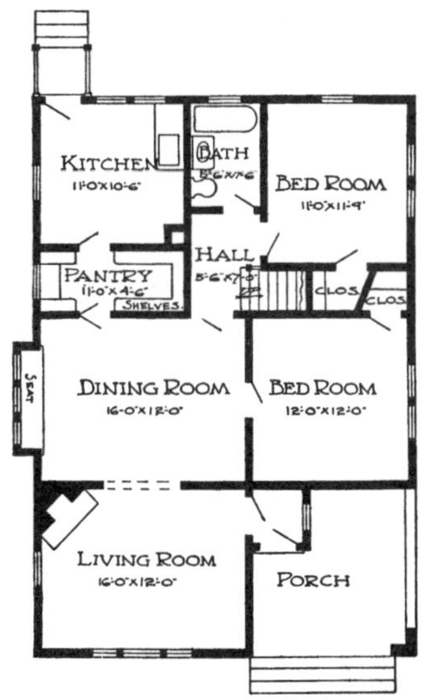

Floor Plan.

This Building is 29 feet 6 inches in width; 41 feet 6 inches in length.

Price of Complete Working Plans and Specifications $10.00

The Blue Printed Working Plans for this House consist of roof plan floor plan; front, right, left and rear elevations; wall sections and all necessary details.

The Typewritten Specifications contain all the necessary information for the proper construction of the House.

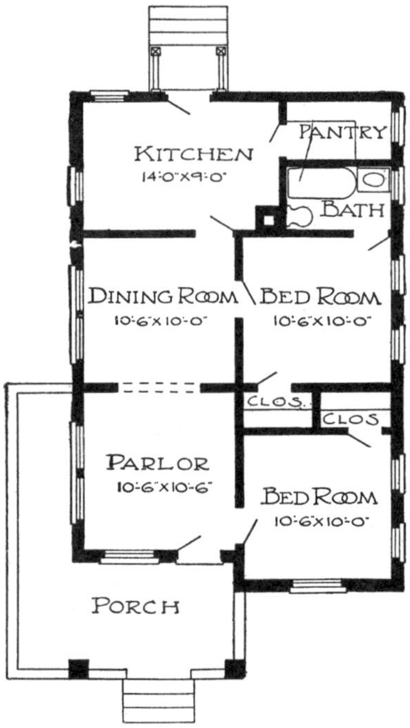

Floor Plan.

This Building is 23 feet 4 inches in width; 34 feet in length.

Design No. 9077

The arrangement of this **House** is as follows:

FLOOR PLAN.

Parlor, 10 feet 6 inches by 10 feet 6 inches.

Dining Room, 10 feet 6 inches by 10 feet.

Kitchen, 14 feet by 9 feet.

Bedroom, 10 feet 6 inches by 10 feet.

Bedroom, 10 feet 6 inches by 10 feet.

Bathroom, 7 feet 6 inches by 4 feet 6 inches

Pantry, Front and Rear Porches.

2 Closets.

Price of Complete Working Plans and Specifications **$12.00**

The Blue Printed Working Plans for this House consist of foundation plan; roof plan and floor plan; front, right, left and rear elevations; wall sections and all necessary details.

The Typewritten Specifications contain all the necessary information for the proper construction of the House.

Design No. 7076

Size: Width, 26 feet; Length, 44 feet 6 inches, exclusive of porch

PRICE

of Blue Prints together with a complete set of typewritten specifications

ONLY TWELVE DOLLARS

We mail Plans and Specifications the same day order is received.

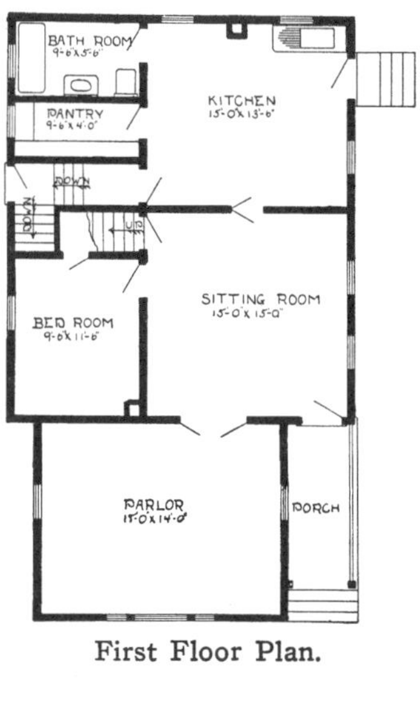

First Floor Plan.

Blue prints consist of basement plan; roof plan; first and second floor plans; front, rear, and two side elevations; wall sections and all necessary interior details. Specifications consist of about twenty pages of typewritten matter.

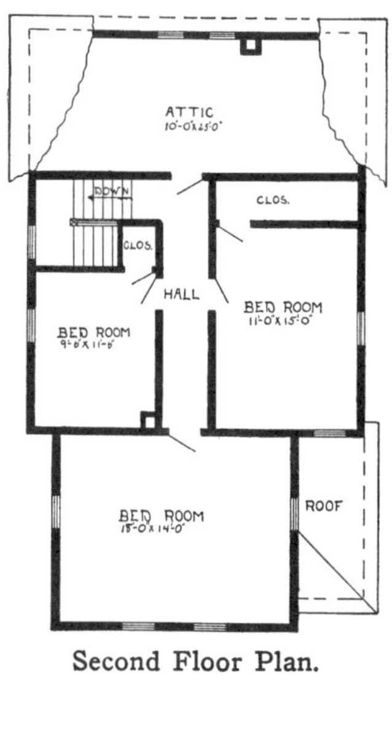

Second Floor Plan.

Design No. 7008

Size: Width, 31 feet 6 inches; Length, 29 feet, exclusive of porches

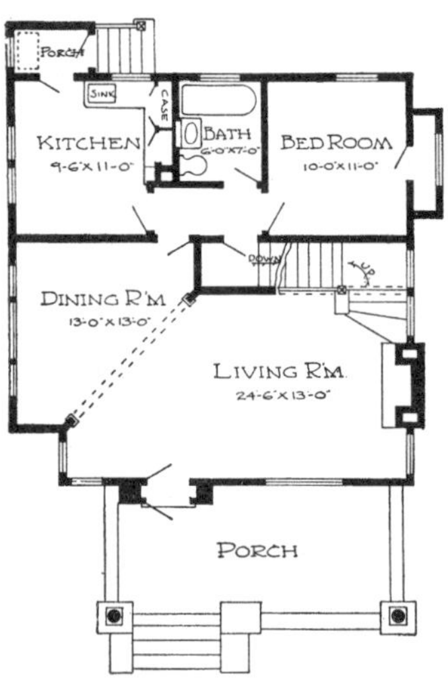

First Floor Plan

Blue prints consist of basement plan; roof plan; first and second floor plans; front, rear, two side elevations; wall sections and all necessary interior details. Specifications consist of about twenty pages of typewritten matter.

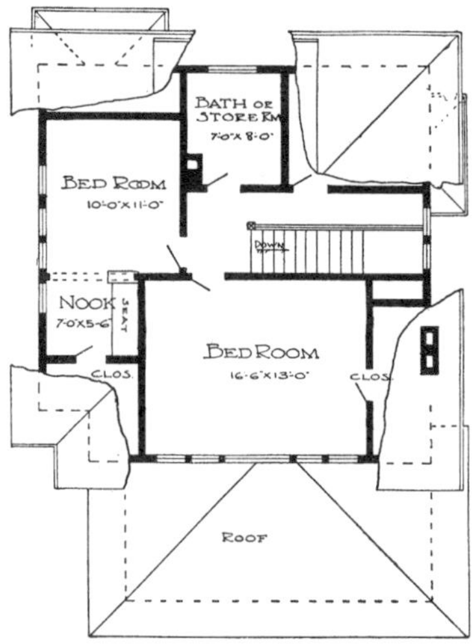

Second Floor Plan

PRICE

of Blue Prints, together with a complete set of typewritten specifications

ONLY FIFTEEN DOLLARS

We mail Plans and Specifications the same day order is received.

Design No. 2021

PRICE

of Blue Prints, together with a complete set of typewritten specifications is

ONLY TWELVE DOLLARS

We mail Plans and Specifications the same day order is received.

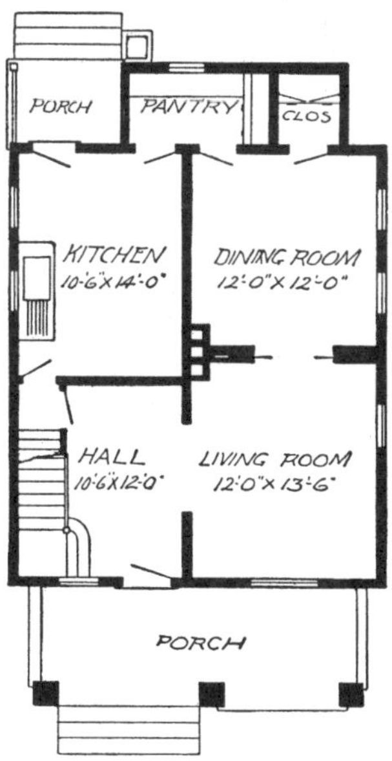

First Floor Plan

Blue prints consist of basement plan; first and second floor plans; front, rear, two side elevations; wall sections and all necessary interior details. Specifications consist of about twenty pages of typewritten matter.

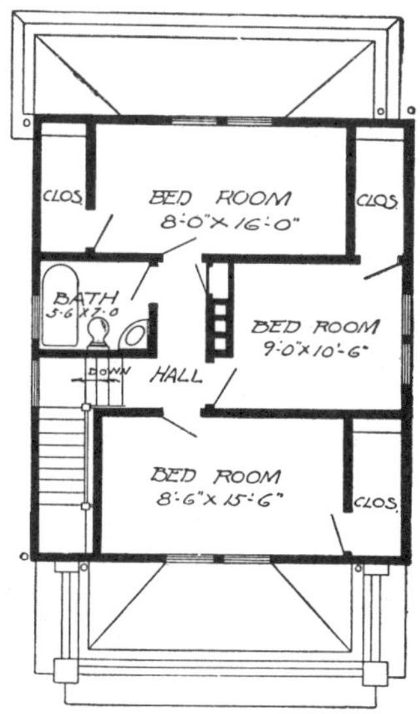

Second Floor Plan

SIZE: Width, 24 feet; length, 32 feet 6 inches, exclusive of porch

Our plans are full, complete and accurate in every particular, and guaranteed. Every plan is designed by a licensed architect, who makes a specialty of this kind of work, and whose experience is very broad.

Every foot of space is utilized in the preparation of our plans. We do not load e contractor and home builder with useless expense, simply to carry out some pet idea. Our plans are practical, modern and attractive.

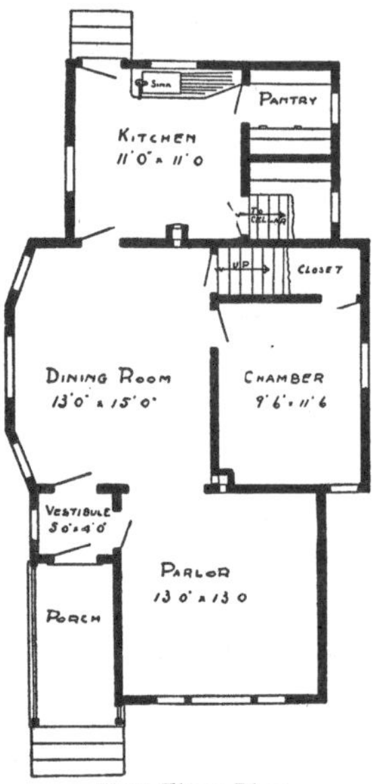

First Floor Plan

Design No. 34

Blue prints consist of cellar and foundation plan; roof plan; first and second floor plans; front, rear, two side elevations; wall sections and all necessary interior details. Specifications consist of about twenty pages of type-written matter.

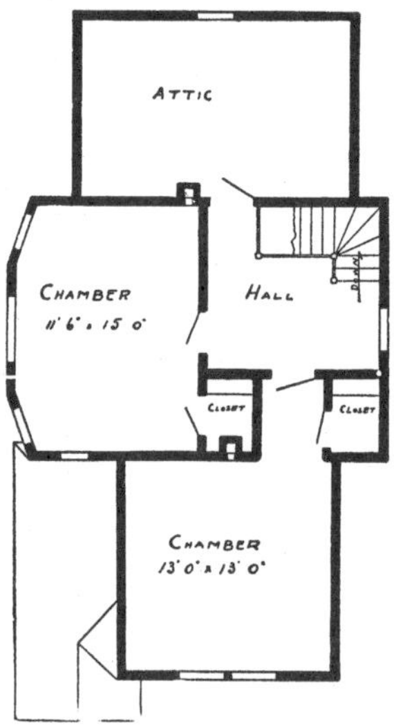

Second Floor Plan

PRICE
of Blue Prints, together with a complete set of typewritten specifications is

ONLY TWELVE DOLLARS

We mail Plans and Specifications the same day order is received.

Size: Width, 24 feet, length, 41 feet.

We do not blame you for wishing to know what you will get for your money. The plans we send out are the reguiar blue printed plans, drawn one-quarter inch scale to the foot, showing all elevatlons, floor plans and necessary interior details.

All our plans are printed by electricity on a circular blue printing machine. We use the very best grade of electric blue printing paper and take great care to have every line perfect and distinct.

DESIGN NUMBER 6012

Size: width, 31 feet, 6 inches; length, 40 feet, exclusive of porches

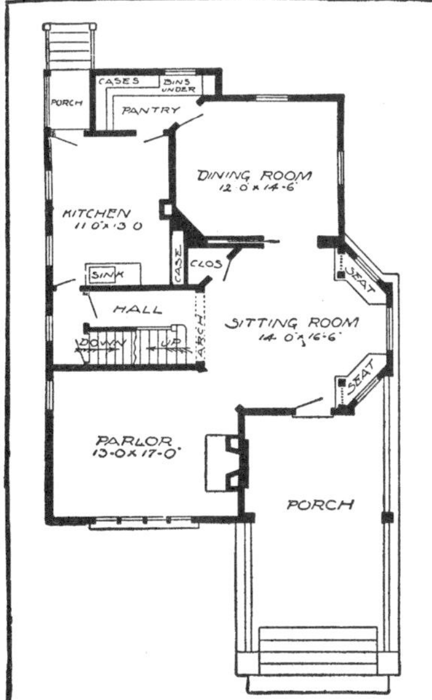

First Floor Plan

BLUE PRINTS consist of basement plan; roof plan; first and second floor plans; front, rear, two side elevations; wall sections and all necessary interior details. Specifications consist of about twenty pages of typewritten matter.

PRICE

of Blue Prints, together with a complete set of typewritten specifications

ONLY FIFTEEN DOLLARS

We mail plans and specifications the same day order is received.

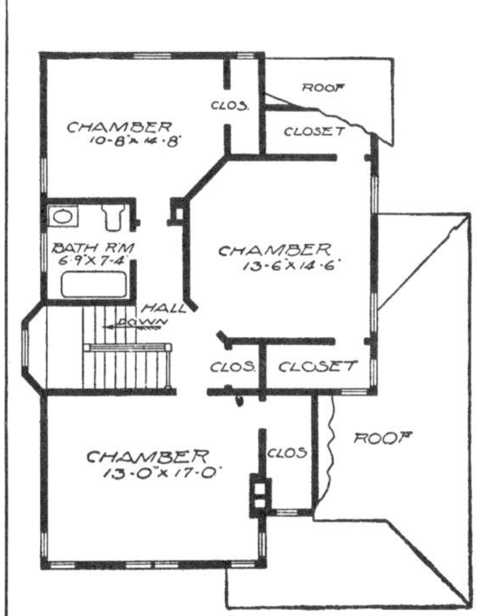

Second Floor Plan

DESIGN NUMBER 6064

Size: width, 31 feet 6 inches; length, 42 feet 6 inches exclusive of porches

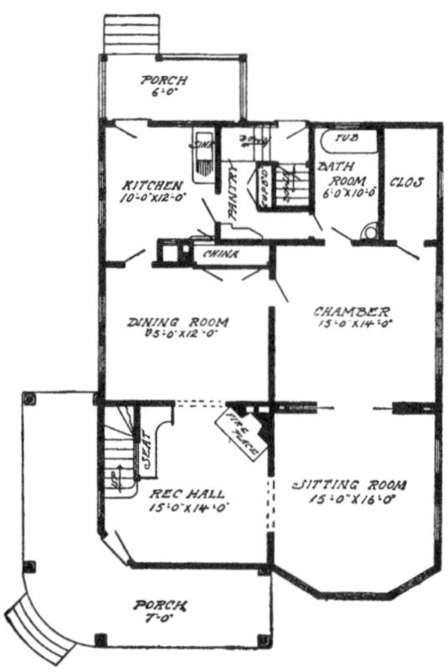

First Floor Plan

BLUE PRINTS consist of basement plan; first and second floor plan; front, rear, two side elevations; wall sections and all necessary interior details. Specifications consist of about twenty pages of typewritten matter.

PRICE

of Blue Prints, together with a complete set of typewritten specifications

ONLY TWELVE DOLLARS

We mail plans and specifications the same day order is received.

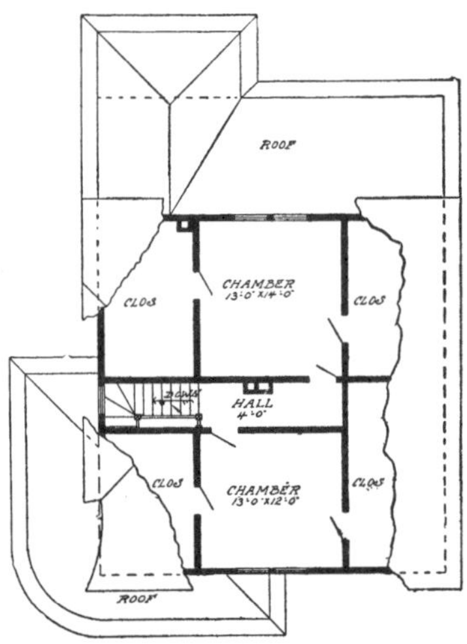

Second Floor Plan

DESIGN NUMBER 6033

Size: width, 23 feet 6 inches; length, 29 feet, exclusive of porches

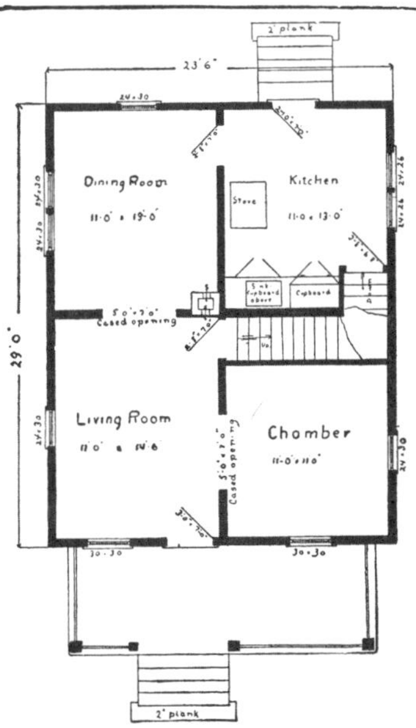

First Floor Plan

BLUE PRINTS consist of basement plan; first and second floor plans; front, rear, two side elevations; wall sections and all necessary interior details. Specifications consist of about twenty pages of typewritten matter.

PRICE

of Blue Prints, together with a complete set of typewritten specifications

ONLY TEN DOLLARS

We mail plans and specifications the same day order is received.

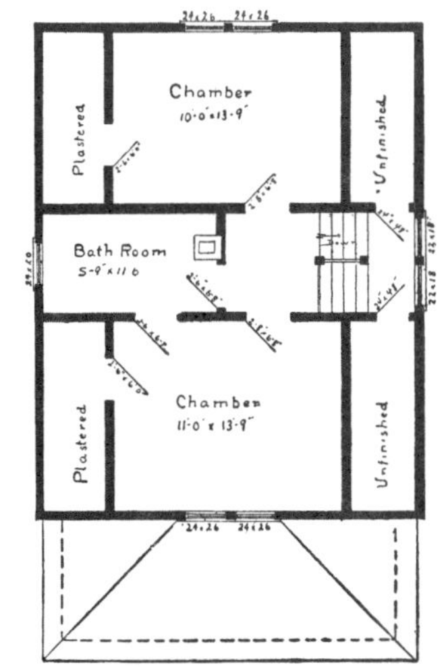

Second Floor Plan

DESIGN NUMBER 6070

Size: width, 32 feet 6 inches; length, 28 feet, exclusive of porches

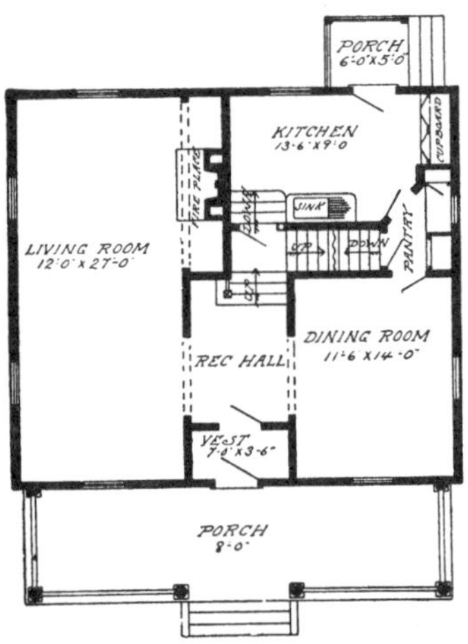

First Floor Plan

BLUE PRINTS consist of basement plan; first and second floor plans; front, rear, two side elevations; wall sections and all necessary interior details. Specifications consist of about twenty pages of typewritten matter.

PRICE

of Blue Prints, together with a complete set of typewritten specifications

ONLY TWELVE DOLLARS

We mail plans and specifications the same day order is received.

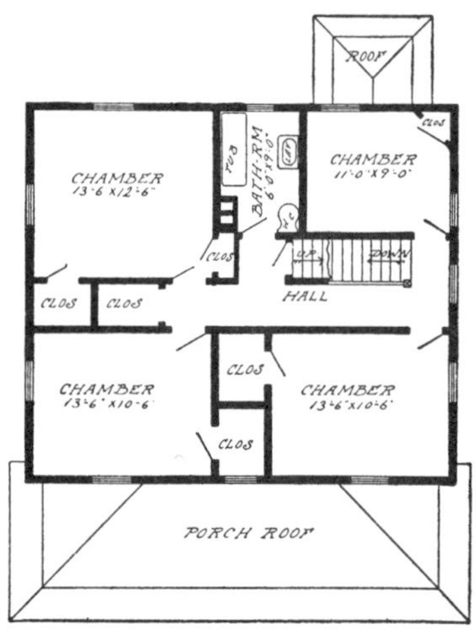

Second Floor Plan

Design No. 7036

Size: Width, 34 feet; Length, 47 feet, exclusive of porches

PRICE

of Blue Prints, together with a complete set of typewritten specifications.

ONLY FIFTEEN DOLLARS

We mail Plans and Specifications the same day order is received.

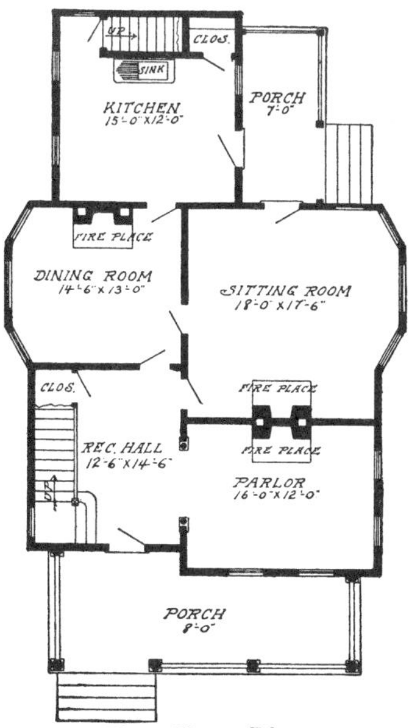

First Floor Plan

Blue Prints consist of basement plan; roof plan; first and second floor plans; front, rear, two side elevations; wall sections and all necessary interior details. Specifications consist of about twenty pages of typewritten matter.

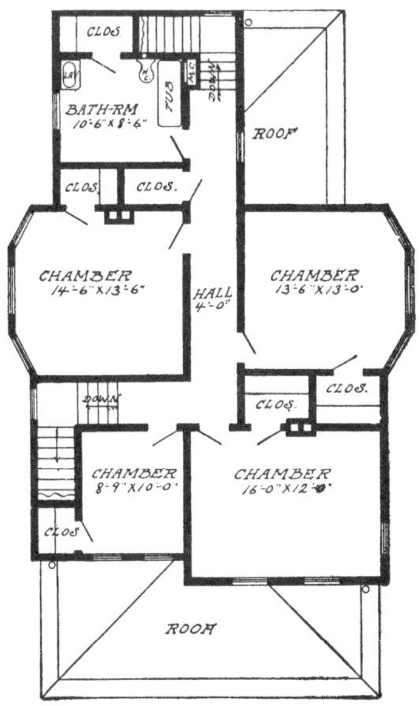

Second Floor Plan

Design No. 7092

Size: Width, 30 feet 6 inches; Length, 34 feet 6 inches, exclusive of porches

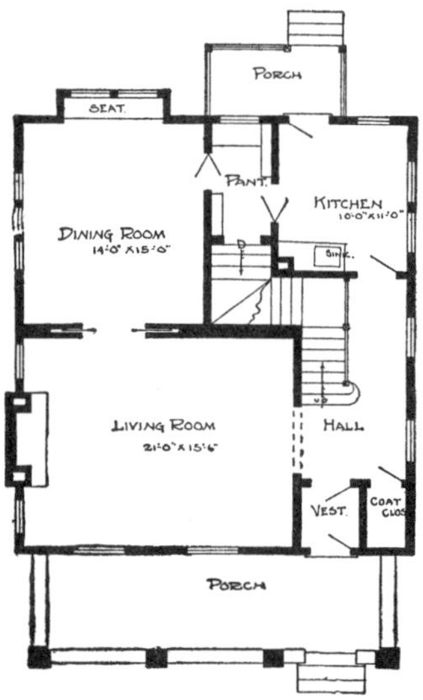

First Floor Plan

Blue prints consist of basement plan; first and second floor plans; front, rear, two side elevations; wall sections and all necessary interior details. Specifications consist of about twenty pages of typewritten matter.

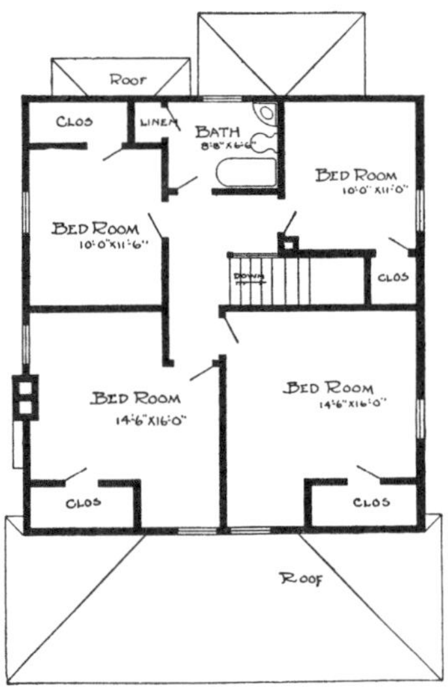

Second Floor Plan

PRICE

of Blue Prints together with a complete set of typewritten specifications

ONLY FIFTEEN DOLLARS

We mail Plans and Specifications the same day orde is received.

PRICE
of Blue Prints, together with a complete set of typewritten specifications is

ONLY TEN DOLLARS

We mail Plans and Specifications the same day order is received.

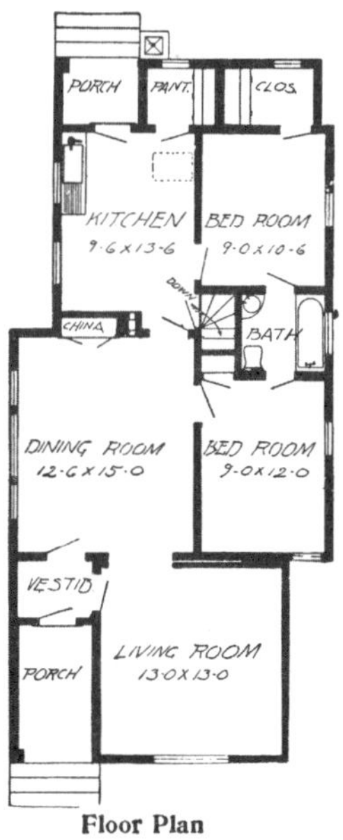

Floor Plan

Design No. 2018

Blue prints consist of foundation plan; roof plan; floor plan; front, rear, two side elevations; wall sections and all necessary interior details. Specifications consist of about fifteen pages of typewritten matter.

SIZE: Width, 25 feet; length, 48 feet 6 inches.

If a plan in this pleases you, if the arrangement of the rooms is satisfactiory, and if the exterior is pleasing and attractive, we claim that it can be built as cheap or cheaper than if any other architect designed it.

"Be it ever so humble, there is no place like home." It is, or should be, the ambition of every one to some day own a home of his own. The plans we illustrate are such as 75 to 90 per cent of the people build

Design No. 2050

Blue prints consist of basement plan; roof plan; floor plan; front, rear, two side elevations; wall sections and all necessary interior details. Specifications consist of about fifteen pages of typewritten matter.

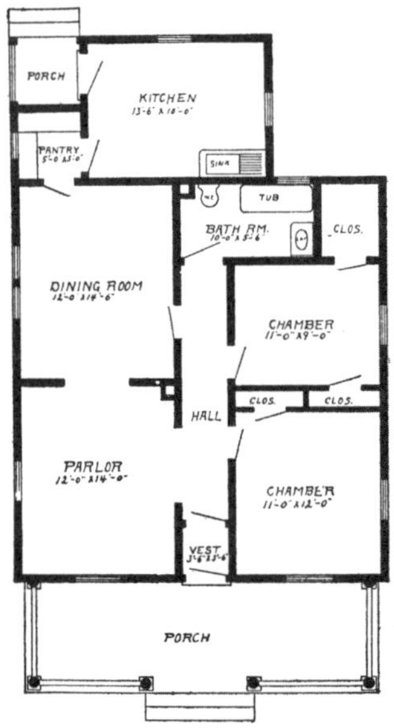

Floor Plan

PRICE

of Blue Prints, together with a complete set of typewritten specifications is

ONLY TEN DOLLARS

We mail Plans and Specifications the same day order is received.

SIZE: Width, 28 feet, 6 inches; length, 40 feet, 6 inches, exclusive of porch.

We do not blame you for wishing to know what you will get for your money. The plans we send out are the regular blue printed plans, drawn one-quarter inch scale to the foot, showing all elevations, floor plans and necessary interior details.

All of our plans are printed by electricity on a circular blue printing machine. We use the very best grade of electric blue printing paper and take great care to have every line perfect and distinct.

DESIGN NUMBER 6080

Size: width, 28 feet, 6 inches; length, 34 feet 6 inches, exclusive ot porches

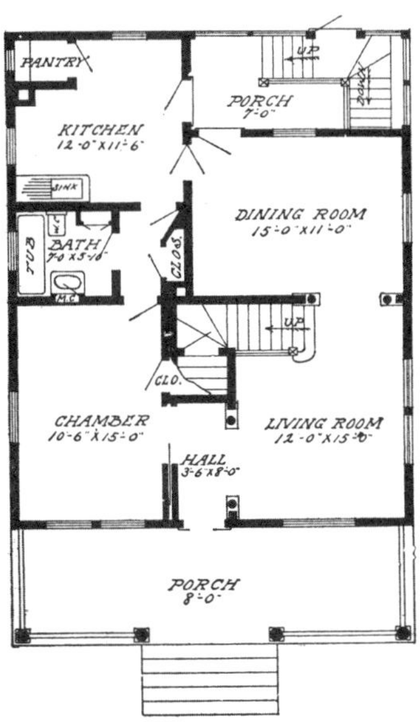

First Floor Plan

BLUE PRINTS consist of basement plan; first and second floor plans; front, rear two side elevations; wall sections and all necessary interior details. Specifications consist of about twenty pages of typewritten matter.

PRICE

of Blue Prints, together with a complete set of typewritten specifications

ONLY TEN DOLLARS

We mail plans and specifications the same day order is received.

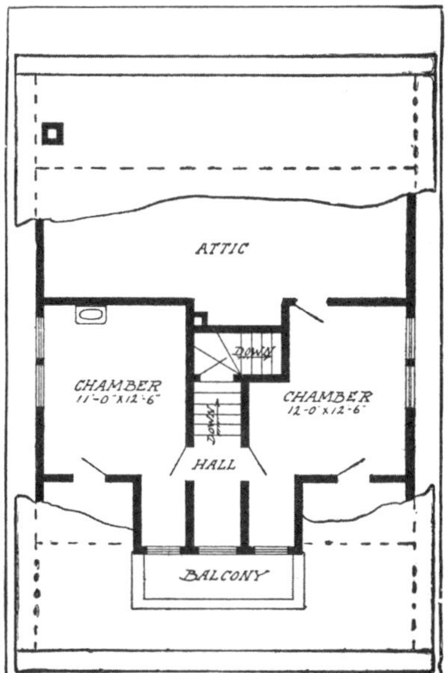

Second Floor Plan

DESIGN NUMBER 6030

Size: width, 34 feet; length, 28 feet, exclusive of porches

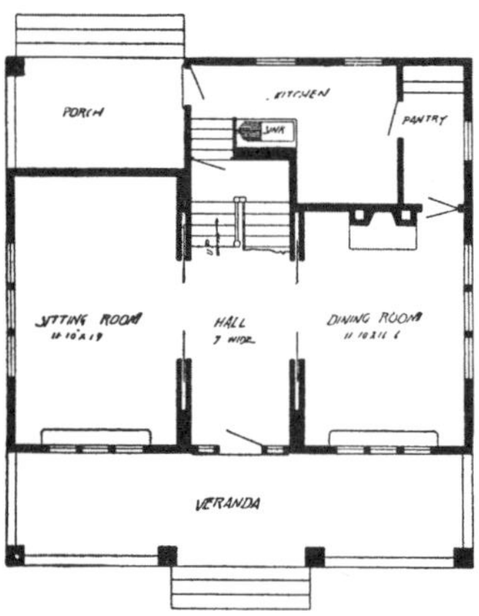

First Floor Plan

BLUE PRINTS consist of foundation plan; roof plan; first and second floor plans; front, rear, two side elevations; wall sections and all necessary interior details. Specifications consist of about twenty pages of typewritten matter.

PRICE

of Blue Prints, together with a complete set of typewritten specifications

ONLY TEN DOLLARS

We mail plans and specifications the same day order is received.

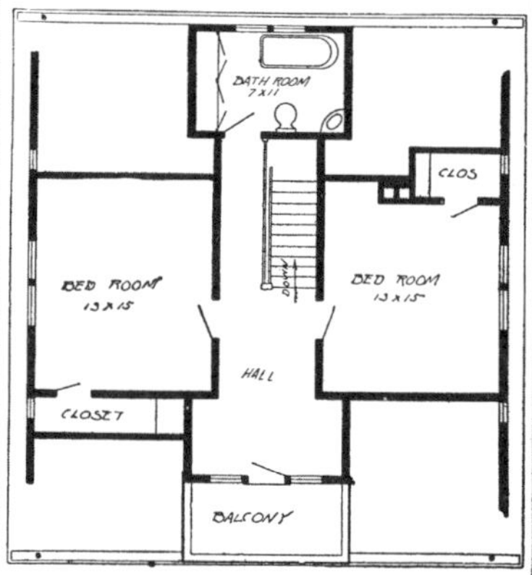

Second Floor Plan

D E S I G N N U M B E R 6 0 3 4

Size: width, 23 feet 10 inches; length, 25 feet, exclusive of porches

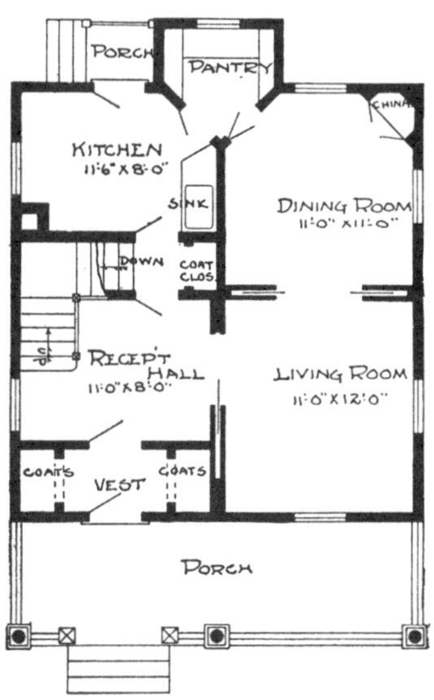

First Floor Plan

BLUE PRINTS consist of basement plan; first and second floor plans; front, rear, two side elevations; wall sections and all necessary interior details. Specifications consist of about twenty pages of typewritten matter.

PRICE

of Blue Prints, together with a complete set of typewritten specifications

ONLY TWELVE DOLLARS

We mail plans and specifications the same day order is received.

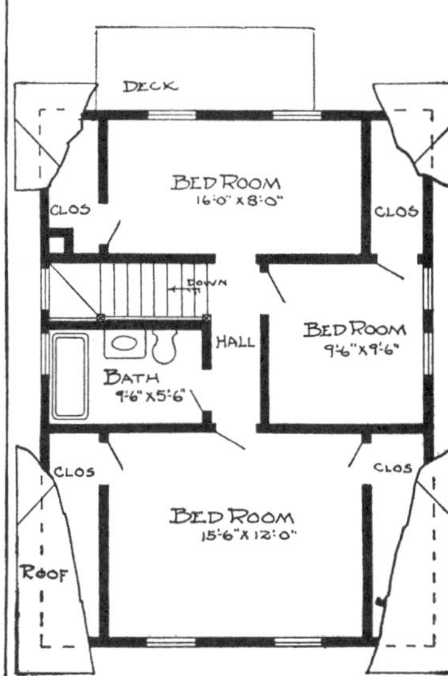

Second Floor Plan

D E S I G N   N U M B E R   6 0 2 9

Size: Width, 30 feet, 4 inches; length, 47 feet, 4 inches exclusive of porches

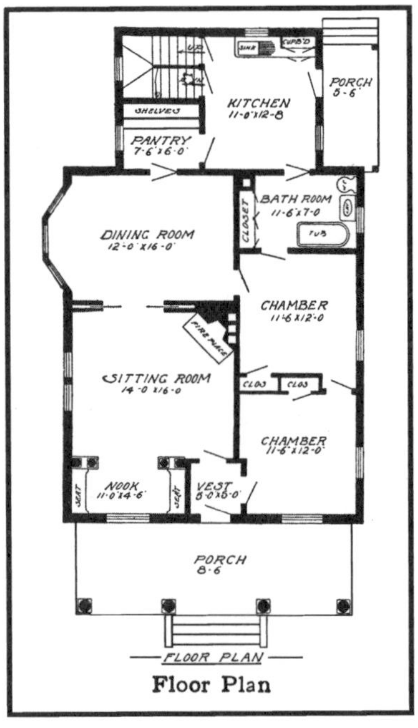

Floor Plan

BLUE PRINTS consist of basement plan; roof plan; floor plan; front, rear, two side elevations; wall sections and all necessary interior details. Specifications consist of about fifteen pages of typewritten matter.

PRICE

of Blue Prints, together with a complete set of typewritten specifications

ONLY TEN DOLLARS

We mail plans and specifications the same day order is received.

Design No. 7022

Size: Width, 30 feet; Length, 47 feet 6 inches, exclusive of porch

PRICE

of Blue Prints, together with a complete set of typewritten specifications.

ONLY FIFTEEN DOLLARS

We mail Plans and Specifications the same day order is received.

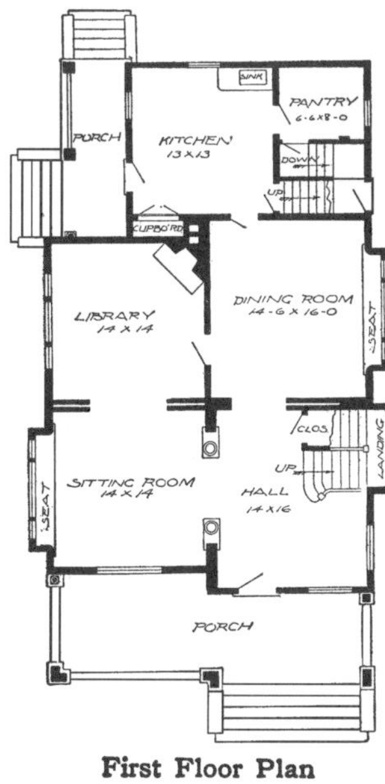

First Floor Plan

Blue prints consist of cellar and foundation plan; roof plan; first and second floor plans; front, rear, two side elevations; wall sections and all necessary interior details. Specifications consist of about twenty pages of typewritten matter.

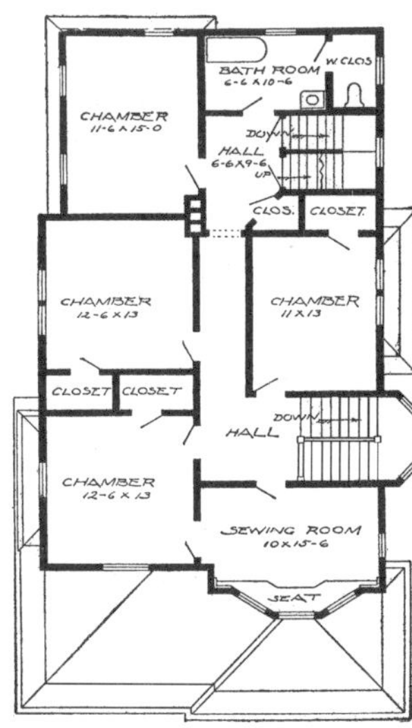

Second Floor Plan

Design No. 7085

Size: Width, 23 feet 6 inches; Length, 27 feet 6 inches, exclusive of porches

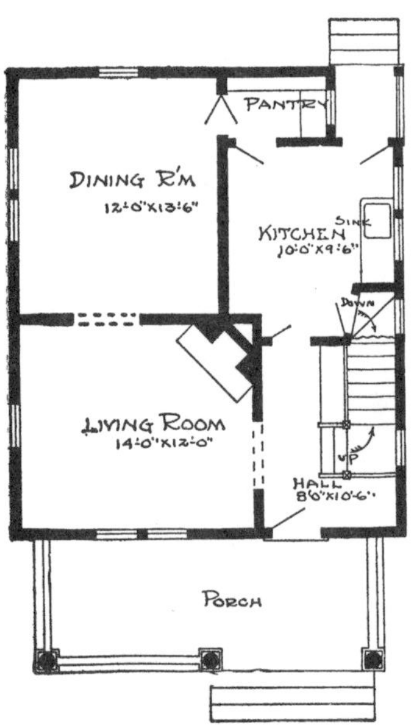

First Floor Plan

Blue prints consist of basement plan; roof plan; first and second floor plans; front, rear, two side elevations; wall sections and all necessary interior details. Specifications consist of about twenty pages of typewritten matter.

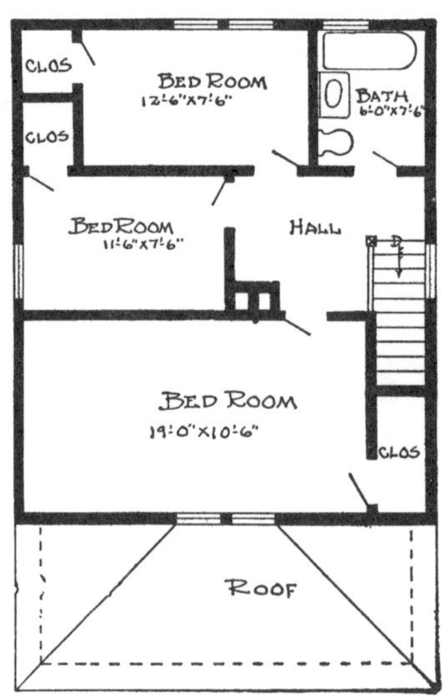

Second Floor Plan

PRICE

of Blue Prints, together with a complete set of typewritten specifications

ONLY TWELVE DOLLARS

We mail **Plans and Specifications** the same day **order** is received.

DESIGN NUMBER 6044

Size: width, 36 feet; length, 45 feet, exclusive of porches

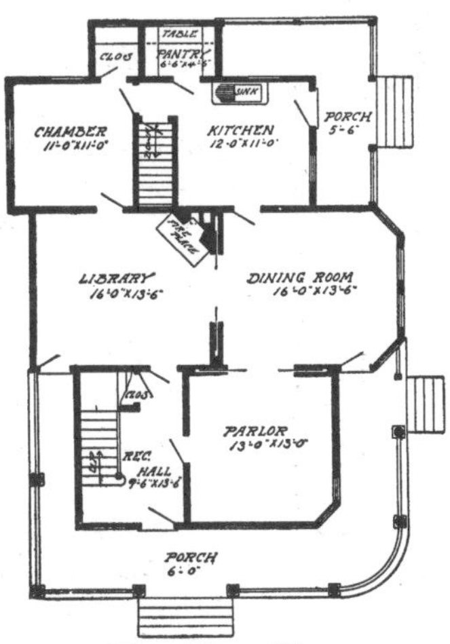

First Floor Plan

BLUE PRINTS consist of cellar and foundation plan; first and second floor plans; front, rear, two side elevations; wall sections and all necessary interior details. Specifications consist of about twenty pages of typewritten matter.

PRICE

of Blue Prints, together with a complete set of typewritten specifications.

ONLY FIFTEEN DOLLARS

We mail plans and specifications the same day order is received.

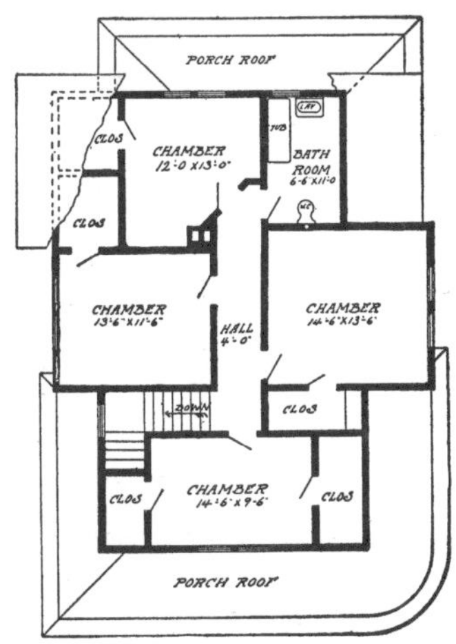

Second Floor Plan

DESIGN NUMBER 6047

Size: width, 25 feet; length, 31 feet, exclusive of porches

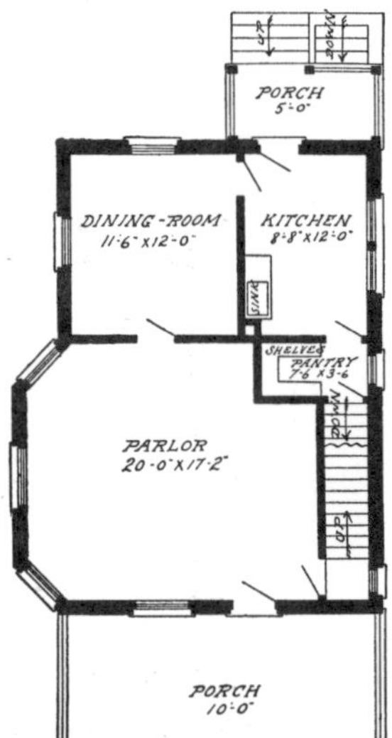

First Floor Plan

BLUE PRINTS consist of cellar and foundation plan, first and second floor plan; front, two side elevations; wall sections and all necessary interior details. Specifications consist of about twenty pages of typewritten matter.

PRICE

of Blue Prints, together with a complete set of typewritten specifications

ONLY TEN DOLLARS

We mail plans and specifications the same day order is received.

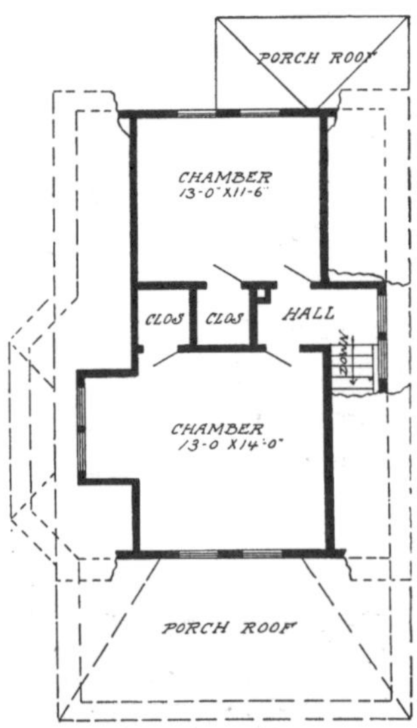

Second Floor Plan

PRICE

of Blue Prints, together with a complete set of type-written specifications is

ONLY TWELVE DOLLARS

We mail Plans and Specifications the same day order is received.

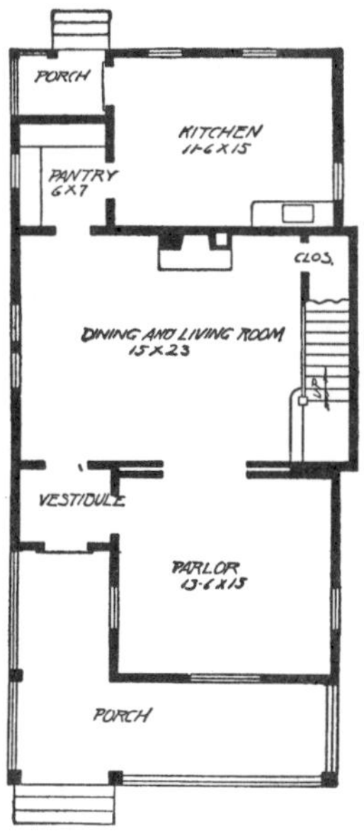

First Floor Plan

Design No. 2022

Blue prints consist of cellar and foundation plan; first and second floor plan; front, two side elevations; wall sections and all necessary interior details. Specifications consist of about twenty pages of type-written matter.

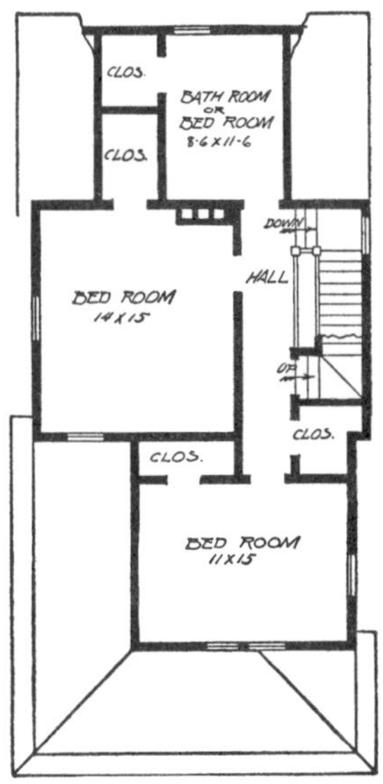

Second Floor Plan

SIZE: Width, 24 feet; length, 43 feet, exclusive of porches

Many have marveled at our ability to furnish such excellent and complete working plans and specifications at such low prices.

We do not wonder at this, because we charge but five dollars for a more complete set of working plans and specifications than you would receive if ordered in the regular manner, and when drawn especially for you, at a cost of from fifty to seventy-five dollars.

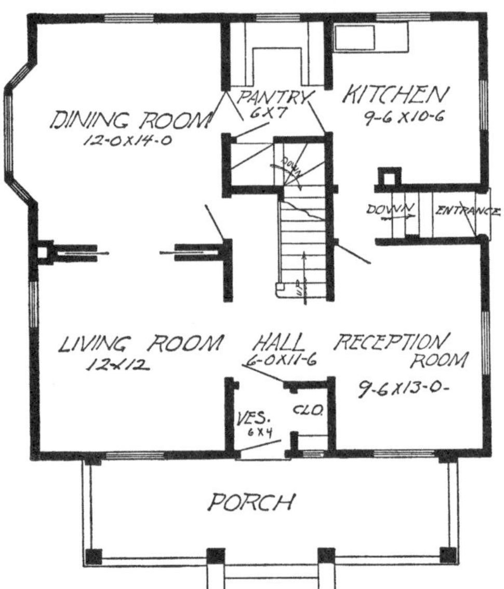

First Floor Plan

Design No. 2026

Blue prints consist of basement plan; roof plan; first and second floor plans; front, rear, and two side elevations; wall sections and all necessary interior details. Specifications consist of about twenty pages of typewritten matter.

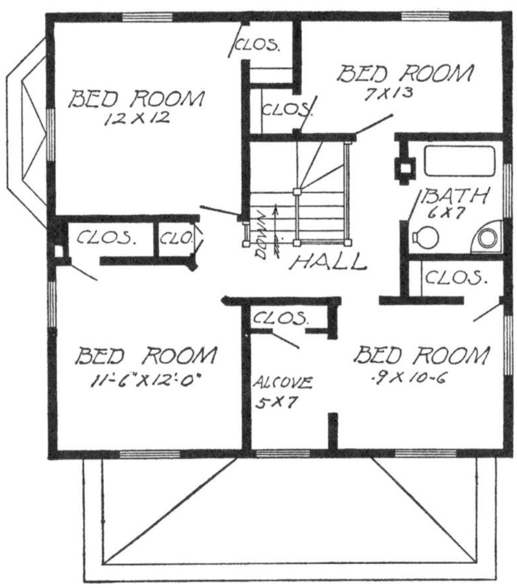

Second Floor Plan

PRICE

of Blue Prints, together with a complete set of typewritten specifications is

ONLY TWELVE DOLLARS

We mail Plans and Specifications the same day order is received.

SIZE: Width, 29 feet 6 inches; length, 28 feet exclusive of porch.

All of our plans are prepared by licensed architects standing at the head of their profession, and the standard of their work is the very highest.

We could not afford to make this guarantee if we were not positive that we were furnishing the best plans put out in this country, even though our price is not more than one-seventh to one-tenth of the price usually charged.

Design No. 9001

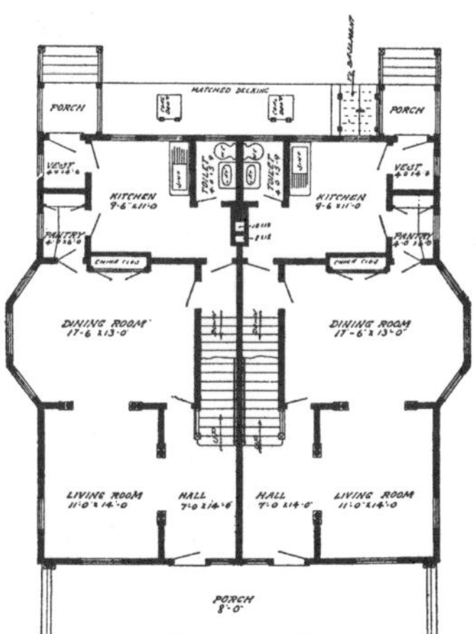

First Floor Plan.

Double House; both sides are the same.

The arrangement of this House is as follows:

FIRST FLOOR.

Reception Hall, 7 feet by 14 feet.
Living Room, 11 feet by 14 feet.
Dining Room, 17 feet 6 inches by 13 feet.
Kitchen, 9 feet 6 inches by 11 feet.
Lavatory, 4 feet by 5 feet 9 inches.
Pantry, Front and Rear Porches.

SECOND FLOOR.

Bedroom, 18 feet 6 inches by 11 feet.
Bedroom, 9 feet 6 inches by 11 feet.
Bedroom, 14 feet by 13 feet.
Bathroom, 6 feet by 7 feet.
3 Closets.

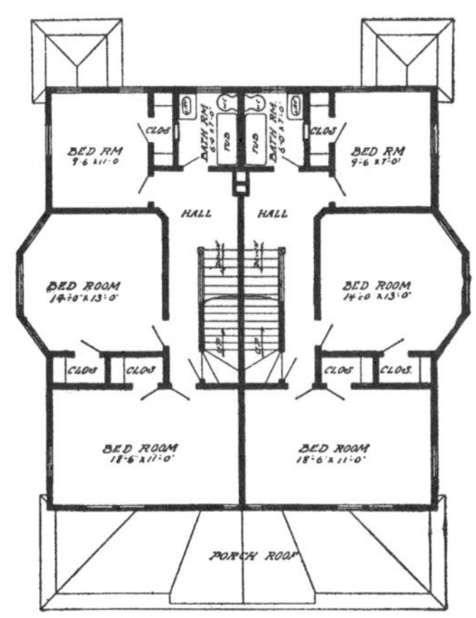

Second Floor Plan.

This building is 44 feet 6 inches in width; 40 feet in length.

Price of Complete Working Plans and Specifications.. $20.00

The Blue Printed Working Plans for this House consist of basement plan, roof plan, first and second floor plans; front, right, left and rear elevations; wall sections and all necessary details.

The Typewritten Specifications contain all the necessary information for the proper construction of the House.

Design No. 9064

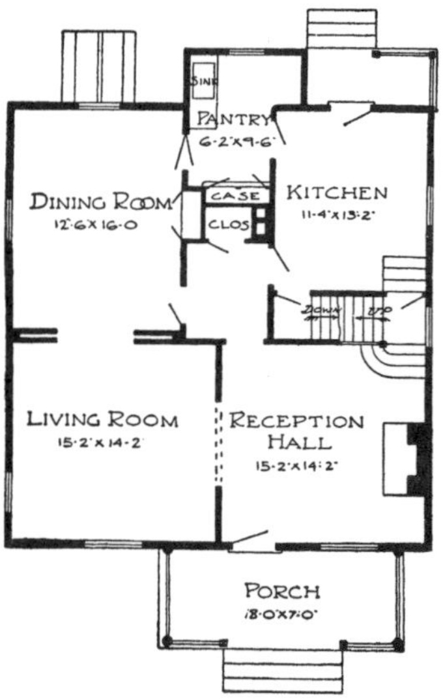

First Floor Plan.

The arrangement of this House is as follows:

FIRST FLOOR.

Reception Hall, 15 feet 2 inches by 14 feet 2 inches.
Living Room, 15 feet 2 inches by 14 feet 2 inches.
Dining Room, 12 feet 6 inches by 16 feet.
Kitchen, 11 feet 4 inches by 13 feet 2 inches.
Pantry, Front and Rear Porches.

SECOND FLOOR.

Bedroom, 12 feet 8 inches by 13 feet 2 inches.
Bedroom, 13 feet 2 inches by 15 feet 2 inches.
Bedroom, 13 feet 2 inches by 13 feet 2 inches.
Bathroom, 12 feet 8 inches by 9 feet 8 inches.
5 Closets.

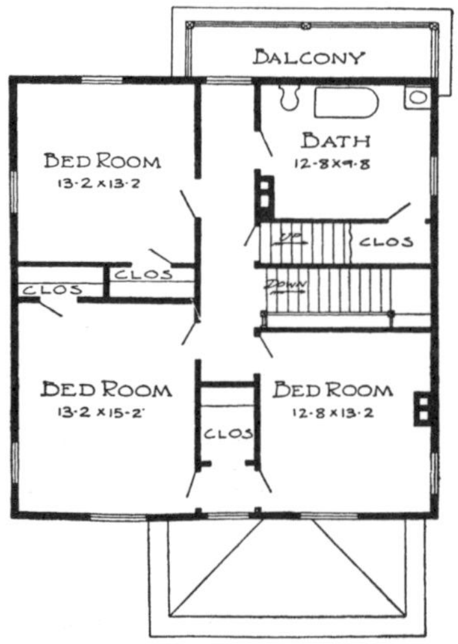

Second Floor Plan.

This Building is 31 feet 6 inches in width; 36 feet in length.

Price of Complete Working Plans and Specifications.. **$12.00**

The Blue Printed Working Plans for this House consist of basement plan; roof plans; first and second floor plans; front, right, left and rear elevations; wall sections and all necessary details.

The Typewritten Specifications contain all the necessary information for the proper construction of the House

DESIGN NUMBER 6071

Size: width, 28 feet; length, 36 feet, exclusive of porches

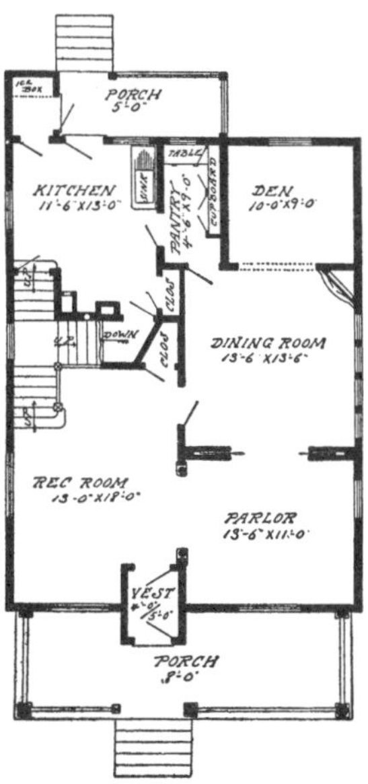

First Floor Plan

BLUE PRINTS consist of basement plan; roof plan; first and second floor plans; front, rear, two side elevations; wall sections and all necessary interior details. Specifications consist of about twenty pages of typewritten matter.

PRICE

of Blue Prints, together with a complete set of typewritten specifications

ONLY TWELVE DOLLARS

We mail plans and specifications the same day order is received.

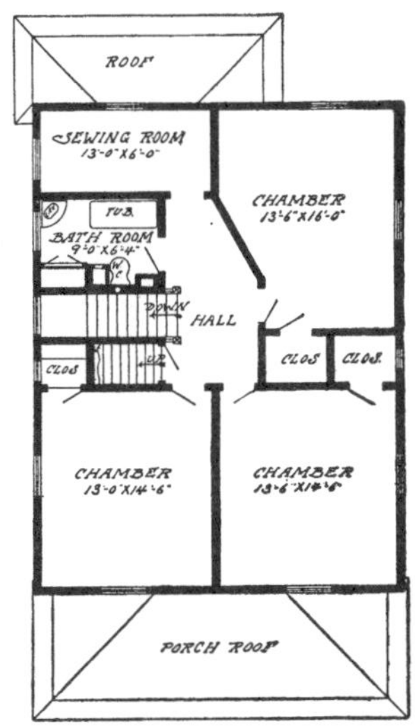

Second Floor Plan

DESIGN NUMBER 6068

Size: width, 32 feet; length, 36 feet, exclusive of porches

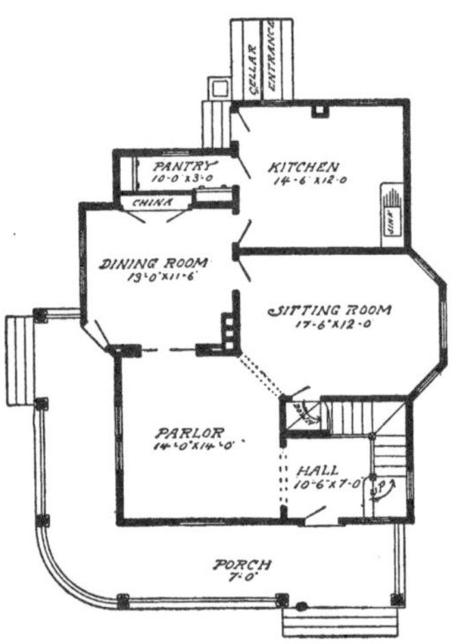

First Floor Plan

BLUE PRINTS consist of basement plan; first and second floor plans; front, rear, two side elevations; wall sections and all necessary interior details. Specifications consist of about twenty pages of typewritten matter.

PRICE

of Blue Prints, together with a complete set of typewritten specifications

ONLY TWELVE DOLLARS

We mail plans and specifications the same day order is received.

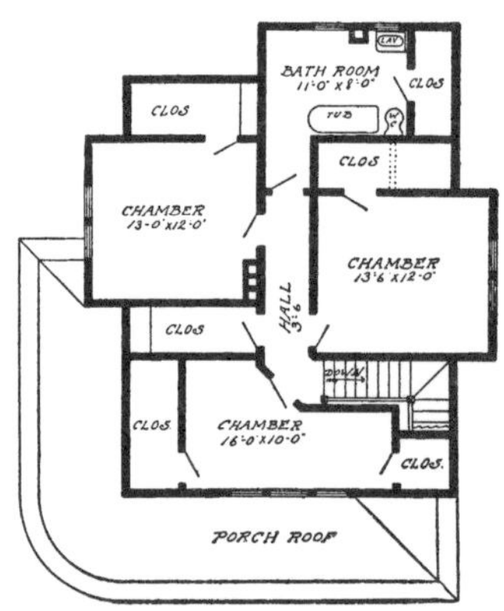

Second Floor Plan

Design No. 9079

The arrangement of this House is as follows:

FLOOR PLAN.

Living Room, 15 feet by 15 feet.

Dining Room, 12 feet by 15 feet.

Kitchen, 12 feet by 8 feet 9 inches.

Bedroom, 10 feet by 12 feet.

Bathroom, 5 feet 6 inches by 8 feet 6 inches.

Pantry, Front and Rear Porches.

2 Closets.

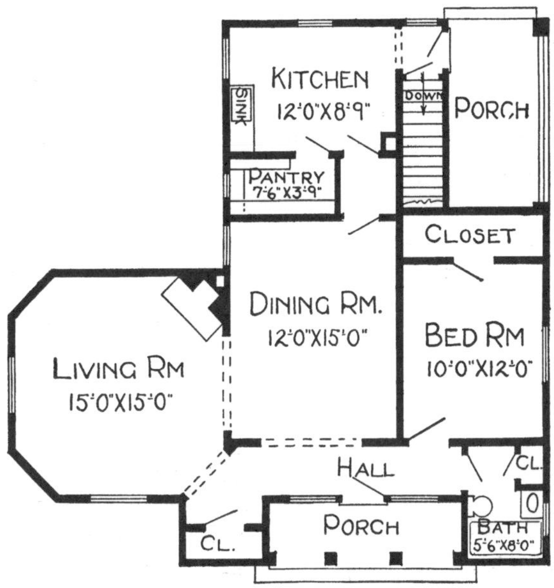

Floor Plan.

This Building is 39 feet in width; 37 feet 6 inches in length.

Price of Complete Working Plans and Specifications $10.00

The Blue Printed Working Plans for this House consist of basement plan; floor plan; front, right, left and rear elevations; wall sections and all necessary details.

The Typewritten Specifications contain all the necessary information for the proper construction of the House

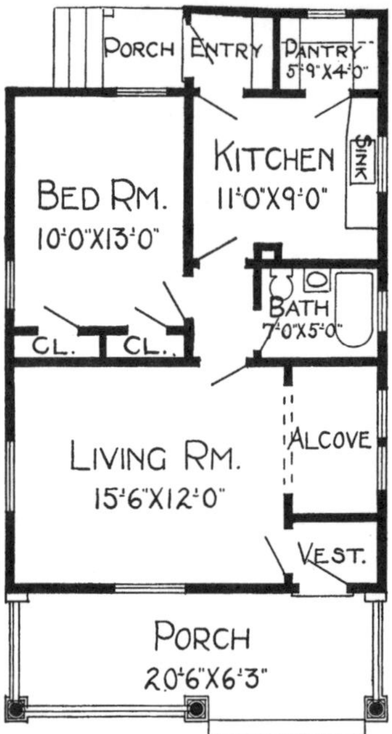

Floor Plan.

Design No. 9081

The arrangement of this House is as follows:

FLOOR PLAN.

Living Room, 15 feet 6 inches by 12 feet.
Kitchen, 11 feet by 9 feet.
Bedroom, 10 feet by 13 feet.
Bathroom, 7 feet by 5 feet.
Pantry, Front and Rear Porches.
Alcove.
2 Closets.

This Building is 22 feet in width; 32 feet in length.

Price of Complete Working Plans and Specifications $10.00

The Blue Printed Working Plans for this House consist of foundation plan; floor plan; front, right, left and rear elevations; wall sections and all necessary details.

The Typewritten Specifications contain all the necessary information for the proper construction of the House.

DESIGN NUMBER 6081

Size: width, 32 feet; length, 43 feet, exclusive of porches

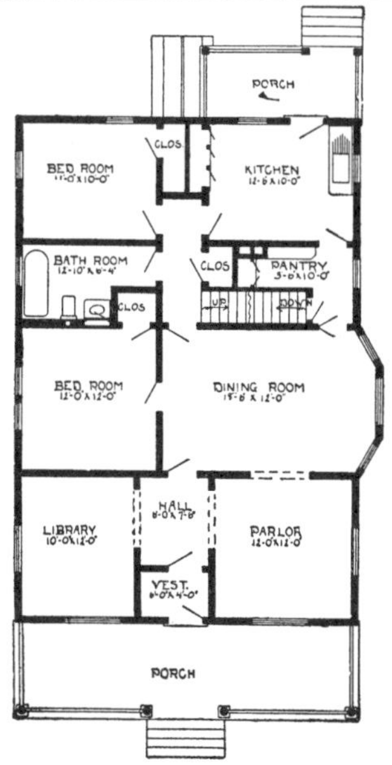

First Floor Plan

BLUE PRINTS consist of cellar and foundation plan; first and second floor plans; front, rear, two side elevations; wall sections and all necessary interior details. Specifications consist of about twenty pages of typewritten matter.

PRICE

of Blue Prints, together with a complete set of typewritten specifications

ONLY TWELVE DOLLARS

We mail plans and specifications the same day order is received.

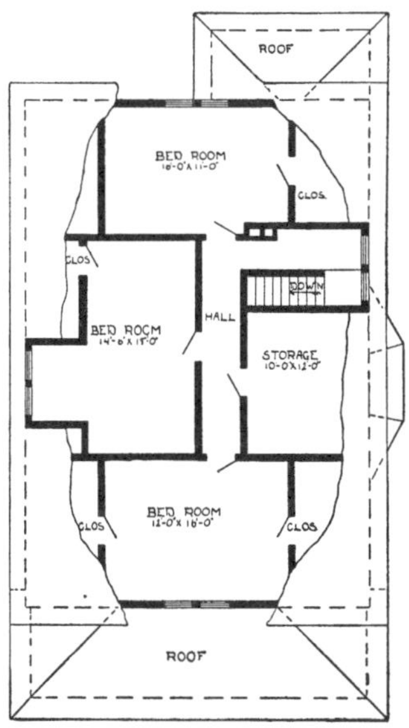

Second Floor Plan

DESIGN NUMBER 6051

Size: width, 31 feet, 6 inches; length, 40 feet, exclusive of porches

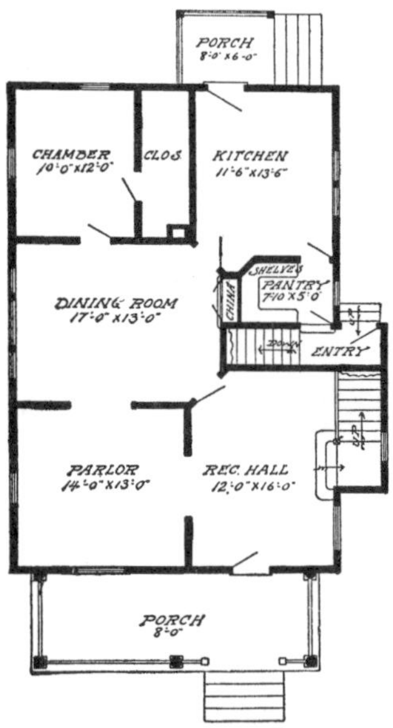

First Floor Plan

BLUE PRINTS consist of basement plan; roof plan; first and second floor plans; front, rear, two side elevations; wall sections and all necessary interior details. Specifications consist of about twenty pages of typewritten matter.

PRICE

of Blue Prints, together with a complete set of typewritten specifications

ONLY TEN DOLLARS

We mail plans and specifications the same day order is received.

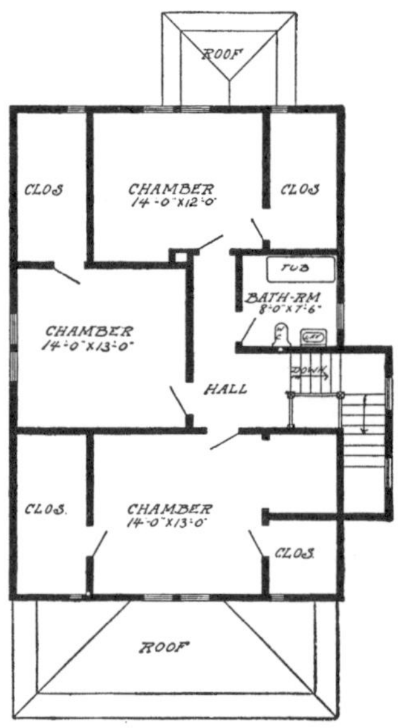

Second Floor Plan

DESIGN NUMBER 6167

Size: width, 25 feet 6 inches; length, 34 feet 6 inches, exclusive of porches

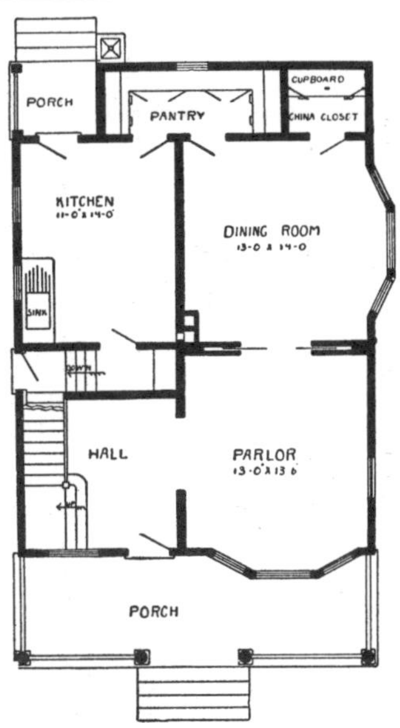

First Floor Plan

BLUE PRINTS consist of cellar and foundation plan; floor plan; front, rear, two side elevations; wall sections and all necessary interior details. Specifications consist of about twenty pages of typewritten matter.

PRICE

of Blue Prints, together with a complete set of typewritten specifications

ONLY TWELVE DOLLARS

We mail plans and specifications the same day order is received.

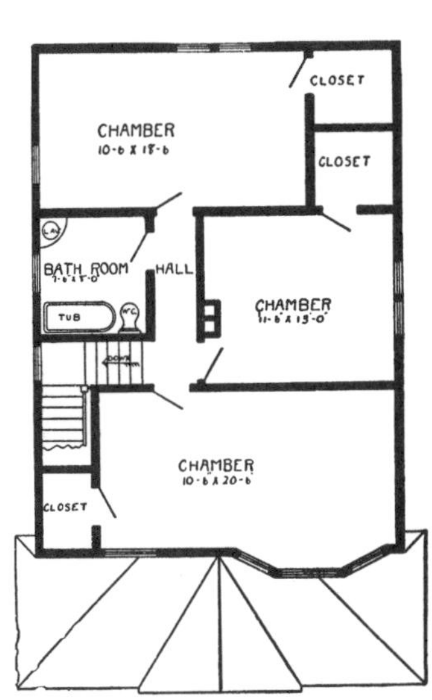

Second Floor Plan

DESIGN NUMBER 6016

Size: Width, 29 feet; length, 38 feet 6 inches exclusive of porches

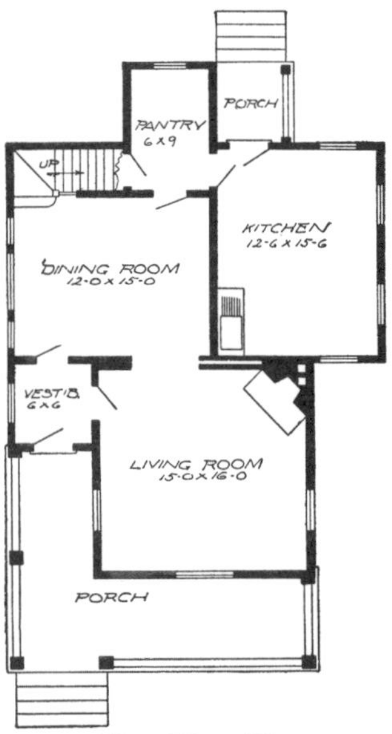

First Floor Plan

BLUE PRINTS consist of basement plan; roof plan; first and second floor plans; front, rear, two side elevations; wall sections and all necessary interior details. Specifications consist of about twenty pages of typewritten matter.

PRICE

of Blue Prints, together with a complete set of typewritten specifications

ONLY TWELVE DOLLARS

We mail plans and specifications the same day order is received.

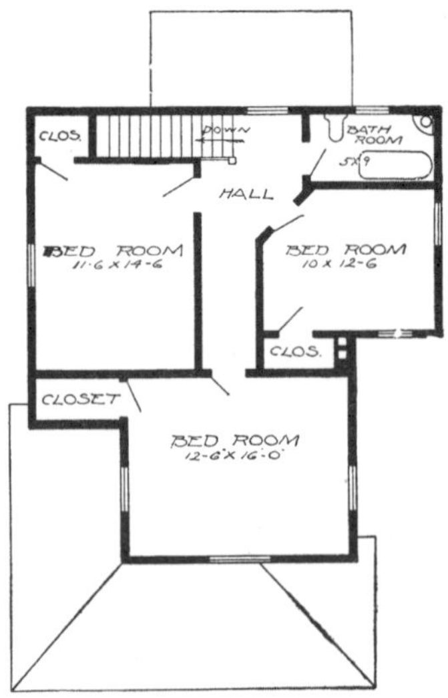

Second Floor Plan

Design No. 7004

Size: Width, 31 feet 6 inches; Length, 40 feet, exclusive of porches

PRICE

of Blue Prints, together with a complete set of typewritten specifications

ONLY FIFTEEN DOLLARS

We mail Plans and Specifications the same day order is received.

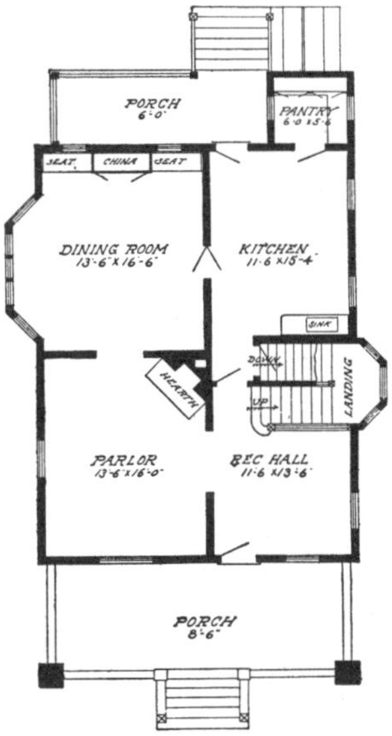

First Floor Plan

Blue Prints consist of basement plan; roof plan; first and second floor plans; front, rear, two side elevations; wall sections and all necessary interior details. Specifications consist of about twenty pages of typewritten matter.

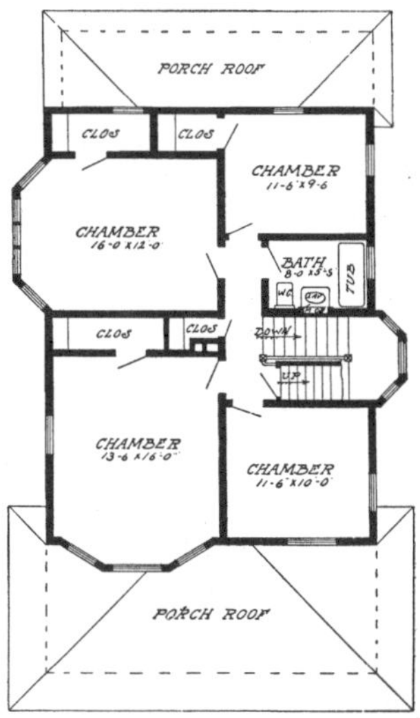

Second Floor Plan

Design No. 7032

Size: Width, 25 feet; Length, 35 feet, exclusive of porches

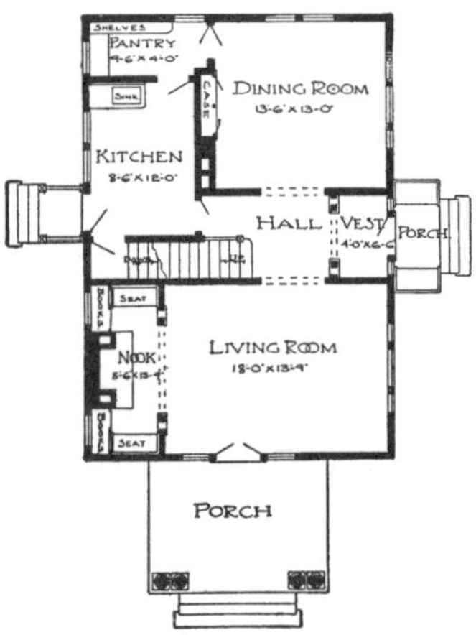

First Floor Plan

Blue prints consist of basement plan; roof plan; first and second floor plans; front, rear, two side elevations; wall sections and all necessary interior details. Specifications consist of about twenty pages of typewritten matter.

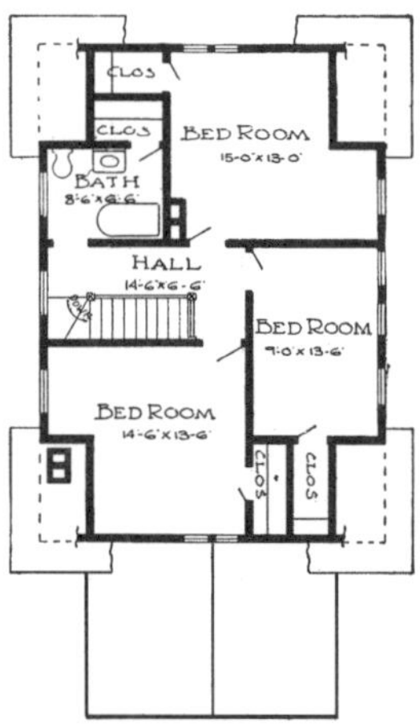

Second Floor Plan

PRICE

of Blue Prints, together with a complete set of typewritten specifications

ONLY FIFTEEN DOLLARS

We mail Plans and Specifications the same day order is received.

DESIGN NUMBER 6011

Size: width, 28 feet 6 inches; length, 33 feet, exclusive of porches

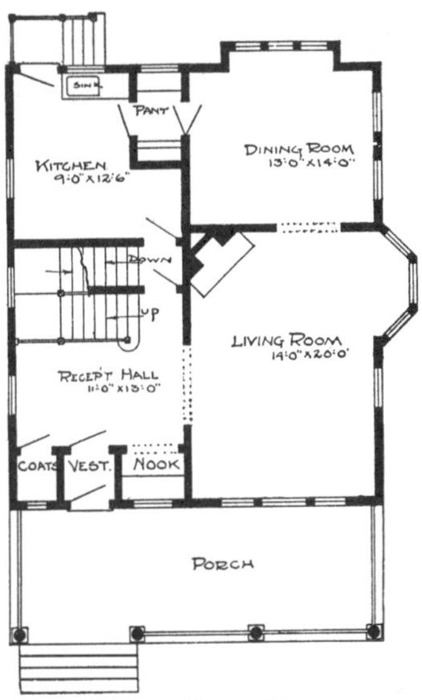

First Floor Plan

BLUE PRINTS consist of basement plan; roof plan; first and second floor plans; front, rear, two side elevations; wall sections and all necessary interior details. Specifications consist of about twenty pages of typewritten matter.

PRICE

of Blue Prints, together with a complete set of typewritten specifications

ONLY TWELVE DOLLARS

We mail plans and specifications the same day order is received.

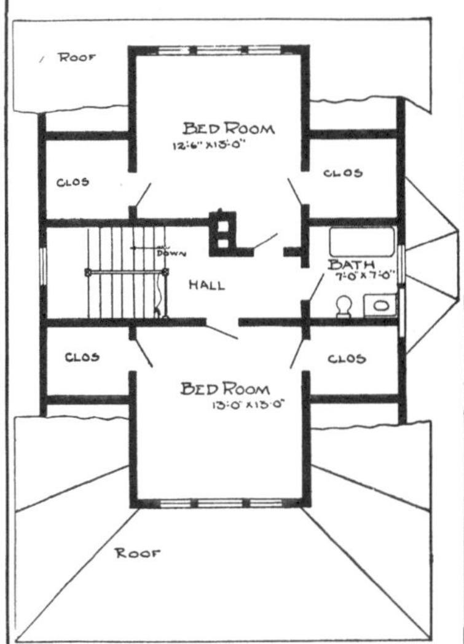

Second Floor Plan

DESIGN NUMBER 6041

Size: Width, 35 feet 6 inches; Length, 40 feet, exclusive of porches

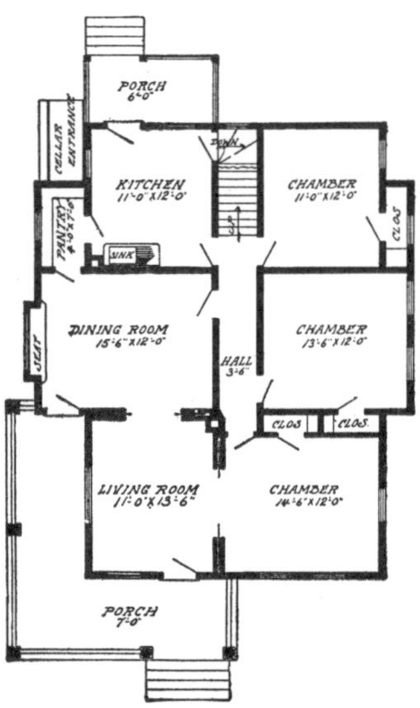

Floor Plan

BLUE PRINTS consist of basement plan; roof plan; floor plan; front, rear, two side elevations; wall sections and all necessary interior details. Specifications consist of about fifteen pages of typewritten matter.

PRICE

of Blue Prints, together with a complete set of typewritten specifications

ONLY TEN DOLLARS

We mail plans and specifications the same day order is received.

Design No. 7083

Size: Width, 36 feet; Length, 45 feet, exclusive of porch

PRICE

of Blue Prints, together with a complete set of typewritten specifications

ONLY TEN DOLLARS

We mail Plans and Specifications the same day order is received.

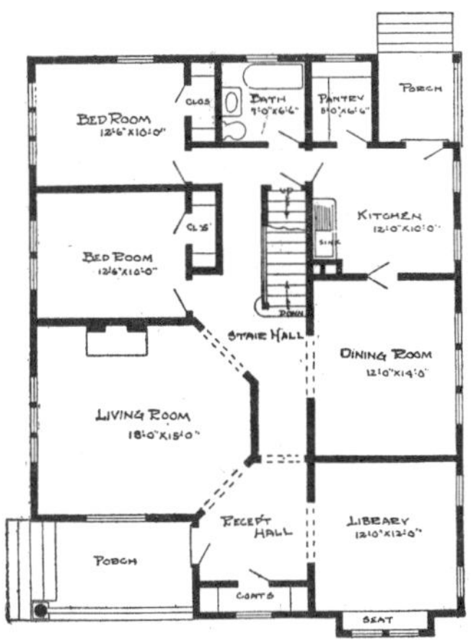

Floor Plan

Blue prints consist of basement plan; roof plan; floor plan; front, rear, two side elevations; wall sections and all necessary interior details. Specifications consist of about fifteen pages of typewritten matter.

Design No. 7086

Size: Width, 23 feet 6 inches; Length, 29 feet 6 inches, exclusive of porches

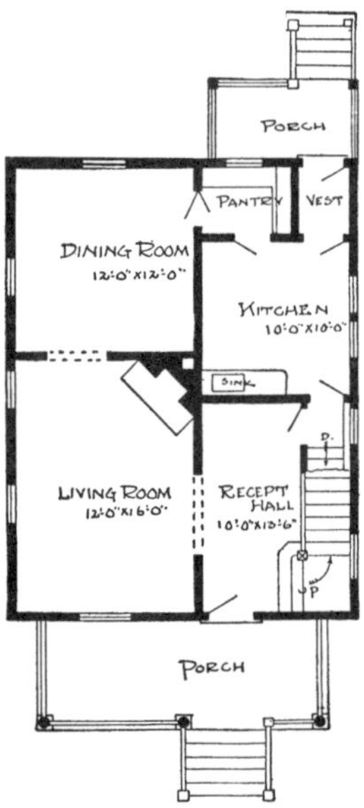

First Floor Plan

Blue prints consist of basement plan; first and second floor plans; front, rear, and two side elevations; wall sections and all necessary interior details. Specifications consist of about twenty pages of typewritten matter.

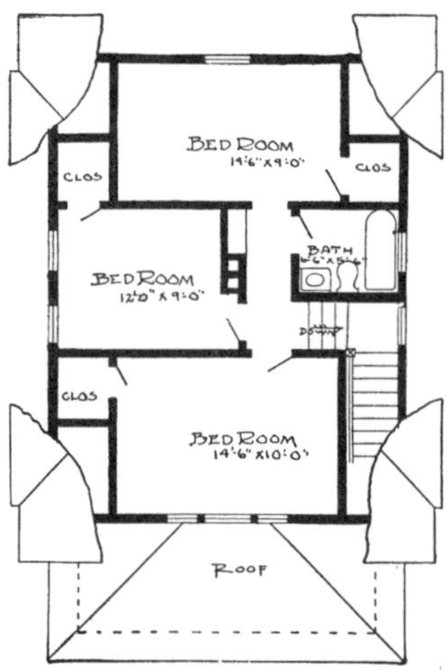

Second Floor Plan

PRICE

of Blue Prints together with a complete set of typewritten specifications

ONLY TWELVE DOLLARS

We mail Plans and Specifications the same day order is received.

Design No. 7066

Size: Width, 30 feet 6 inches; Length, 29 feet, exclusive of porches

PRICE

of Blue Prints, together with a complete set of typewritten specifications

ONLY TWELVE DOLLARS

We mail Plans and Specifications the same day order is received.

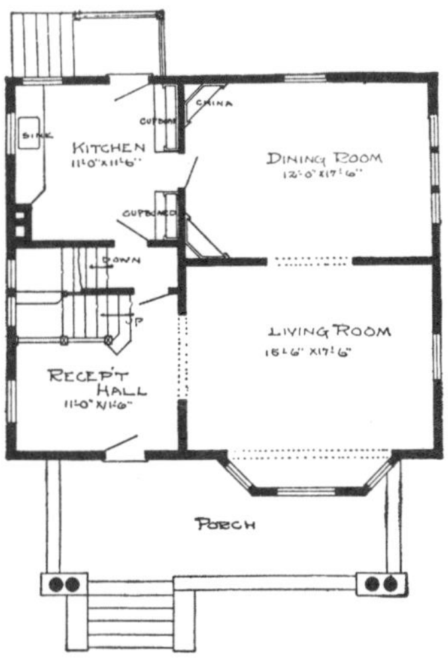

First Floor Plan

Blue prints consist of basement plan; roof plan; first and second floor plans; front, rear, two side elevations; wall sections and all necessary interior details. Specifications consist of about twenty pages of typewritten matter.

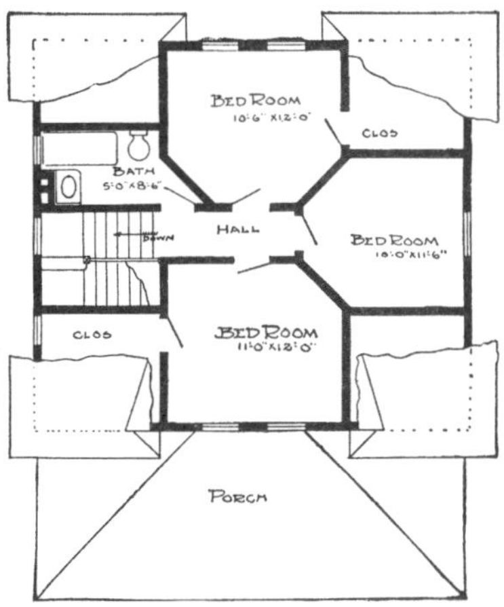

Second Floor Plan

Design No. 7017

Size: Width, 23 feet; Length, 35 feet, exclusive of porches

First Floor Plan

Blue prints consist of basement plan; roof plan. first and second floor plans; front, rear, two side elevations; wall sections and all necessary interior details. Specifications consist of about twenty pages of typewritten matter.

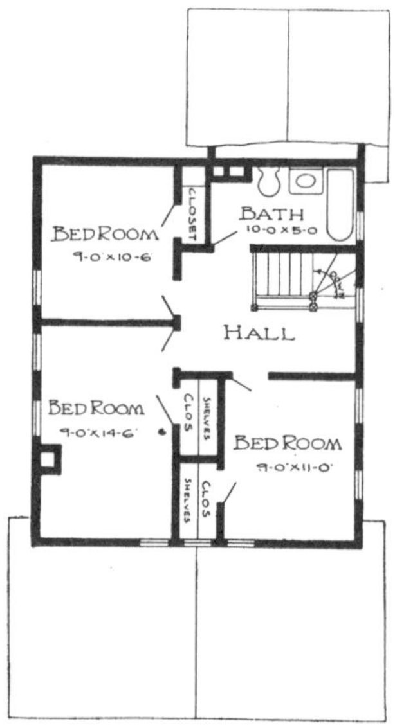

Second Floor Plan

PRICE

of Blue Prints, together with a complete set of typewritten specifications

ONLY FIFTEEN DOLLARS

We mail Plan. and Specifications the same day order is received.

DESIGN NUMBER 6076

Size: width, 30 feet 6 inches; length, 32 feet 6 inches exclusive of porches

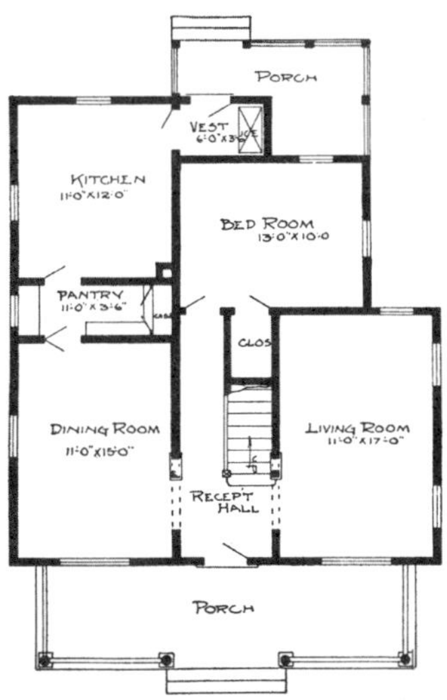

First Floor Plan

BLUE PRINTS consist of foundation plan; roof plan; first and second floor plans; front, rear, two side elevations; wall sections and all necessary interior details. Specifications consist of about twenty pages of typewritten matter.

PRICE

of Blue Prints, together with a complete set of typewritten specifications

ONLY TWELVE DOLLARS

We mail plans and specifications the same day order is received.

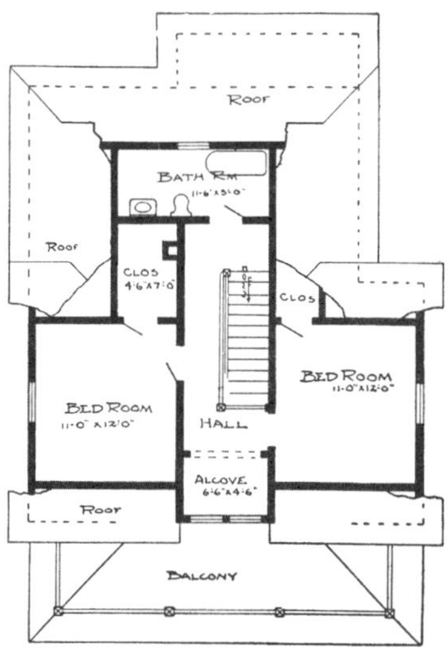

Second Floor Plan

DESIGN NUMBER 6089

Size: width, 36 feet; length, 36 feet, exclusive of porches

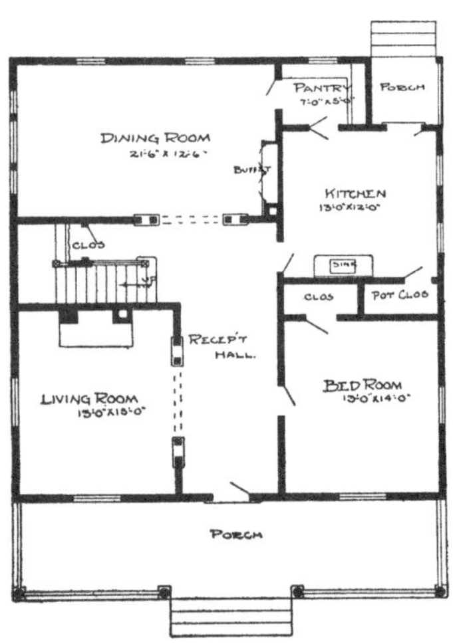

First Floor Plan

BLUE PRINTS consist of basement plan; roof plans; first and second floor plans; front, rear, two side elevations; wall sections and all necessary interior details. Specifications consist of about twenty pages of typewritten matter.

PRICE

of Blue Prints, together with a complete set of typewritten specifications

ONLY TEN DOLLARS

We mail plans and specifications the same day order is received.

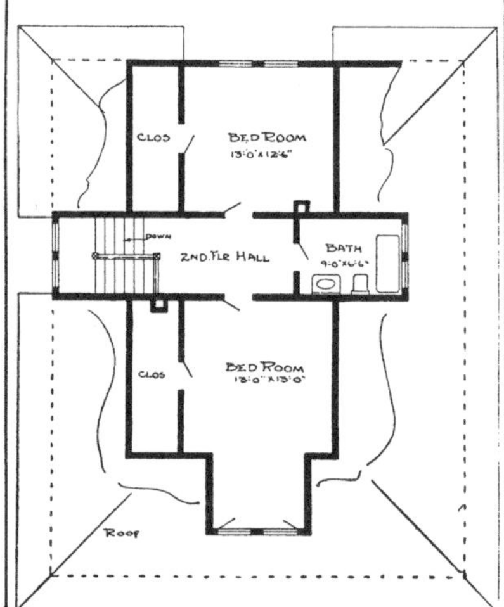

Second Floor Plan

DESIGN NUMBER 6009

Size: Width, 26 feet; Length, 45 feet, exclusive of porch

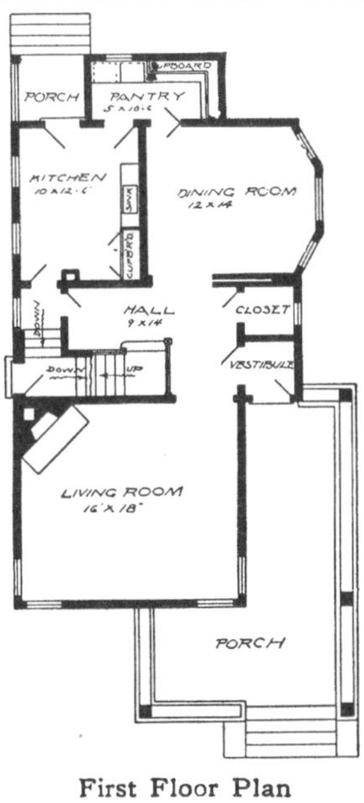

First Floor Plan

BLUE PRINTS consist of cellar and foundation plan; roof plan; first and second floor plans; front, rear, two side elevations; wall sections and all necessary interior details. Specifications consist of about twenty pages of type-written matter.

PRICE

of Blue Prints, together with a complete set of typewritten specifications

ONLY FIFTEEN DOLLARS

We mail plans and specifications the same day order is received.

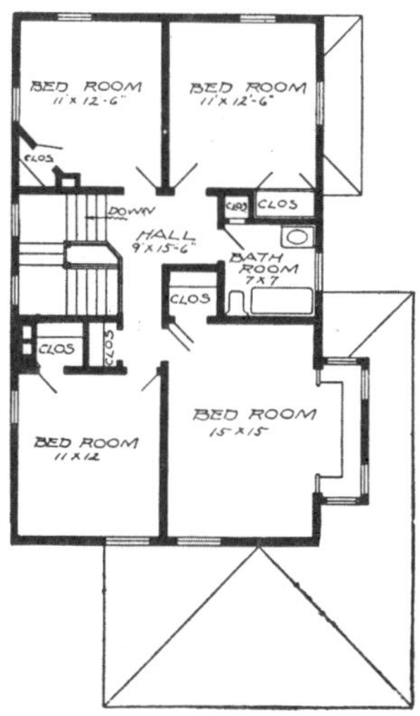

Second Floor Plan

DESIGN NUMBER 6003

Size: width, 45 feet 9 inches; length, 32 feet 6 inches exclusive of porches

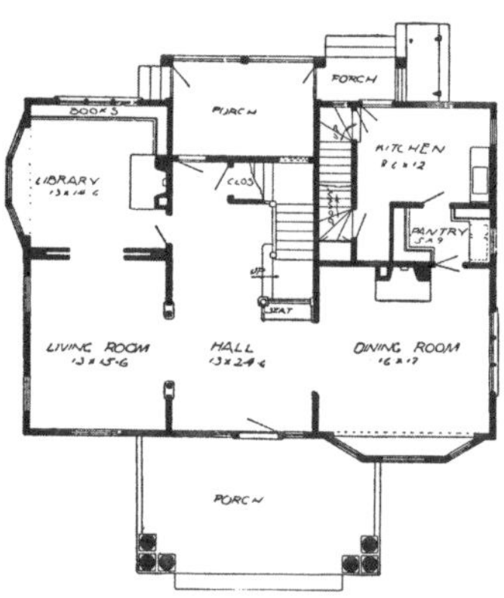

First Floor Plan

BLUE PRINTS consist of basement plan; roof plan; first and second floor plans; front, rear, two side elevations; wall sections and all necessary interior details. Specifications consist of about twenty pages of typewritten matter.

PRICE

of Blue Prints, together with a complete set of typewritten specifications

ONLY FIFTEEN DOLLARS

We mail plans and specifications the same day order is received.

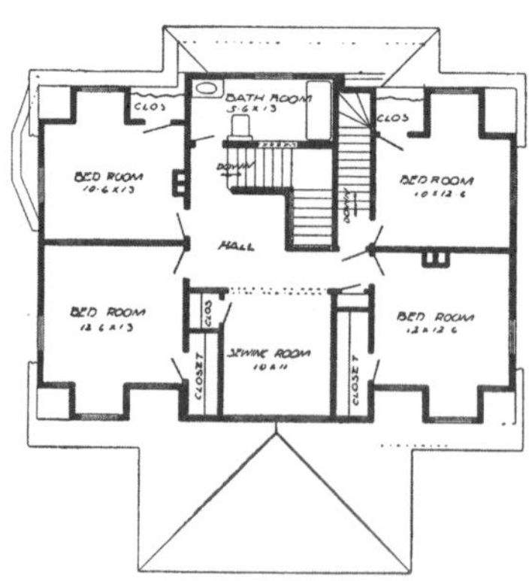

Second Floor Plan

Design No. 9019

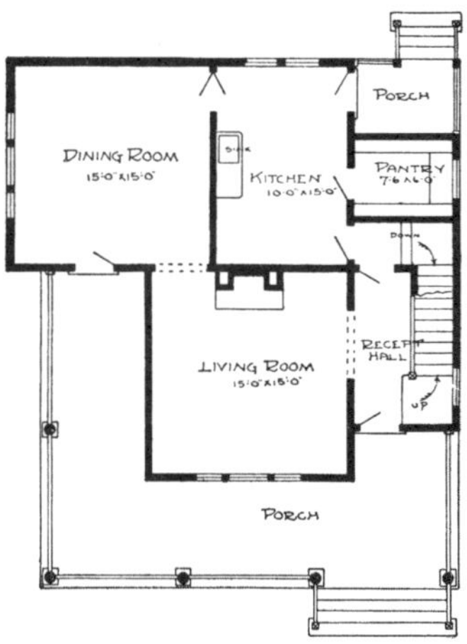

First Floor Plan.

The arrangement of this House is as follows:

FIRST FLOOR.

Reception Hall, 7 feet 6 inches by 11 feet 6 inches.
Living Room, 15 feet by 15 feet.
Dining Room, 15 feet by 15 feet.
Kitchen, 10 feet by 15 feet.
Pantry, Front and Rear Porches.

SECOND FLOOR.

Bedroom, 15 feet by 12 feet 6 inches.
Bedroom, 10 feet by 11 feet.
Bedroom, 12 feet 6 inches by 15 feet.
Bathroom, 7 feet 6 inches by 5 feet 6 inches.
4 Closets.

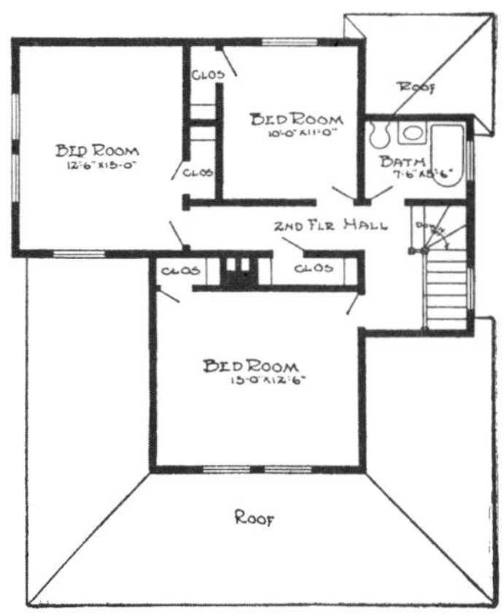

Second Floor Plan.

This Building is 31 feet 6 inches in width; 34 feet 6 inches in length.

Price of Complete Working Plans and Specifications.. $12.00

The Blue Printed Working Plans for this House consist of basement plan; first and second floor plans; front, right, left and rear elevations; wall sections and all necesary details.

The Typewritten Specifications contain all the necessary information for the proper construction of the House.

Design No. 9016

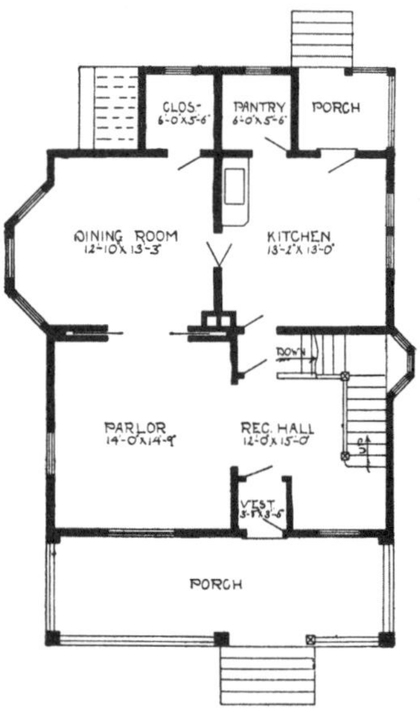

First Floor Plan.

The arrangement of this House is as follows:

FIRST FLOOR.

Reception Hall, 12 feet by 15 feet.
Parlor, 14 feet by 14 feet 9 inches.
Dining Room, 12 feet 10 inches by 13 feet 3 inches.
Kitchen, 13 feet 2 inches by 13 feet.
Pantry, Front and Rear Porches.

SECOND FLOOR.

Bedroom, 13 feet by 8 feet.
Bedroom, 13 feet by 12 feet 6 inches.
Bedroom, 9 feet 3 inches by 13 feet.
Bedroom, 11 feet 9 inches by 13 feet.
Bathroom, 4 feet 6 inches by 7 feet.
3 Closets.

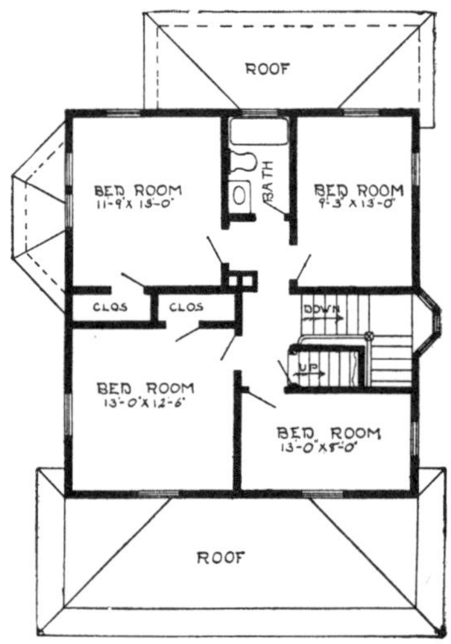

Second Floor Plan.

This Building is 30 feet 6 inches in width; 34 feet in length.

Price of Complete Working Plans and Specifications **$12.00**

The Blue Printed Working Plans for this House consist of basement plan; roof plan; first and second floor plans; front, right, left and rear elevations; wall sections and all necessary details.

The Typewritten Specifications contain all the necessary information for the proper construction of the House.

Design No. 9028

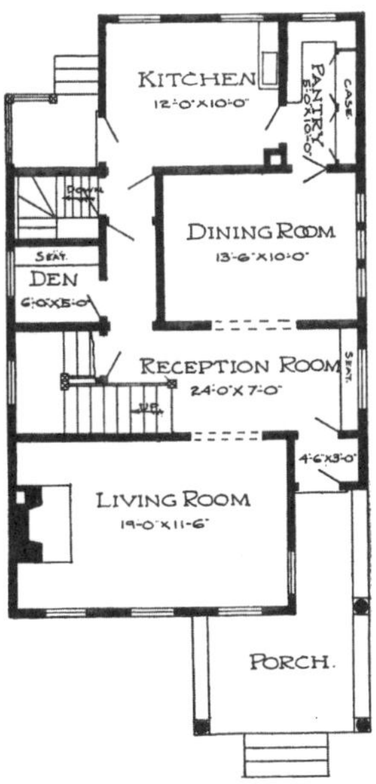

First Floor Plan.

The arrangement of this House is as follows:

FIRST FLOOR.

Reception Room, 24 feet by 7 feet.
Living Room, 19 feet by 11 feet 6 inches.
Den, 6 feet by 5 feet.
Dining Room, 13 feet 6 inches by 10 feet.
Kitchen, 12 feet by 10 feet.
Pantry, Front and Rear Porches.

SECOND FLOOR.

Den, 10 feet by 10 feet.
Bedroom, 11 feet 6 inches by 11 feet 6 inches.
Bedroom, 12 feet by 11 feet 6 inches.
Bedroom, 10 feet by 11 feet 6 inches.
Bedroom, 10 feet by 8 feet 6 inches.
Bathroom, 7 feet by 8 feet 6 inches.
4 Closets.

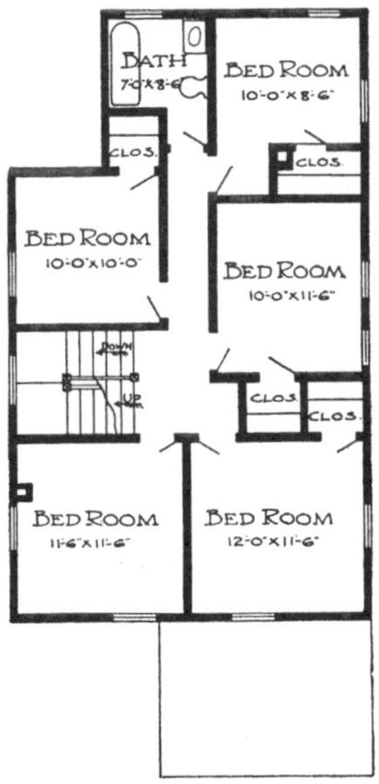

Second Floor Plan.

This Building is 25 feet in width: 41 feet in length.

Price of Complete Working Plans and Specifications.. **$15.00**

The Blue Printed Working Plans for this House consist of basement plan; first and second floor plans, front, right, left and rear elevations; wall sections and all necessary details.

The Typewritten Specifications contain all the necessary information for the proper construction of the House.

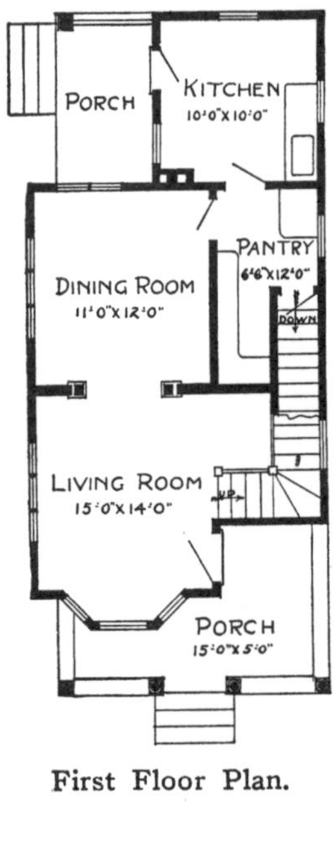

First Floor Plan.

Design No. 9049

The arrangement of this House is as follows:

FIRST FLOOR.

Living Room, 15 feet by 14 feet.

Dining Room, 11 feet by 12 feet.

Kitchen, 10 feet by 10 feet.

Pantry, Front and Rear Porches.

SECOND FLOOR.

Bedroom, 11 feet by 9 feet 6 inches.

Bedroom, 10 feet by 9 feet 6 inches.

Bathroom, 8 feet 6 inches by 4 feet 6 inches.

2 Closets.

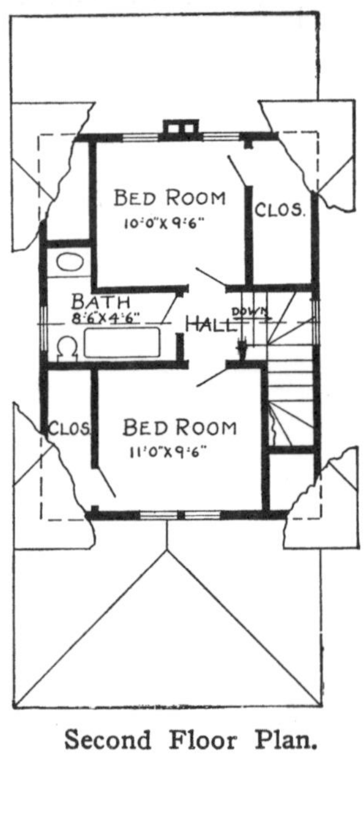

Second Floor Plan.

This Building is 19 feet in width; 38 feet in length.

Price of Complete Working Plans and Specifications.. $12.00

The Blue Printed Working Plans for this House consist of basement plan; first and second floor plans, front. right, left and rear elevations; wall sections and all necessary details.

The Typewritten Specifications contain all the necessary information for the proper construction of the House.

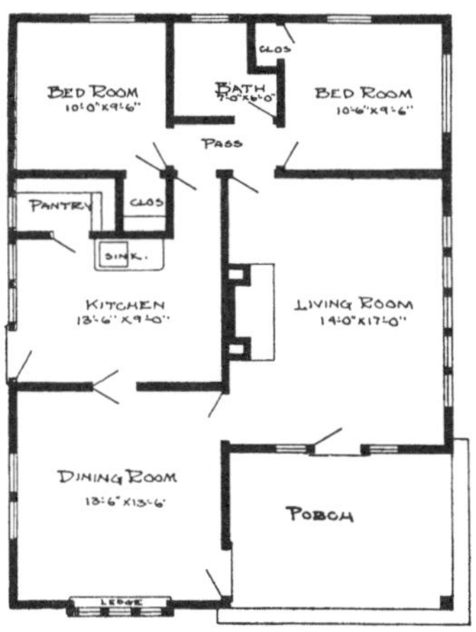

Floor Plan.

Design No. 9060

The arrangement of this House is as follows:

Living Room, 14 feet by 17 feet.

Dining Room, 13 feet 6 inches by 13 feet 6 inches.

Kitchen, 13 feet 6 inches by 9 feet.

Bedroom, 10 feet by 9 feet 6 inches.

Bedroom, 10 feet by 9 feet 6 inches.

Bathroom, 7 feet by 6 feet.

Pantry and Front Porch.

2 Closets.

This Building is 29 feet in width; 38 feet 6 inches in length.

Price of Complete Working Plans and Specifications $10.00

The Blue Printed Working Plans for this House consist of foundation plan; roof plan; floor plan; front, right, left and rear elevations; wall sections and all necessary details:

The Typewritten Specifications contain all the necessary information for the proper construction of the House.

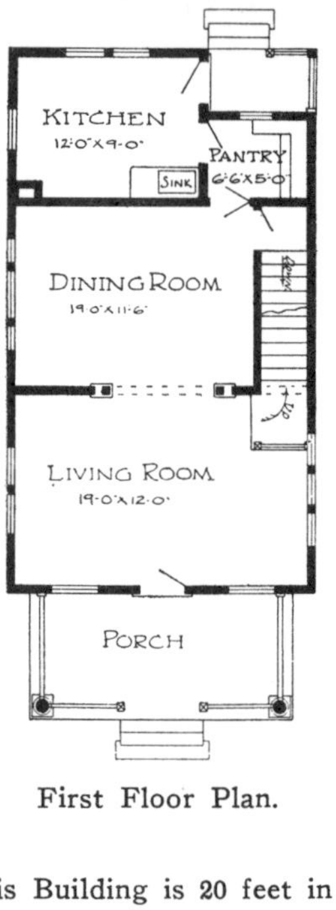

First Floor Plan.

Design No. 9037

The arrangement of this House is as follows:

FIRST FLOOR.

Living Room, 19 feet by 12 feet.

Dining Room, 15 feet 6 inches by 11 feet 6 inches.

Kitchen, 12 feet by 9 feet.

Pantry, Front and Rear Porches.

SECOND FLOOR.

Bedroom, 12 feet by 12 feet.

Bedroom, 8 feet 6 inches by 9 feet.

Bedroom, 12 feet by 11 feet 6 inches.

Bathroom, 6 feet 6 inches by 9 feet.

4 Closets.

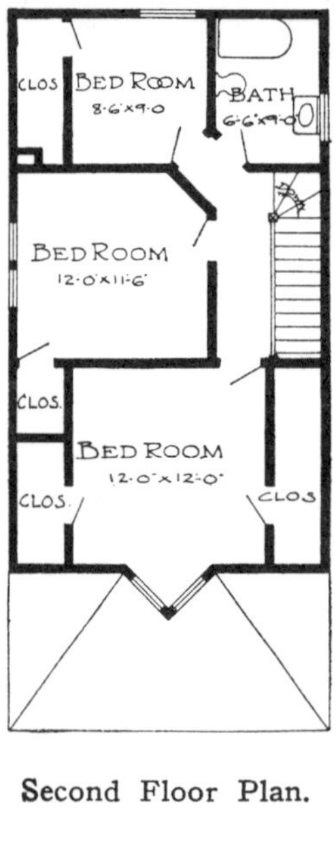

Second Floor Plan.

This Building is 20 feet in width; 34 feet 6 inches in length.

Price of Complete Working Plans and Specifications.......... $12.00

The Blue Printed Working Plans for this House consist of basement plan, roof plan, first and second floor plans; front, right, left and rear elevations; wall sections and all necessary details.

The Typewritten Specifications contain all the necessary information for the proper construction cf the House.

PRICE
of Blue Prints, together with a complete set of typewritten specifications is

ONLY TWELVE DOLLARS

We mail Plans and Specifications the same day order is received.

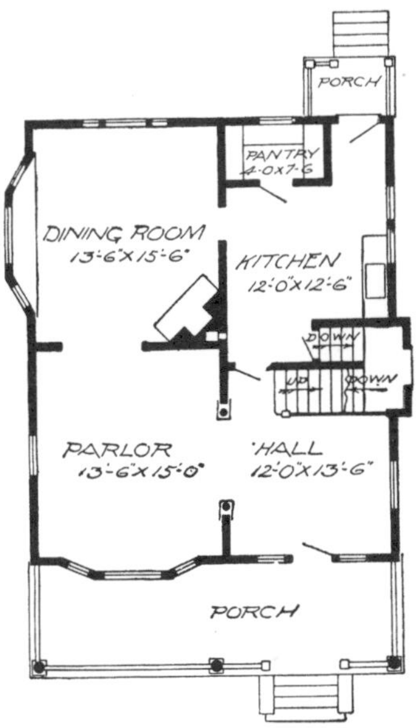

First Floor Plan

Design No. 2007

Blue prints consist of basement plan; first and second floor plans; front, rear, two side elevations; wall sections and all necessary interior details. Specifications consist of about twenty pages of typewritten matter.

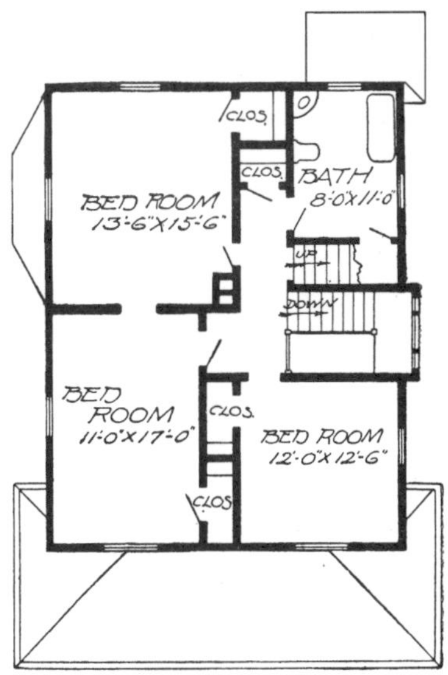

Second Floor Plan

SIZE: Width, 29 feet 6 inches; length, 33 feet, exclusive of porches

It costs but little more to have a modern, convenient and pretty home than an old-style box house. Our plans are so complete and clear that there will be no difficulty in building the most expensive illustrated.

This perspective view has been accurately drawn to show the house exactly as it will appear when built. No liberties bave been taken to have it appear otherwise. This is an exact reproduction of this house.

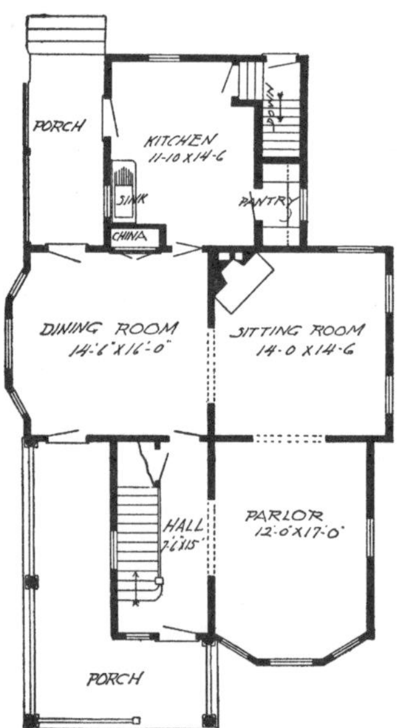

First Floor Plan

Design No. 2047

Blue prints consist of basement plan; roof plan; first and second floor plans; front, rear, two side elevations; wall sections and all necessary interior details. Specifications consist of about twenty pages of typewritten matter.

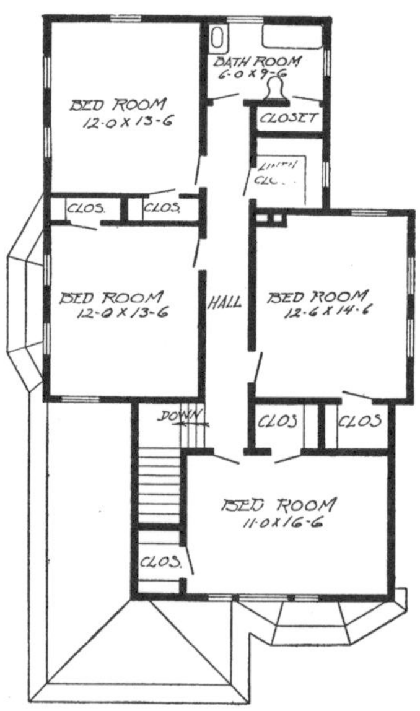

Second Floor Plan

PRICE

of Blue Prints, together with a complete set of typewritten specifications is

ONLY FIFTEEN DOLLARS

We mail Plans and Specifications the same day order is received.

SIZE: Width, 30 feet; length, 46 feet, exclusive of porches.

The prospective builder should not lose sight of the fact that some day it may be necessary or desirable to sell the house, and, if it is attractive and artistic, it can always be disposed of and at a profit to the owner.

The houses we illustrate have been designed by licensed architects to meet the needs of the people and they have a reputation for being practical, attractive and artistic.

DESIGN NUMBER 6072

Size: width, 29 feet 6 inches; length, 56 feet, exclusive of porches

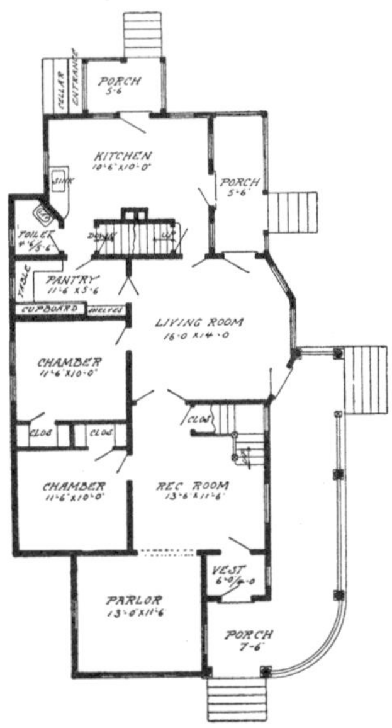

First Floor Plan

BLUE PRINTS consist of basement plan; first and second floor plans; front, rear, two side elevations; wall sections and all necessary interior details. Specifications consist of about twenty pages of typewritten matter.

PRICE

of Blue Prints, together with a complete set of typewritten specifications

ONLY TWELVE DOLLARS

We mail plans and specifications the same day order is received.

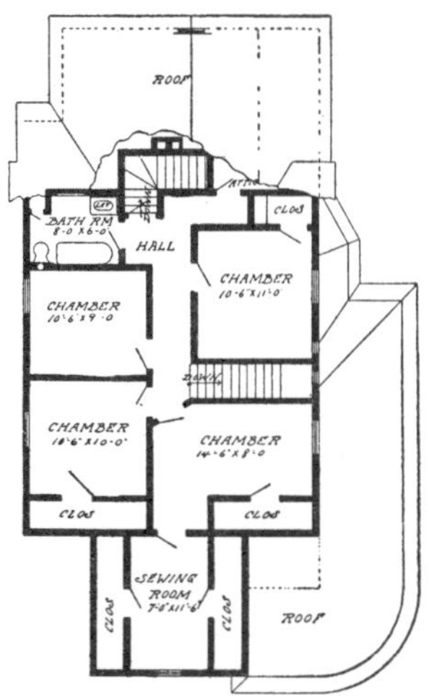

Second Floor Plan

DESIGN NUMBER 6037

Size: width, 41 feet; length 56 feet, 6 inches, exclusive of porches

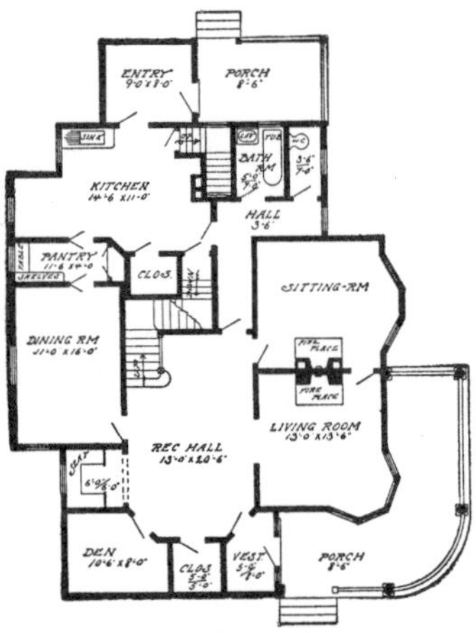

First Floor Plan

BLUE PRINTS consist of basement plan; roof plan; first and second floor plans; front, rear, two side elevations; wall sections and all necessary interior details. Specifications consist of about twenty pages of typewritten matter.

PRICE

of Blue Prints, together with a complete set of typewritten specifications.

ONLY FIFTEEN DOLLARS

We mail plans and specifications the same day order is received.

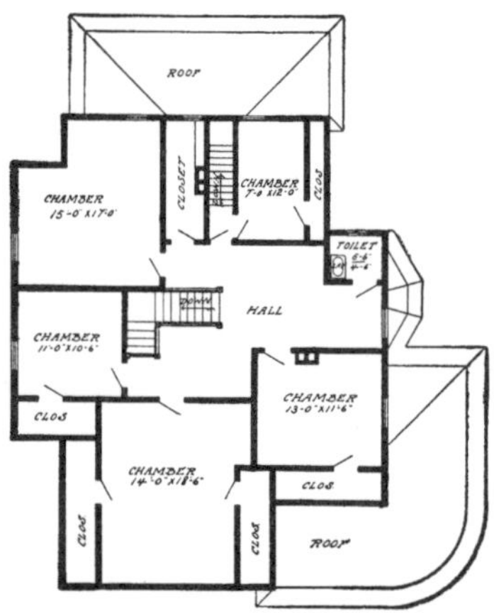

Second Floor Plan

Design No. 7068

Size: Width, 32 feet 6 inches; Length, 42 feet 6 inches, exclusive of porches

PRICE

of Blue Prints, together with a complete set of typewritten specifications

ONLY TWELVE DOLLARS

We mail Plans and Specifications the same day order is received.

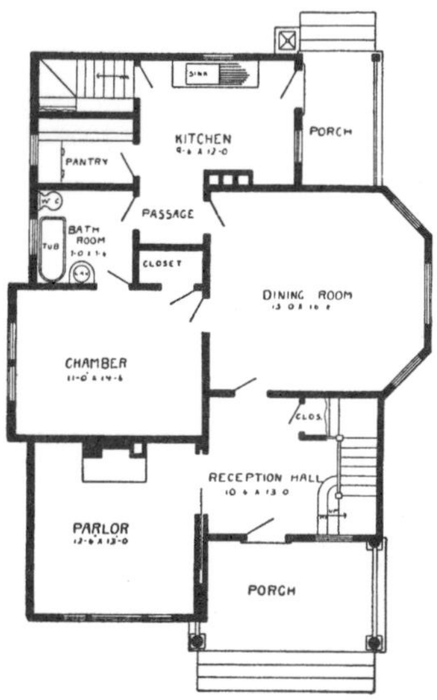

First Floor Plan

Blue prints consist of basement plan; first and second floor plans; front, rear, two side elevations; wall sections and all necessary interior details. Specifications consist of about twenty pages of typewritten matter.

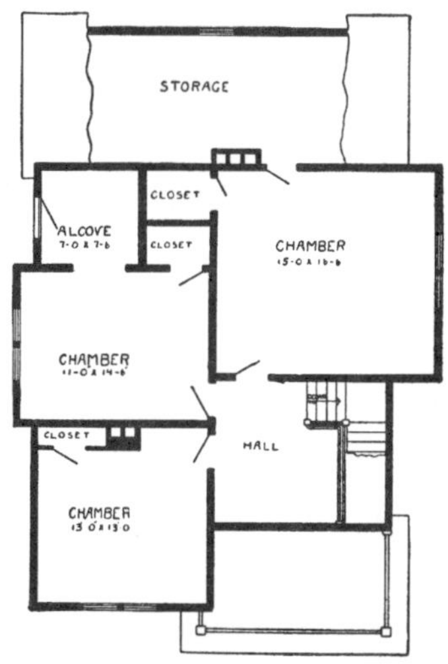

Second Floor Plan

Design No. 7034

Size: Width, 27. feet; Length, 49 feet, exclusive of porches

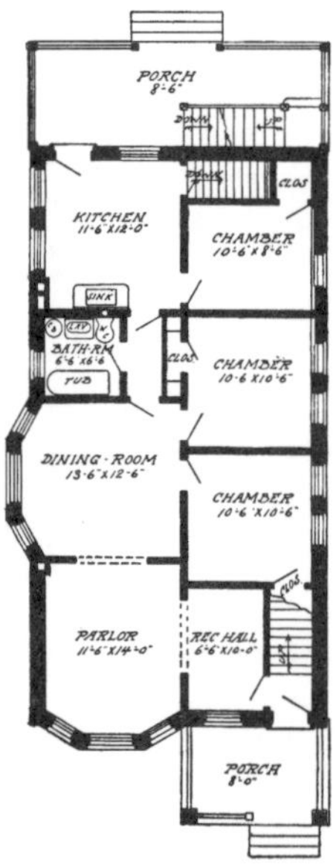

First Floor Plan

Blue prints consist of basement plan; first and second floor plans; front, rear, two side elevations; wall sections and all necessary interior details. Specifications consist of about twenty pages of typewritten matter.

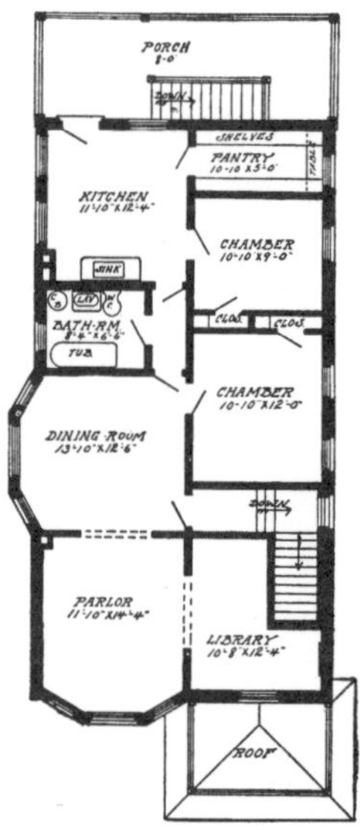

Second Floor Plan

PRICE

of Blue Prints, together with a complete set of typewritten specifications.

ONLY FIFTEEN DOLLARS

We mail Plans and Specifications the same day order is received.

DESIGN NUMBER 6057

Size: width, 24 feet; length, 38 feet, exclusive of porch

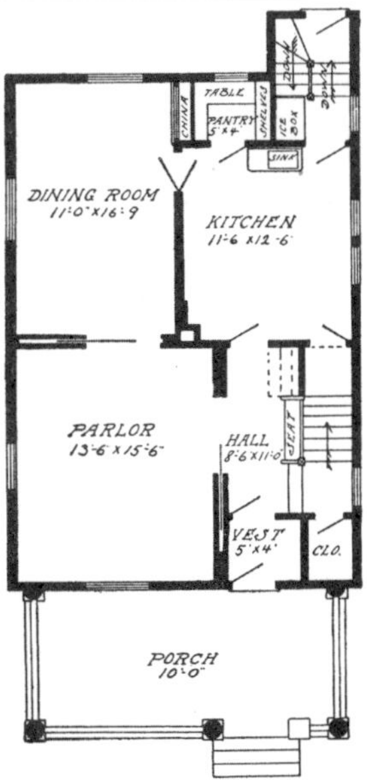

First Floor Plan

BLUE PRINTS consist of cellar and foundation plan; roof plan; first and second floor plans; front, two side elevations; wall sections and all necessary interior details. Specifications consist of about twenty pages of typewritten matter.

PRICE

of Blue Prints, together with a complete set of typewritten specifications

ONLY TWELVE DOLLARS

We mail plans and specifications the same day order is received.

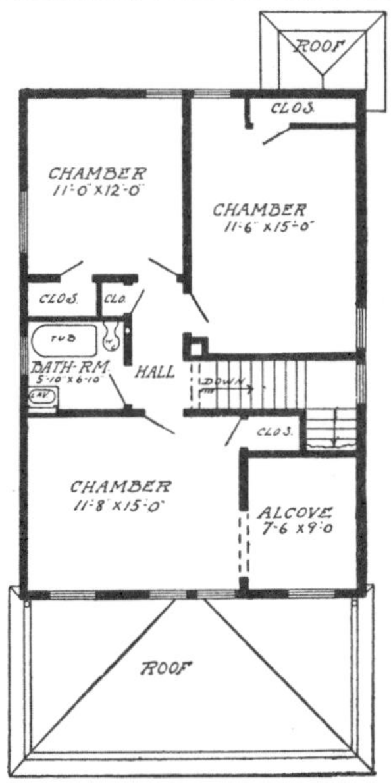

Second Floor Plan

DESIGN NUMBER 6067

Size: width, 28 feet; length, 40 feet, exclusive of porch

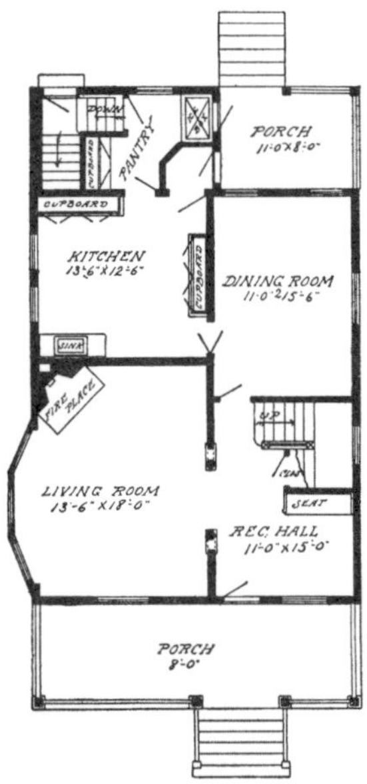

First Floor Plan

BLUE PRINTS consist of basement plan; roof plan; first and second floor plans; front, rear, two side elevations; wall sections and all necessary interior details. Specifications consist of about twenty pages of typewritten matter.

PRICE

of Blue Prints, together with a complete set of typewritten specifications

ONLY FIFTEEN DOLLARS

We mail plans and specifications the same day order is received.

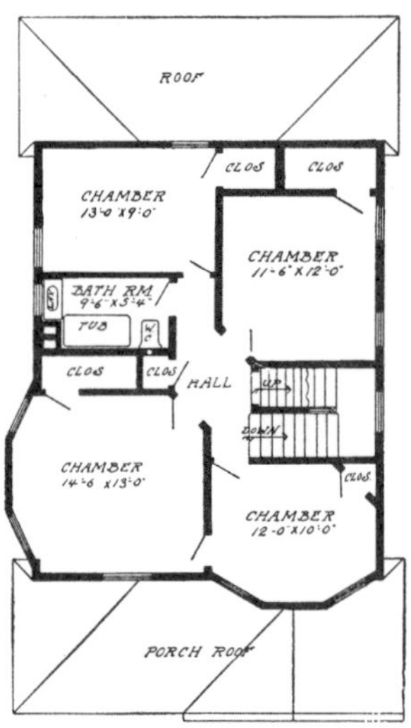

Second Floor Plan

Design No. 9030

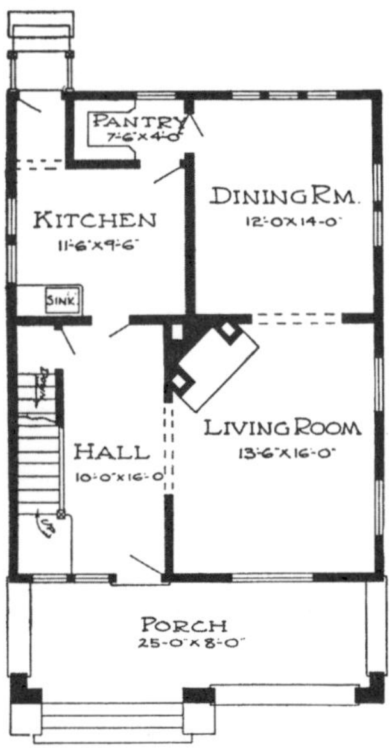

First Floor Plan.

The arrangement of this House is as follows:

FIRST FLOOR.

Reception Hall, 10 feet by 16 feet.
Living Room, 13 feet 6 inches by 16 feet.
Dining Room, 12 feet by 14 feet.
Kitchen, 11 feet 6 inches by 9 feet 6 inches.
Pantry, Front and Rear Porches.

SECOND FLOOR.

Bedroom, 17 feet 6 inches by 13 feet.
Bedroom, 13 feet 6 inches by 10 feet 6 inches.
Bedroom, 10 feet by 14 feet.
Bathroom, 5 feet 6 inches by 7 feet.
4 Closets.

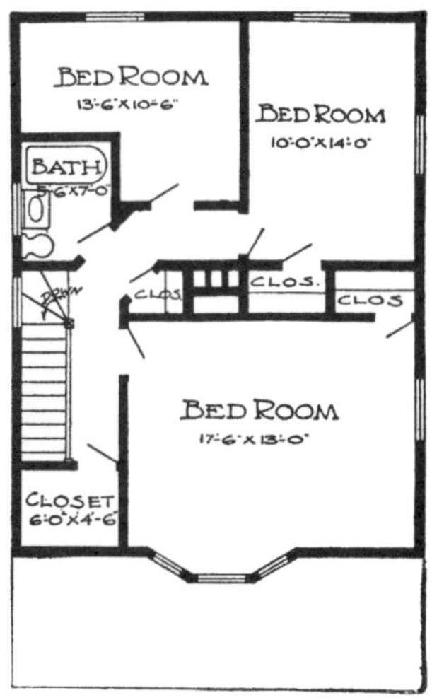

Second Floor Plan.

This Building is 25 feet in width; 32 feet in length.

Price of Complete Working Plans and Specifications **$12.00**

The Blue Printed Working Plans for this House consist of basement plan; first and second floor plans, front, right, left and rear elevations; wall sections and all necessary details.

The Typewritten Specifications contain all the necessary information for the proper construction of the House.

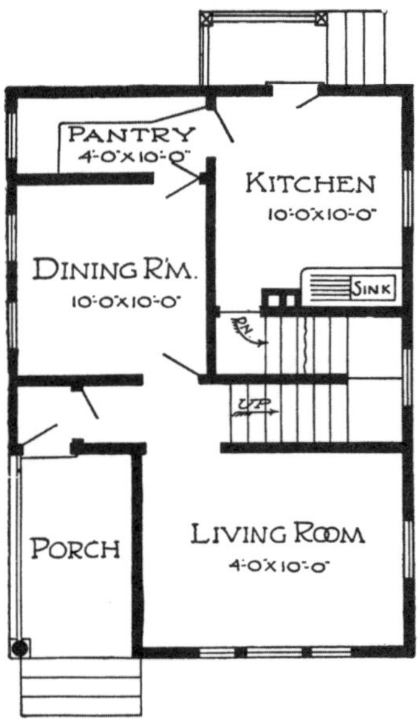

First Floor Plan.

Design No. 9083

The arrangement of this House is as follows:

FIRST FLOOR.

Living Room, 14 feet by 10 feet.
Dining Room, 10 feet by 10 feet.
Kitchen, 10 feet by 10 feet.
Pantry, Front and Rear Porches.

SECOND FLOOR.

Bedroom, 11 feet 6 inches by 10 feet.
Bedroom, 11 feet by 11 feet 6 inches.
Bathroom, 6 feet by 6 feet 6 inches.
4 Closets.

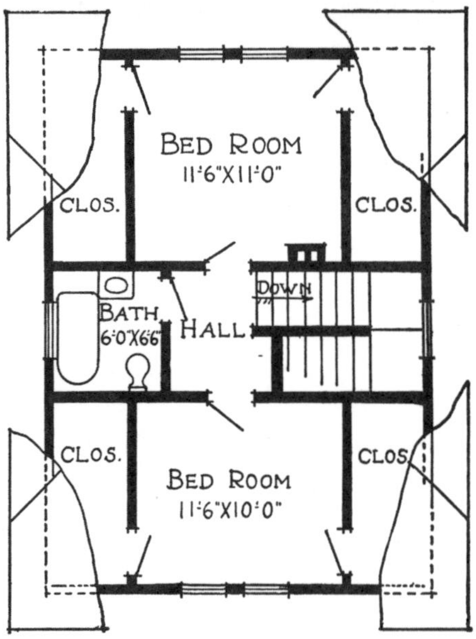

Second Floor Plan.

This Building is 21 feet 6 inches in width; 29 feet 6 inches in length.

Price of Complete Working Plans and Specifications **$12.00**

The Blue Printed Working Plans for this House consist of basement plan; first and second floor plans, front, right, left and rear elevations; wall sections and all necessary details.

The Typewritten Specifications contain all the necessary information for the proper construction of the House.

Design No. 9078

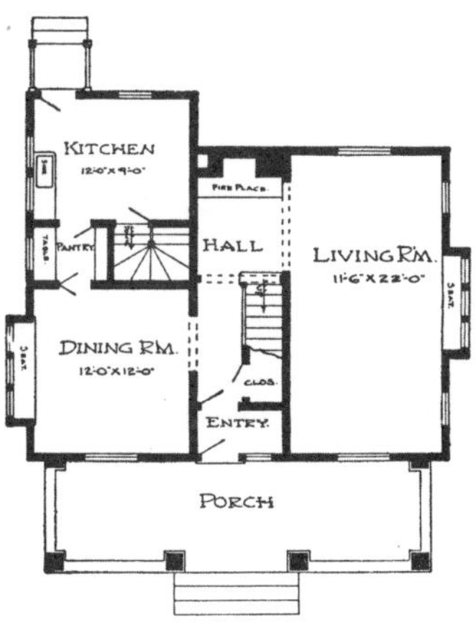

First Floor Plan.

The arrangement of this House is as follows:

FIRST FLOOR.

Living Room, 11 feet 6 inches by 22 feet.
Dining Room, 12 feet by 12 feet.
Kitchen, 12 feet by 9 feet.
Pantry, Front and Rear Porches.

SECOND FLOOR.

Bedroom, 11 feet 6 inches by 19 feet.
Bedroom, 12 feet by 11 feet 6 inches.
Bedroom, 12 feet by 11 feet.
Bathroom, 6 feet 6 inches by 7 feet 6 inches.
3 Closets.

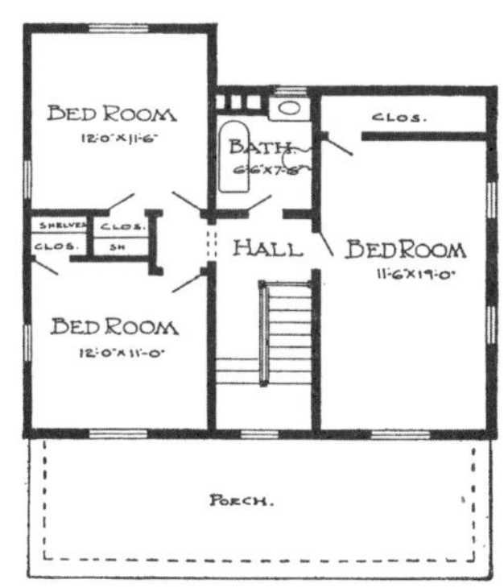

Second Floor Plan.

This Building is 35 feet in width; 27 feet in length.

Price of Complete Working Plans and Specifications $12.00

The Blue Printed Working Plans for this House consist of basement plan, roof plan, first and second floor plans; front, right, left and rear elevations; wall sections and all necessary details.

The Typewritten Specifications contain all the necessary information for the proper construction of the House.

PLACE
STAMP
HERE

SCHIFFER PUBLISHING LTD
4880 LOWER VALLEY ROAD
ATGLEN, PA 19310-9717 USA

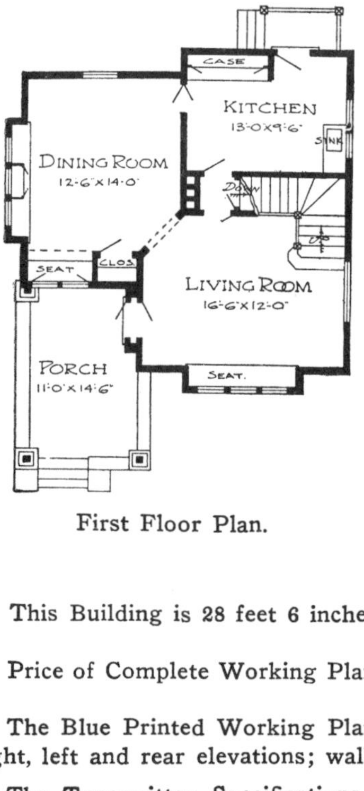

First Floor Plan.

Design No. 9061

The arrangement of this House is as follows:

FIRST FLOOR.

Living Room, 16 feet 6 inches by 12 feet.
Dining Room, 12 feet 6 inches by 14 feet.
Kitchen, 13 feet by 9 feet 6 inches.
Front and Rear Porches.

SECOND FLOOR.

Bedroom, 11 feet by 11 feet.
Bedroom, 14 feet 6 inches by 11 feet.
Bathroom, 10 feet 6 inches by 7 feet 6 inches.
4 Closets.

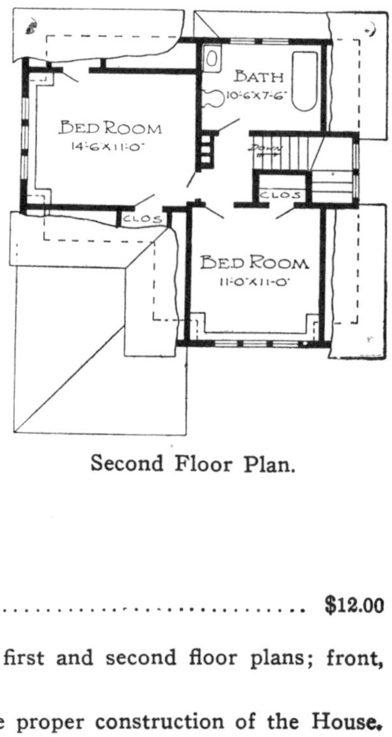

Second Floor Plan.

This Building is 28 feet 6 inches in width; 27 feet 6 inches in length.

Price of Complete Working Plans and Specifications $12.00

The Blue Printed Working Plans for this House consist of basement plan; first and second floor plans; front, right, left and rear elevations; wall sections and all necessary details.

The Typewritten Specifications contain all the necessary information for the proper construction of the House.

Design No. 2028

Blue prints consist of basement plan; roof plan; floor plan; front, rear, two side elevations; wall sections and all necessary interior details. Specifications consist of about fifteen pages of typewritten matter.

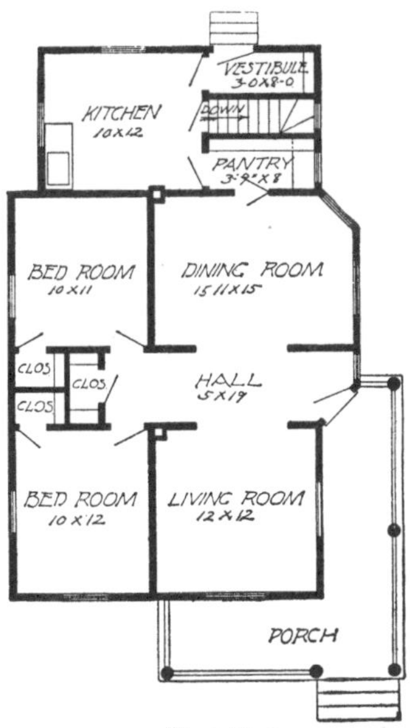

Floor Plan

PRICE

of Blue Prints, together with a complete set of typewritten specifications is

ONLY TEN DOLLARS

We mail Plans and Specifications the same day order is received.

SIZE: Width, 26 feet 6 inches; length, 40 feet 6 inches exclusive of porches.

Why attempt building without plans, when you can secure a complete set of plans and specifications that are guaranteed to be thoroughly accurate in every particular, at such reasonable prices.

These working plans and specificationns can be made the basis of contract between contractor and home builder. They will prevent mistakes which cost money. and disputes, that are never settled satisfactorily to both parties

PRICE

of Blue Prints, together with a complete set of typewritten specifications is

ONLY TWELVE DOLLARS

We mail Plans and Specifications the same day order is received.

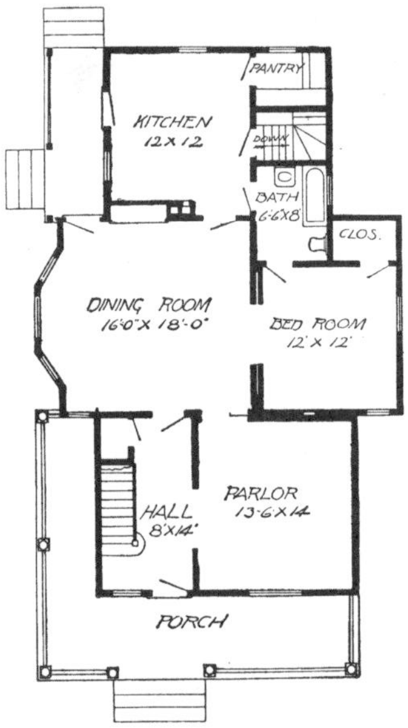

First Floor Plan

Design No. 2023

Blue prints consist of basement plan; first and second floor plans; front, rear, two side elevations; wall sections and all necessary interior details. Specifications consist of about twenty pages of typewritten matter.

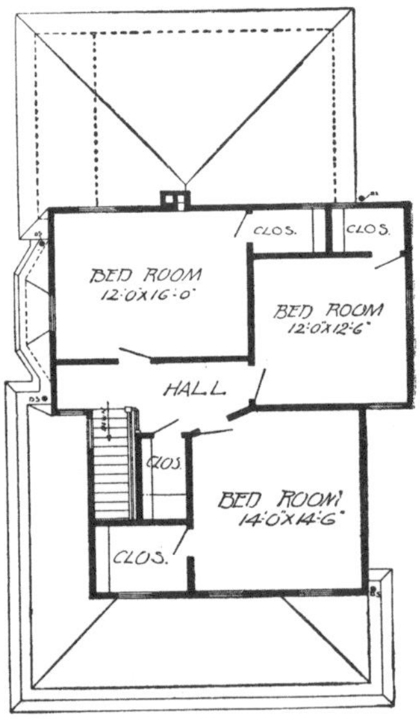

Second Floor Plan

SIZE: Width, 32 feet; length, 46 feet, exclusive of porches

All the houses we illustrate are either low or medium priced. These are the most difficult houses to design. Nearly any acrhitect can design an expensive house, where the saving in cost is not the most important factor.

Every plan in this book is designed by a licensed architect, standing at the head of his profession. We do not furnish any plans which will not stand the closest inspection in every respect.

Design No. 7062

Size: Width, 30 feet; Length, 34 feet, exclusive of porch

PRICE

of Blue Prints, together with a complete set of typewritten specifications

ONLY TWELVE DOLLARS

We mail Plans and Specifications the same day order is received.

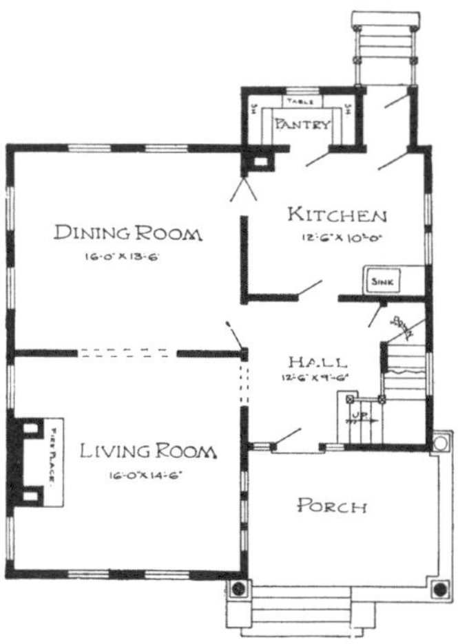

First Floor Plan

Blue prints consist of basement plan; roof plan; first and second floor plans; front, rear, two side elevations; wall sections and all necessary interior details. Specifications consist of about twenty pages of typewritten matter.

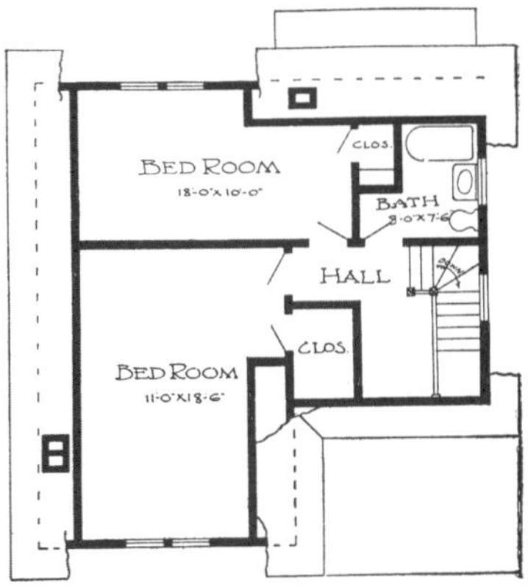

Second Floor Plan

Design No. 7037

Size: Width, 29 feet 6 inches; Length, 28 feet 6 inches, exclusive of porch

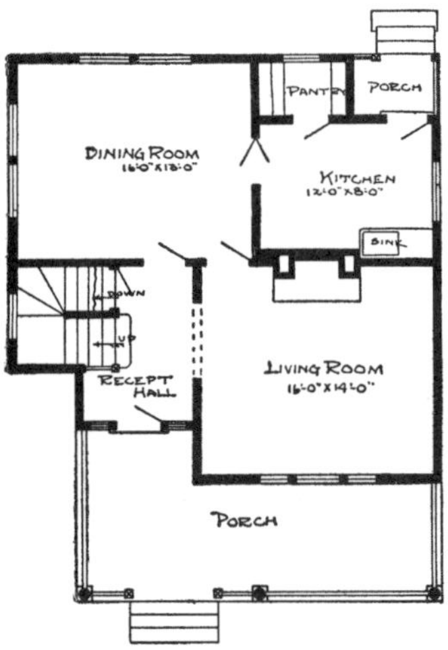

First Floor Plan

Blue prints consist of basement plan; roof plan; first and second floor plans; front, rear, two side elevations; wall sections and all necessary interior details. Specifications consist of about twenty pages of typewritten matter.

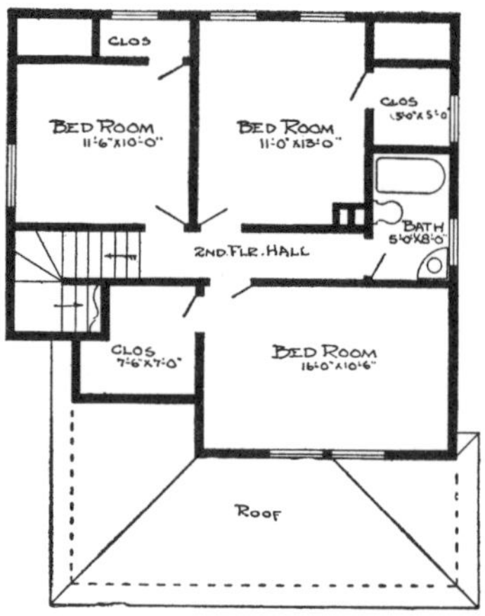

Second Floor Plan

PRICE

of Blue Prints, together with a complete set of typewritten specifications.

ONLY TWELVE DOLLARS

We mail Plans nd Specitications the same day order is received.

Design No. 7072

Size: Width, 32 feet. Length, 28 feet, exclusive of porch

PRICE

of Blue Prints, together with a complete set of typewritten specificarions

ONLY FIFTEEN DOLLARS

We mail Plans and Specifications the same day order is received.

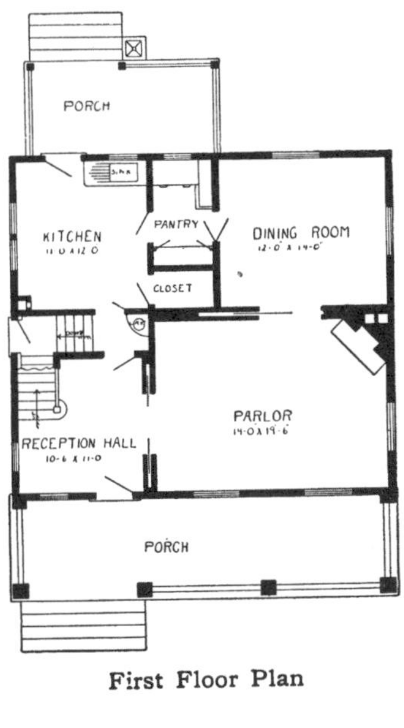

First Floor Plan

Blue prints consist of basement plan; roof plan; first and second floor plans; front, rear, two side elevations; wall sections and all necessary interior details. Specifications consist of about twenty pages of typewritten matter.

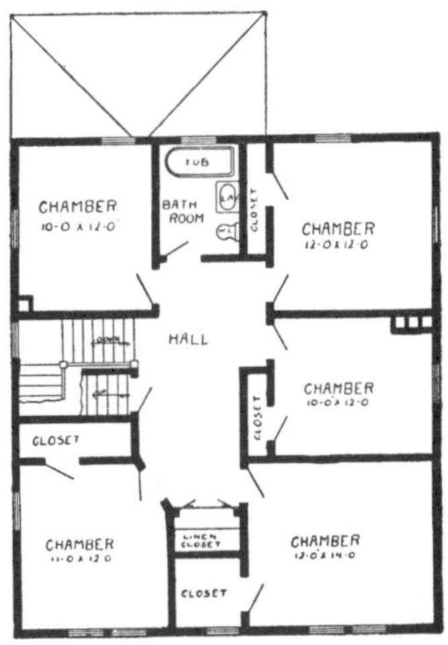

Second Floor Plan

Design No. 7048

Size: Width, 31 feet 6 inches; Length, 45 feet, exclusive of porches

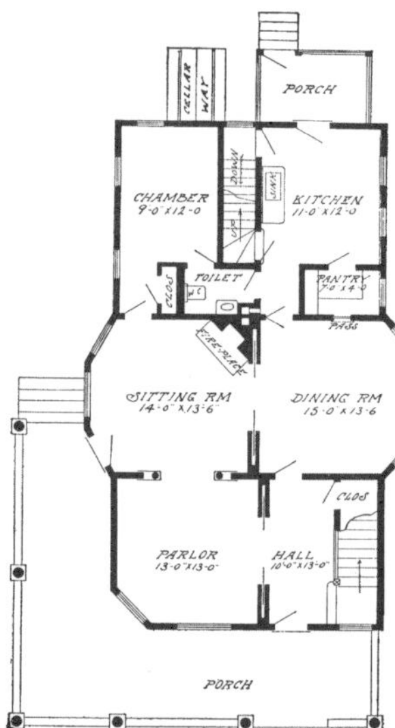

First Floor Plan

Blue prints consist of basement plan; roof plan; first and second floor plans; front, rear, two side elevations; wall sections and all necessary interior details. Specifications consist of about twenty pages of typewritten matter.

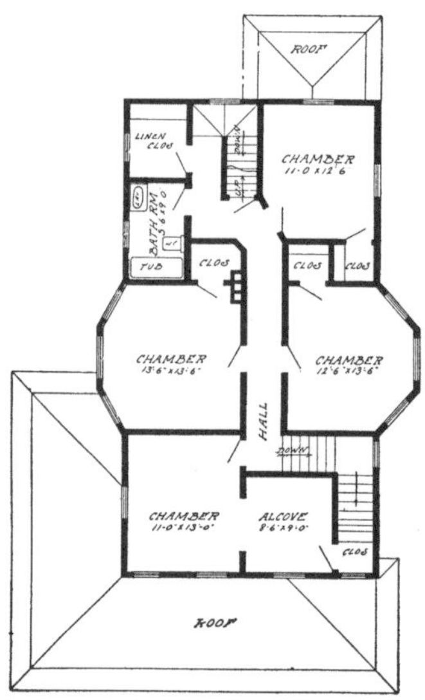

Second Floor Plan

PRICE

of Blue Prints, together with a complete set of typewritten specifications

ONLY FIFTEEN DOLLARS

We mail Plans and Specifications the same day order is received.

DESIGN NUMBER 6046

Size: width, 27 feet, 6 inches; length, 43 feet, exclusive of porches

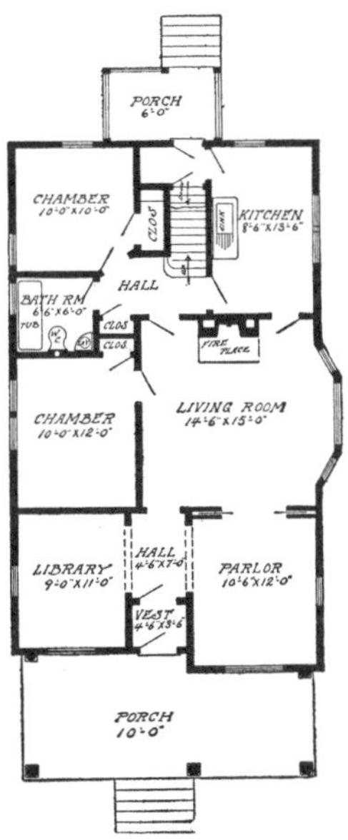

Floor Plan

BLUE PRINTS consist of basement plan, roof plan; first and second floor plans; front, rear, two side elevations; wall sections and all necessary interior details. Specifications consist of about twenty pages of typewritten matter.

PRICE

of Blue Prints, together with a complete set of typewritten specifications

ONLY TEN DOLLARS

We mail plans and specifications the same day order is received.

DESIGN NUMBER 6028

Size: width, 35 feet; length, 28 feet 6 inches, exclusive of porches

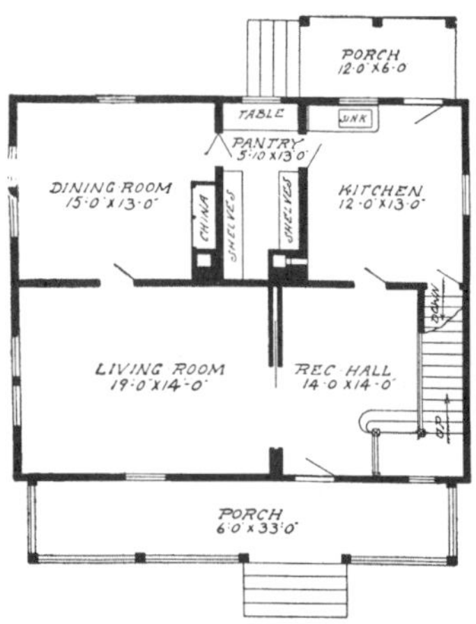

First Floor Plan

BLUE PRINTS consist of basement plan; first and second floor plans; front, rear, two side elevations; wall sections and all necessary interior details. Specifications consist of about twenty pages of typewritten matter.

PRICE

of Blue Prints, together with a complete set of typewritten specifications

ONLY TWELVE DOLLARS

We mail plans and specifications the same day order is received.

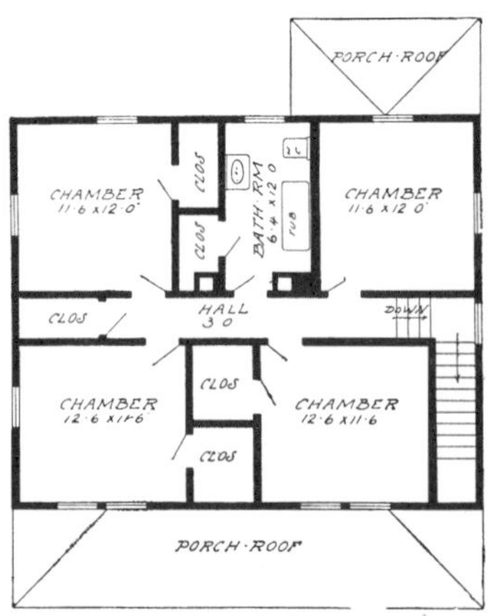

Second Floor Plan

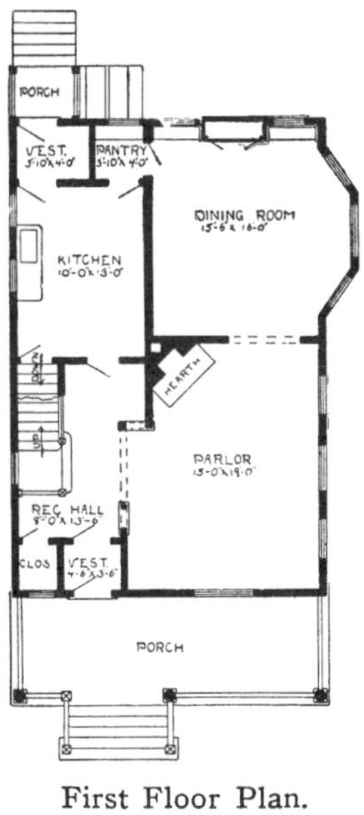

First Floor Plan.

Design No. 9006

The arrangement of this House is as follows:

FIRST FLOOR.

Reception Hall, 8 feet by 13 feet 6 inches.
Parlor, 15 feet by 19 feet.
Dining Room, 15 feet 6 inches. by 16 feet.
Kitchen, 10 feet by 13 feet.
Pantry, Front and Rear Porches.

SECOND FLOOR.

Bedroom, 15 feet by 12 feet.
Bedroom, 10 feet 6 inches by 15 feet.
Bedroom, 11 feet 9 inches by 12 feet.
Bathroom, 6 feet 6 inches by 7 feet 6 inches.
6 Closets.

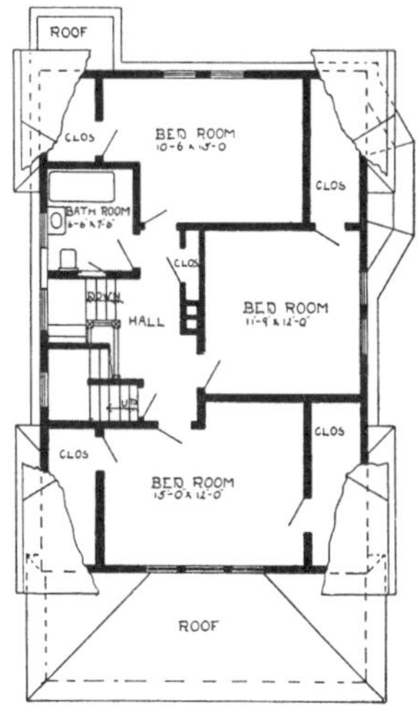

Second Floor Plan.

This Building is 27 feet in width; 36 feet 6 inches in length.

Price of Complete Working Plans and Specifications.. $12.00

The Blue Printed Working Plans for this House consist of basement plan; roof plan; first and second floor plans; front, right, left and rear elevations; wall sections and all necessary details.

The Typewritten Specifications contain all the necessary information for the proper construction of the House.

Design No. 9069

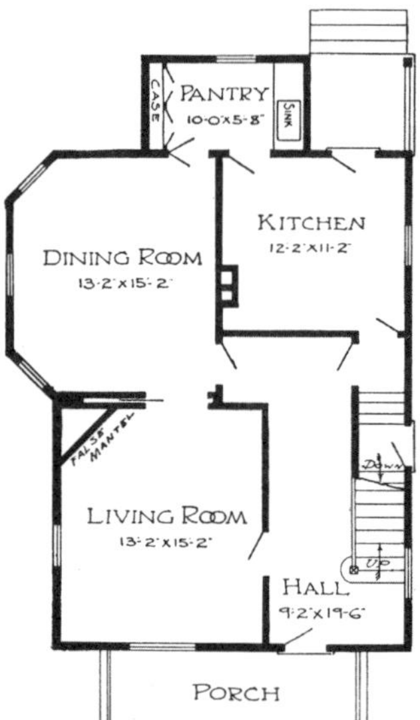

First Floor Plan.

The arrangement of this House is as follows:

FIRST FLOOR.

Reception Hall, 9 feet 2 inches by 19 feet 6 inches.
Living Room, 13 feet 2 inches by 15 feet 2 inches.
Dining Room, 13 feet 2 inches by 15 feet 2 inches.
Kitchen, 12 feet 2 inches by 11 feet 2 inches.
Pantry, Front and Rear Porches.

SECOND FLOOR.

Sewing Room, 9 feet 2 inches by 9 feet 2 inches.
Bedroom, 13 feet 2 inches by 13 feet 2 inches.
Bedroom, 12 feet 2 inches by 10 feet.
Bedroom, 13 feet 2 inches by 15 feet 2 inches.
Bathroom, 7 feet 8 inches by 6 feet 2 inches.
4 Closets.

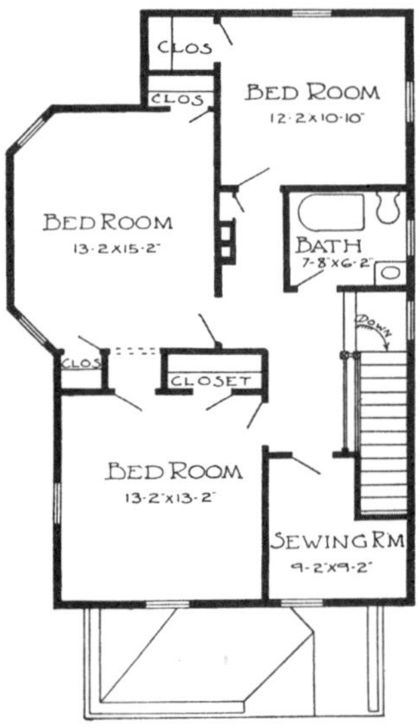

Second Floor Plan.

This Building is 26 feet 6 inches in width; 38 feet in length.

Price of Complete Working Plans and Specifications........ **$12.00**

The Blue Printed Working Plans for this House consist of basement plan; roof plan; first and second floor plans; front, right, left and rear elevations; wall sections and all necessary details.

The Typewritten Specifications contain all the necessary information for the proper construction of the House

Design No. 9519

Size: Width, 28 feet; Length, 48 feet

Blue prints consist of basement plan; roof plan; floor plan; front, rear, two side elevations; wall sections and all necessary interior details. Specifications consist of twenty-two pages of typewritten matter.

PRICE

of Blue Prints, together with a complete set of typewritten specifications

ONLY

$22.00

We mail Plans and Specifications the same day order is received.

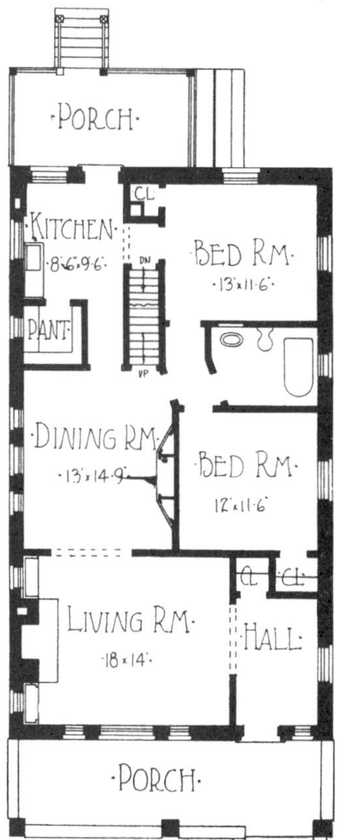

Floor Plan

Design No. 9515

Size: Width, 47 feet 6 inches; Length, 46 feet

Blue prints consist of basement plan; floor plan; front, rear, two side elevations; wall sections and all necessary interior details. Specifications consist of twenty-two pages of typewritten matter.

PRICE

of Blue Prints, together with a complete set of typewritten specifications

ONLY

$26.00

We mail Plans and Specifications the same day order is received.

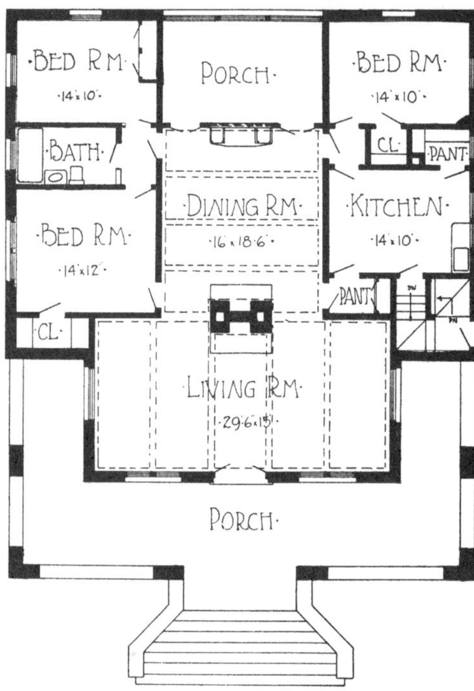

Floor Plan

ALTERATIONS. We can change any plans to suit your requirements, at a reasonable extra charge depending on amount of work involved.

PRICE of Blue Prints, together with a complete set of typewritten specifications is

ONLY TEN DOLLARS

We mail Plans and Specifications the same day order is received.

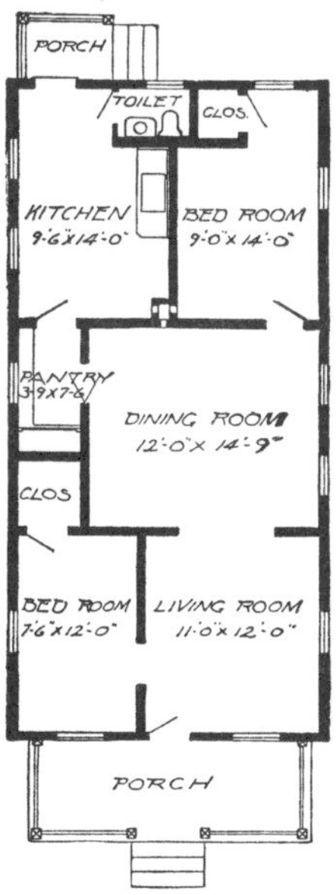

Floor Plan

Design No. 2001

Blue prints consist of foundation plan, roof plan; floor plan; front, rear, two side elevations, wall sections and all necessary interior details. Specifications consist of about fifteen pages of typewritten matter.

SIZE: Width, 20 feet; length, 40 feet, exclusive of porches

Our plans are all substantially and artistically bound in cloth and waterproof paper. The specifications are bound in the same manner, and the two make a uniform set, worth many times the cost.

The first question you will ask is, What do we get in these working plans and specifications? We furnish the best blue printed plans ever sent out. We do not give you the cheap tissue paper plans.

Design No. 2020

Blue prints consist of foundation plan; floor plan; front, rear. two side elevations; wall sections and all necessary interior details. Specifications consist o about fifteen pages of typewritten matter.

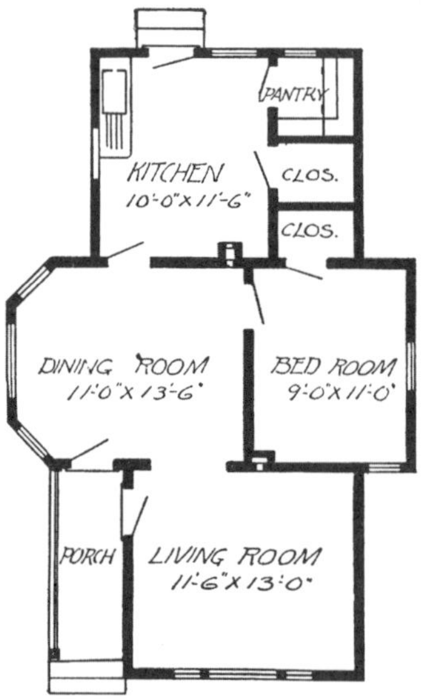

PRICE

of Blue Prints, together with a complete set of typewritten specifications is

ONLY TEN DOLLARS

We mail Plans and Specifications the same day order is received.

SIZE: Width, 24 feet; length, 36 feet.

All of the plans illustrated in this book have been prepared by licensed architects standing at the head of their profession, and the standard of their work is of the very highest.

We could not afford to make this guarantee if we were not positive that we were furnishing the best plans put out in this country, even though our price is not more than one-seventh to one-tenth the price usually charged.

Design No. 7009

Size: Width, 27 feet 6 inches; Length, 43 feet, exclusive of porches

PRICE

of Blue Prints, together with a complete set of typewritten specifications

ONLY TWELVE DOLLARS

We mail Plans and Specifications the same day order is received.

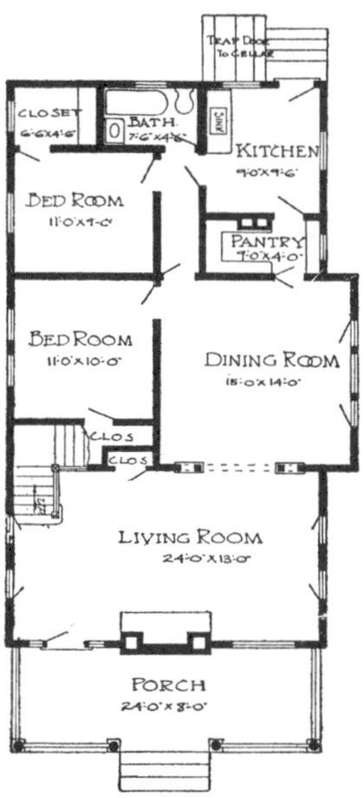

First Floor Plan

Blue Prints consist of basement plan; first and second floor plans; front, rear, two side elevations; wall sections and all necessary interior details. Specifications consist of about twenty pages of typewritten matter.

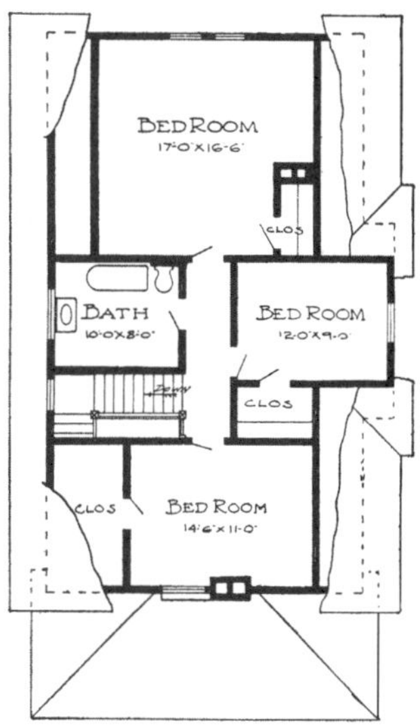

Second Floor Plan

Design No. 7095

Size: Width, 26 feet; Length, 29 feet 6 inches, exclusive of porches

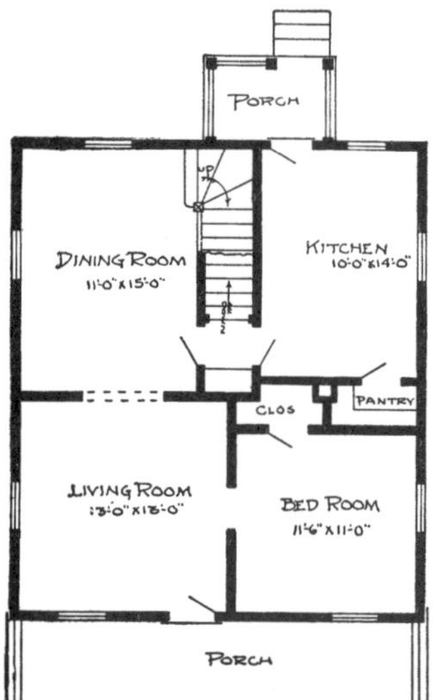

First Floor Plan

Blue prints consist of basement plan; first and second floor plans; front, two side elevations; wall sections and all necessary interior details. Specifications consist of about twenty pages of typewritten matter.

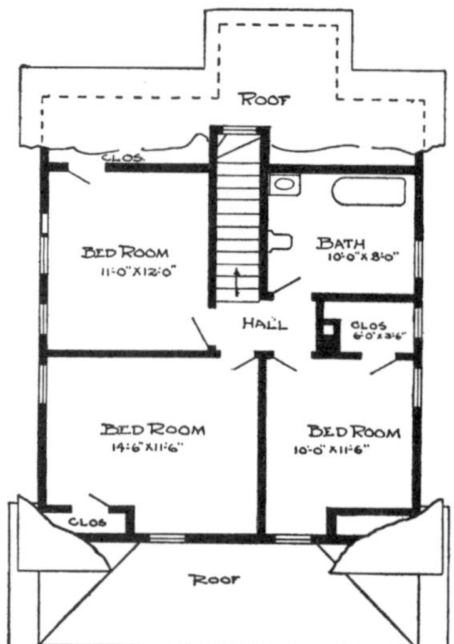

Second Floor Plan

PRICE

of Blue Prints together with a complete set of typewritten specifications

ONLY TWELVE DOLLARS

We mail Plans and Specifications the same day order is received.

Design No. 7056

Size: Width, 30 feet. Length, 44 feet, exclusive of porches

PRICE

of Blue Prints, together with a complete set of typewritten specifications.

ONLY FIFTEEN DOLLARS

We mail Plans and Specifications the same day order is received.

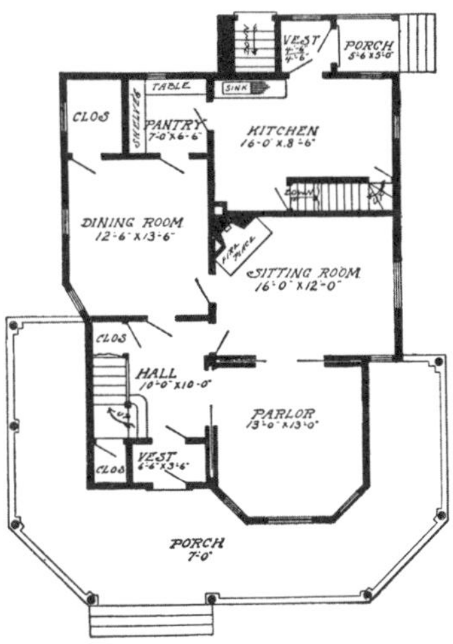

First Floor Plan

Blue prints consist of basement plan; roof plan; first and second floor plans; front, rear, two side elevations; wall sections and all necessary interior details. Specifications consist of about twenty pages of typewritten matter.

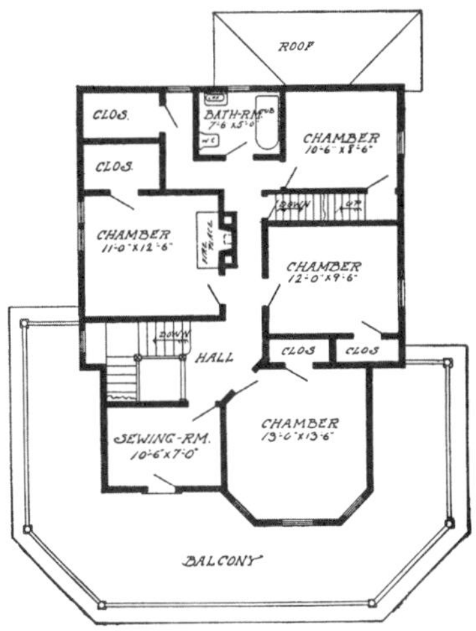

Second Floor Plan

Design No. 7065

Size: Width, 35 feet 6 inches; Length, 49 feet, exclusive of porches

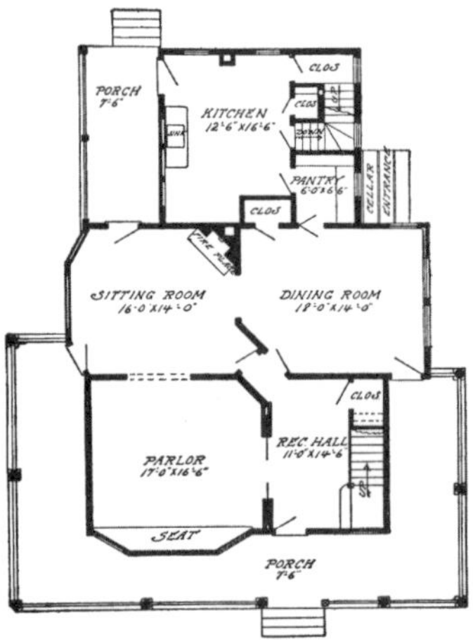

First Floor Plan

Blue prints consist of cellar and foundation plan; roof plan; first and second floor plans; front, rear, two side elevations; wall sections and all necessary interior details. Specifications consist of about twenty pages of typewritten matter.

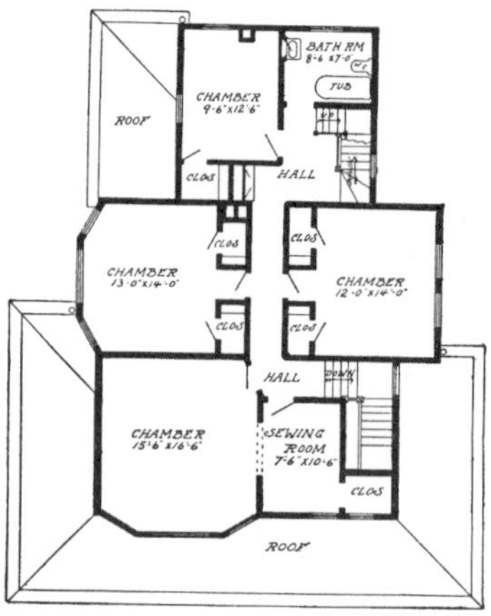

Second Floor Plan

PRICE

of Blue Prints, together with a complete set of typewritten specifications

ONLY FIFTEEN DOLLARS

We mail Plans and Specifications the same day order is received.

DESIGN NUMBER 6013

Size: width, 28 feet 9 inches; length, 30 feet 9 inches, exclusive of porches

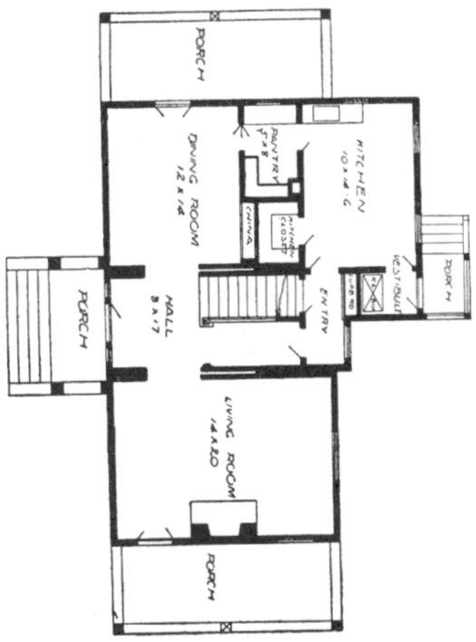

First Floor Plan

BLUE PRINTS consist of basement plan; roof plan; first and second floor plans; front, rear two side elevations; wall sections and all necessary interior details. Specifications consist of about twenty pages of typewritten matter.

PRICE

of Blue Prints, together with a complete set of typewritten specifications

ONLY FIFTEEN DOLLARS

We mail plans and specifications the same day order is received.

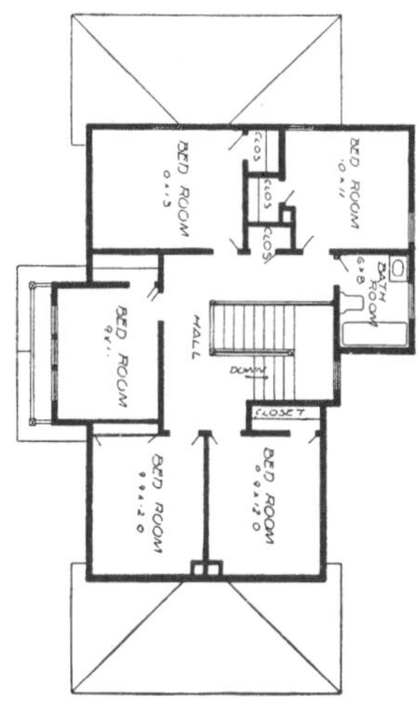

Second Floor Plan

DESIGN NUMBER 6026

Size: width, 28 feet; length, 42 feet, exclusive of porches

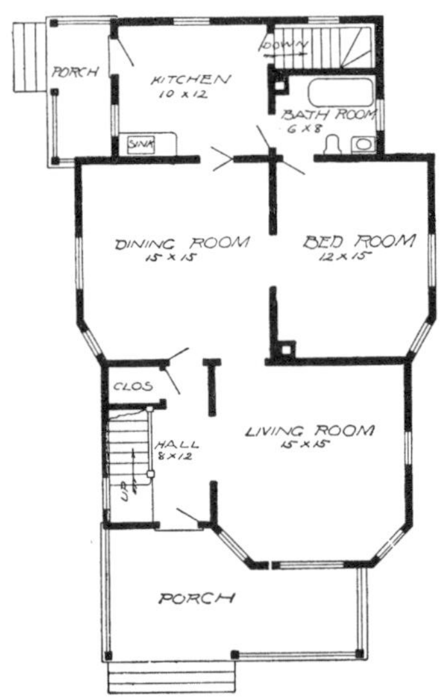

First Floor Plan

BLUE PRINTS consist of cellar and foundation plan; roof plan; first and second floor plans; front, rear, two side elevations; wall sections and all necessary interior details. Specifications consist of about twenty pages of typewritten matter.

PRICE

of Blue Prints, together with a complete set of typewritten specifications

ONLY TWELVE DOLLARS

We mail plans and specifications the same day order is received.

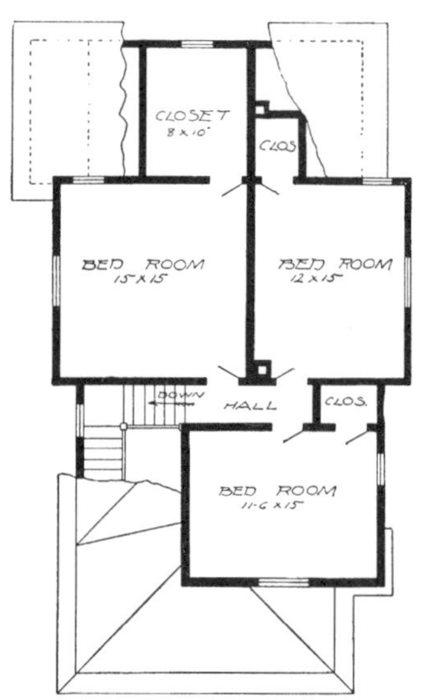

Second Floor Plan

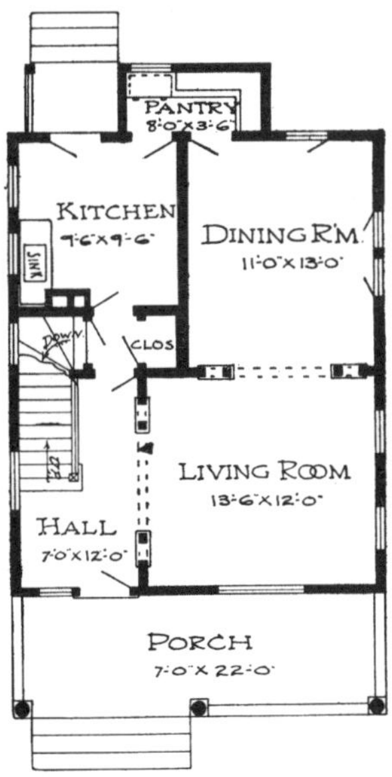

First Floor Plan.

Design No. 9045

The arrangement of this House is as follows:

FIRST FLOOR.

Reception Hall, 7 feet by 12 feet.
Living Room, 13 feet 6 inches by 12 feet.
Dining Room, 11 feet by 13 feet.
Kitchen, 9 feet 6 inches by 9 feet 6 inches.
Pantry, Front and Rear Porches.

SECOND FLOOR.

Bedroom, 17 feet by 9 feet 6 inches.
Bedroom, 17 feet by 9 feet 6 inches.
Bathroom, 8 feet by 5 feet 6 inches.
3 Closets.

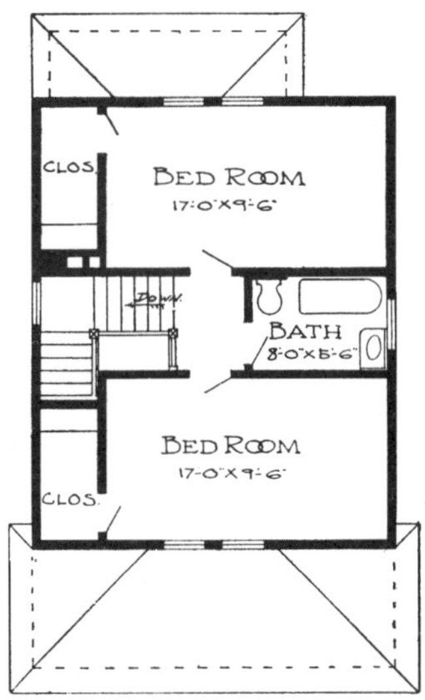

Second Floor Plan.

This Building is 22 feet in width; 30 feet 6 inches in length.

Price of Complete Working Plans and Specifications.. $10.00

The Blue Printed Working Plans for this House consist of basement plan; first and second floor plans, front, right, left and rear elevations; wall sections and all necessary details.

The Typewritten Specifications contain all the necessary information for the proper construction of the House.

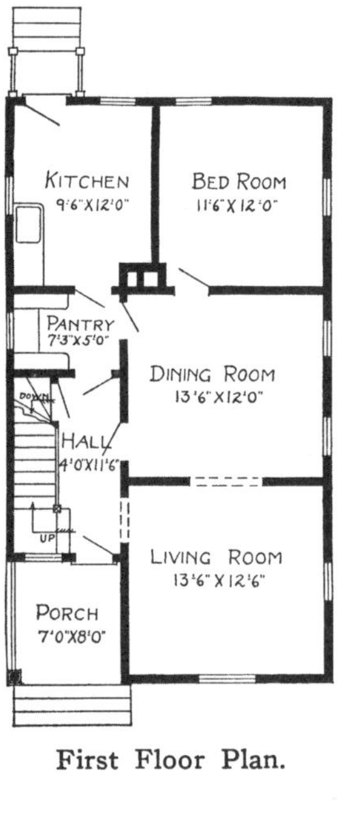

First Floor Plan.

Design No. 9053

The arrangement of this House is as follows:

FIRST FLOOR.

Reception Hall, 4 feet by 11 feet 6 inches.
Living Room, 13 feet 6 inches by 12 feet 6 inches.
Dining Room, 13 feet 6 inches by 12 feet.
Kitchen, 9 feet 6 inches by 12 feet.
Bedroom, 11 feet 6 inches by 12 feet.
Pantry, Front and Rear Porches.

SECOND FLOOR.

Bedroom, 13 feet 6 inches by 12 feet 6 inches.
Bedroom, 9 feet 6 inches by 12 feet.
Bathroom, 7 feet 9 inches by 5 feet.
2 Closets and Storeroom.

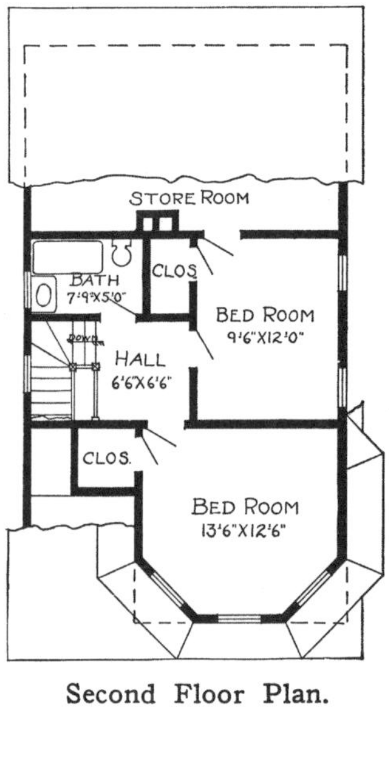

Second Floor Plan.

This Building is 22 feet 6 inches in width; 38 feet 6 inches in length.

Price of Complete Working Plans and Specifications.. **$12.00**

The Blue Printed Working Plans for this House consist of basement plan, roof plan, first and second floor plans; front, right, left and rear elevations; wall sections and all necessary details.

The Typewritten Specifications contain all the necessary information for the proper construction of the House.

Design No. 9003

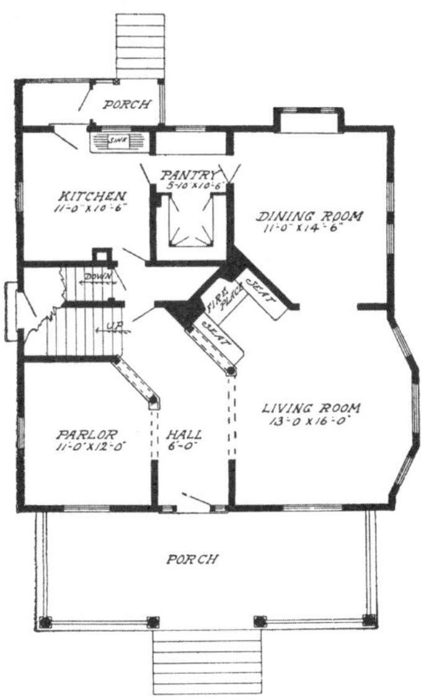

First Floor Plan.

This House is arranged in the following manner:

FIRST FLOOR.

Reception Hall, 6 feet.
Parlor, 11 feet by 12 feet.
Living Room, 13 feet by 16 feet.
Dining Room, 11 feet by 14 feet 6 inches.
Kitchen, 11 feet by 10 feet 6 inches.
Pantry, Front and Rear Porches.

SECOND FLOOR.

Bedroom, 11 feet by 12 feet.
Bedroom, 14 feet 6 inches by 15 feet.
Bedroom, 11 feet 6 inches by 10 feet 6 inches.
Bedroom, 12 feet 6 inches by 12 feet 6 inches.
Bathroom, 6 feet by 7 feet 8 inches.
6 Closets.

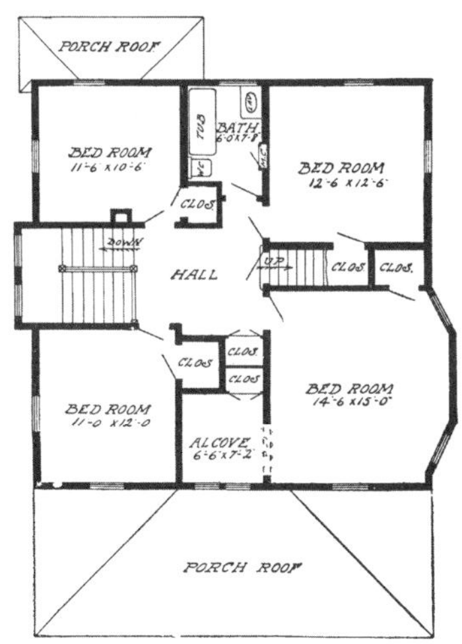

Second Floor Plan.

This Building is 34 feet in width; 32 feet in length.

Price of Complete Working Plans and Specifications.......... **$15.00**

The Blue Printed Working Plans for this House consist of basement plan; roof plan; first and second floor plans; front, right, left and rear elevations; wall sections and all necessary details.

The Typewritten Specifications contain all the necessary information for the proper construction of the House.

Design No. 9004

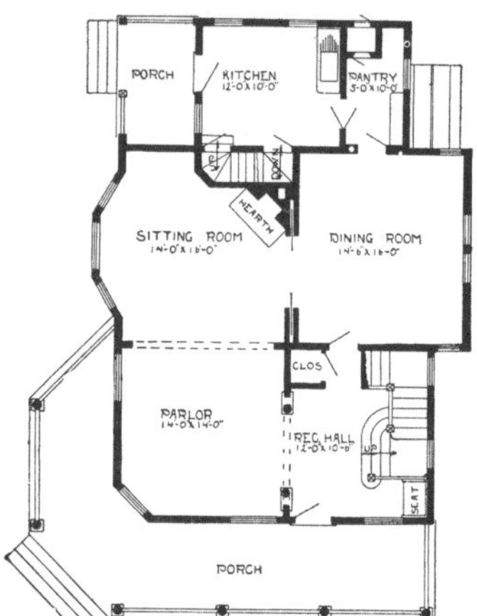

First Floor Plan.

The arrangement of this House is as follows:

FIRST FLOOR.

Reception Hall, 12 feet by 10 feet 6 inches.
Parlor, 14 feet by 14 feet.
Living Room, 14 feet by 16 feet.
Dining Room, 14 feet 6 inches by 16 feet.
Kitchen, 12 feet by 10 feet.
Pantry, Front and Rear Porches.

SECOND FLOOR.

Bedroom, 12 feet by 11 feet 6 inches.
Bedroom, 14 feet by 14 feet.
Bedroom, 16 feet by 14 feet.
Sewing Room, 11 feet by 10 feet.
Bathroom, 11 feet by 5 feet 6 inches.
4 Closets.

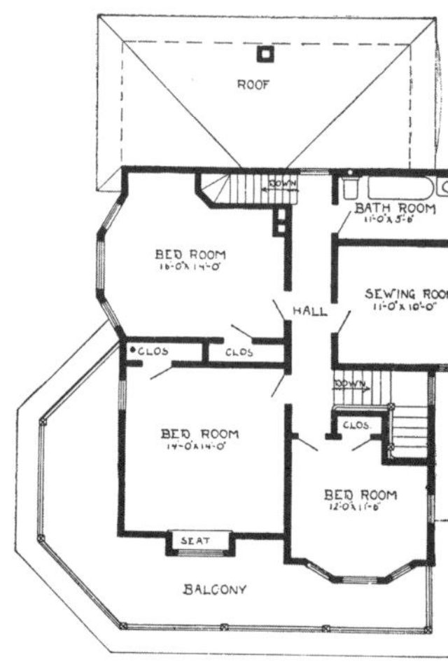

Second Floor Plan.

This Building is 32 feet 6 inches in width; 42 feet in length.

Price of Complete Working Plans and Specifications **$15.00**

The Blue Printed Working Plans for this House consist of basement plan; roof plan; first and second floor plans; front, right, left and rear elevations; wall sections and all necessary details.

The Typewritten Specifications contain all the necessary information for the proper construction of the House.

PRICE
of Blue Prints, together with a complete set of typewritten specifications is

ONLY TEN DOLLARS

We mail Plans and Specifications the same day order is received.

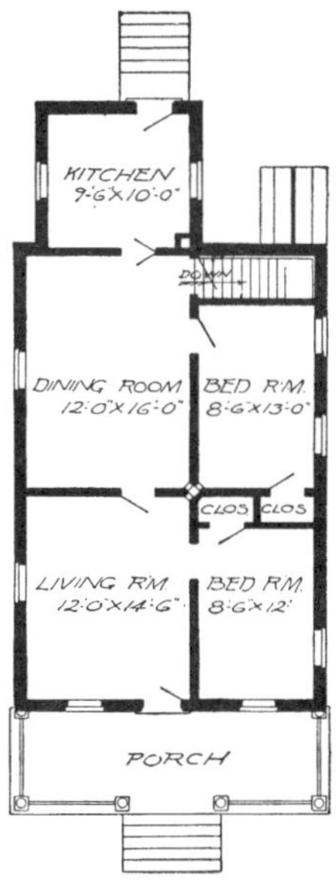

Floor Plan

Design No. 2010

Blue prints consist of basement plan; roof plan; floor plan; front, rear, two side elevations; wall sections and all necessary interior details. Specifications consist of about fifteen pages of typewritten matter.

SIZE: Width, 22 feet 8 inches; length, 42 feet 8 inches, exclusive of porch

Our plans are so clear and explicit that no carpenter or contractor will have the least difficulty in understanding them. We aim to make our plans so plain that there will be a minimum of mistakes.

In drawing these plans special care has been taken to provide for the most economical construction, thereby giving the contractor and the home builder the benefit of the saving of many dollars in material and wages.

Design No. 2045

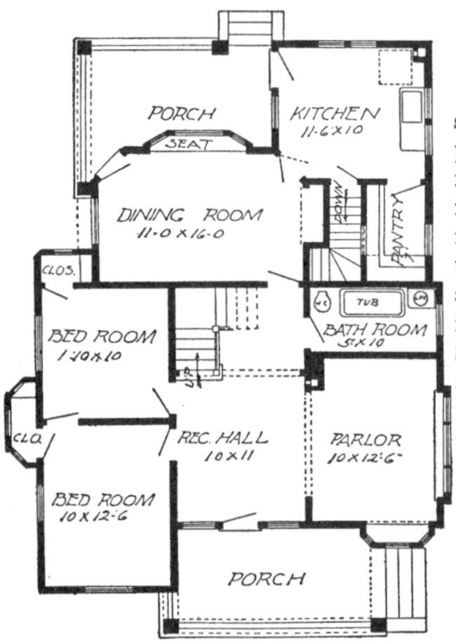

First Floor Plan

Blue prints consist of basement plan; roof plan; first and second floor plans; front, rear, two side elevations; wall sections and all necessary interior details. Specifications consist of about twenty pages of typewritten matter.

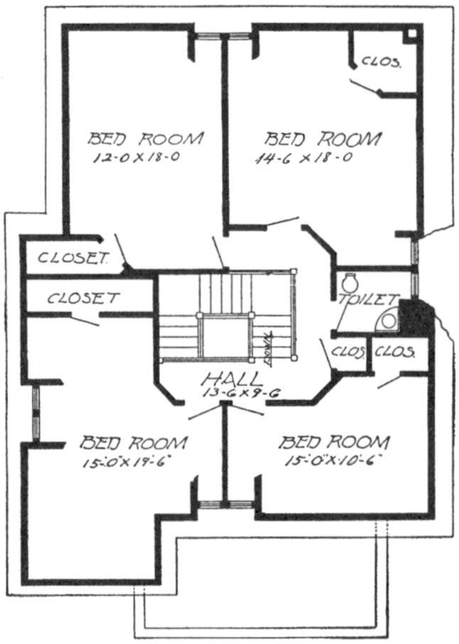

Second Floor Plan

PRICE

of Blue Prints, together with a complete set of typewritten specifications is

ONLY TWELVE DOLLARS

We mail Plans and Specifications the same day order is received.

SIZE: Width, 32 feet; length, 42 feet 6 inches exclusive of porches.

The majority of the people build only one house in a life time, therefore, it is the duty of every prospective builder to make his home as comfortable and attractive as possible.

This kind of a home costs no more to build than the ordinary structures usually seen in towns and villages, and the prospective builder can well afford to take a little time and investigate the latest designs.

Design No. 7050

Size: Width, 30 feet 6 inches; Length, 39 feet, exclusive of porches

PRICE

of Blue Prints, together with a complete set of typewritten specifications.

ONLY TWELVE DOLLARS

We mail Plans and Specifications the same day order is received.

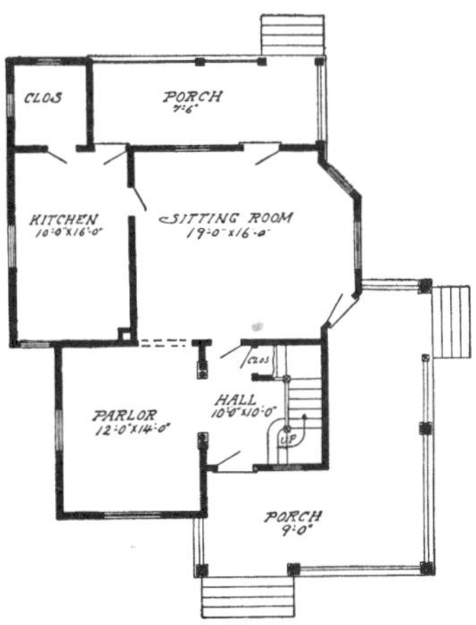

First Floor Plan

Blue prints consist of foundation plan; first and second floor plans; front, rear, two side elevations; wall sections and all necessary interior details. Specifications consist of about twenty pages of typewritten matter.

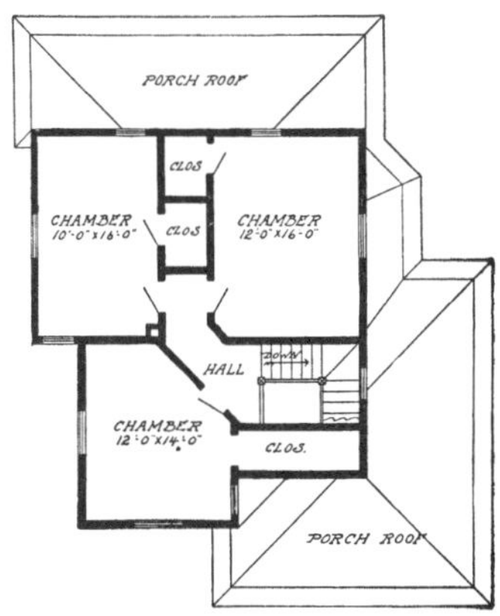

Second Floor Plan

Design No. 7071

Size: Width, 38 feet 6 inches; Length, 51 feet, exclusive of porches

Blue prints consist of basement plan; floor plan; front, rear, two side elevations; wall sections and all necessary interior details. Specifications consist of about fifteen pages of typewritten matter.

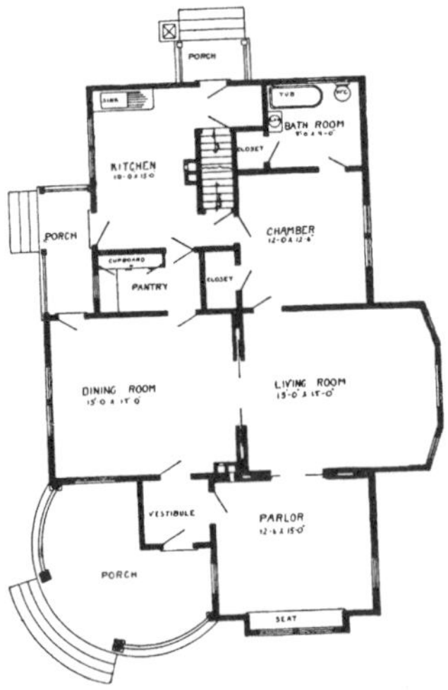

Floor Plan

PRICE

of Blue Prints, together with a complete set of typewritten specifications

ONLY TEN DOLLARS

We mail Plans and Specifications the same day order is received.

Design No. 7094

Size: Width, 29 feet 6 inches; Length, 35 feet 6 inches, exclusive of porches

PRICE

of Blue Prints, together with a complete set of typewritten specifications

ONLY TWELVE DOLLARS

We mail Plans and Specifications the same day order is received.

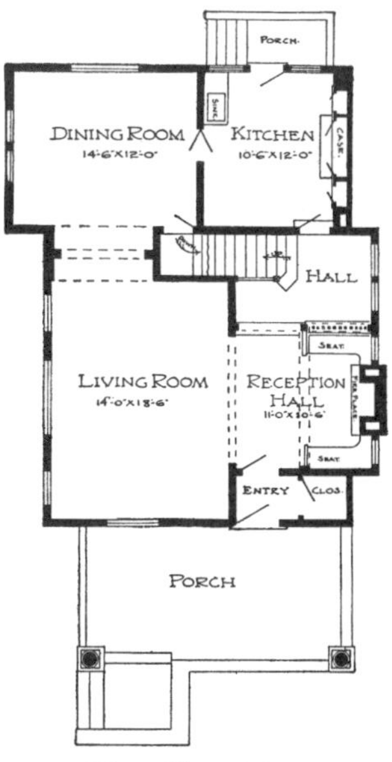

First Floor Plan

Blue prints consist of basement plan; roof plan; first and second floor plans; front, rear, two side elevations; wall sections and all necessary interior details. Specifications consist of about twenty pages of typewritten matter.

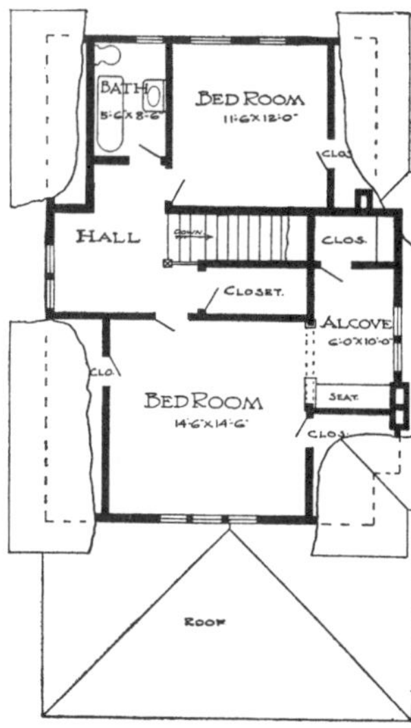

Second Floor Plan

Design No. 7060

Size: Width, 29 feet 6 inches; Length, 35 feet 6 inches, exclusive of porches

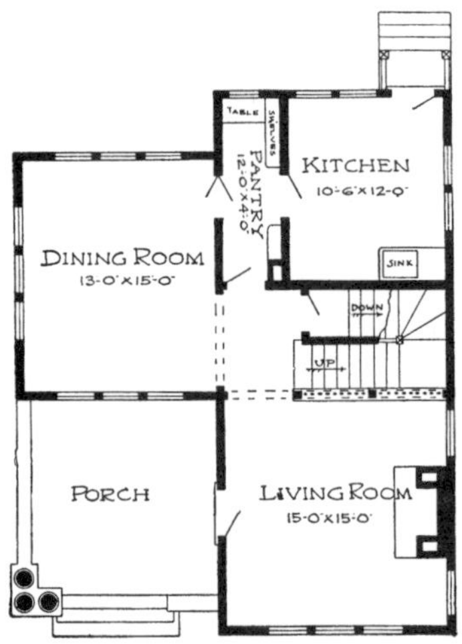

First Floor Plan

Blue prints consist of basement plan; roof plan; first and second floor plans; front, rear, two side elevations; wall sections and all necessary interior details. Specifications consist of about twenty pages of typewritten matter.

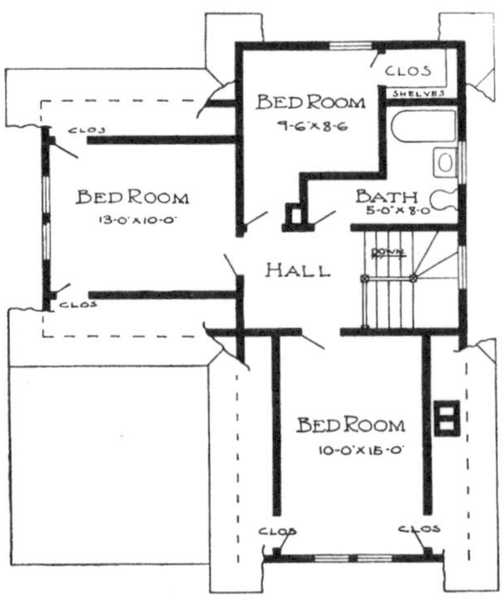

Second Floor Plan

PRICE

of Blue Prints, together with a complete set of typewritten specifications

ONLY FIFTEEN DOLLARS

We mail Plans and Specifications the same day order is received.

DESIGN NUMBER 6050

Size: width, 36 feet; length, 36 feet, exclusive of porches

BLUE PRINTS consist of foundation plan; floor plan; front, rear, two side elevations; wall sections and all necessary interior details. Specifications consist of about fifteen pages of typewritten matter.

Floor Plan

PRICE

of Blue Prints, together with a complete set of typewritten specifications

ONLY TEN DOLLARS

We mail plans and specifications the same day order is received.

DESIGN NUMBER 6043

Size: width, 26 feet 6 inches; length, 30 feet 6 inches exclusive of porches

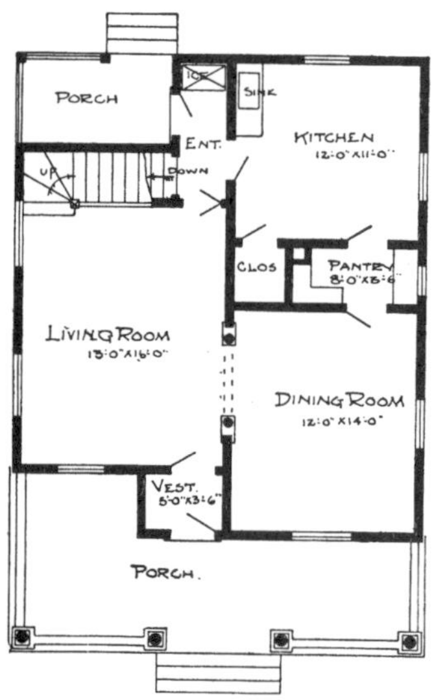

First Floo Plan

BLUE PRINTS consist of basement plan; roof plan; first and second floor plans; front, rear, two side elevations; wall sections and all necessary interior details. Specifications consist of about twenty pages of typewritten matter.

PRICE

of Blue Prints, together with a complete set of typewritten specifications

ONLY TEN DOLLARS

We mail plans and specifications the same day order is received.

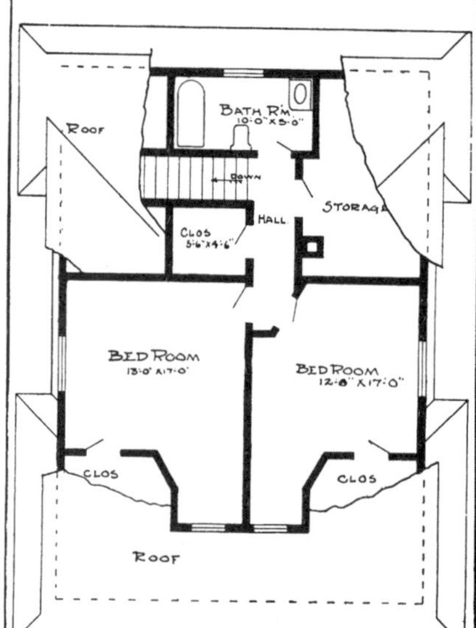

Second Floor Plan

Design No. 9011

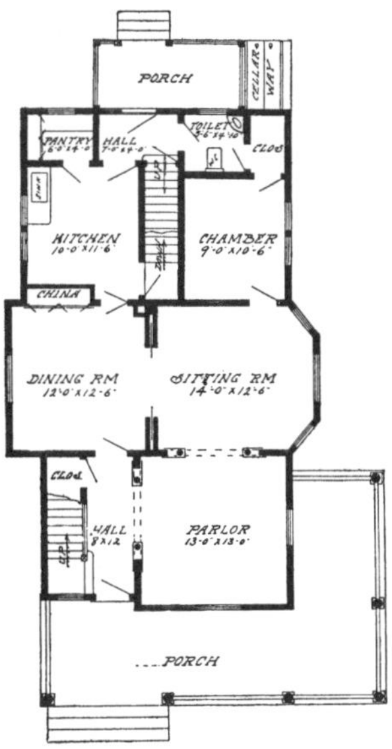

First Floor Plan.

The arrangement of this House is as follows:

FIRST FLOOR.

Reception Hall, 8 feet by 12 feet.
Parlor, 13 feet by 13 feet.
Living Room, 14 feet by 12 feet 6 inches.
Dining Room, 12 feet by 12 feet 6 inches.
Kitchen, 10 feet by 11 feet 6 inches.
Lavatory, 5 feet 6 inches by 4 feet 10 inches.
Bedroom, 9 feet by 10 feet 6 inches.
Pantry, Front and Rear Porches.

SECOND FLOOR.

Bedroom, 13 feet by 13 feet.
Alcove, 8 feet by 8 feet.
Bedroom, 13 feet by 12 feet 6 inches.
Bedroom, 13 feet 6 inches by 11 feet 6 inches.
Bedroom, 9 feet 6 inches by 12 feet 6 inches.
Bathroom, 8 feet 10 inches by 11 feet 6 inches.
5 Closets.

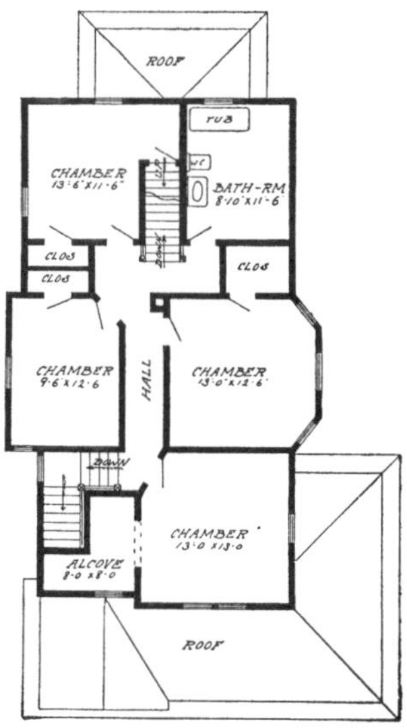

Second Floor Plan.

This Building is 28 feet in width; 43 feet 6 inches in length.
Price of Complete Working Plans and Specifications.................... $15.00
The Blue Printed Working Plans for this House consist of basement plan; roof plan; first and second floor plans; front, right, left and rear elevations; wall sections and all necessary details.
The Typewritten Specifications contain all the necessary information for the proper construction of the House.

Design No. 9013

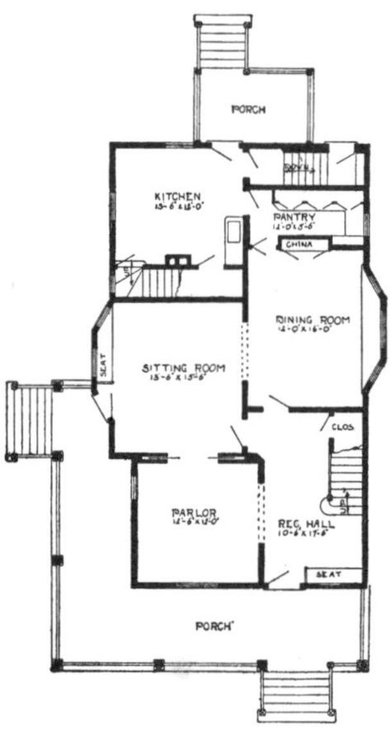

First Floor Plan.

The arrangement of this House is as follows:

FIRST FLOOR.

Reception Hall, 10 feet 6 inches by 17 feet 6 inches.
Parlor, 12 feet 6 inches by 12 feet.
Living Room, 13 feet 6 inches by 15 feet 6 inches.
Dining Room, 12 feet by 16 feet.
Kitchen, 13 feet 6 inches by 12 feet.
Pantry, Front and Rear Porches.

SECOND FLOOR.

Bedroom, 10 feet 6 inches by 9 feet 6 inches.
Bedroom, 12 feet 6 inches by 12 feet 6 inches.
Bedroom, 15 feet 3 inches by 12 feet.
Bedroom, 13 feet 6 inches by 12 feet.
Bedroom, 8 feet 6 inches by 14 feet.
Bathroom, 12 feet by 8 feet.
6 Closets.

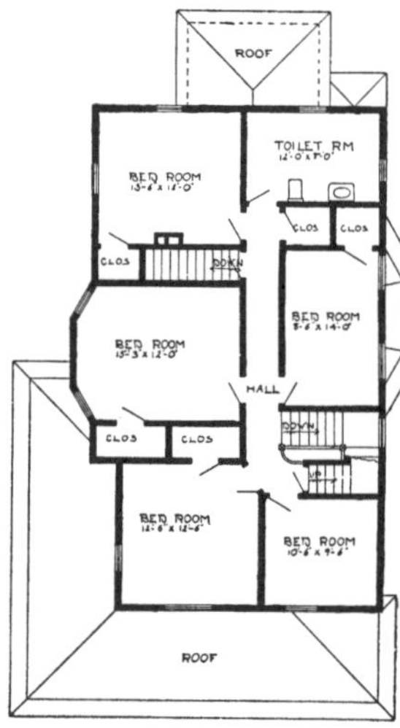

Second Floor Plan.

This Building is 30 feet 6 inches in width; 45 feet 6 inches in length.
Price of Complete Working Plans and Specifications........ $15.00
The Blue Printed Working Plans for this House consist of foundation plan; roof plan; first and second floor plans; front, right, left and rear elevations; wall sections and all necessary details.
The Typewritten Specifications contain all the necessary information for the proper construction of the House.

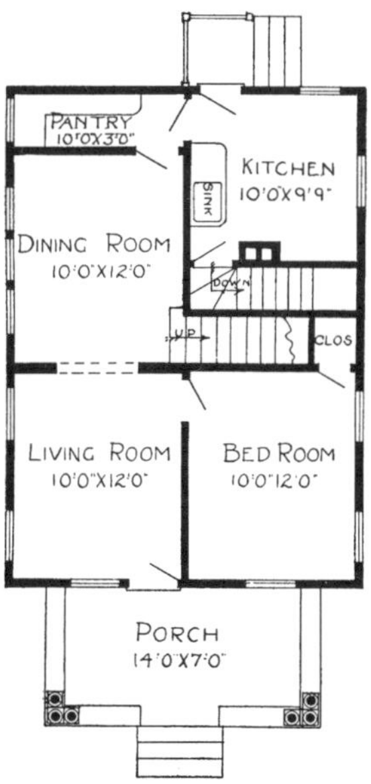

First Floor Plan.

Design No. 9054

The arrangement of this House is as follows:

FIRST FLOOR.

Living Room, 10 by 12 feet.
Dining Room, 10 feet by 12 feet.
Kitchen, 10 feet by 9 feet 9 inches.
Bedroom, 10 feet by 12 feet.
Pantry, Front and Rear Porches.

SECOND FLOOR.

Bedroom, 13 feet 6 inches by 11 feet 6 inches.

Bedroom, 13 feet 6 inches by 10 feet.

Bathroom, 5 feet 6 inches by 5 feet 6 inches.

3 Closets.

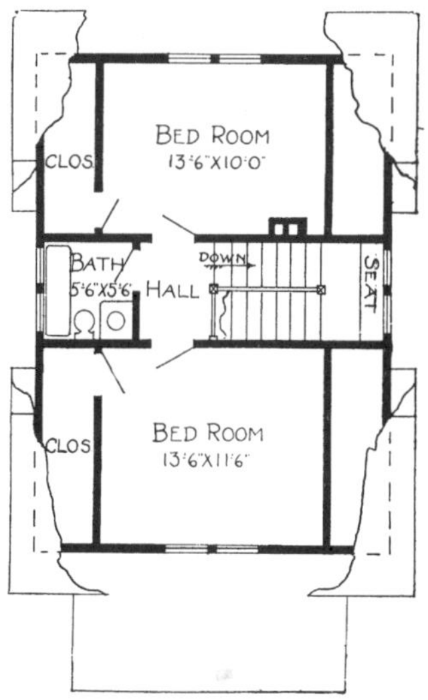

Second Floor Plan.

This Building is 21 feet 6 inches in width; 29 feet in length.

Price of Complete Working Plans and Specifications.. $12.00

The Blue Printed Working Plans for this House consist of basement plan; first and second floor plans, front right, left and rear elevations; wall sections and all necessary details.

The Typewritten Specifications contain all the necessary information for the proper construction of the House.

Design No. 9056

The arrangement of this House is as follows:

FIRST FLOOR.

Parlor, 18 feet by 12 feet.

Dining Room, 14 feet by 14 feet.

Kitchen, 10 feet 6 inches by 9 feet 6 inches.

Pantry and Front Porch.

SECOND FLOOR.

Bedroom, 21 feet by 12 feet.

Bedroom, 13 feet 6 inches by 10 feet 6 inches.

Bathroom, 7 feet by 10 feet 6 inches.

3 Closets.

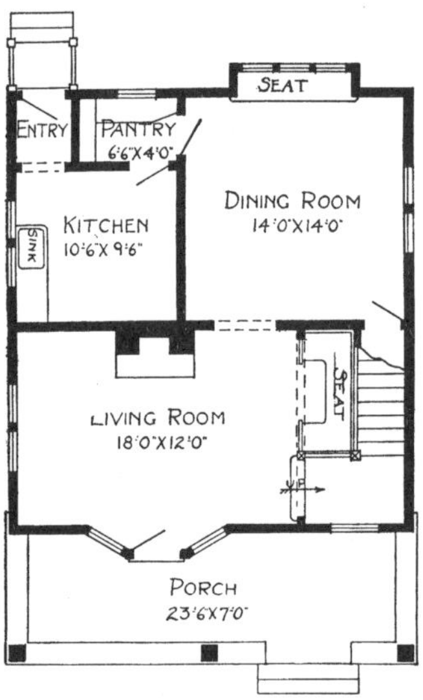

First Floor Plan.

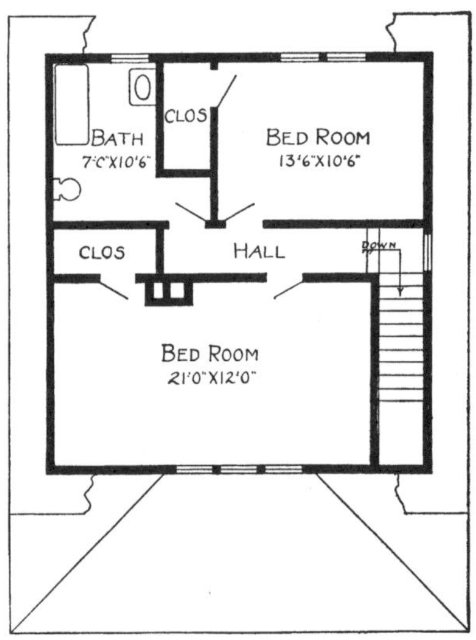

Second Floor Plan.

This Building is 26 feet in width; 30 feet 6 inches in length.

Price of Complete Working Plans and Specifications $12.00

The Blue Printed Working Plans for this House consist of foundation plan; first and second floor plans; front, right, lett and rear elevations; wall sections and all necessary details.

The Typewritten Specifications contain all the necessary information for the proper construction of the House.

PRICE
of Blue Prints, together with a complete set of typewritten specifications is

ONLY TWELVE DOLLARS

We mail Plans and Specifications the same day order is received

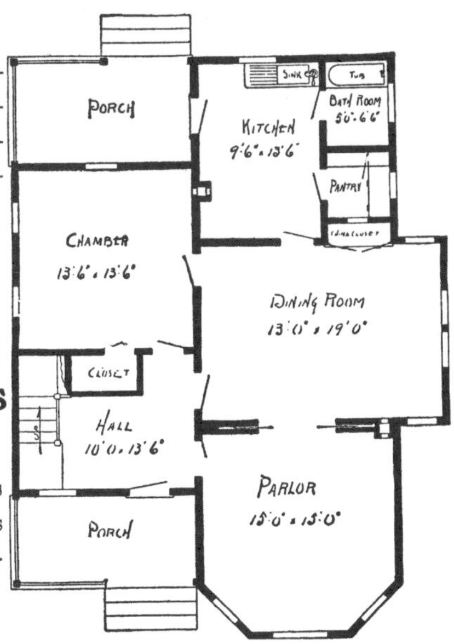

First Floor Plan

Design No. 133

Blue prints consist of foundation plan; first and second floor plans; front, two side elevations; wall sections and all necessary interior details. Specifications consist of about fifteen pages of typewritten matter.

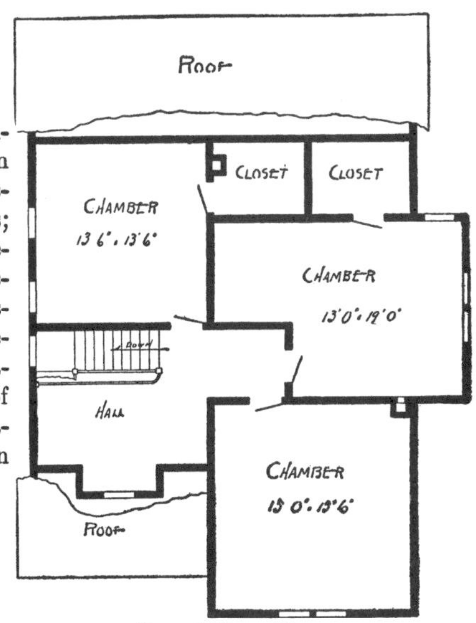

Second Floor Plan

Size: Width, 34 feet; length, 44 feet, exclusive of porch.

The prospective builder should not lose sight of the fact that some day it may be necessary or desirable to sell the house, and, if it is attractive and artistic, it can always be disposed of and at a profit to the owner.

The houses we illustrate have been designed by licensed architects to meet the needs of the people and they have a reputation for being practical, attractive and artistic.

PRICE
of Blue Prints, together with a complete set of typewritten specifications is

ONLY TEN DOLLARS

We mail Plans and Specifications the same day order is received.

Design No. 2029

Blue prints consist of basement plan; roof plan; floor plan, front, rear, two side elevations; wall sections and all necessary interior details. Specifications consist of about fifteen pages of typewritten matter.

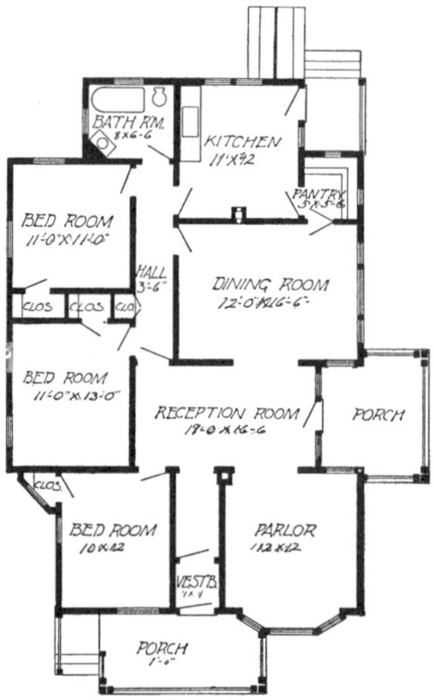

Floor Plan

SIZE: Width, 32 feet, 6 inches; length, 47 feet, 6 inches, exclusive of porch.

With all of our plans we furnish a front, right, left and rear elevation. These drawings are complete and accurate in every respect. They show the shape, size and location of all doors and windows, porches, cornices, towers, bays and the like, and, in fact, give you an exact scale picture of the house as it should be at completion.

Full wall sections are given showing the construction from foundation to roof, the height of stories between joists. height of plates, pitch of roof, etc.

Design No. 7011

Size: Width, 42 feet; Length, 30 feet, exclusive of porches

PRICE

of Blue Prints, together with a complete set of typewritten specifications

ONLY FIFTEEN DOLLARS

We mail Plans and Specifications the same day order is received.

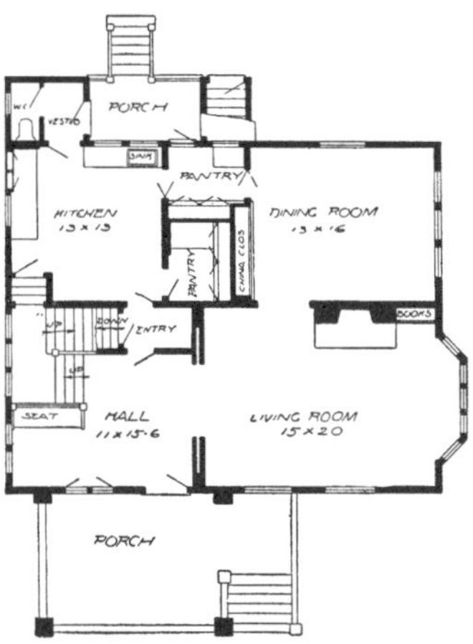

First Floor Plan

Blue prints consist of cellar and foundation plan; roof plan; first and second floor plans; front, two side elevations; wall sections and all necessary interior details. Specifications consist of about twenty pages of type written matter.

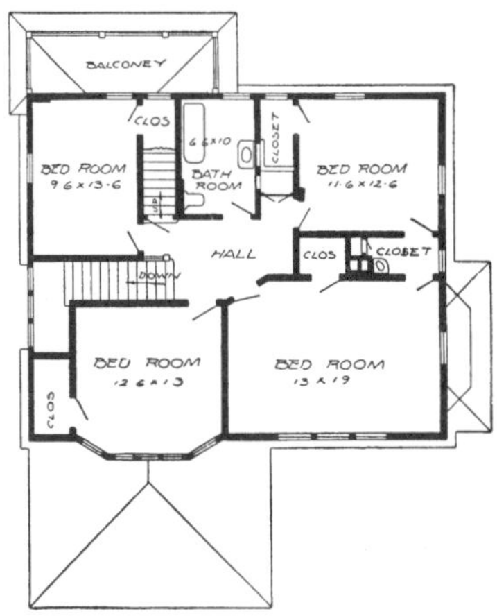

Second Floor Plan

Design No. 7096

Size: Width, 33 feet 6 inches; Length, 23 feet, exclusive of porches

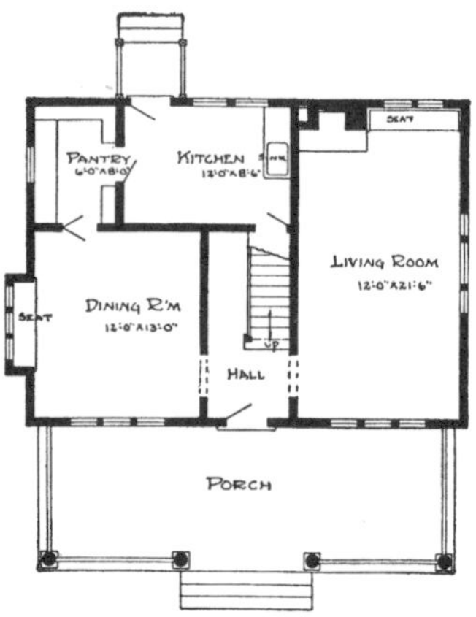

First Floor Plan

Blue prints consist of basement plan; roof plan; first and second floor plans; front, rear, two side elevations; wall sections and all necessary interior details. Specifications consist of about twenty pages of typewritten matter.

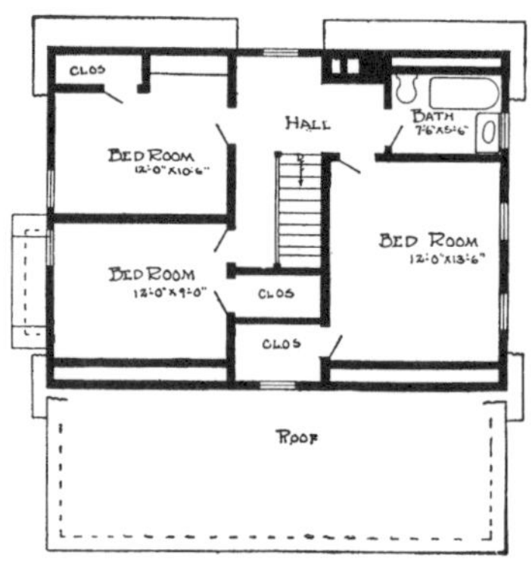

Second Floor Plan

PRICE

of Blue Prints, together with a complete set of typewritten specifications

ONLY TWELVE DOLLARS

We mail Plans and Specifications the same day order is received.

Design No. 7002

Size: Width, 22 feet 6 inches; Length, 30 feet, exclusive of porches

PRICE

of Blue Prints, together with a complete set of typewritten specifications.

ONLY TWELVE DOLLARS

We mail Plans and Specifications the same day order is received.

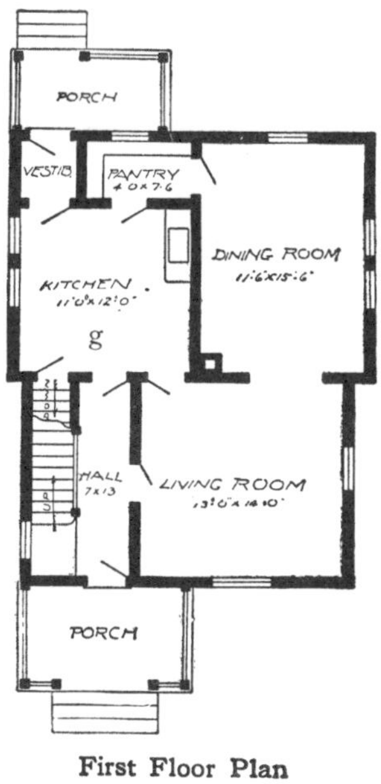

First Floor Plan

Blue prints consist of cellar and foundation plan; first and second floor plans; front, rear, two side elevations; wall sections and all necessary interior details. Specifications consist of about twenty pages of typewritten matter.

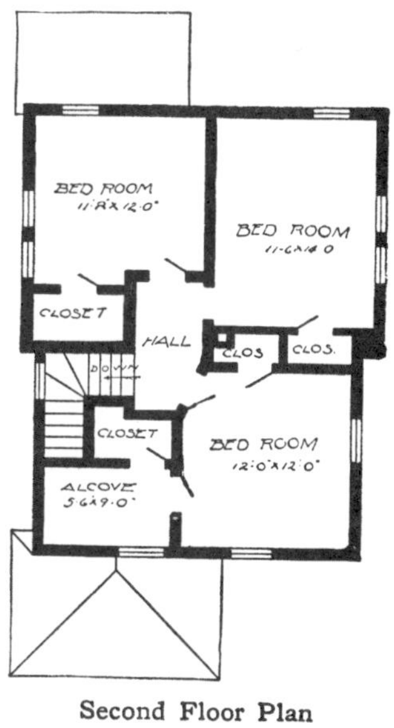

Second Floor Plan

Design No. 7080

Size: Width, 29 feet 6 inches; Length, 26 feet, exclusive of porches

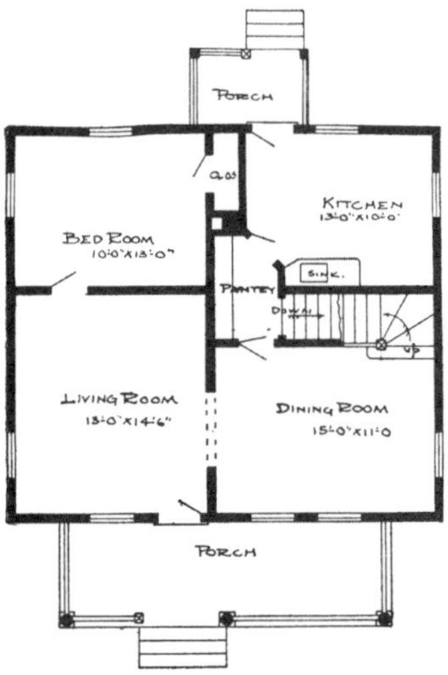

First Floor Plan

Blue prints consist of basement plan; roof plan; floor plan; front, rear, two side elevations; wall sections and all necessary interior details. Specifications consist of about fifteen pages of typewritten matter.

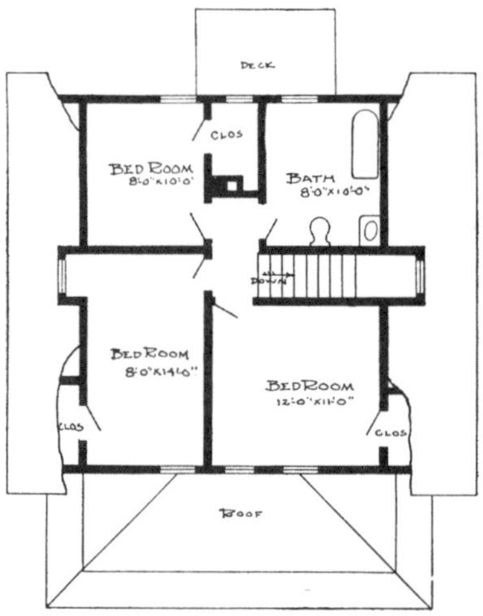

Second Floor Plan

PRICE

of Blue Prints, together with a complete set of typewritten specifications

ONLY TWELVE DOLLARS

We mail Plans and Specifications the same day order is received.

D E S I G N   N U M B E R   6 0 2 2

Size: width, 40 feet; length, 31 feet, exclusive of porches

BLUE PRINTS consist of foundation plan; floor plan; front, rear, two side elevations; wall sections and all necessary interior details. Specifications consist of about fifteen pages of typewritten matter.

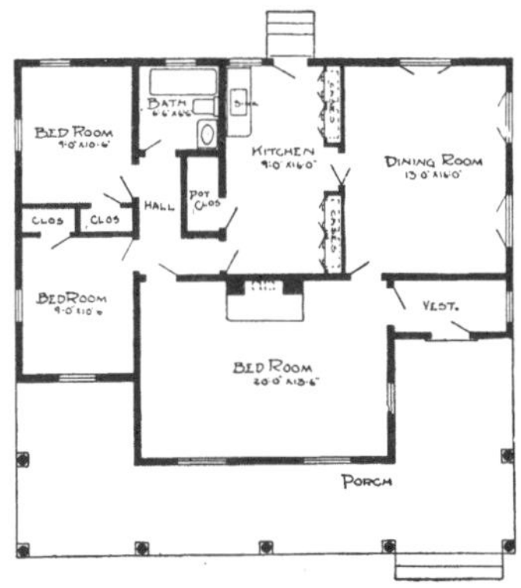

Floor Plan

PRICE

of Blue Prints, together with a complete set of typewritten specifications

ONLY TEN DOLLARS

We mail plans and specifications the same day order is received.

DESIGN NUMBER 6083

Size: width, 33 feet, 6 inches; length, 29 feet, exclusive of porches

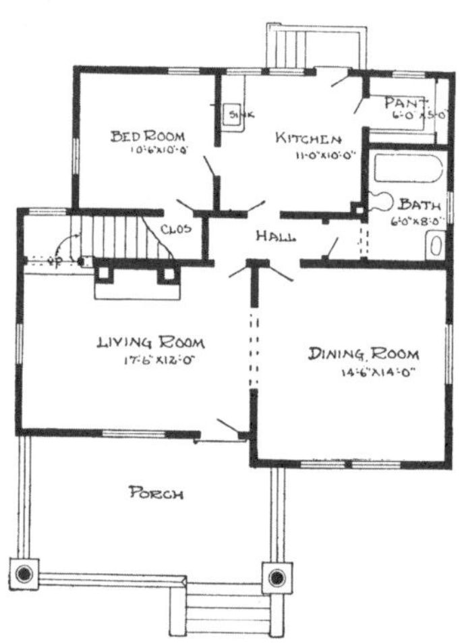

Floor Plan

BLUE PRINTS consist of basement plan; floor plan; front, rear, two side elevations; wall sections and all necessary interior details. Specifications consist of about fifteen pages of typewritten matter.

PRICE

of Blue Prints, together with a complete set of typewritten specifications

ONLY TEN DOLLARS

We mail plans and specifications the same day order is received.

Design No. 9044

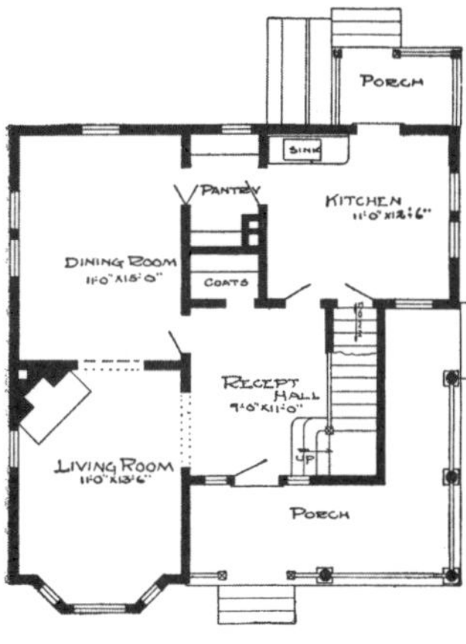

First Floor Plan.

The arrangement of this House is as follows:

FIRST FLOOR.

Reception Hall, 9 feet by 11 feet.
Living Room, 11 feet by 13 feet 6 inches.
Dining Room, 11 feet by 15 feet.
Kitchen, 11 feet by 12 feet 6 inches.
Pantry, Front and Rear Porches.

SECOND FLOOR.

Bedroom, 11 feet by 12 feet 6 inches.
Bedroom, 11 feet by 11 feet.
Bedroom, 12 feet by 11 feet.
Bedroom, 11 feet by 15 feet.
Bathroom, 5 feet by 7 feet 6 inches.
3 Closets.

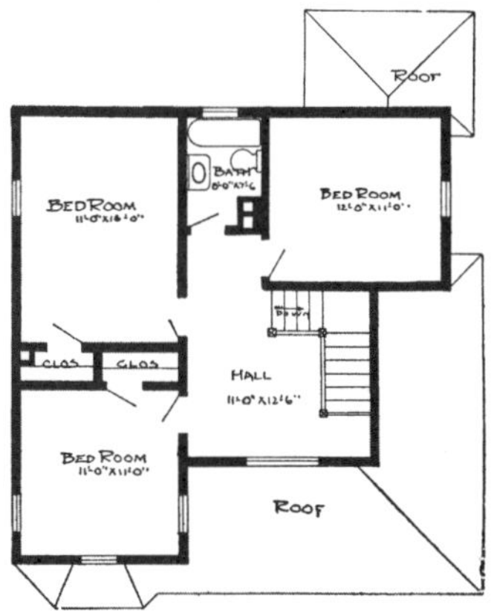

Second Floor Plan.

This Building is 30 feet in width; 32 feet in length.

Price of Complete Working Plans and Specifications.. **$12.00**

The Blue Printed Working Plans for this House consist of basement plan; roof plan; first and second floor plans; front, right, left and rear elevations; wall sections and all necessary details.

The Typewritten Specifications contain all the necessary information for the proper construction of the House.

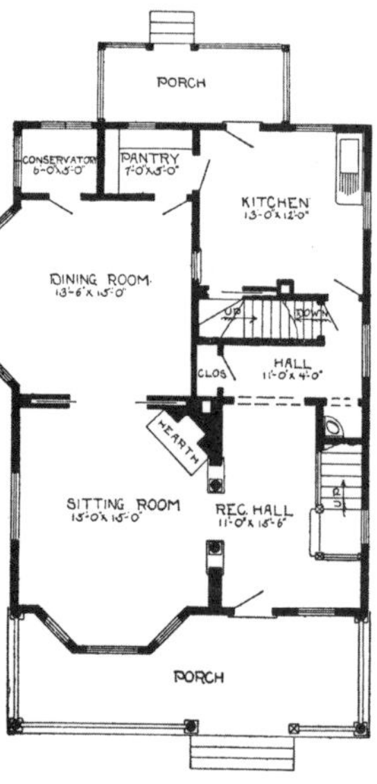

First Floor Plan.

Design No 9005

The arrangement of this House is as follows:

FIRST FLOOR.

Reception Hall, 11 feet by 15 feet 6 inches.
Living Room, 15 feet by 15 feet.
Dining Room, 13 feet 6 inches by 15 feet.
Kitchen, 13 feet by 12 feet.
Conservatory, 6 feet by 5 feet.
Pantry, Front and Rear Porches.

SECOND FLOOR.

Bedroom, 13 feet by 10 feet.
Bedroom, 13 feet 6 inches by 15 feet 6 inches.
Bedroom, 16 feet by 12 feet.
Bathroom, 8 feet 6 inches by 12 feet 6 inches.
5 Closets.

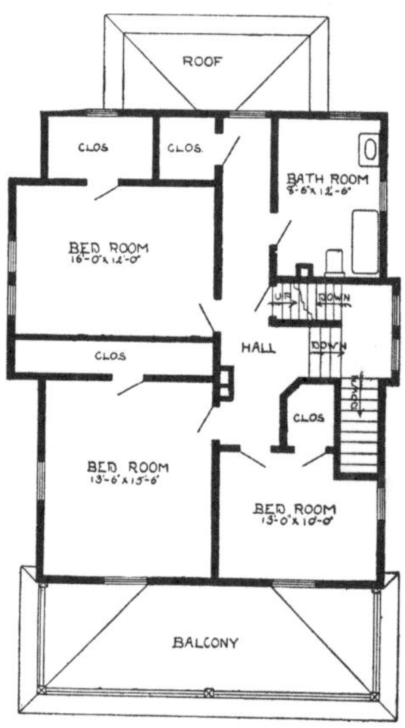

Second Floor Plan.

This Building is 30 feet 6 inches in width; 40 feet 6 inches in length.

Price of Complete Working Plans and Specifications **$15.00**

The Blue Printed Working Plans for this House consist of basement plan; roof plan; first and second floor plans; front, right, left and rear elevations; wall sections and all necessary details.

The Typewritten Specifications contain all the necessary information for the proper construction of the House.

Design No. 9092

The arrangement of this House is as follows:

Living Room, 13 feet by 15 feet.

Dining Room, 16 feet by 13 feet.

Kitchen, 11 feet 6 inches by 12 feet.

Bedroom, 9 feet 6 inches by 13 feet.

Bedroom, 13 feet by 9 feet 6 inches.

Bathroom, 5 feet 6 inches by 8 feet 6 inches.

Pantry, Front and Rear Porches.

2 Closets.

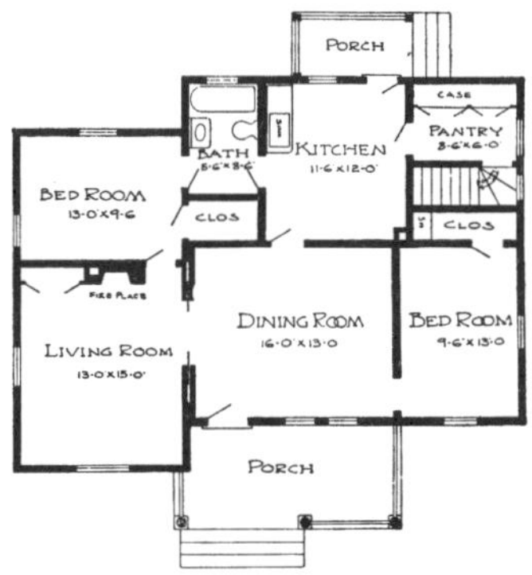

Floor Plan.

This Building is 41 feet in width; 30 feet in length.

Price of Complete Working Plans and Specifications **$10.00**

The Blue Printed Working Plans for this House consist of basement plan; floor plan; front, right, left and rear elevations; wall sections and all necessary details.

The Typewritten Specifications contain all the necessary information for the proper construction of the House.

Design No. 9057

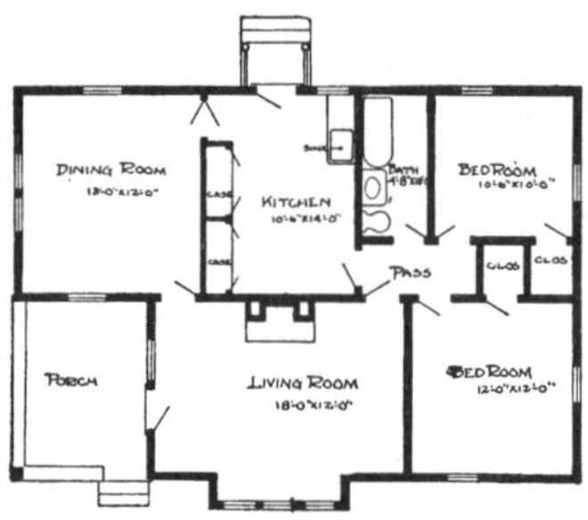

Floor Plan

The arrangement of this House is as follows:

Living Room, 18 feet by 12 feet.
Dining Room, 13 feet by 12 feet.
Kitchen, 10 feet 6 inches by 14 feet.
Bedroom, 10 feet 6 inches by 10 feet.
Bathroom, 4 feet 8 inches by 10 feet.
Front and Rear Porches.
4 Closets.

This Building is 41 feet 6 inches in width; 29 feet 6 inches in length.

Price of Complete Working Plans and Specifications.. $10.00

The Blue Printed Working Plans for this House consist of foundation plan; floor plan; front, right, left and rear elevations; wall sections and all necessary details.

The Typewritten Specifications contain all the necessary information for the proper construction of the House.

PRICE

of Blue Prints, together with a complete set of typewritten specifications is

ONLY TWELVE DOLLARS

We mail Plans and Specifications the same day order is received.

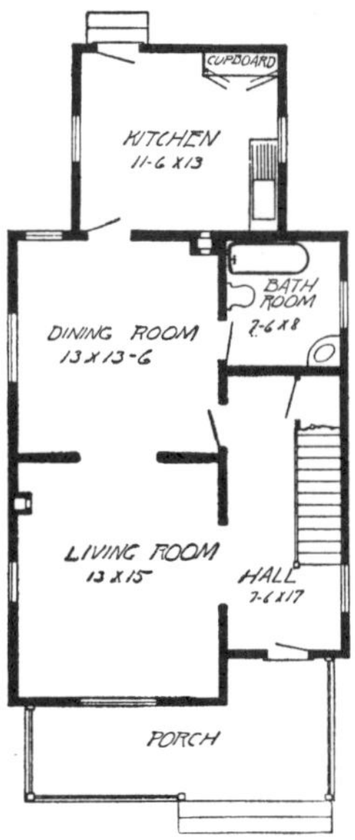

First Floor Plan

Design No. 2025

Blue prints consist of foundation plan; first and second floor plans; front, rear, two side elevations; wall sections and all necessary interior details. Specifications consist of about twenty pages of typewritten matter.

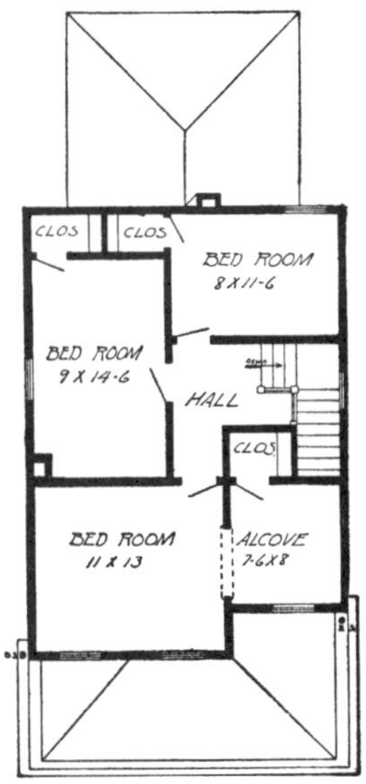

Second Floor Plan

SIZE: Width, 22 feet; length, 52 feet, exclusive of porch

When designing our houses, we have kept in mind the fact that some day the owner may wish to get his money out of his home. We design only practical houses, out of which the owner can readily get his money.

Our plans prevent mistakes in cutting lumber, in placing door and window frames, and in many other places, when the contractor is not on the job, and the men have received only partial or indefinite instruction.

Design No. 2015

Blue prints consist of basement plan; roof plan; first and second floor plans; front, rear, two side elevations; wall sections and all necessary interior details. Specifications consist of about twenty pages of typewritten matter.

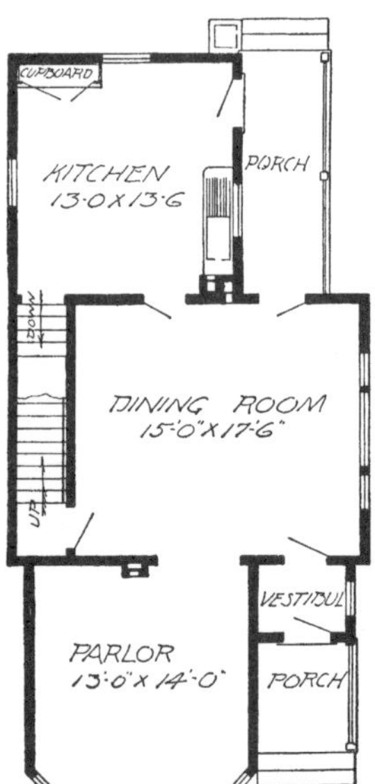

First Floor Plan

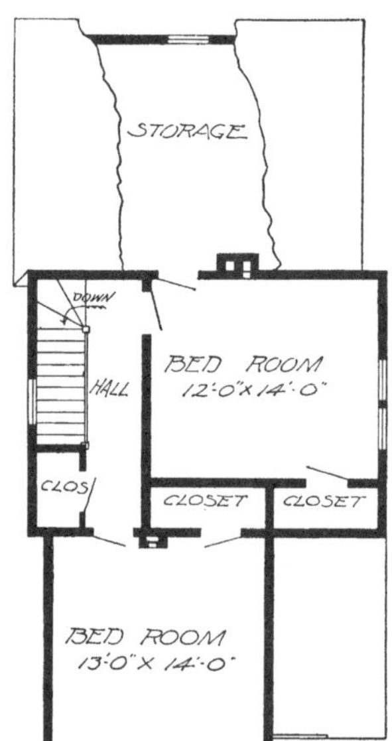

Second Floor Plan

PRICE

of Blue Prints, together with a complete set of typewritten specifications is

ONLY TWELVE DOLLARS

We mail Plans and Specifications the same day order is received.

SIZE: Width, 22 feet; length, 44 feet, 6 inches.

All of our plans are printed by electricity on a circular blue printing machine. We use the very best grade of electric blue printing paper and take great care to have every line perfect and distinct.

We do not blame you for wishing to know what you will get for your money. The plans we send out are the regular blue printed plans, drawn one-quarter inch scale to the foot, showing all elevations, floor plans and necessary interior details.

Design No. 7026

Size: Width, 25 feet 6 inches; Length, 41 feet 6 inches, exclusive of porch

PRICE

of Blue Prints, together with a complete set of typewritten specifications

ONLY TWELVE DOLLARS

We mail Plans and Specifications the same day order is received.

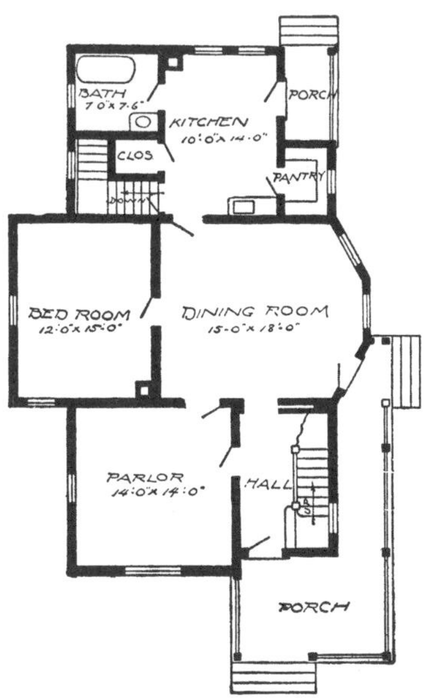

First Floor Plan

Blue prints consist of cellar and foundation plan; roof plan; first and second floor plans; front, rear, two side elevations; wall sections and all necessary interior details. Specifications consist of about twenty pages of typewritten matter.

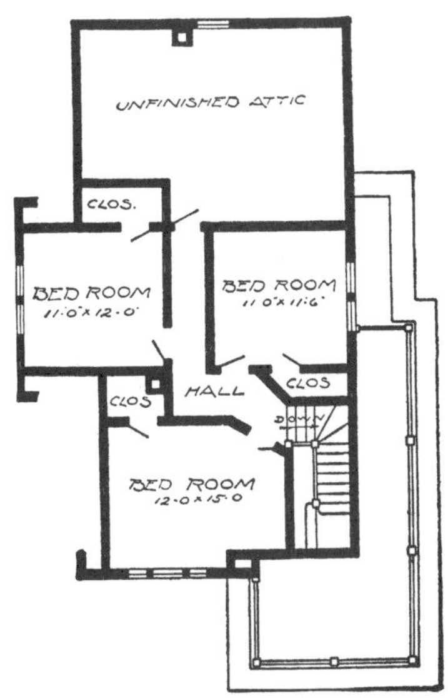

Second Floor Plan

Design No. 7090

Size: Width, 26 feet 6 inches; Length, 27 feet 6 inches, exclusive of porches

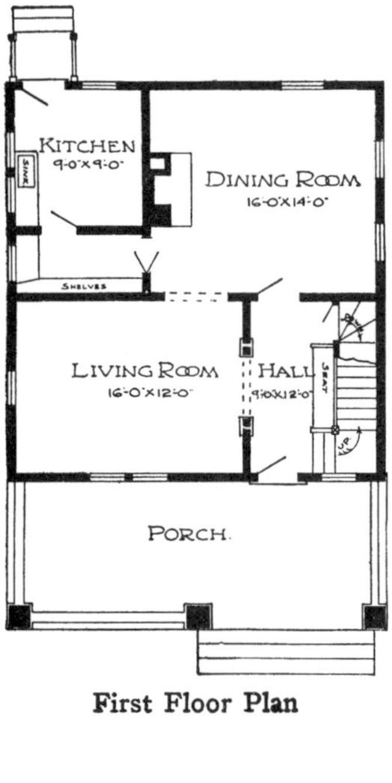

First Floor Plan

Blue prints consist of basement plan; roof plan; first and second floor plans; front, rear and two side elevations; wall sections and all necessary interior details. Specifications consist of about twenty pages of typewritten matter.

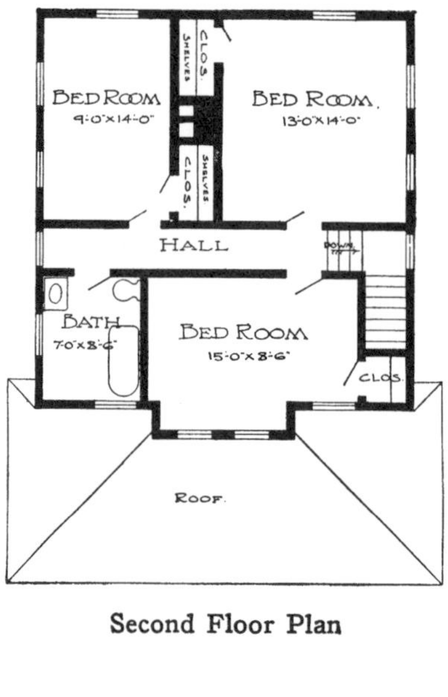

Second Floor Plan

PRICE

of Blue Prints, together with a complete set of typewritten specifications

ONLY TWELVE DOLLARS

We mail Plans and Specifications the same day order is received.

Design No. 7006

Size: Width, 16 feet 6 inches; Length, 28 feet 6 inches, exclusive of porches

PRICE

of Blue Prints, together with a complete set of typewritten specifications

ONLY EIGHT DOLLARS

We mail Plans and Specifications the same day order is received.

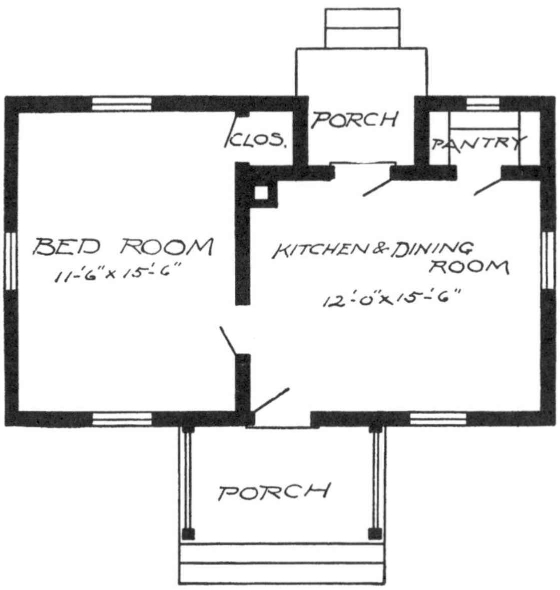

Floor Plan

Blue prints consist of foundation plan; floor plan; front, rear, two side elevations; wall sections and all necessary interior details. Specifications consist of about twelve pages of typewriter matter.

Design No. 7088

Size: Width, 40 feet; Length, 32 feet 6 inches, exclusive of porch

Blue prints consist of foundation plan; roof plan; floor plan; front, rear, two side elevations; wall sections and all necessary interior details. Specifications consist of about fifteen pages of lypewritten matter.

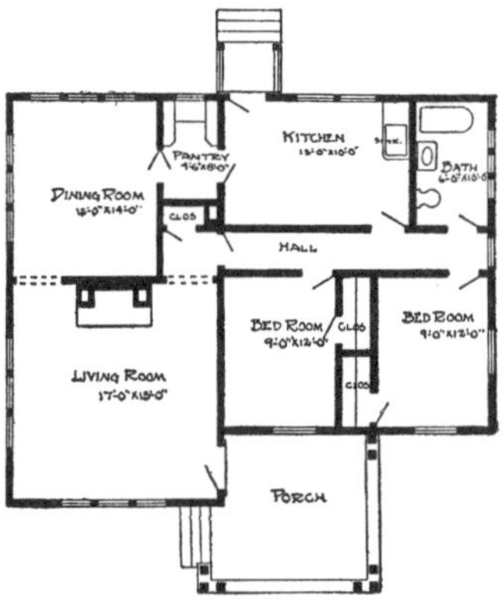

Floor Plan

PRICE

of Blue Prints, together with a complete set of typewritten specifications

ONLY TEN DOLLARS

We mail Plans and Specifications the same day ordes is received.

DESIGN NUMBER 6040

Size: width, 31 feet 6 inches; length, 51 feet, exclusive of porches

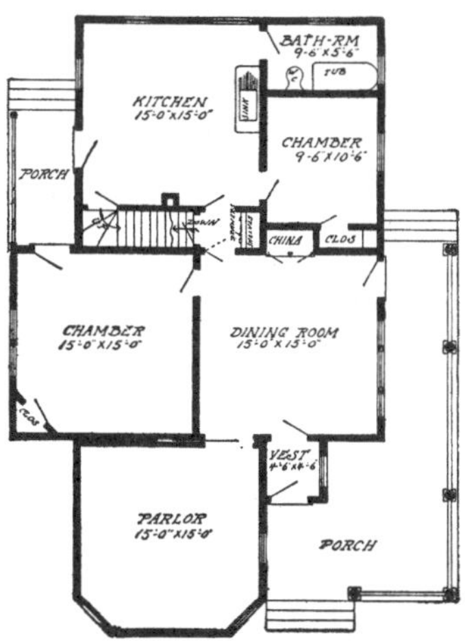

Floor Plan

BLUE PRINTS consist of basement plan; first floor plan; roof plan; front, right and left side elevations; wall sections and all necessary interior details. Specifications consist of about fifteen pages of typewritten matter.

PRICE

of Blue Prints, together with a complete set of typewritten specifications

ONLY TEN DOLLARS

We mail plans and specifications the same day order is received

DESIGN NUMBER 6075

Size: width, 26 feet; length, 44 feet, exclusive of porches

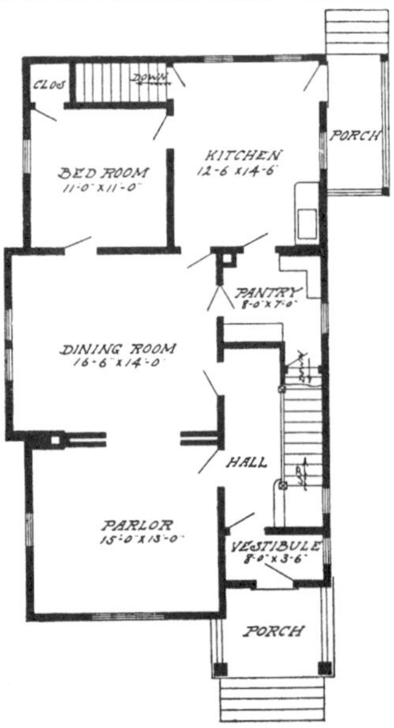

First Floor Plan

BLUE PRINTS consist of basement plan; roof plan; first and second floor plans; front, rear, two side elevations; wall sections and all necessary interior details. Specifications consist of about twenty pages of typewritten matter.

PRICE

of Blue Prints, together with a complete set of typewritten specifications

ONLY TEN DOLLARS

We mail plans and specifications the same day order is received.

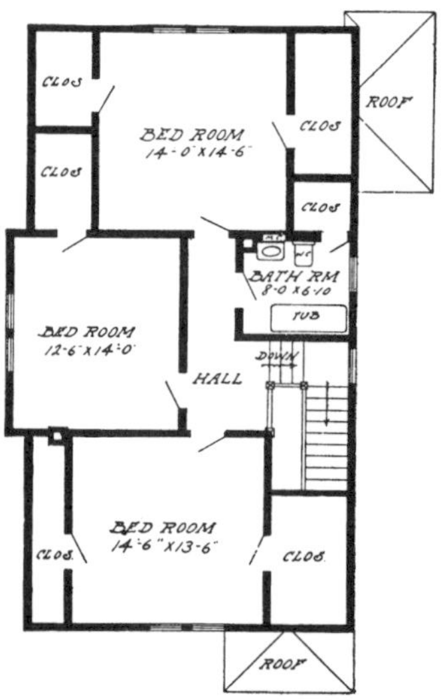

Second Floor Plan

Design No. 9067

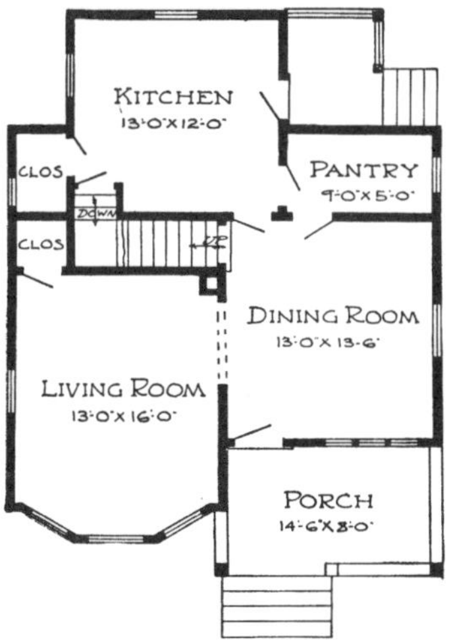

First Floor Plan.

The arrangement of this House is as follows:

FIRST FLOOR.

Living Room, 13 feet by 16 feet.
Dining Room, 13 feet by 13 feet 6 inches.
Kitchen, 13 feet by 12 feet.
Pantry, Front and Rear Porches.

SECOND FLOOR.

Bedroom, 13 feet by 11 feet 6 inches.
Bedroom, 13 feet by 12 feet.
Bedroom, 13 feet by 13 feet 6 inches.
4 Closets.

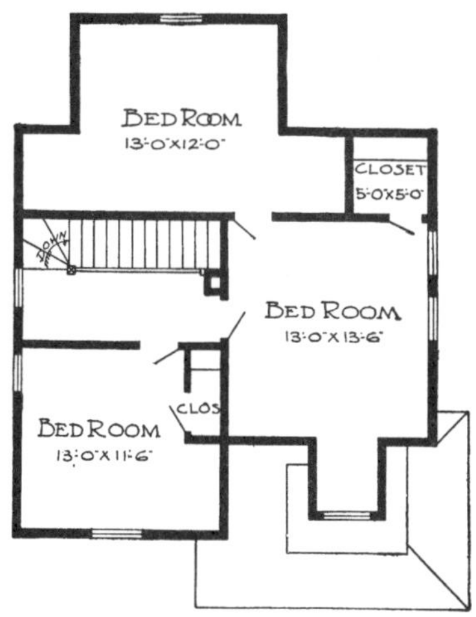

Second Floor Plan.

This Building is 27 feet 6 inches in width; 33 feet in length.

Price of Complete Working Plans and Specifications.. $15.00

The Blue Printed Working Plans for this House consist of basement plan; roof plan; first and second floor plans; front, right, left and rear elevations; wall sections and all necessary details.

The Typewritten Specifications contain all the necessary information for the proper construction of the House.

Design No. 9002

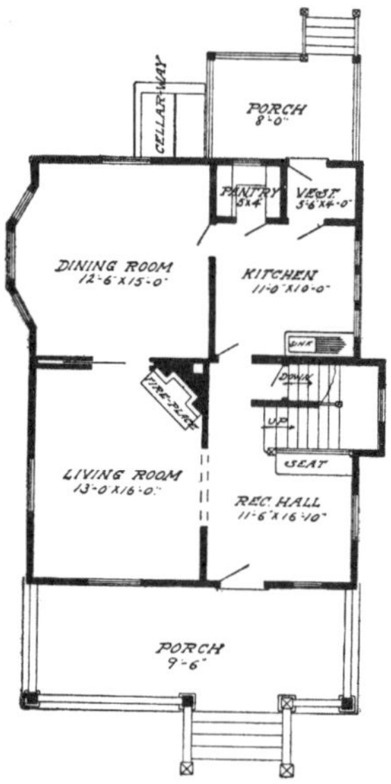

First Floor Plan.

This House is arranged in the following manner:

FIRST FLOOR.

Reception Hall, 11 feet 6 inches by 16 feet 10 inches.
Living Room, 13 feet by 16 feet.
Dining Room, 12 feet 6 inches by 15 feet.
Kitchen, 11 feet by 10 feet.
Pantry, Front and Rear Porches.

SECOND FLOOR.

Bedroom 9 feet 6 inches by 12 feet.
Bedroom, 11 feet 3 inches by 13 feet 9 inches.
Bedroom, 13 feet 10 inches by 15 feet 9 inches.
Sewing Room, 12 feet 2 inches by 9 feet 6 inches.
Bathroom, 8 feet by 5 feet 10 inches.
4 Closets.

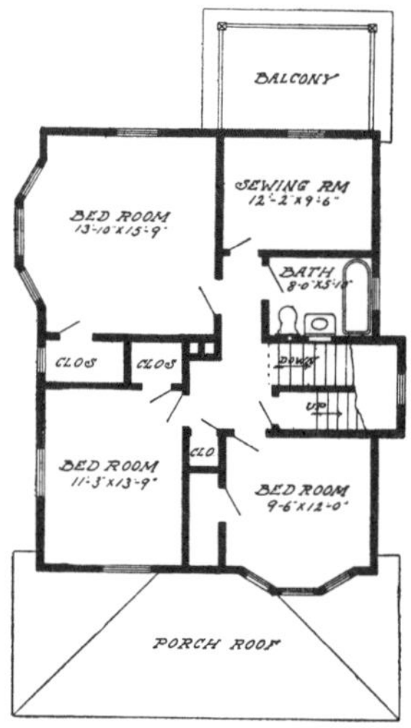

Second Floor Plan.

This Building is 30 feet in width; 33 feet in length.
Price of Complete Working Plans and Specifications.. **$15.00**
The Blue Printed Working Plans for this House consist of basement plan; roof plan; first and second floor plans; front, right, left and rear elevations; wall sections and all necessary details.
The Typewritten Specifications contain all the necessary information for the proper construction of the House.

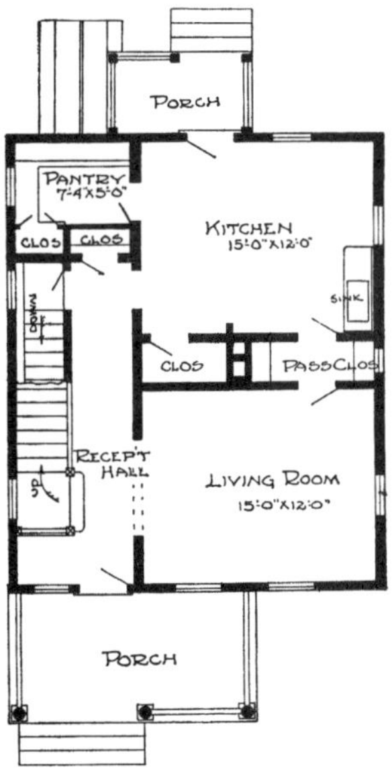

First Floor Plan.

Design No. 9015

The arrangement of this House is as follows:

FIRST FLOOR.

Reception Hall, 7 feet 6 inches.
Living Room, 15 feet by 12 feet.
Kitchen, 15 feet by 12 feet.
Pantry, Front and Rear Porches.

SECOND FLOOR.

Bedroom, 18 feet 6 inches by 12 feet.
Bedroom, 14 feet by 12 feet.
Bathroom, 8 feet by 7 feet.
8 Closets.

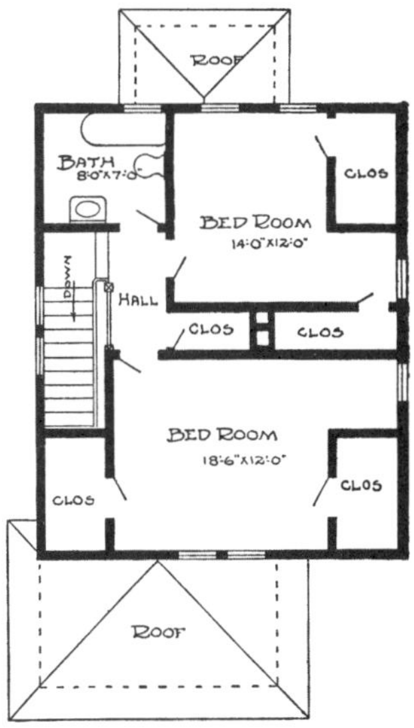

Second Floor Plan.

This Building is 24 feet in width; 28 feet 6 inches in length.

Price of Complete Working Plans and Specifications $12.00

The Blue Printed Working Plans for this House consist of basement plan; roof plan; first and second floor plans; front, right, left and rear elevations; wall sections and all necessary details.

The Typewritten Specifications contain all the necessary information for the proper construction of the House.

Design No. 9051

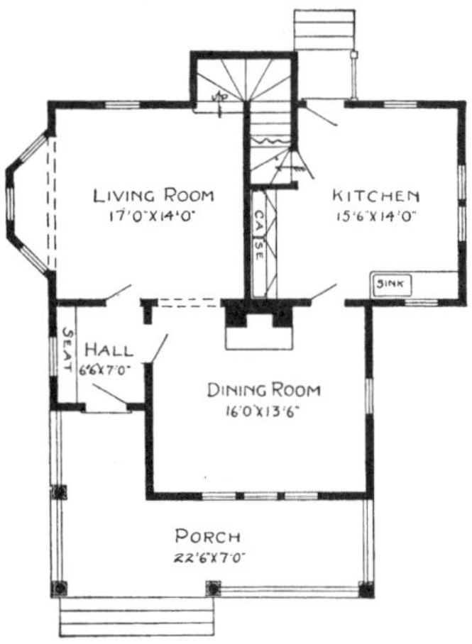

First Floor Plan.

The arrangement of this House is as follows:

FIRST FLOOR.

Reception Hall, 6 feet 6 inches by 7 feet.
Living Room, 17 feet by 14 feet.
Dining Room, 16 feet by 13 feet 6 inches.
Kitchen, 15 feet 6 inches by 14 feet.
Front and Rear Porches.

SECOND FLOOR.

Bedroom, 14 feet by 11 feet.
Bedroom, 12 feet by 14 feet.
Bedroom, 14 feet by 13 feet 6 inches.
Bathroom, 8 feet 6 inches by 8 feet.
3 Closets.

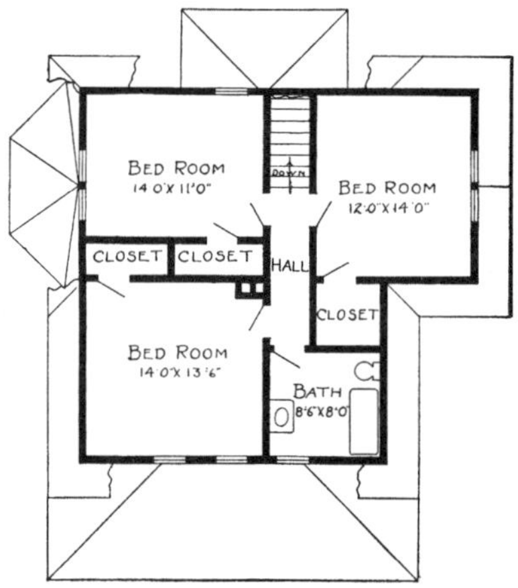

Second Floor Plan.

This Building is 34 feet in width; 32 feet 6 inches in length.

Price of Complete Working Plans and Specifications.. **$12.00**

The Blue Printed Working Plans for this House consist of basement plan, roof plan, first and second floor plans; front, right, left and rear elevations; wall sections and all necessary details.

The Typewritten Specifications contain all the necessary information for the proper construction of the House

PRICE

of Blue Prints, together with a complete set of typewritten specifications is

ONLY TWELVE DOLLARS

We mail Plans and Specifications the same day order is received.

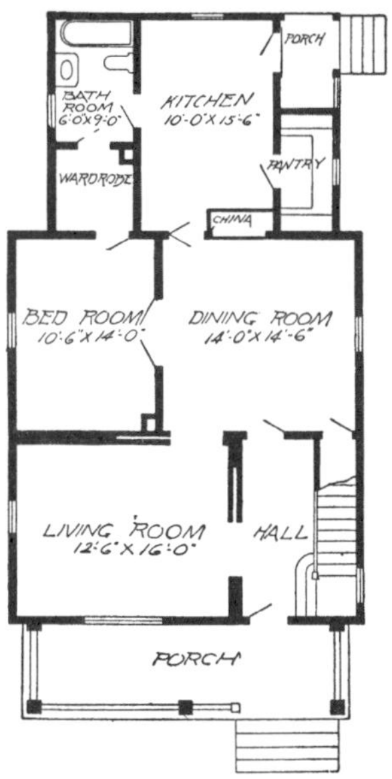

First Floor Plan

Design No. 2013

Blue prints consist of cellar and foundation plan; roof plan; first and second floor plans; front, rear, two side elevations; wall sections and all necessary interior details. Specifications consist of about twenty pages of typewritten matter.

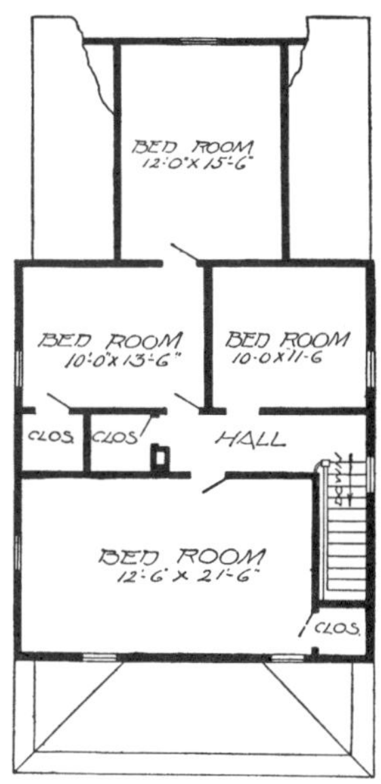

Second Floor Plan

SIZE: Width, 26 feet; length, 44 feet 6 inches, exclusive of porch

The floor plans we furnish show the shape and size of all rooms, halls and closets; the location and size of all doors and windows; the position of all plumbing fixtures, gas lights, registers, pantry work, etc., and all the measurements that are necessary are given.

All necessary details of interior work, such as door and window casings and trim, base, stools, picture moulding, doors, newel posts, balusters, rail, etc., accompany each set of plans. Part is shown in full size, while some of the larger work, such as stair construction, is drawn to a scale of one and one half-inch to the foot.

Design No. 2044

Blue prints cousist of basement plan; roof plan; first and second floor plans; front, rear and two side elevations; wall sections and all necessary interior details. Specifications consist of about twenty pages of typewritten matter.

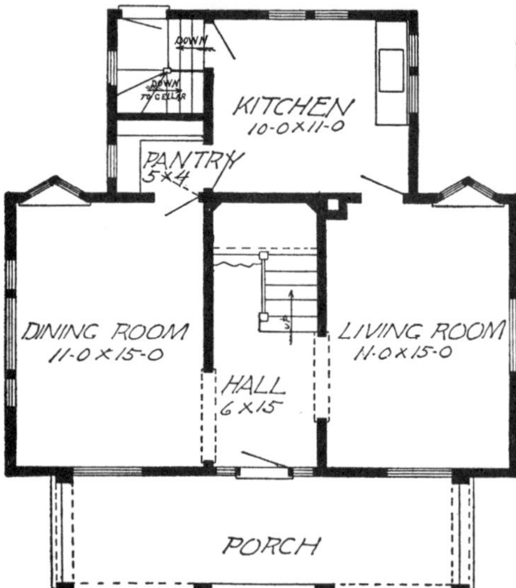

First Floor Plan

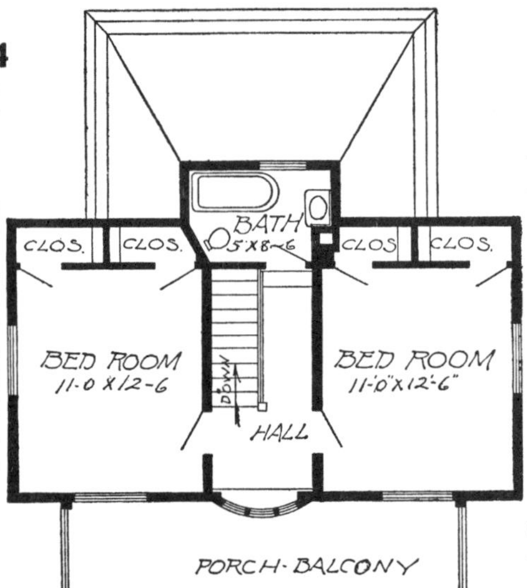

Second Floor Plan

PRICE

of Blue Prints, together with a complete set of typewritten specifications is

ONLY TWELVE DOLLARS

We mail Plans and Specifications the same day order is received.

SIZE: Width, 30 feet; length, 26 feet, 6 inches, exclusive of porch.

On account our large business and unusual equipment, and owing to the fact that we divide the expense among so many, it is possible to sell at these low prices, give such excellent plans and immediate shipment.

The home builder will derive a great deal of satisfaction in watching the construction of his house if he has a set of complete working plans to examine as the work progresses.

Design No. 7087

Size: Width, 28 feet 6 inches; Length, 34 feet, exclusive of porches

PRICE

of Blue Prints, together with a complete set of typewritten specifications.

ONLY FIFTEEN DOLLARS

We mail Plans and Specifications the same day order is received.

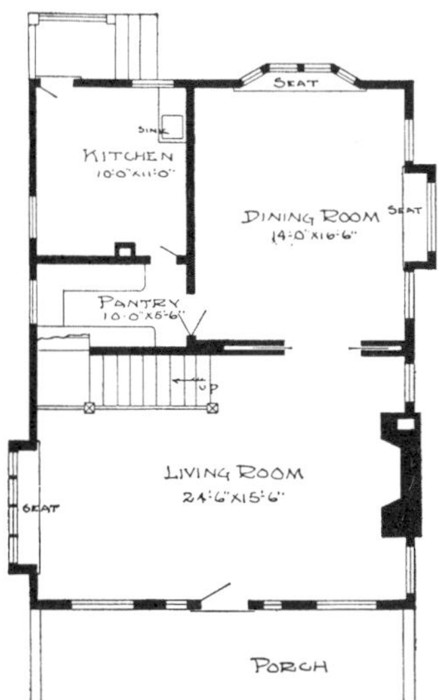

First Floor Plan

Blue prints consist of foundation plan; first and second floor plans; front, rear, two side elevations; wall sections and all necessary interior details. Specifications consist of about twenty pages of typewritten matter.

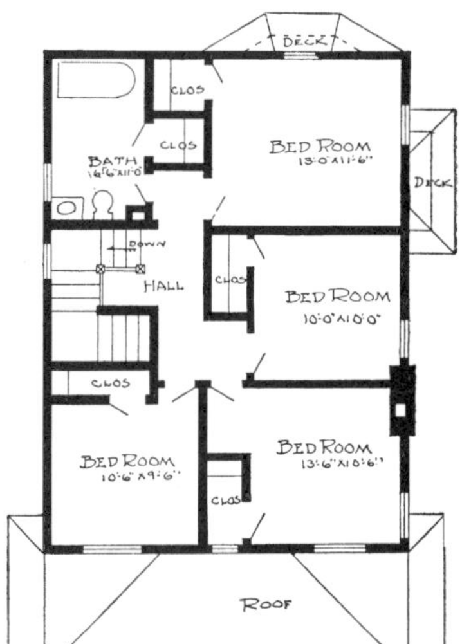

Second Floor Plan

Design No. 7089

Size: Width, 26 feet; Length, 29 feet 6 inches, exclusive of porches

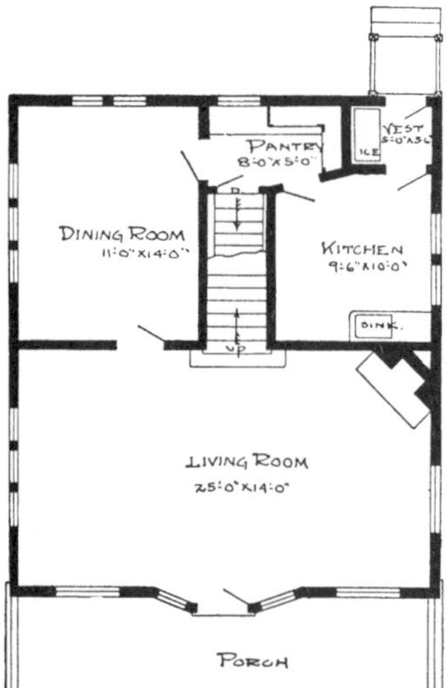

First Floor Plan

Blue prints consist of basement plan; first and second floor plans; front, rear, two side elevations; wall sections and all necessary interior details. Specifications consist of about twenty pages of typewritten matter.

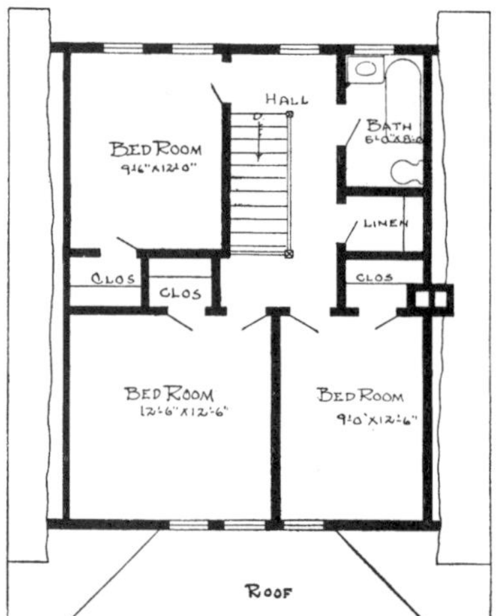

Second Floor Plan

PRICE

of Blue Prints, together with a complete set of typewritten specifications.

ONLY TWELVE DOLLARS

We mail Plans and Specifications the same day order is received.

Design No. 7046

Size: Width, 33 feet 6 inches; Length, 46 feet, exclusive of porches

PRICE

of Blue Prints, together with a complete set of typewritten specifications.

ONLY FIFTEEN DOLLARS

We mail Plans and Specifications the same day order is received.

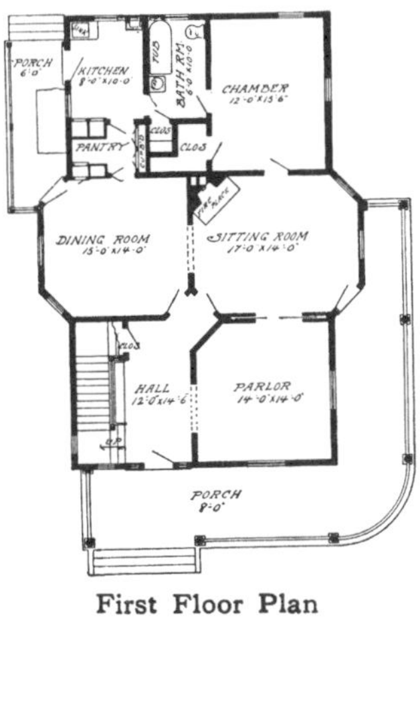

First Floor Plan

Blue prints consist of basement plan; roof plan; first and second floor plans; front, rear, two side elevations; wall sections and all necessary interior details. Specifications consist of about twenty pages of typewritten matter.

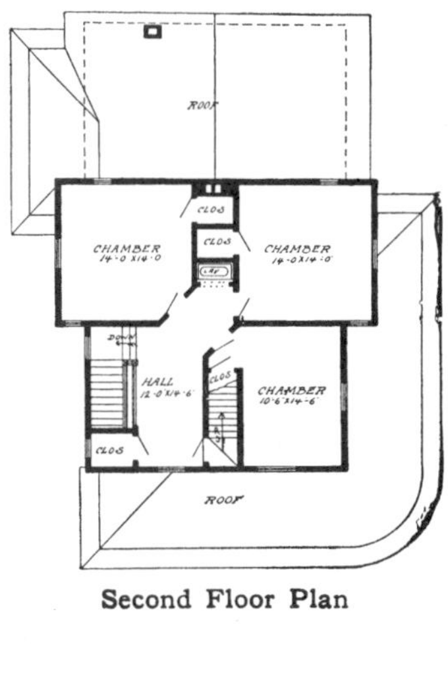

Second Floor Plan

Design No. 7069

Size: Width, 28 feet; Length, 37 feet, exclusive of porches

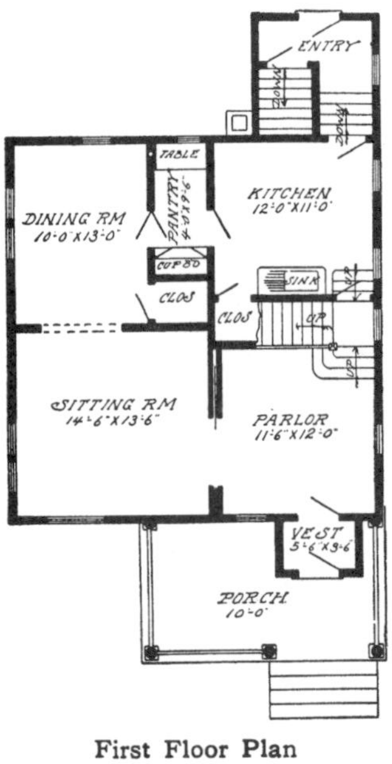

First Floor Plan

Blue prints consist of basement plan; first and second floor plans; front, rear, two side elevations; wall sections and all necessary interior details. Specifications consist of about twenty pages of typewritten matter.

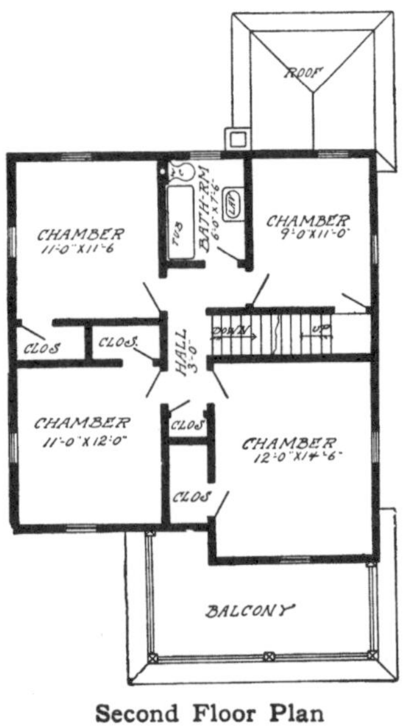

Second Floor Plan

PRICE

of Blue Prints, together with a complete set of typewritten specifications.

ONLY TWELVE DOLLARS

We mail Plans and Specifications the same day order is received.

DESIGN NUMBER 6048

Size: width, 28 feet; length, 30 feet, exclusive of porches

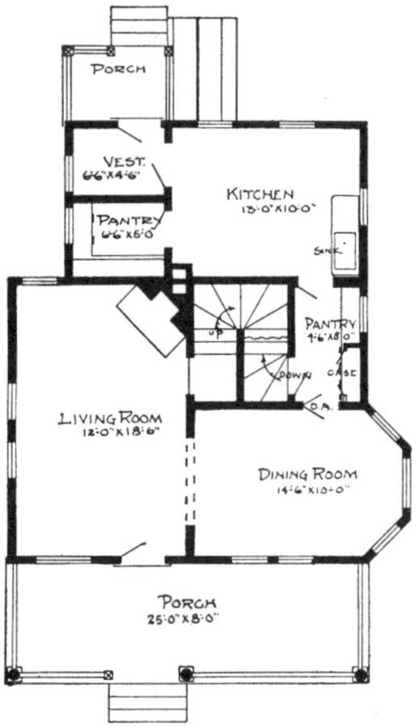

First Floor Plan

BLUE PRINTS consist of basement plan; first and second floor plans; front, rear, two side elevations; wall sections and all necessary interior details. Specifications consist of about twenty pages of typewritten matter.

PRICE

of Blue Prints, together with a complete set of typewritten specifications

ONLY TWELVE DOLLARS

We mail plans and specifications the same day order is received.

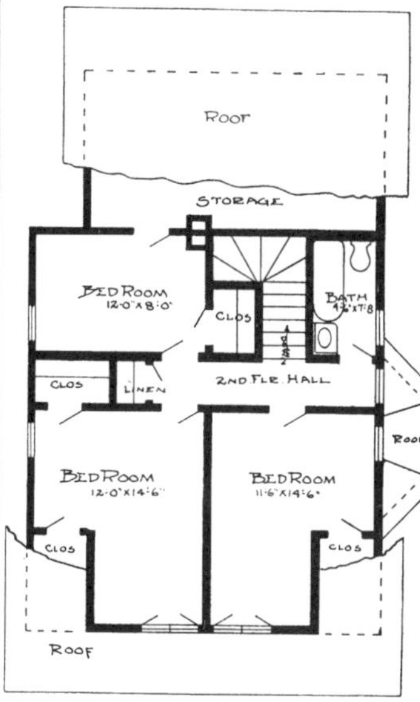

Second Floor Plan

DESIGN NUMBER 6063

Size: width, 28 feet; length, 47 feet 6 inches, exclusive of porches

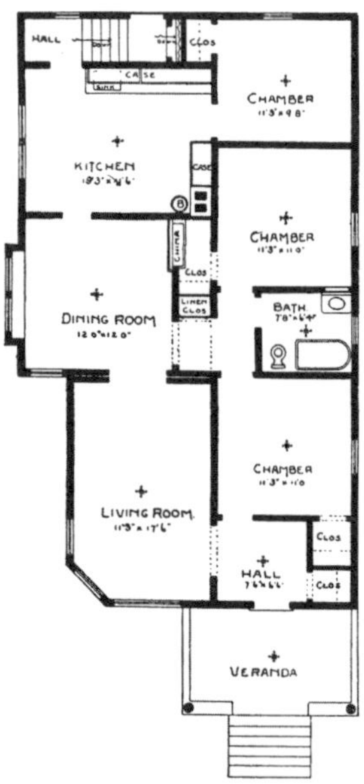

Floor Plan

BLUE PRINTS consist of basement plan; roof plan; floor plan; front, rear, two side elevations; wall sections and all necessary interior details. Specifications consist of about fifteen pages of typewritten matter.

PRICE

of Blue Prints, together with a complete set of typewritten specifications

ONLY TEN DOLLARS

We mail plans and specifications the same day order is received.

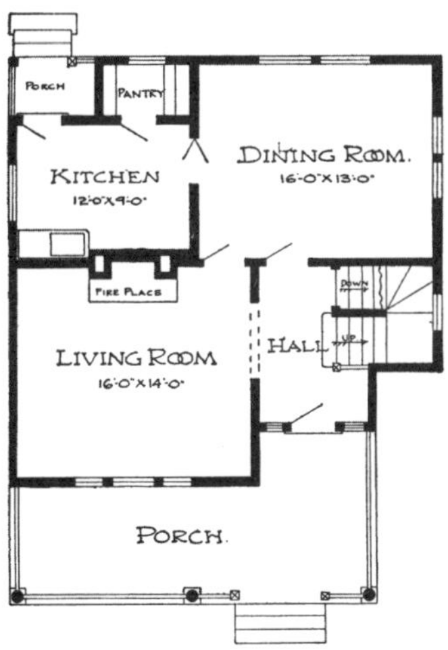

First Floor Plan.

Design No. 9094

The arrangement of this House is as follows:

FIRST FLOOR.

Reception Hall, 7 feet 6 inches by 10 feet 6 inches.
Living Room, 16 feet by 14 feet.
Dining Room, 16 feet by 13 feet.
Kitchen, 12 feet by 9 feet.
Pantry, Front and Rear Porches.

SECOND FLOOR.

Alcove, 7 feet 6 inches by 10 feet 6 inches.
Bedroom, 16 feet by 10 feet 6 inches.
Bedroom, 11 feet by 13 feet.
Bedroom, 11 feet 6 inches by 10 feet.
Bathroom, 5 feet by 8 feet.
2 Closets.

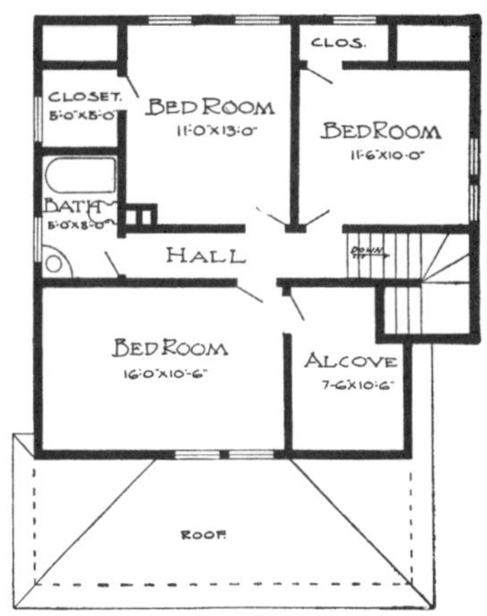

Second Floor Plan.

This Building is 29 feet 6 inches in width; 28 feet 6 inches in length.

Price of Complete Working Plans and Specifications.. $12.00

The Blue Printed Working Plans for this House consist of basement plan; first and second floor plans; front, right, left and rear elevations; wall sections and all necessary details.

The Typewritten Specifications contain all the necessary information for the proper construction of the House.

Design No. 9063

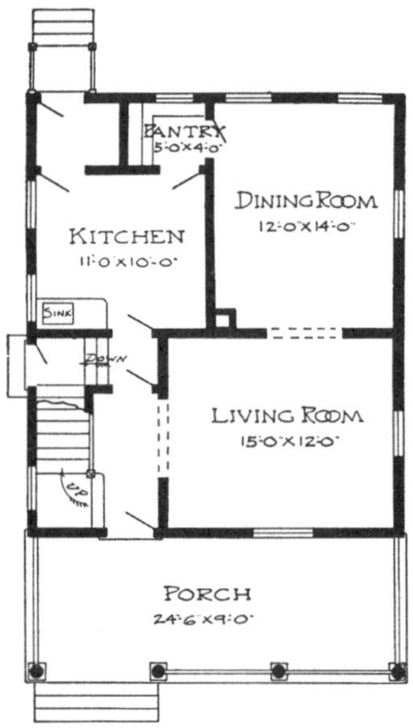

First Floor Plan.

The arrangement of this House is as follows:

FIRST FLOOR.

Reception Hall, 8 feet by 8 feet 6 inches.
Living Room, 15 feet by 12 feet.
Dining Room, 12 feet by 14 feet.
Kitchen, 11 feet by 10 feet.
Pantry, Front and Rear Porches.

SECOND FLOOR.

Bedroom, 16 feet by 10 feet.
Bedroom, 16 feet by 8 feet 6 inches.
Bedroom, 10 feet by 8 feet 6 inches.
Bathroom, 7 feet by 5 feet 6 inches.
4 Closets.

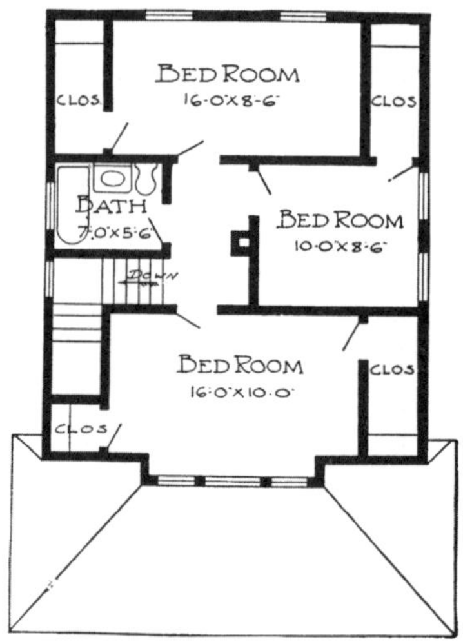

Second Floor Plan.

This Building is 24 feet 6 inches in width; 28 feet in length.

Price of Complete Working Plans and Specifications........ $12.00

The Blue Printed Working Plans for this House consist of basement plan; first and second floor plans; front, right, left and rear elevations; wall sections and all necessary details.

The Typewritten Specifications contain all the necessary information for the proper construction of the House.

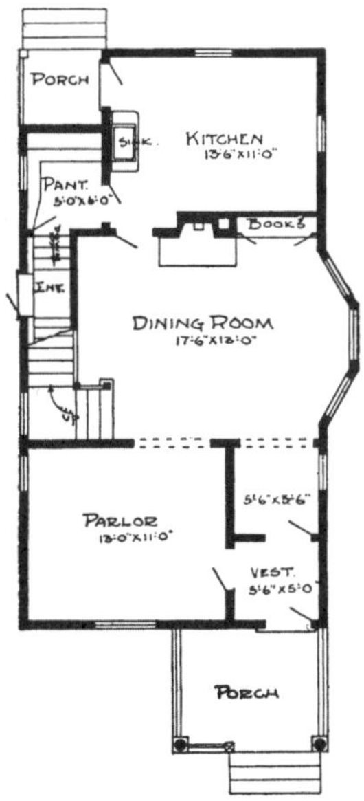

First Floor Plan.

Design No. 9021

The arrangement of this House is as follows:

FIRST FLOOR.

Reception Hall, 5 feet 6 inches by 5 feet.
Parlor, 13 feet by 11 feet.
Dining Room, 17 feet 6 inches by 13 feet.
Kitchen, 13 feet 6 inches by 11 feet.
Alcove, 5 feet 6 inches by 5 feet 6 inches.
Pantry, Front and Rear Porches.

SECOND FLOOR.

Bedroom, 12 feet by 11 feet.
Bedroom, 10 feet by 10 feet.
Bedroom, 12 feet by 13 feet.
Bathroom, 5 feet by 8 feet 6 inches.
3 Closets.

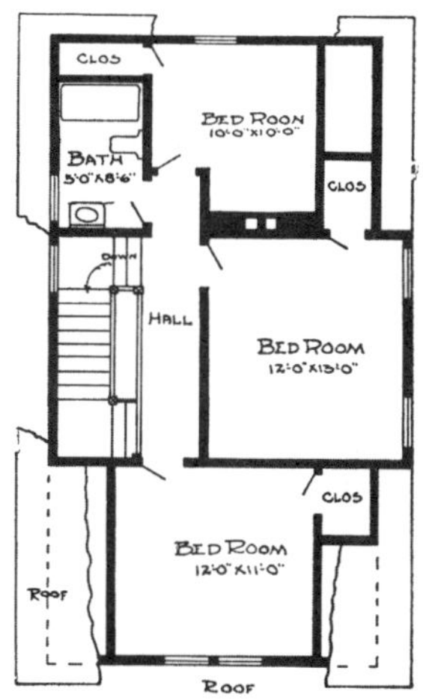

Second Floor Plan.

This Building is 22 feet in width; 37 feet in length.

Price of Complete Working Plans and Specifications **$12.00**

The Blue Printed Working Plans for this House consist of basement plan; roof plan; first and second floor plans; front, right, left and rear elevations; wall sections and all necessary details.

The Typewritten Specifications contain all the necessary information for the proper construction of the House.

Design No. 9038

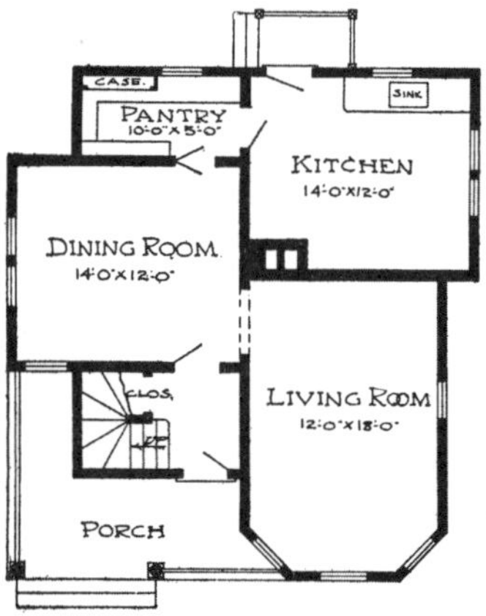

First Floor Plan.

The arrangement of this House is as follows:

FIRST FLOOR.

Reception Hall, 10 feet by 6 feet 6 inches.
Living Room, 12 feet by 18 feet.
Dining Room, 14 feet by 12 feet.
Kitchen, 14 feet by 12 feet.
Pantry, Front and Rear Porches.

SECOND FLOOR.

Bedroom, 12 feet by 14 feet 6 inches.
Bedroom, 12 feet by 12 feet 6 inches.
Bedroom, 11 feet 6 inches by 12 feet.
Bathroom, 11 feet by 5 feet.
3 Closets.

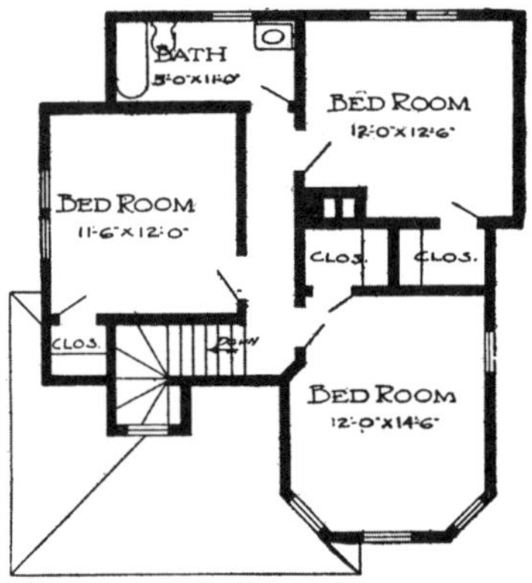

Second Floor Plan.

This Building is 29 feet 6 inches in width; 31 feet 6 inches in length.

Price of Complete Working Plans and Specifications.......... **$15.00**

The Blue Printed Working Plans for this House consist of foundation plan, roof plan, first and second floor plans; front, right, left and rear elevations; wall sections and all necessary details.

The Typewritten Specifications contain all the necessary information for the proper construction of the House.

Design No. 2024

Blue prints consist of basement plan; first and second floor plans; front, rear, two side elevations; wall sections and all necessary interior details. Specifications consist of about twenty pages of typewritten matter.

PRICE

of Blue Prints, together with a complete set of typewritten specifications is

ONLY TWELVE DOLLARS

We mail Plans and Specifications the same day order is received.

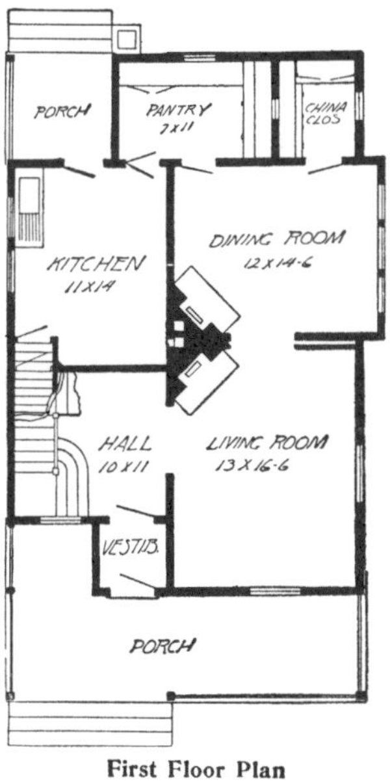

First Floor Plan

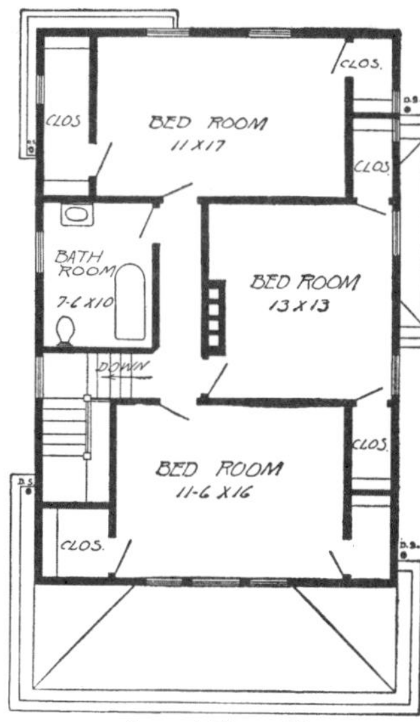

Second Floor Plan

SIZE: **Width, 26 feet 9 inches; length, 44 feet 6 inches, exclusive of porch**

Our plans are so clear and explicit that no carpenter or contractor will have the least difficulty in understanding them We aim to make our plans so plain that there will be a minimum of mistakes.

Long experience has taught the contractor that he should not build even the smallest house without working plans The lack of experience of the average home builder makes plans necessary for the understanding of the work.

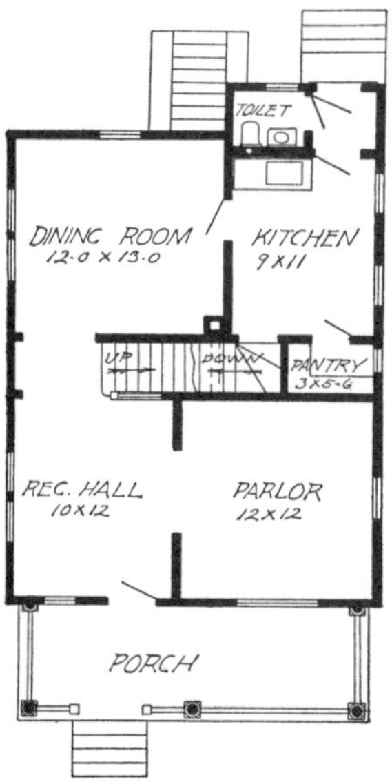

First Floor Plan

Design No. 2041

Blue prints consist of basement plan; roof plan; first and second floor plans; front, rear, two side elevations; wall sections and all necessary interior details. Specifications consist of about twenty pages of typewritten matter.

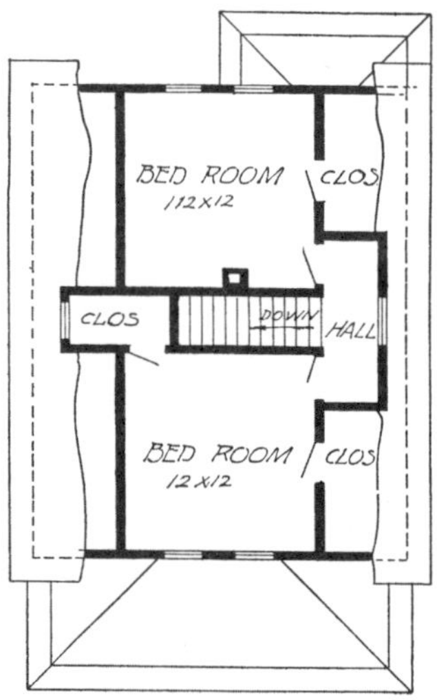

Second Floor Plan

PRICE

of Blue Prints, together with a complete set of typewritten specifications is

ONLY TEN DOLLARS

We mail Plans and Specifications the same day order is received.

SIZE: Width, 23 feet 6 inches; length 32 feet exclusive of porch.

Every house illustrated will show by the complete working plans and specifications that we give you designs that will work out to the best advantage and will give you the most for your money; besides, every bit of space nas been utilized to the best advantage.

In the plans we illustrate, the prospective builder is sure to find some plan which will meet his requirements. If, however no plan proves satisfactory, the ideas advanced in these illustrations are well worth the price of the book.

Design No. 7070

Size: Width, 20 feet; Length, 31 feet 6 inches, exclusive of porches

PRICE

of Blue Prints, together with a complete set of typewritten specifications

ONLY TWELVE DOLLARS

We mail Plans and Specifications the same day order is received.

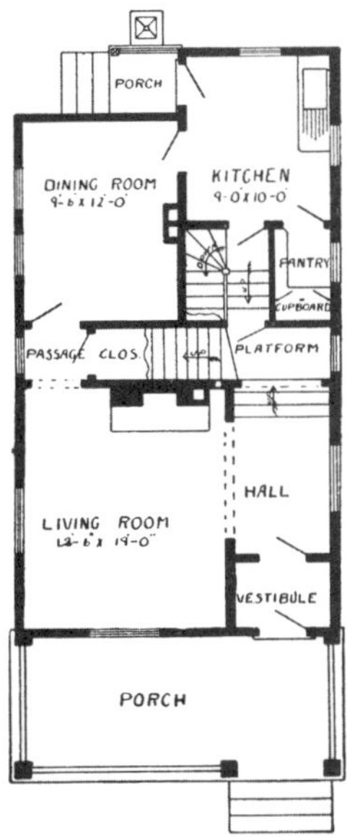

First Floor Plan

Blue prints consist of cellar and foundation plan; first and second floor plans; front, rear, two side elevations; wall sections and all necessary interior details. Specifications consist of about twenty pages of typewritten matter.

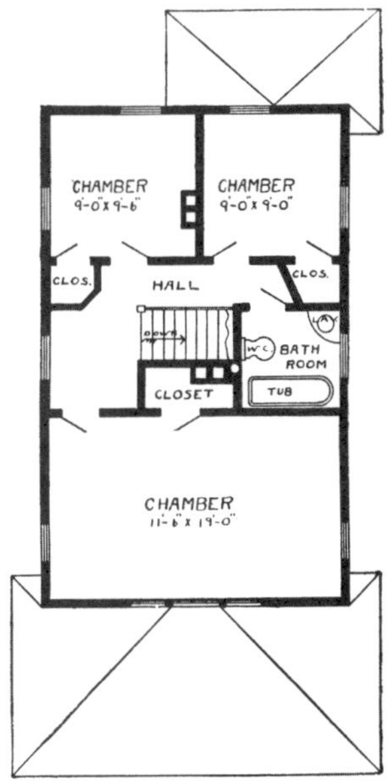

Second Floor Plan

Design No. 7039

Size: Width, 28 feet; Length, 40 feet 6 inches, exclusive of porch

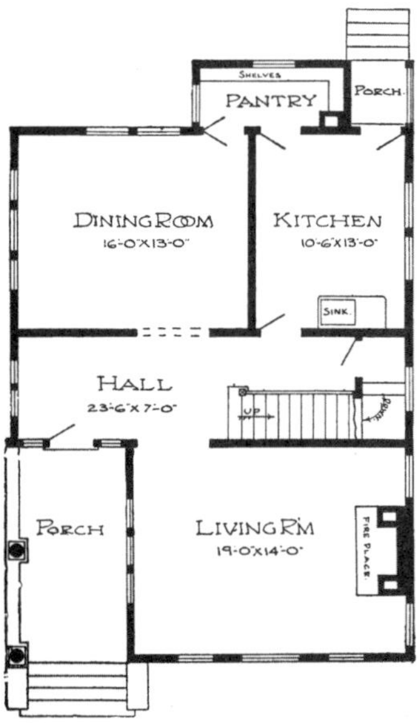

First Floor Plan

Blue prints consist of basement plan; roof plan; first and second floor plans; front, rear, two side elevations; wall sections and all necessary interior details. Specifications consist of about twenty pages of typewritten matter.

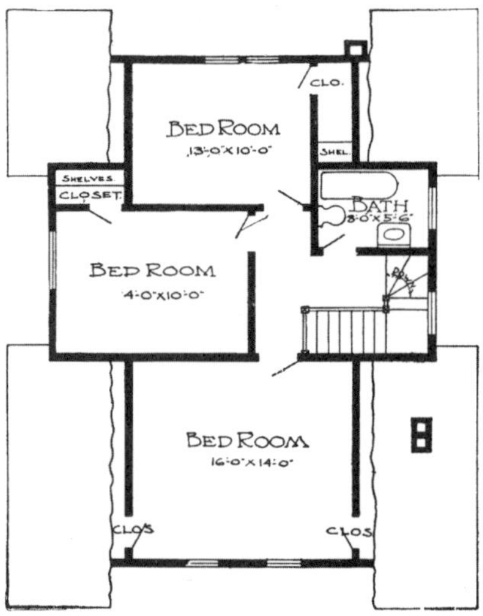

Second Floor Plan

PRICE

of Blue Prints, together with a complete set of typewritten specifications

ONLY FIFTEEN DOLLARS

We mail Plans and Specifications the same day order is received.

DESIGN NUMBER 6018

Size: width, 32 feet 6 inches; length, 40 feet, exclusive of porches

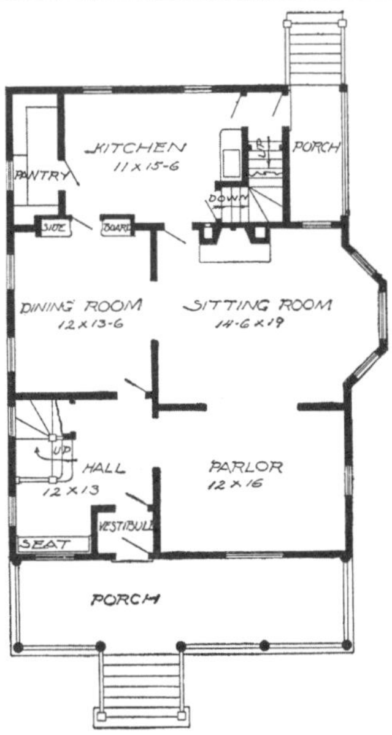

First Floor Plan

BLUE PRINTS consist of basement plan; roof plan; first and second floor plans; front, rear, two side elevations; wall sections and all necessary interior details. Specifications consist of about twenty pages of typewritten matter.

PRICE

of Blue Prints, together with a complete set of typewritten specifications

ONLY FIFTEEN DOLLARS

We mail plans and specifications the same day order is received.

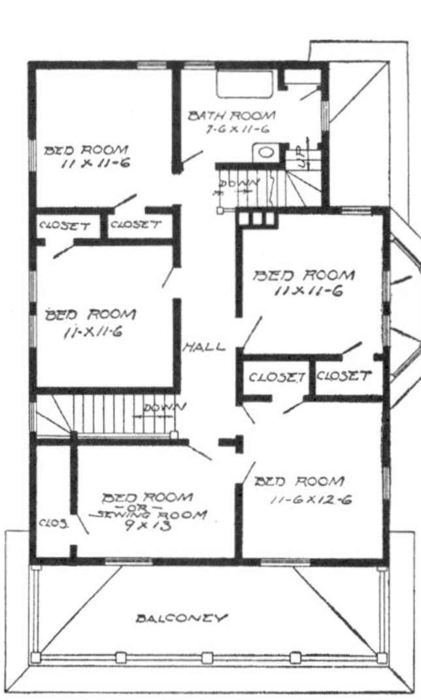

Second Floor Plan

DESIGN NUMBER 6010

Size: width, 33 feet; length, 42 feet 6 inches, exclusive of porch

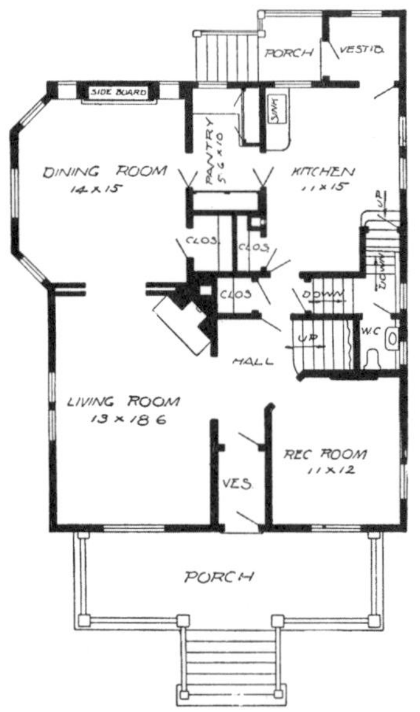

First Floor Plan

BLUE PRINTS consist of basement plan; roof plan; first and second floor plans; front, rear, two side elevations; wall sections and all necessary interior details. Specifications consist of about twenty pages of typewritten matter.

PRICE

of Blue Prints, together with a complete set of typewritten specifications

ONLY FIFTEEN DOLLARS

We mail plans and specifications the same day order is received.

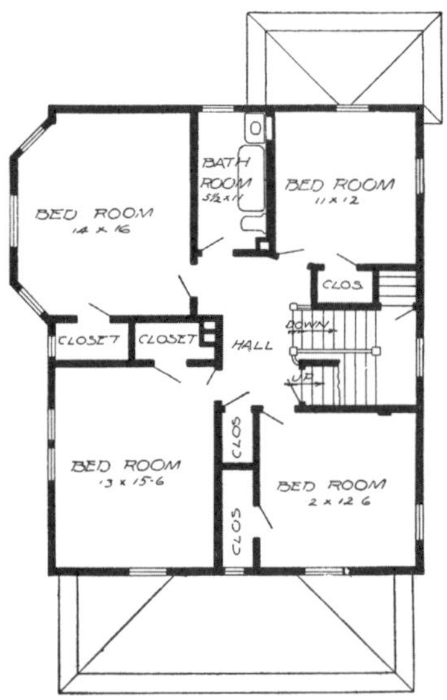

Second Floor Plan

Design No. 9040

The arrangement of this House is as follows:

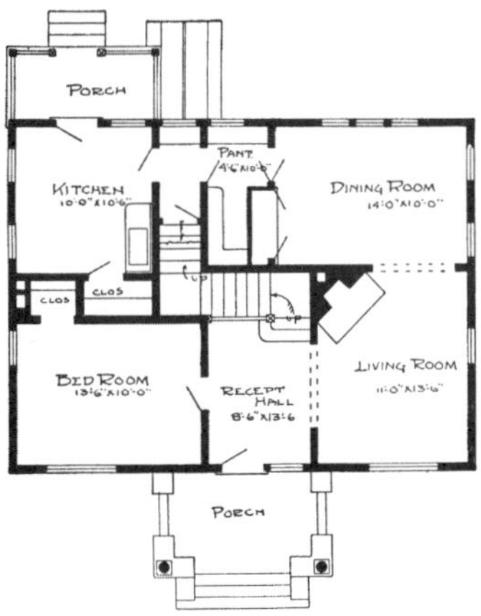

First Floor Plan.

FIRST FLOOR.

Reception Hall, 8 feet 6 inches by 13 feet 6 inches.
Living Room, 11 feet by 13 feet 6 inches.
Dining Room, 14 feet by 10 feet.
Kitchen, 10 feet by 10 feet 6 inches.
Bedroom, 13 feet 6 inches by 10 feet.
Pantry, Front and Rear Porches.

SECOND FLOOR.

Sewing Room, 7 feet 6 inches by 6 feet.
Bedroom, 11 feet by 13 feet 6 inches.
Bedroom, 10 feet by 10 feet 6 inches.
Bedroom, 13 feet 6 inches by 10 feet.
Bathroom, 11 feet by 6 feet.
6 Closets.

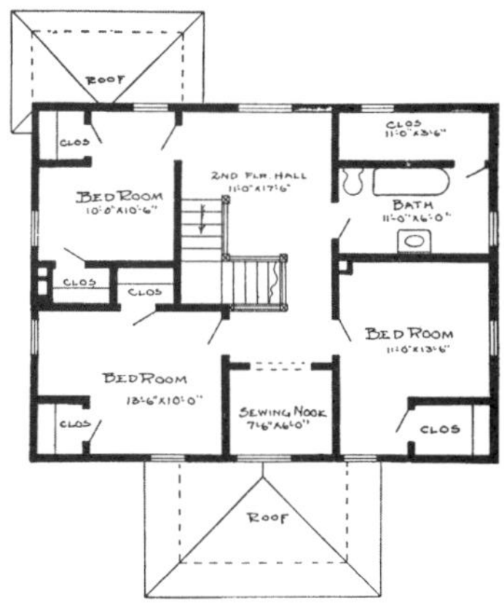

Second Floor Plan.

This Building is 34 feet in width; 25 feet in length.

Price of Complete Working Plans and Specifications $12.00

The Blue Printed Working Plans for this House consist of basement plan; roof plan; first and second floor plans; front, right, left and rear elevations; wall sections and all necessary details.

The Typewritten Specifications contain all the necessary information for the proper construction of the House

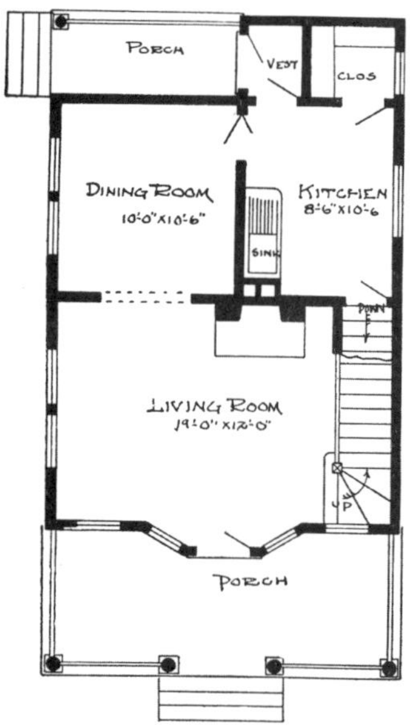

First Floor Plan.

Design No. 9084

The arrangement of this House is as follows:

FIRST FLOOR.

Living Room, 19 feet by 12 feet.
Dining Room, 10 feet by 10 feet 6 inches.
Kitchen, 8 feet 6 inches by 10 feet 6 inches.
Pantry, Front and Rear Porches.

SECOND FLOOR.

Bedroom, 12 feet 6 inches by 8 feet 6 inches.
Bedroom, 12 feet 6 inches by 14 feet.
Bathroom, 6 feet by 9 feet 6 inches.
4 Closets.

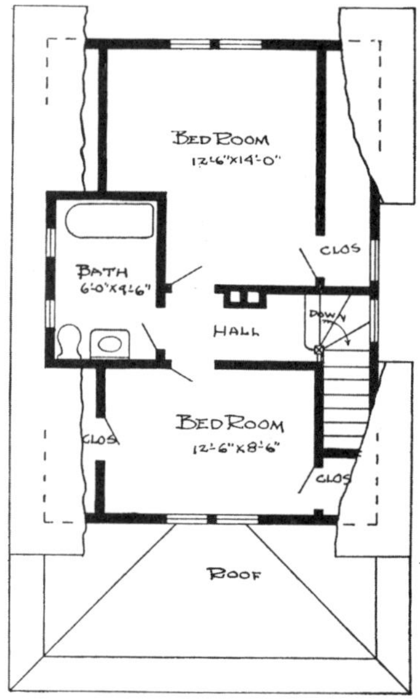

Second Floor Plan.

This Building is 20 feet in width; 30 feet in length.

Price of Complete Working Plans and Specifications.. **$10.00**

The Blue Printed Working Plans for this House consist of basement plan; first and second floor plans: front, right, left and rear elevations; wall sections and all necessary details.

The Typewritten Specifications contain all the necessary information for the proper construction of the House.

Design No. 9012

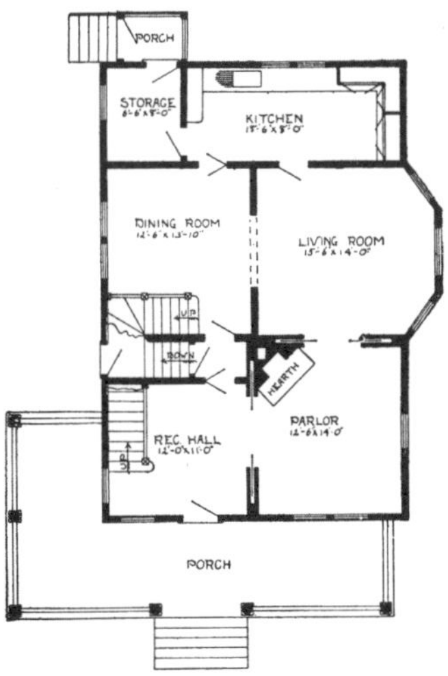

First Floor Plan.

The arrangement of this House is as follows:

FIRST FLOOR.

Reception Hall, 12 feet by 11 feet.
Parlor, 12 feet 6 inches by 14 feet.
Living Room, 15 feet 6 inches by 14 feet.
Dining Room, 12 feet 6 inches by 13 feet 10 inches.
Kitchen, 18 feet 6 inches by 8 feet.
Store Room, 6 feet 6 inches by 8 feet.
Front and Back Porches.

SECOND FLOOR.

Bedroom, 12 feet 6 inches by 11 feet 6 inches.
Bedroom, 15 feet 6 inches by 14 feet.
Bedroom, 12 feet 6 inches by 12 feet.
Alcove, 9 feet 6 inches by 8 feet.
Sewing Room, 12 feet 6 inches by 6 feet.
Bathroom, 8 feet by 5 feet 10 inches.
4 Closets.

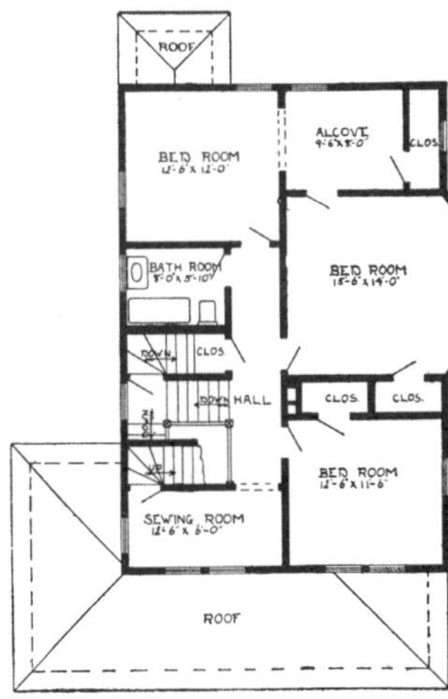

Second Floor Plan.

This Building is 29 feet 6 inches in width; 38 feet 6 inches in length.

Price of Complete Working Plans and Specifications.. **$15.00**

The Blue Printed Working Plans for this House consist of basement plan; roof plan; first and second floor plans; front, right, left and rear elevations; wall sections and all necessary details.

The Typewritten Specifications contain all the necessary information for the proper construction of the House.

Design No. 9034

The arrangement of this House is as follows:

FIRST FLOOR.

Living Room, 19 feet by 12 feet.

Dining Room, 12 feet 6 inches by 12 feet 6 inches.

Kitchen, 9 feet by 11 feet.

Nook, 6 feet by 9 feet.

Pantry, Front and Rear Porches.

SECOND FLOOR.

Bedroom, 15 feet 6 inches by 12 feet.

Bedroom, 11 feet by 10 feet.

Bathroom, 7 feet 6 inches by 6 feet.

3 Closets.

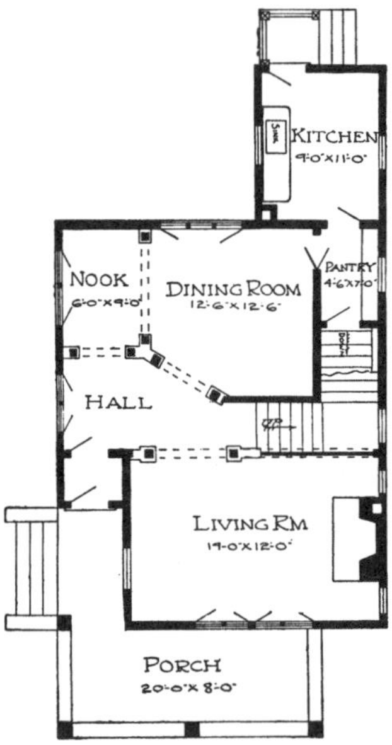

First Floor Plan.

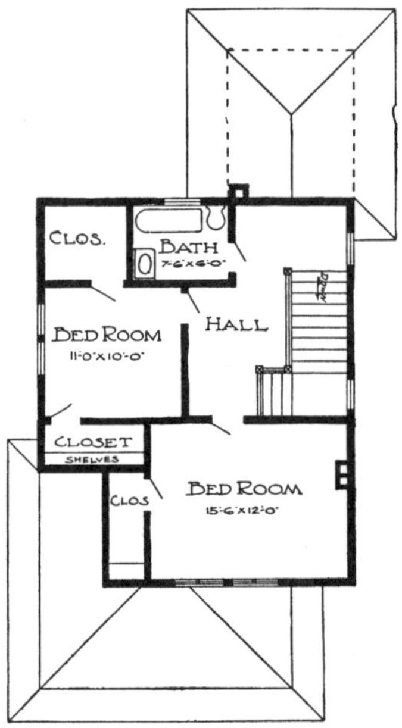

Second Floor Plan.

This Building is 25 feet in width; 41 feet 6 inches in length.

Price of Complete Working Plans and Specifications.. **$12.00**

The Blue Printed Working Plans for this House consist of basement plan, roof plan, first and second floor plans; front, right, left and rear elevations; wall sections and all necessary details.

The Typewritten Specifications contain all the necessary information for the proper construction of the House.

Design No. 2019

PRICE
of Blue Prints, together with a complete set of typewritten specifications is

ONLY TEN DOLLARS

We mail Plans and Specifications the same day order is received.

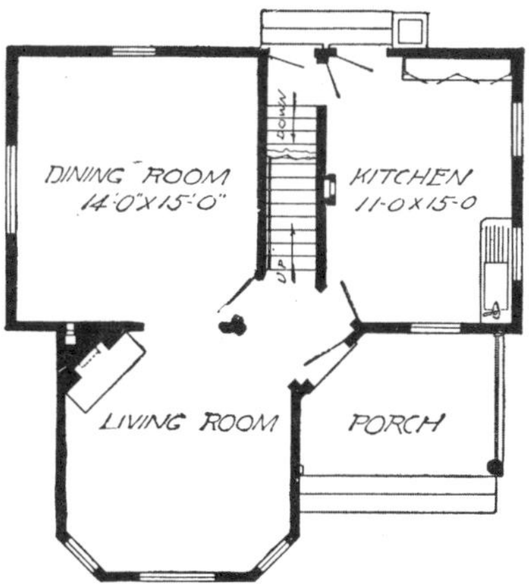

First Floor Plan

Blue Prints consist of basement plan; first and second floor plans; front, rear, two side elevations; wall sections and all necessary interior details. Specifications consist of about twenty pages of typewritten matter

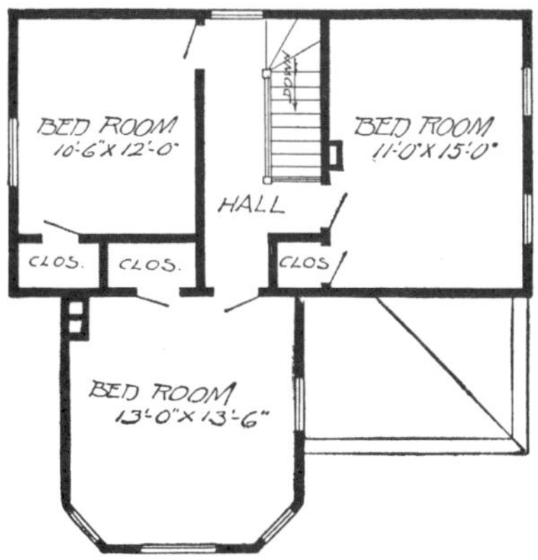

Second Floor Ploor

SIZE: Width, 30 feet; length, 30 feet

We have boiled down everything in this book so that the readers can see at a glance what is necessary. We do not give long descriptions of each house, which are valueless to the prospective builder.

Start right. Get plans before you break ground. We have heard of a few cases where our houses have been built without the complete plans. It always proves expensive, as every good contractor can testify. It is never satisfactory to either contractor or home builder

Design No. 2042

Blue prints consist of basement plan; roof plan; first and second floor plans; front, rear, two side elevations; wall sections and all necessary interior details. Specifications consist of about twenty pages of typewritten matter.

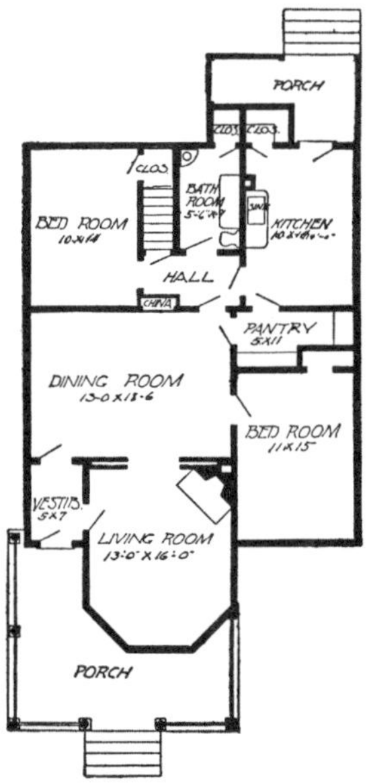

Floor Plan

PRICE

of Blue Prints, together with a complete set of typewritten specifications is

ONLY TEN DOLLARS

We mail Plans and Specifications the same day order is received.

SIZE: Width, 31 feet; length, 45 feet 6 inches exclusive of porches.

The majority of the people build only one house in a life time, therefore, it is the duty of every prospective builder to make his home as comfortable and attractive as possible.

This kind of a home costs no more to build than the ordinary structures usually seen in towns and villages, and the prospective builder can well afford to take a little time and investigate the latest designs.

Design No. 7078

Size: Width, 27 feet; Length, 35 feet, exclusive of porches

PRICE

of Blue Prints, together with a complete set of typewritten specifications

ONLY TWELVE DOLLARS

We mail Plans and Specifications **the** same day order **is** received.

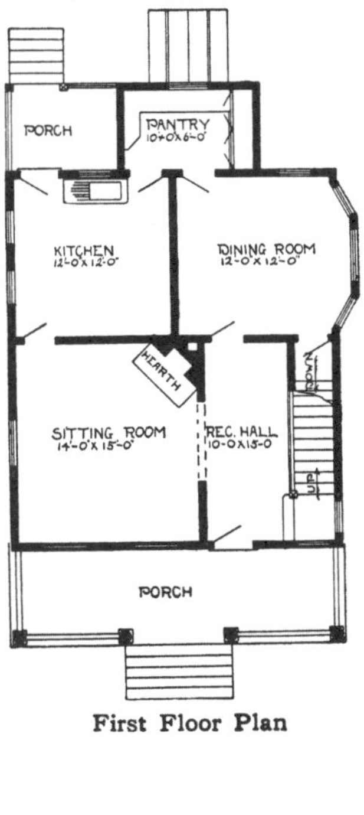

First Floor Plan

Blue prints consist of basement plan; first and second floor plans; front, two side elevations; wall sections and all necessary interior details. Specifications consist of about twenty pages of typewritten matter.

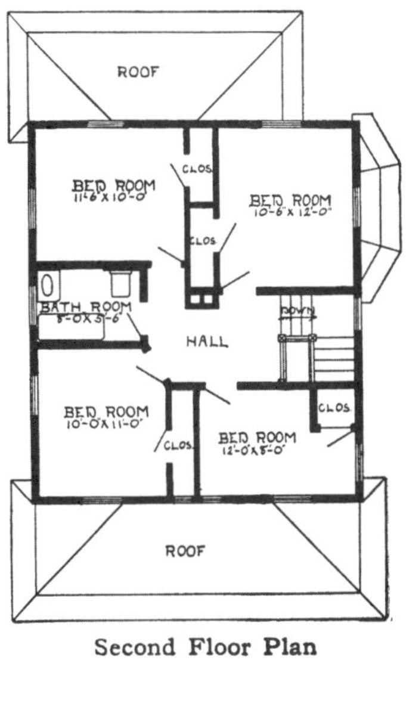

Second Floor Plan

Design No. 7049

Size: Width, 34 feet; Length, 42 feet 6 inches, exclusive of porches

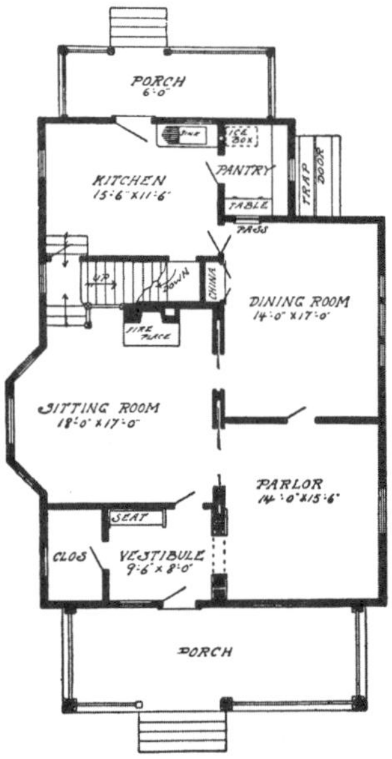

First Floor Plan

Blue prints consist of cellar and foundation plan; first and second floor plans; front, rear, two side elevations; wall sections and all necessary interior details. Specifications consist of about twenty pages of typewritten matter.

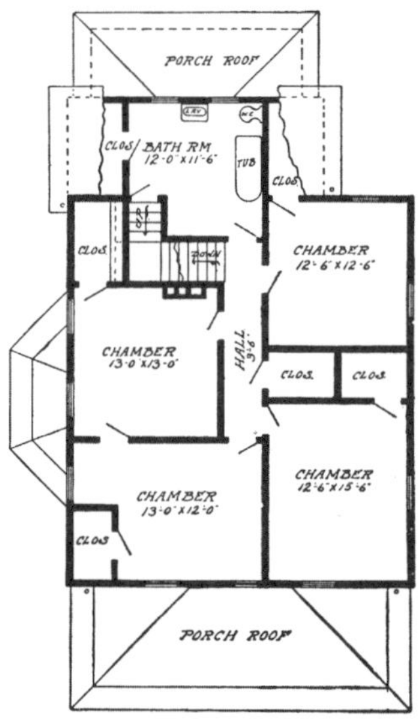

Second Floor Plan

PRICE

of Blue Prints, together with a complete set of typewritten specifications.

ONLY FIFTEEN DOLLARS

We mail Plans and Specifications the same day order is received.

DESIGN NUMBER 6066

Size: width, 27 feet 6 inches; length, 35 feet, exclusive of porches

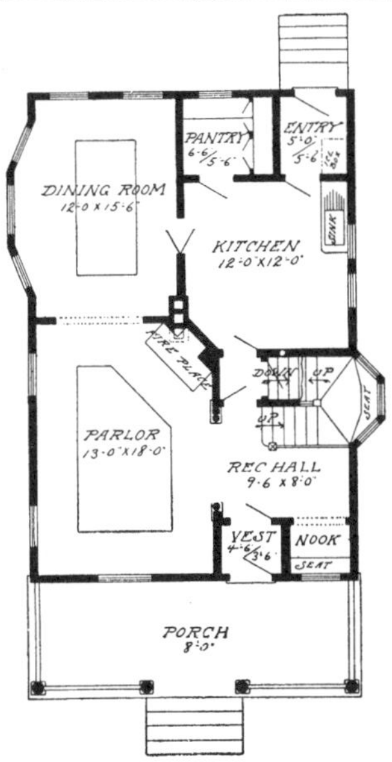

First Floor Plan

BLUE PRINTS consist of basement plan; roof plan; first and second floor plans; front, rear, two side elevations; wall sections and all necessary interior details. Specifications consist of about twenty pages of typewritten matter.

PRICE

of Blue Prints, together with a complete set of typewritten specifications

ONLY TWELVE DOLLARS

We mail plans and specifications the same day order is received.

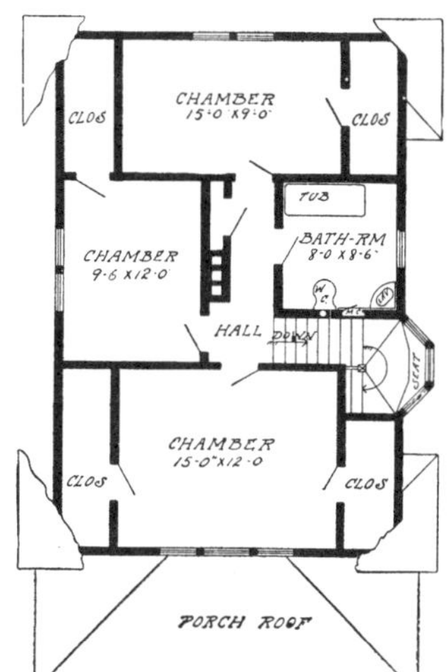

Second Floor Plan

DESIGN NUMBER 6007

Size: width, 46 feet 6 inches; length, 34 feet 6 inches, exclusive of porches

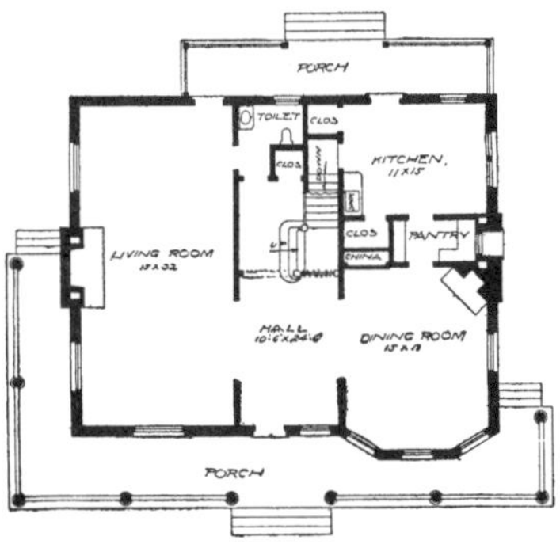

First Floor Plan

BLUE PRINTS consist of basement plan; roof plan; first and second floor plans; front, rear, and two side elevations; wall sections and all necessary interior details. Specifications consist of about twenty pages of typewritten matter.

PRICE

of Blue Prints, together with a complete set of typewritten specifications

ONLY FIFTEEN DOLLARS

We mail plans and specifications the same day order is received.

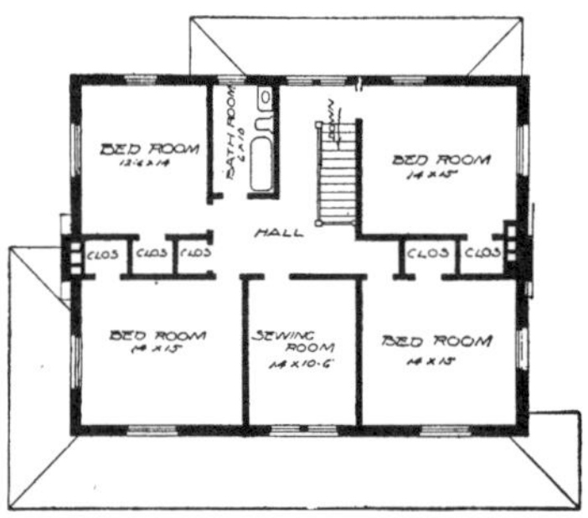

Second Floor Plan

First Floor Plan.

Design No. 9025

The arrangement of this House is as follows:

FIRST FLOOR.

Living Room, 23 feet by 12 feet.

Dining Room, 12 feet 6 inches by 12 feet.

Kitchen, 10 feet by 10 feet.

Pantry, Front and Rear Porches.

SECOND FLOOR.

Bedroom, 10 feet 6 inches by 8 feet 6 inches.

Bedroom, 8 feet 6 inches by 15 feet 6 inches.

Bedroom, 15 feet by 8 feet.

Bathroom, 7 feet 6 inches by 7 feet.

3 Closets.

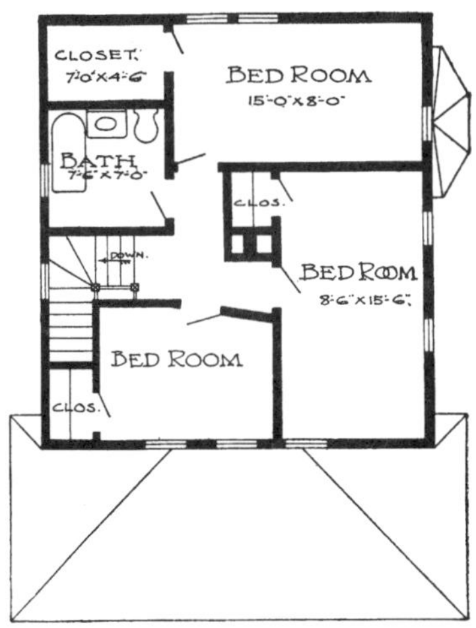

Second Floor Plan.

This Building is 25 feet in width; 28 feet in length.

Price of Complete Working Plans and Specifications **$12.00**

The Blue Printed Working Plans for this House consist of basement plan; first and second floor plans, front, right, left and rear elevations; wall sections and all necessary details.

The Tvpewritten Specifications contain all the necessary information for the proper construction of the House.

Design No. 9055

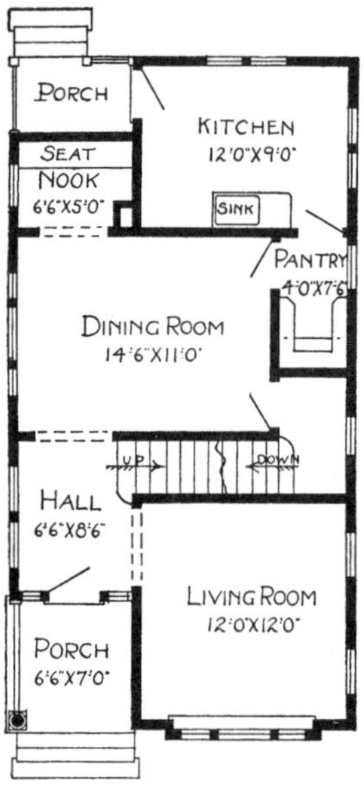

First Floor Plan.

The arrangement of this House is as follows:

FIRST FLOOR.

Reception Hall, 6 feet 6 inches by 8 feet 6 inches.
Living Room, 12 feet by 12 feet.
Dining Room, 14 feet 6 inches by 11 feet.
Kitchen, 12 feet by 9 feet.
Nook, 6 feet 6 inches by 5 feet.
Pantry, Front and Rear Porches.

SECOND FLOOR.

Bedroom, 14 feet by 12 feet.
Bedroom, 14 feet by 9 feet.
Bedroom, 7 feet 6 inches by 11 feet.
Bathroom, 7 feet 6 inches by 7 feet 6 inches.
3 Closets.

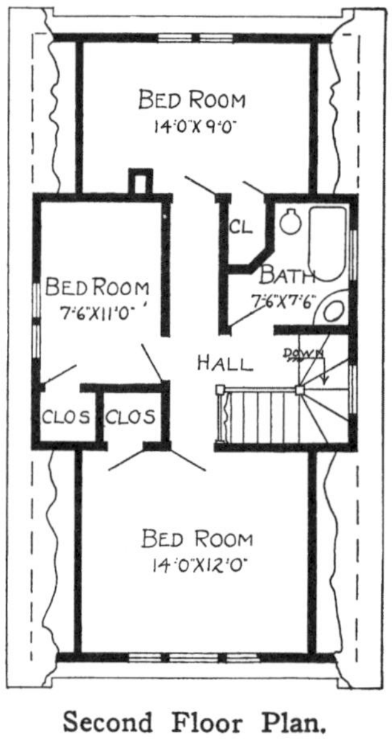

Second Floor Plan.

This Building is 20 feet in width; 38 feet in length.

Price of Complete Working Plans and Specifications.. $12.00

The Blue Printed Working Plans for this House consist of basement plan, roof plan, first and second floor plans; front, right, left and rear elevations; wall sections and all necessary details.

The Typewritten Specifications contain all the necessary info mation for the proper construction of the House.

Design No. 7020

Size: Width, 23 feet 6 inches; Length, 29 feet 6 inches, exclusive of porch

PRICE

of Blue Prints, together with a complete set of typewritten specifications

ONLY TWELVE DOLLARS

We mail Plan. and Specifications the same day order is received.

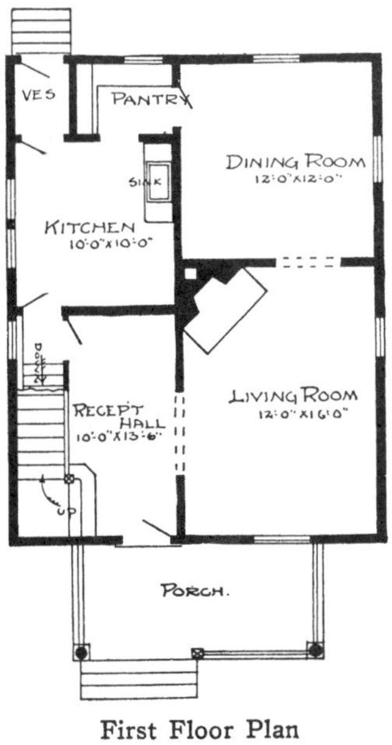

First Floor Plan

Blue prints consist of basement plan; roof plan; first and second floor plans; front, rear, two side elevations; wall sections and all necessary interior details. Specifications consist of about twenty pages of typewritten matter.

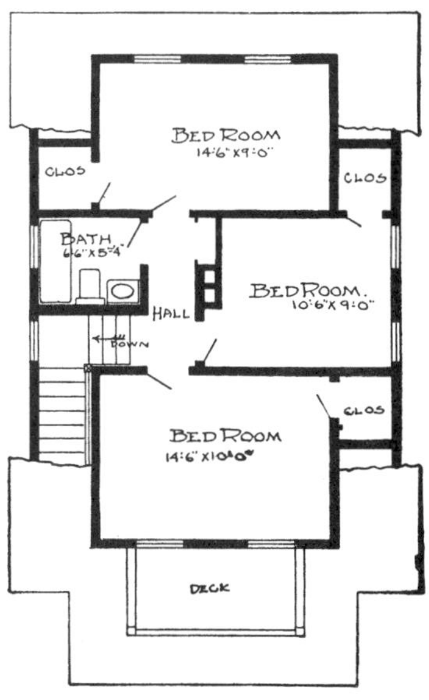

Second Floor Plan

Design No. 7005

Size: Width, 28 feet; 6 inches; Length, 25 feet, 6 inches, exclusive of porch

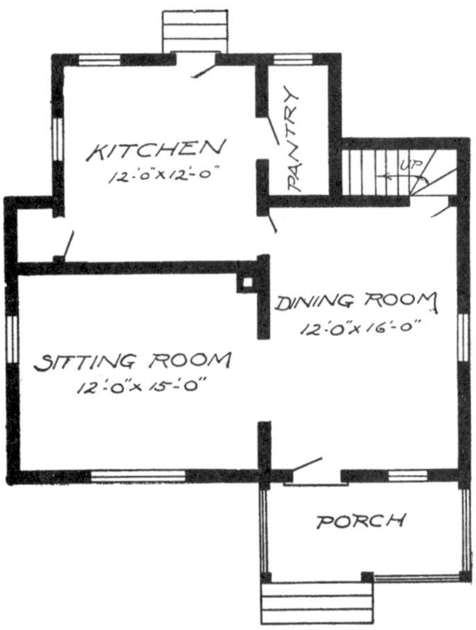

First Floor Plan

Blue prints consist of foundation plan; roof plan; first and second floor plans; front, rear, two side elevations; wall sections and all necessary interior details. Specifications consist of about twenty pages of typewritten matter.

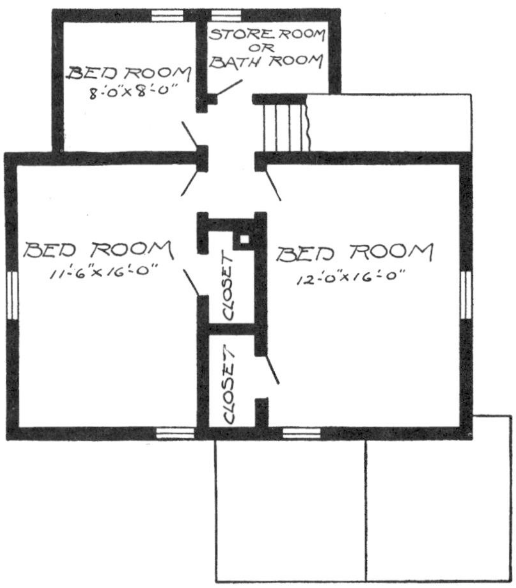

Second Floor Plan

PRICE
of Blue Prints, together with a complete set of typewritten specifications

ONLY TWELVE DOLLARS

We mail Plans and Specifications the same day order is received.

DESIGN NUMBER 6055

Size: width, 28 feet; length, 29 feet 6 inches, exclusive of porches

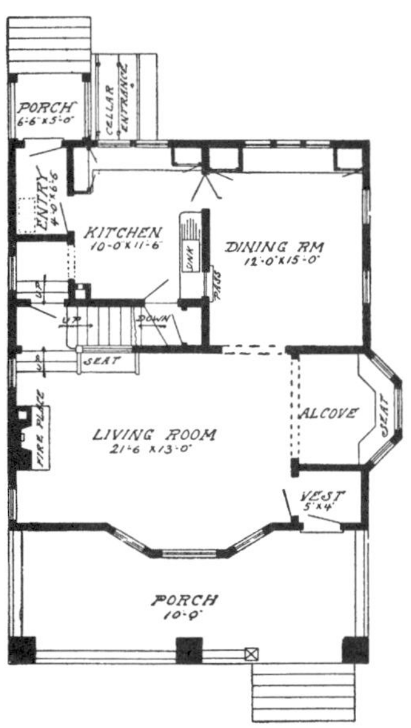

First Floor Plan

BLUE PRINTS consist of basement plan; roof plan; first and second floor plans; front, rear, two side elevations; wall sections and all necessary interior details. Specifications consist of about twenty pages of typewritten matter.

PRICE

of Blue Prints, together with a complete set of typewritten specifications

ONLY FIFTEEN DOLLARS

We mail plans and specifications the same day order is received.

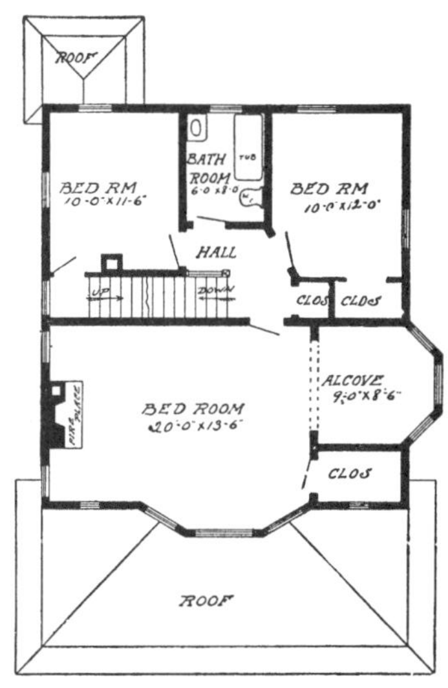

Second Floor Plan

DESIGN NUMBER 6052

Size: width, 36 feet 8 inches; length, 34 feet 8 inches, exclusive of porches

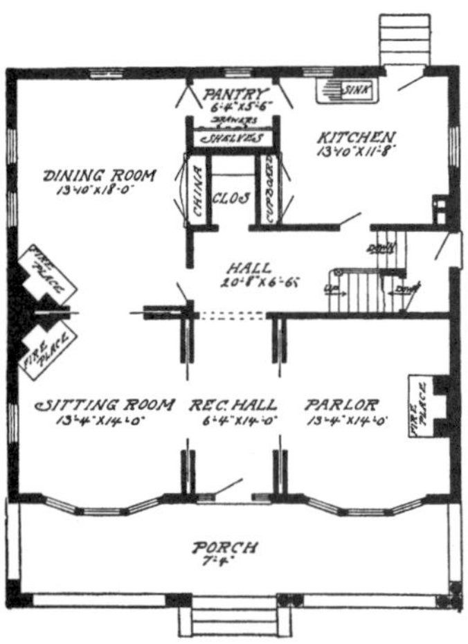

First Floor Plan

BLUE PRINTS consist of basement plan; roof plan; first and second floor plans; front, rear, two side elevations; wall sections and all necessary interior details. Specifications consist of about twenty pages of typewritten matter.

PRICE

of Blue Prints, together with a complete set of typewritten specifications

ONLY FIFTEEN DOLLARS

We mail plans and specifications the same day order is received.

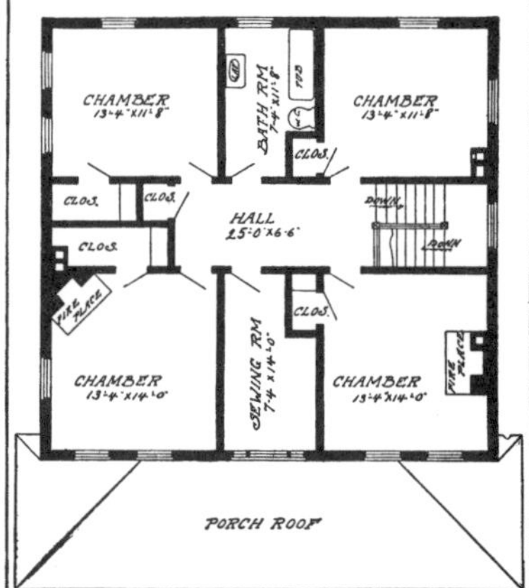

Second Floor Plan

Design No. 9041

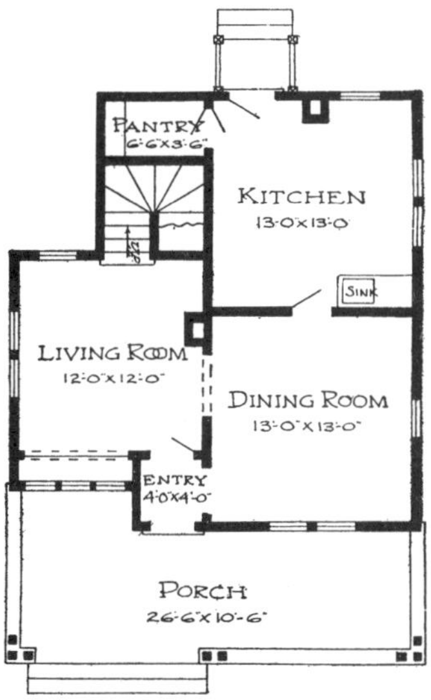

First Floor Plan.

The arrangement of this House is as follows:

FIRST FLOOR.

Entry, 4 feet by 4 feet.
Living Room, 12 feet by 12 feet.
Dining Room, 13 feet by 13 feet.
Kitchen, 13 feet by 13 feet.
Pantry and Front Porch.

SECOND FLOOR.

Bedroom, 12 feet by 14 feet.
Bedroom, 13 feet by 10 feet.
Bedroom, 13 feet by 10 feet.
Bathroom, 9 feet by 5 feet 6 inches.
2 Closets.

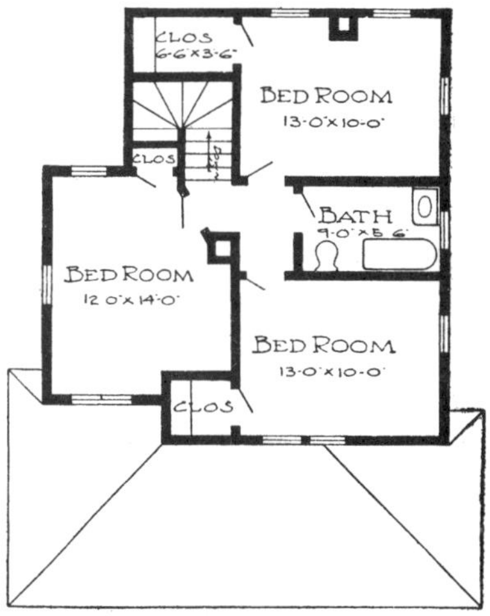

Second Floor Plan.

This Building is 26 feet 6 inches in width; 27 feet 6 inches in length.

Price of Complete Working Plans and Specifications.. **$12.00**

The Blue Printed Working Plans for this House consist of foundation plan, roof plan, first and second floor plans; front, right, left and rear elevations; wall sections and all necessary details.

The Typewritten Specifications contain all the necessary information for the proper construction of the House.

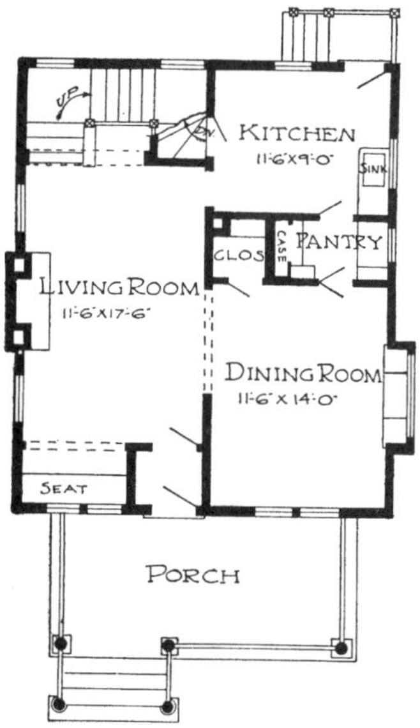

First Floor Plan.

Design No. 9076

The arrangement of this House is as follows:

FIRST FLOOR.

Living Room, 11 feet 6 inches by 17 feet 6 inches.

Dining Room, 11 feet 6 inches by 14 feet.

Kitchen, 11 feet 6 inches by 9 feet.

Pantry, Front and Rear Porches.

SECOND FLOOR.

Bedroom, 11 feet 6 inches by 13 feet.

Bedroom, 11 feet 6 inches by 9 feet.

Bedroom, 11 feet 6 inches by 13 feet.

Bathroom, 7 feet 6 inches by 7 feet.

6 Closets.

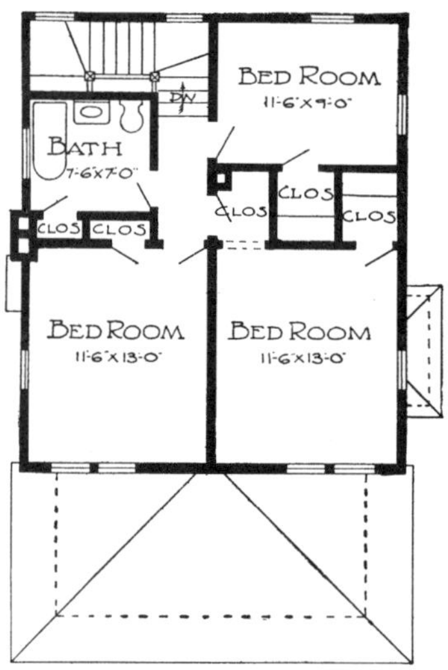

Second Floor Plan.

This Building is 26 feet in width; 28 feet 6 inches in length.

Price of Complete Working Plans and Specifications.. $12.00

The Blue Printed Working Plans for this House consist of basement plan; first and second floor plans; front, right, left and rear elevations; wall sections and all necessary details.

The Typewritten Specifications contain all the necessary information for the proper construction of the House.

Design No. 7007

Size: Width, 27 feet 6 inches; Length, 20 feet

PRICE

of Blue Prints, together with a complete set of typewritten specifications

ONLY EIGHT DOLLARS

We mail Plan. and Specifications the same day order is received.

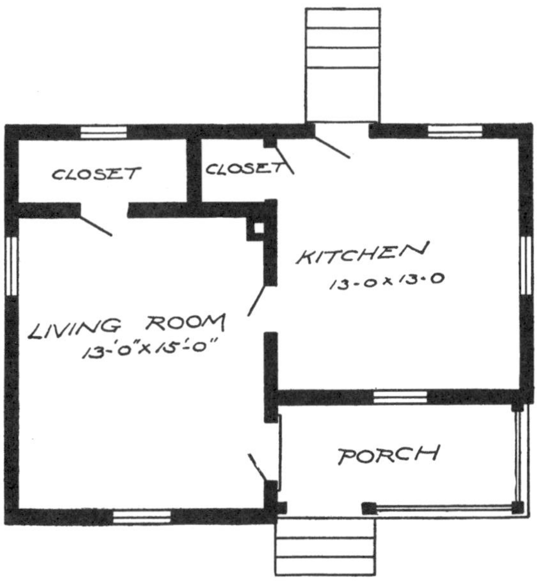

Floor Plan

Blue Prints consist of foundation plan; floor plan; front, rear, two side elevations; wall sections and all necessary interior details. Specifications consist of about fifteen pages of typewritten matter.

Design No. 7099

Size: Width, 41 feet; Length, 25 feet, exclusive of porch

PRICE

of Blue Prints together with a complete set of typewritten specifications

ONLY TEN DOLLARS

We mail Plans and Specifications the same day order is received.

Blue Prints consist of foundation plan; floor plan; front, rear, two side elevations; wall sections and all necessary interior details. Specifications consist of about fifteen pages of typewritten matter.

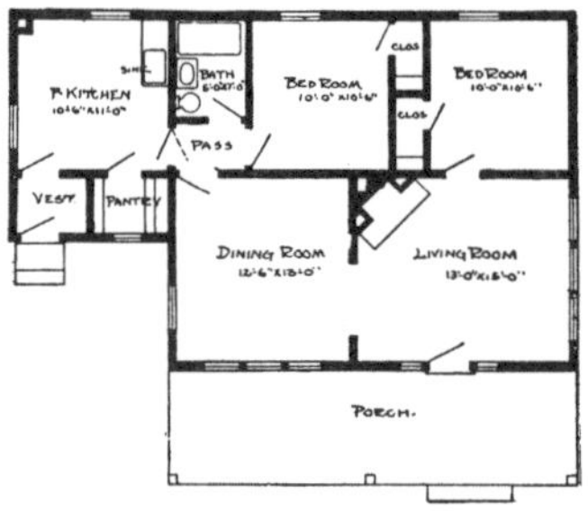

Floor Plan

DESIGN NUMBER 6174

Size: width, 25 feet; length, 37 feet, 6 inches, exclusive of porches

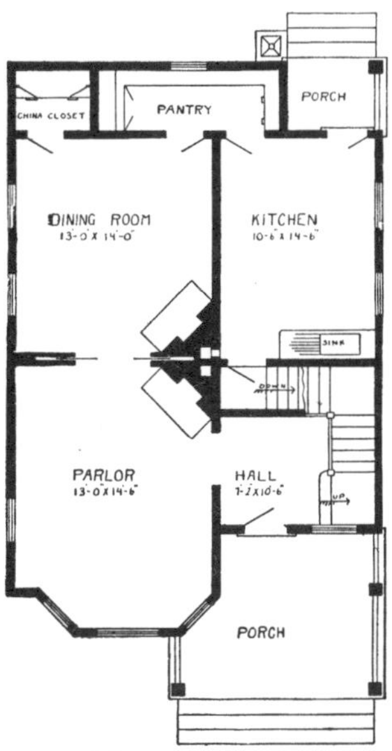

First Floor Plan

BLUE PRINTS consist of basement plan; first and second floor plans; front, rear, two side elevations; wall sections and all necessary interior details. Specifications consist of about twenty pages of typewritten matter.

PRICE

of Blue Prints, together with a complete set of typewritten specifications

ONLY TWELVE DOLLARS

We mail plans and specifications the same day order is received.

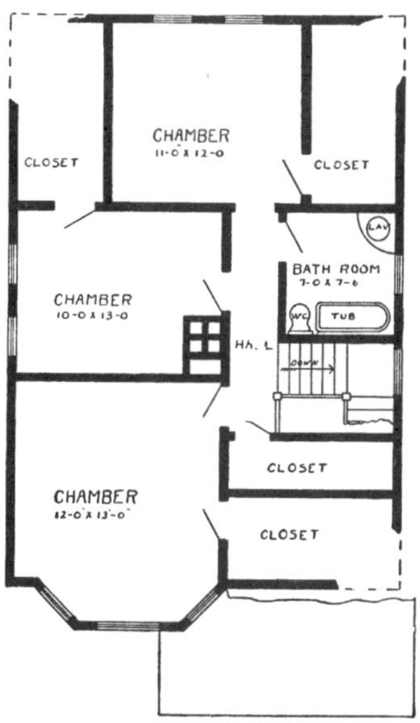

Second Floor Plan

DESIGN NUMBER 6027

Size: width, 29 feet, length, 31 feet exclusive of porches

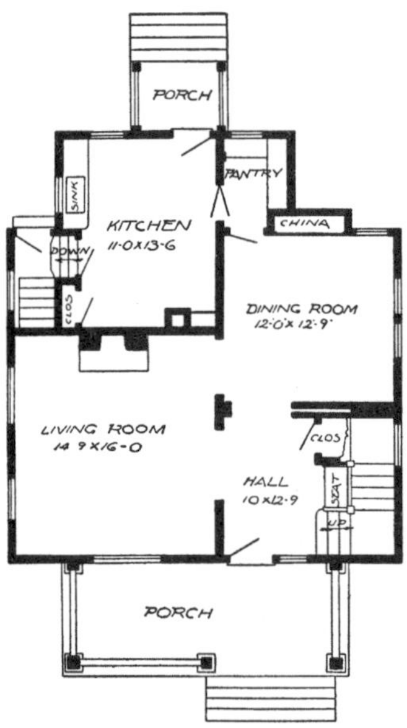

First Floor Plan

BLUE PRINTS consist of cellar and foundation plan; roof plan; first and second floor plans; front, rear, two side elevations; wall sections and all necessary interior details. Specifications consist of about twenty pages of typewritten matter.

PRICE

of Blue Prints, together with a complete set of typewritten specifications

ONLY TWELVE DOLLARS

We mail plans and specifications the same day order is received.

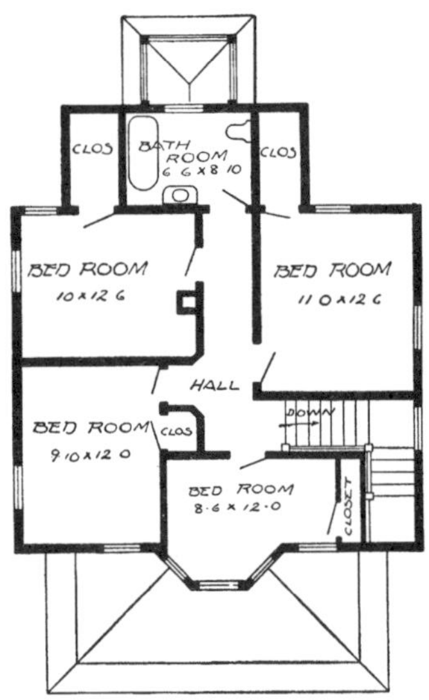

Second Floor Plan

DESIGN NUMBER 6023

Size: width, 31 feet 6 inches; length, 23 feet 6 inches, exclusive of porches

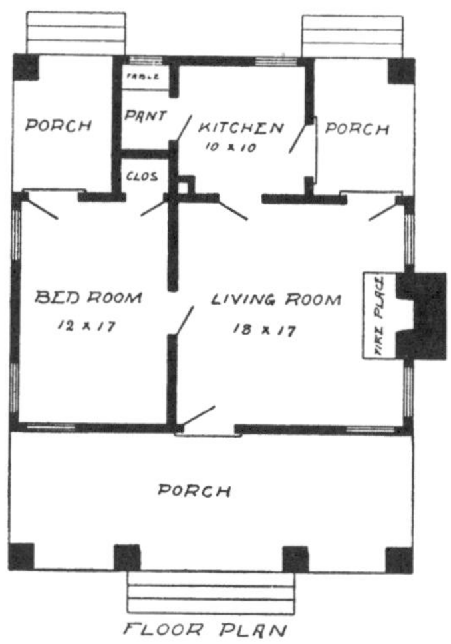

Floor Plan

BLUE PRINTS consist of foundation plan, floor plan; front, rear, two side elevations; wall sections and all necessary interior details. Specifications consist of about fifteen pages of typewritten matter.

PRICE

of Blue Prints, together with a complete set of typewritten specifications

ONLY EIGHT DOLLARS

We mail plans and specifications the same day order is received.

DESIGN NUMBER 6062

Size width, 29 feet 6 inches; length, 43 feet 6 inches, exclusive of porches

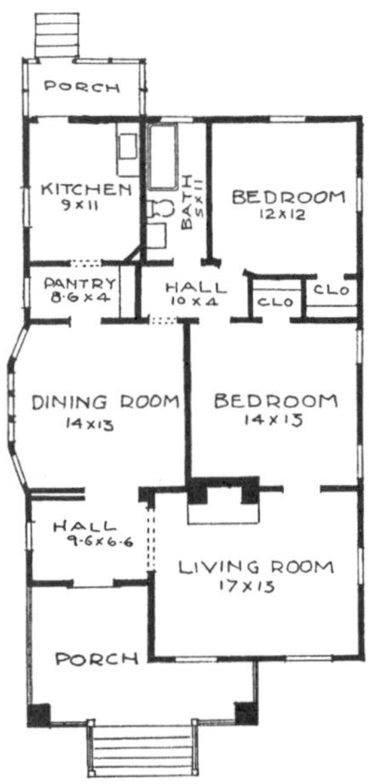

Floor Plan

BLUE PRINTS consist of foundation plan; floor plan; front, rear, two side elevations; wall sections and all necessary interior details. Specifications consist of about fifteen pages of type-written matter.

PRICE

of Dlue Prints, together with a complete set of typewritten specifications

ONLY TEN DOLLARS

We mail plans and specifications the same day order is received.

Design No. 7058

Size: Width, 24 feet; Length, 28 feet, exclusive of porches

PRICE

of Blue Prints, together with a complete set of typewritten specifications.

ONLY TWELVE DOLLARS

We mail Plans and Specifications the same day order is received.

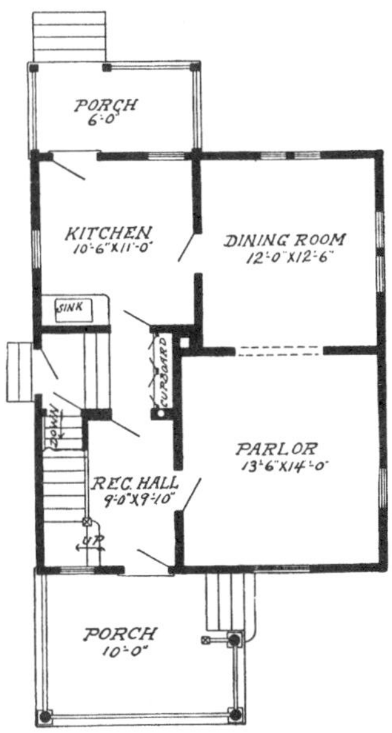

First Floor Plan

Blue prints consist of basement plan; first and second floor plans; front, rear, two side elevations; wall sections and all necessary interior details. Specifications consist of about twenty pages of typewritten matter.

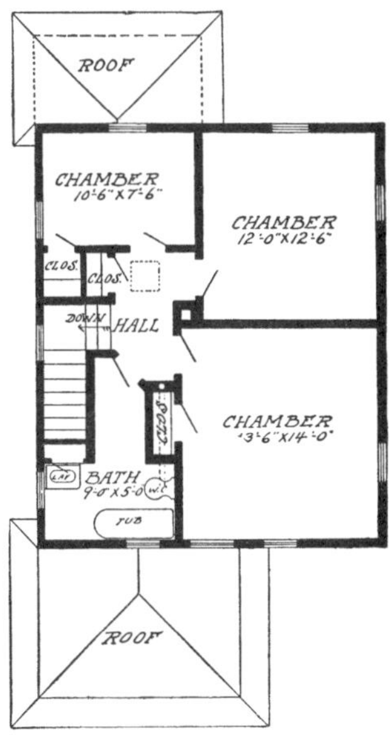

Second Floor Plan

Design No. 7077

Size: Width, 33 feet; Length, 46 feet 6 inches, exclusive of porches

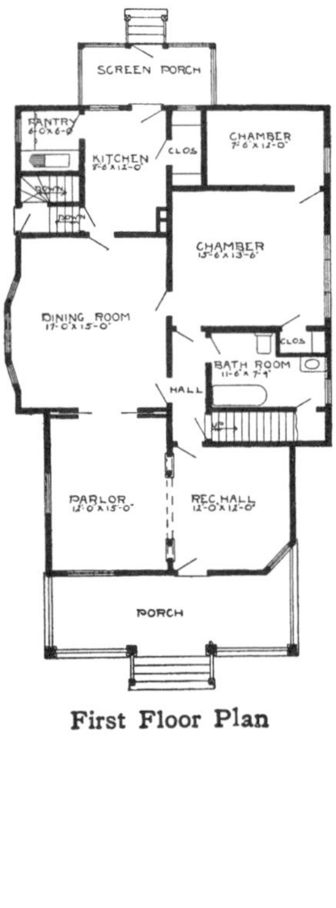

First Floor Plan

Blue prints consist of basement plan; roof plan; first and second floor plans; front, rear, two side elevations; wall sections and all necessary interioı details. Specifications consist of about twenty pages of typewritten matter.

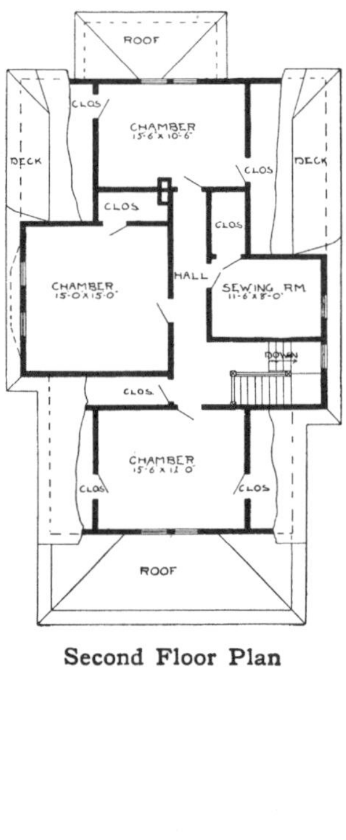

Second Floor Plan

PRICE

of Blue Prints, together with a complete set of typewritten specifications

ONLY TWELVE DOLLARS

We mail Plans and Specifications the same day order is received.

Design No. 7003

Size: Width, 27 feet 6 inches; Length, 20 feet, exclusive of porches

PRICE

of Blue Prints, together with a complete set of typewritten specifications

ONLY EIGHT DOLLARS

We mail Plans and Specifications the same day order is received.

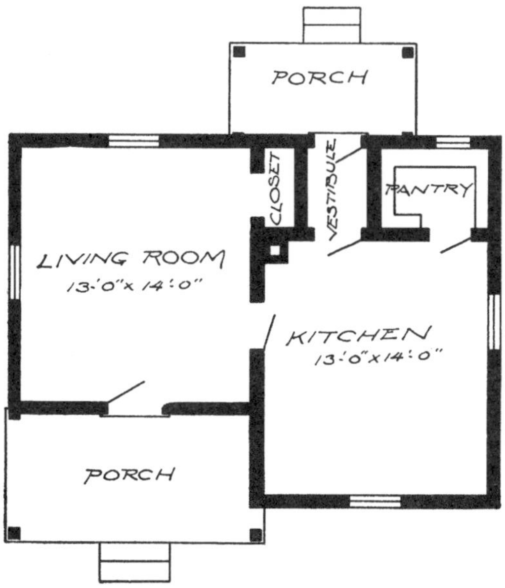

Floor Plan

Blue prints consist of foundation plan; floor plan; front, two side elevations; wall sections and all necessary interior details. Specifications consist of about twelve pages of typewritten matter.

Design No. 7091

Size: Width, 41 feet 6 inches; Length, 30 feet, exclusive of porch

Blue Prints consist of foundation plan; floor plan; front, rear, two side elevations; wall sections and all necessary interior details. Specifications consist of about fifteen pages of typewritten matter.

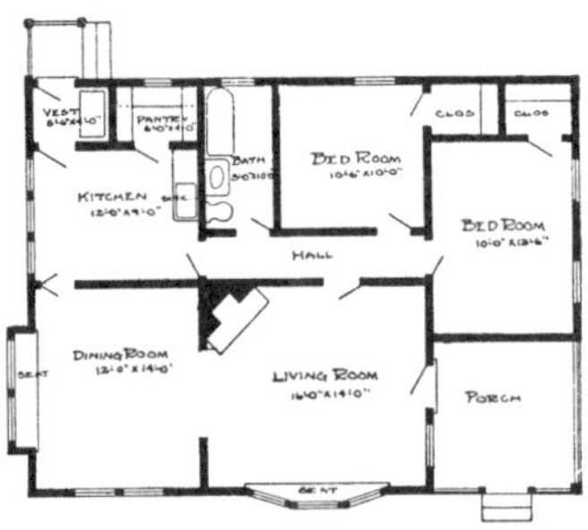

Floor Plan

PRICE

of Blue Prints together with a complete set of typewritten specifications

ONLY TEN DOLLARS

We mail Plans and Specifications the same day orde. is received.

DESIGN NUMBER 6019

Size: width, 26 feet; length, 43 feet, exclusive of porches

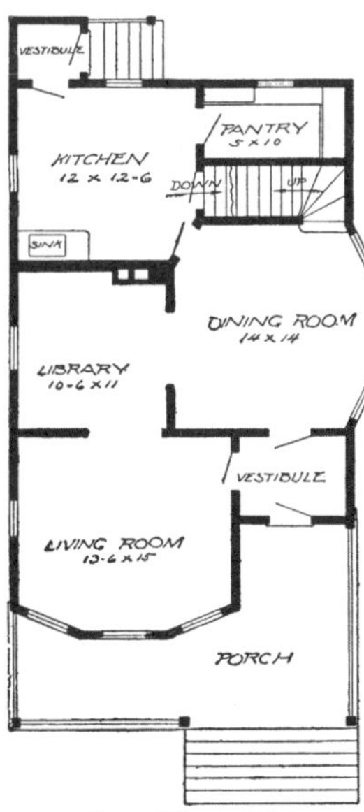

First Floor Plan

BLUE PRINTS consist of basement plan; roof plan; first and second floor plans; front, rear, two side elevations; wall sections and all necessary interior details. Specifications consist of about twenty pages of typewritten matter.

PRICE

of Blue Prints, together with a complete set of typewritten specifications

ONLY TWELVE DOLLARS

We mail plans and specifications the same day order is received.

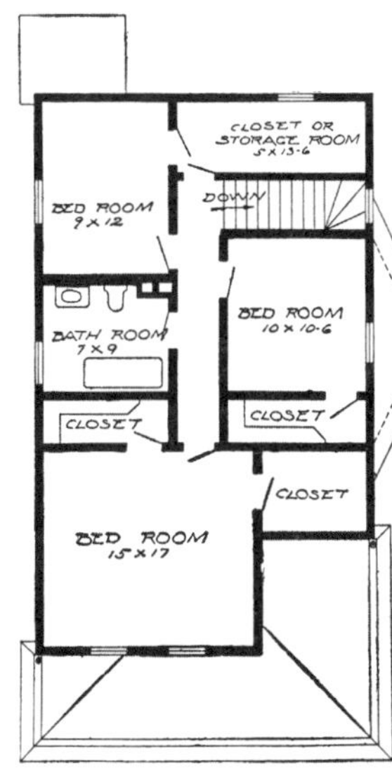

Second Floor Plan

DESIGN NUMBER 6036

Size: width, 32 feet; length, 28 feet, exclusive of porches

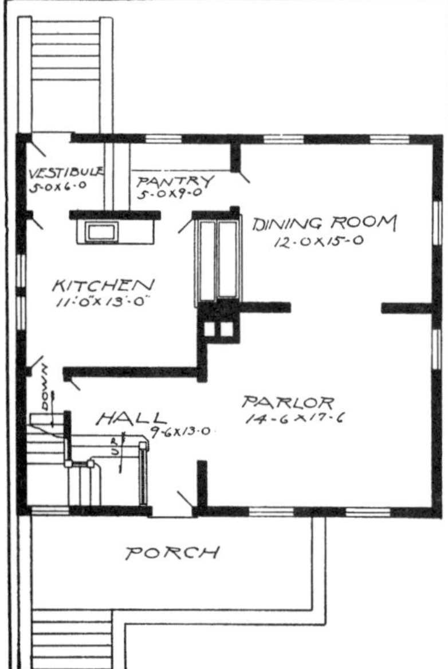

First Floor Plan

BLUE PRINTS consist of cellar and foundation plan; roof plan; first and second floor plans; front, rear, two side elevations; wall sections and all necessary interior details. Specifications consist of about twenty pages of typewritten matter.

PRICE

of Blue Prints, together with a complete set of typewritten specifications

ONLY TWELVE DOLLARS

We mail plans and specifications the same day order is received.

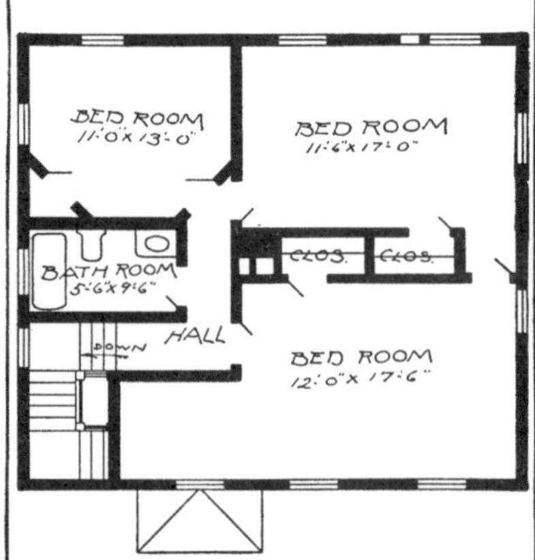

Second Floor Plan

DESIGN NUMBER 6006

Size: width, 29 feet 6 inches; length, 30 feet 6 inches

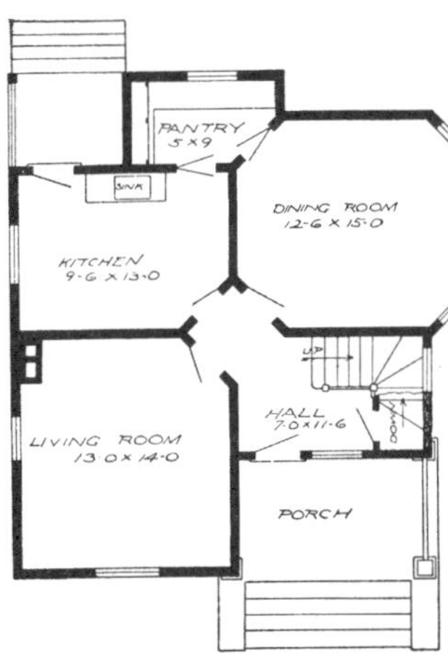

First Floor Plan

BLUE PRINTS consist of basement plan; roof plan; first and second floor plans; front, rear, two side elevations; wall sections and all necessary interior details. Specifications consist of about twenty pages of typewritten matter.

PRICE

of Blue Prints, together with a complete set of typewritten specifications

ONLY TWELVE DOLLARS

We mail plans and specifications the same day order is received.

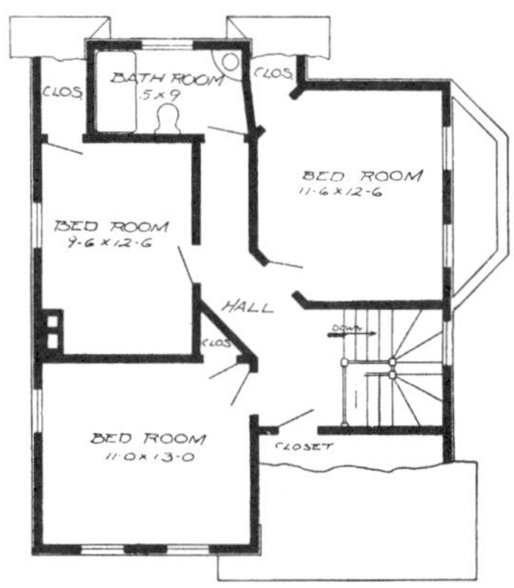

Second Floor Plan

DESIGN NUMBER 6020

Size: width, 32 feet; length, 31 feet, exclusive of porches

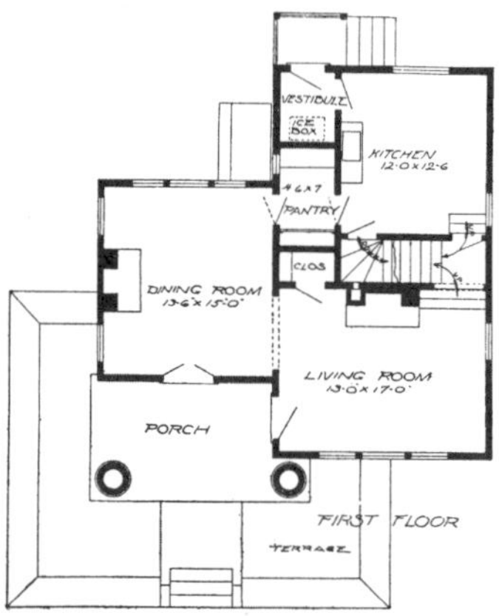

First Floor Plan

BLUE PRINTS consist of cellar and foundation plan; roof plan; first and second floor plans; front, two side elevations; wall sections and all necessary interior details. Specifications consist of about twenty pages of typewritten matter.

PRICE

of Blue Prints, together with a complete set of typewritten specifications

ONLY TWELVE DOLLARS

We mail plans and specifications the same day order is received.

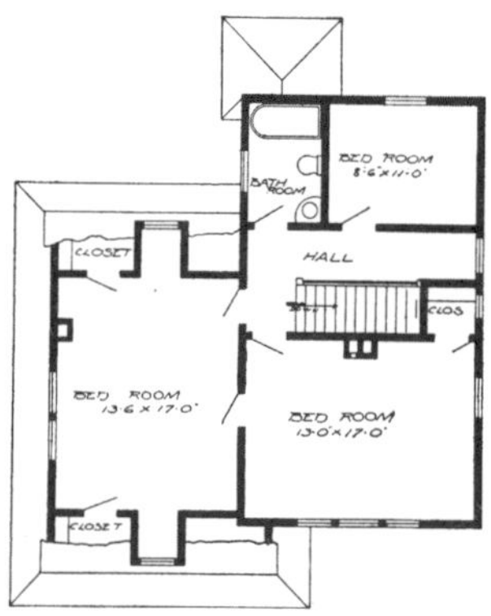

Second Floor Plan

Design No. 7042

Size: Width, 34 feet; Length, 31 feet 6 inches, exclusive of porches

PRICE

of Blue Prints, together with a complete set of typewritten specifications

ONLY TWELVE DOLLARS

We mail Plans and Specifications the same day order is received.

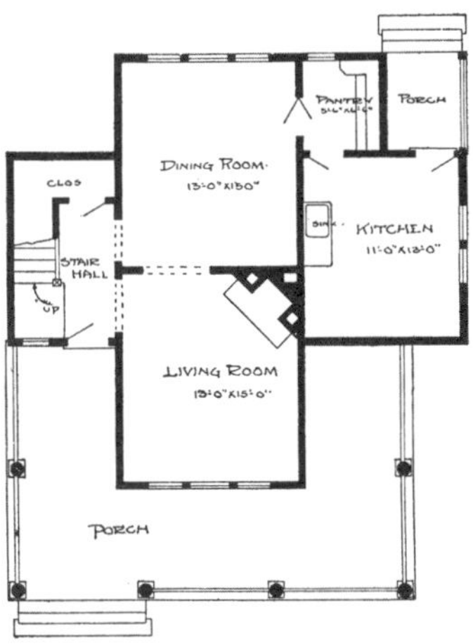

First Floor Plan

Blue Prints consist of basement plan; first and second floor plans; front, rear, two side elevations; wall sections and all necessary interior details. Specifications consist of about twenty pages of typewritten matter.

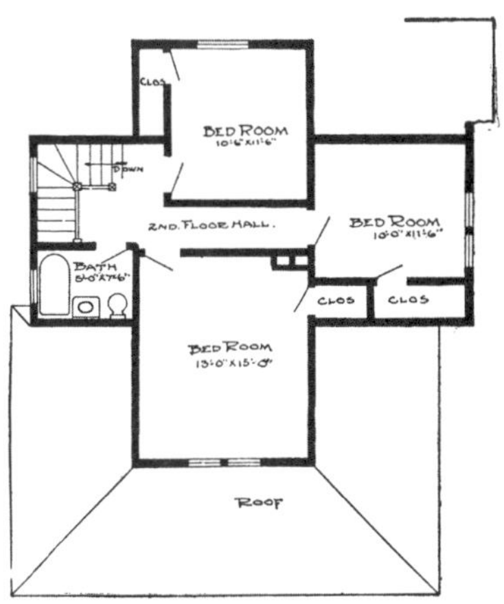

Second Floor Plan

Design No. 7025

Size: Width, 25 feet 6 inches; Length, 29 feet 6 inches, exclusive of porches

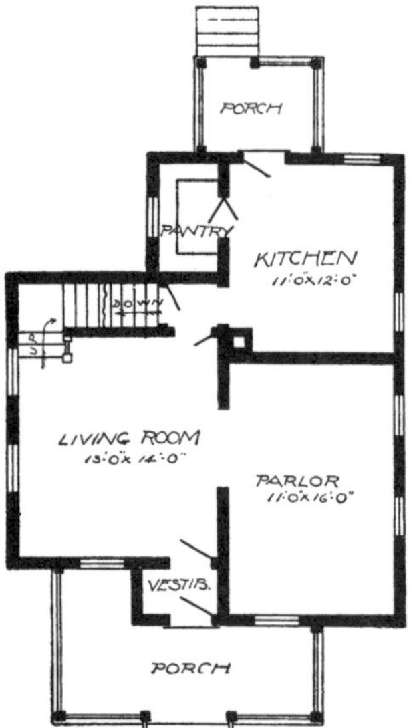

First Floor Plan

Blue prints consist of cellar and foundation plan; first and second floor plans; front, rear, two side elevations; wall sections and all necessary interior details. Specifications consist of about twenty pages of typewritten matter.

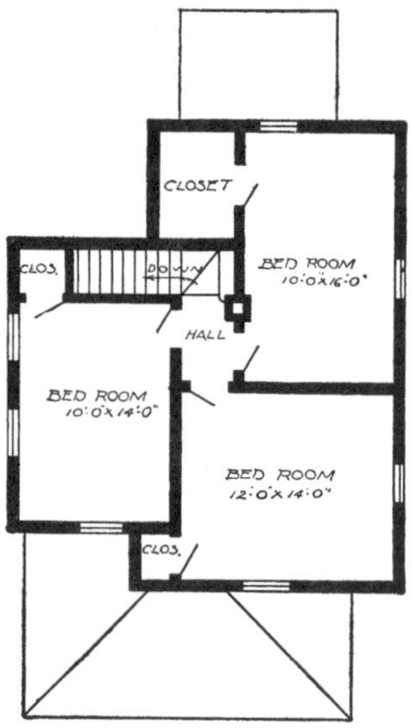

Second Floor Plan

PRICE

of Blue Prints, together with a complete set of typewritten specifications

ONLY TWELVE DOLLARS

We mail Plans and Specifications the same day order is received.

Design No. 2011

Blue prints consist of foundation plan; roof plan; floor plan; front, rear, two side elevations, wall sections and all necessary interior details. Specifications consist of about fifteen pages of typewritten matter

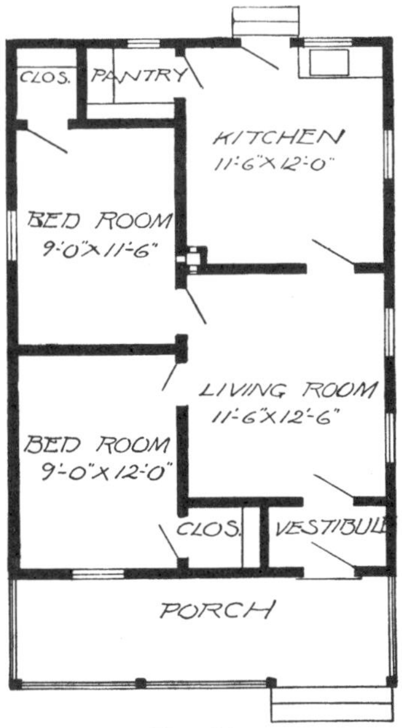

Floor Plan

PRICE

of Blue Prints, together with a complete set of typewritten specifications is

ONLY SEVEN DOLLARS

We mail Plans and Specifications the same day order is received.

SIZE: Width, 22 feet; length 30 feet exclusive of porch.

If a plan in this pleases you, if the arrangement of the rooms is satisfactory, and if the exterior is pleasing and attractive, we claim that it can be built as cheap or cheaper than if any other architect designed it.

"Be it ever so humble, there is no place like home." It is, or should be, the ambition of every one to some day own a home of his own. The plans we illustrate are such as 75 to 90 per cent of the people build.

Design No. 2049

Blue prints consist of basement plan; roof plan; floor plan; front, rear, two side elevations; wall sections and all necessary interior details. Specifications consist of about fifteen pages of typewritten matter.

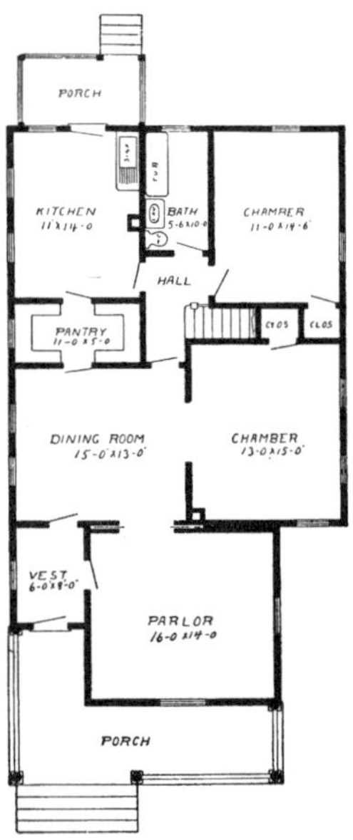

Floor Plan

PRICE

of Blue Prints, together with a complete set of typewritten specifications is

ONLY
EIGHT
DOLLARS

We mail Plans and Specifications the same day order is received.

SIZE: Width, 29 feet 6 inches; length, 49 feet exclusive of porches.

It is not uncommon to hear of disputes, and even lawsuits, between owners and contractors. It is usually occasioned by lack of plans and proper understanding. One party is probably as much in error as the other.

Don't proceed with the construction of your house until you get complete plans. Experienced contractors are the most particular in this respect, knowing the advantage and saving to both themselves and the home builder.

DESIGN NUMBER 6014

Size: width, 22 feet; length, 33 feet, exclusive of porches

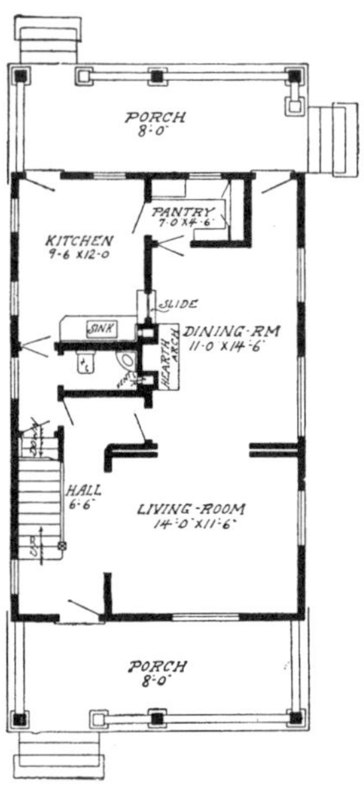

First Floor Plan

BLUE PRINTS consist of basement plan; first and second floor plans; front, two side elevations; wall sections and all necessary interior details. Specifications consist of about twenty pages of typewritten matter.

PRICE

of Blue Prints, together with a complete set of typewritten specifications

ONLY TWELVE DOLLARS

We mail plans and specifications the same day order is received.

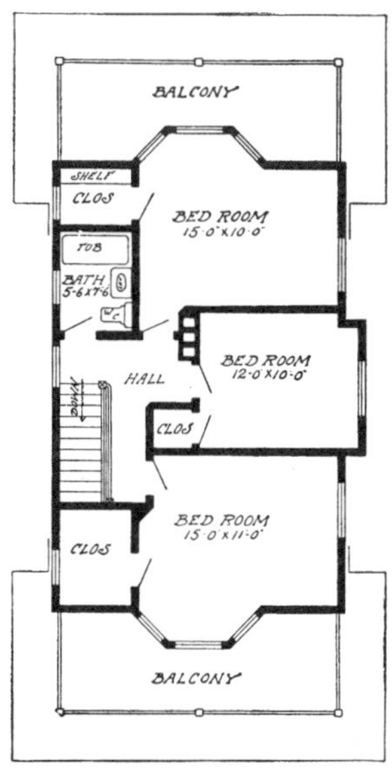

Second Floor Plan

DESIGN NUMBER 6015

Size: width, 27 feet; length, 43 feet, exclusive of porches

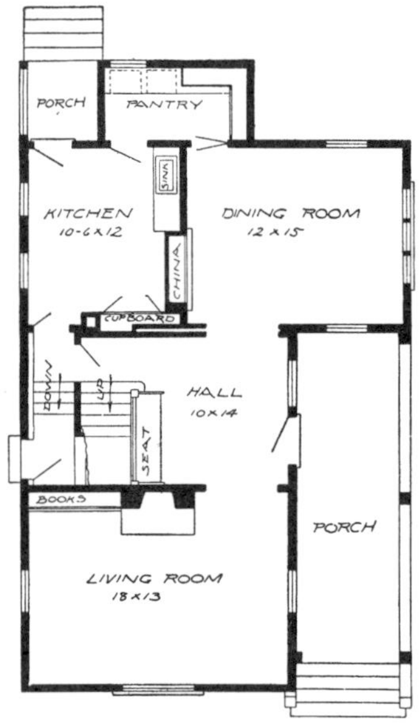

First Floor Plan

BLUE PRINTS consist of basement plan; first and second floor plans; front, rear, two side elevations; wall sections and all necessary interior details. Specifications consist of about twenty pages of typewritten matter.

PRICE

of Blue Prints, together with a complete set of typewritten specifications

ONLY TWELVE DOLLARS

We mail plans and specifications the same day order is received.

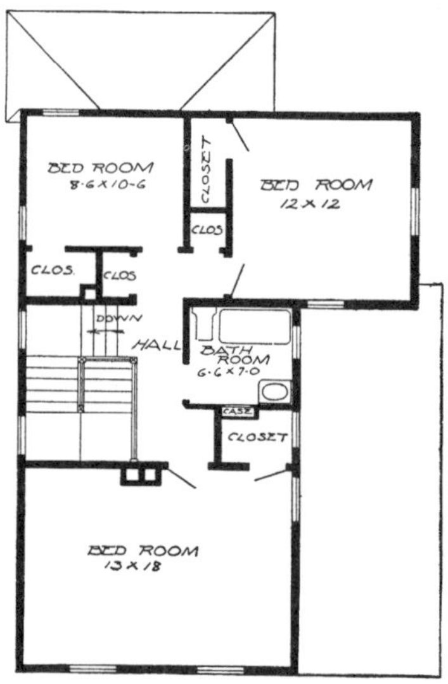

Second Floor Plan

Design No. 7059

Size: Width, 43 feet 6 inches; Length, 54 feet 6 inches, exclusive of porches

PRICE

of Blue Prints, together with a complete set of typewritten specifications.

ONLY TWENTY DOLLARS

We mail Plans and Specifications the same day order is received.

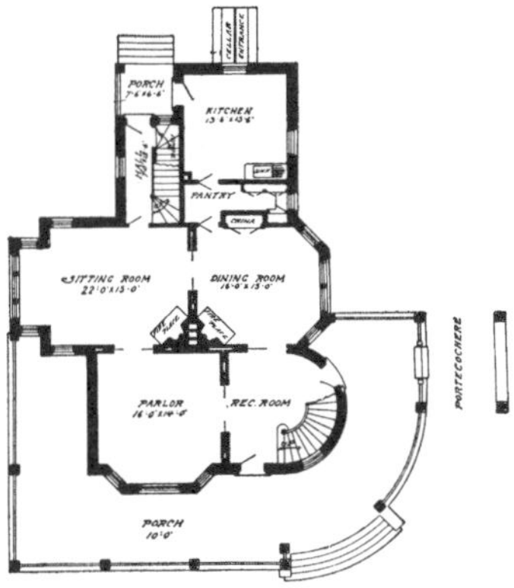

First Floor Plan

Blue prints consist of basement plan; roof plan; first and second floor plans; front, rear, two side elevations; wall sections and all necessary interior details. Specifications consist of about twenty pages of type written matter.

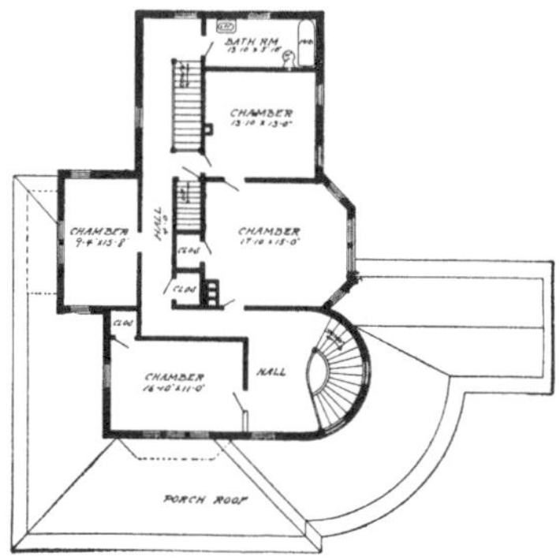

Second Floor Plan

Design No. 7075

Size: Width, 43 feet; Length, 49 feet, exclusive of porch

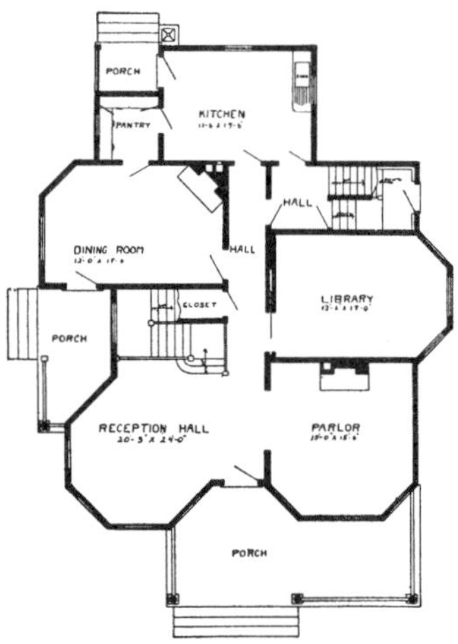

First Floor Plan

Blue prints consist of cellar and foundation plan; first and second floor plans; front, two side elevations; wall sections and all necessary interior details. Specifications consist of about twenty pages of typewritten matter.

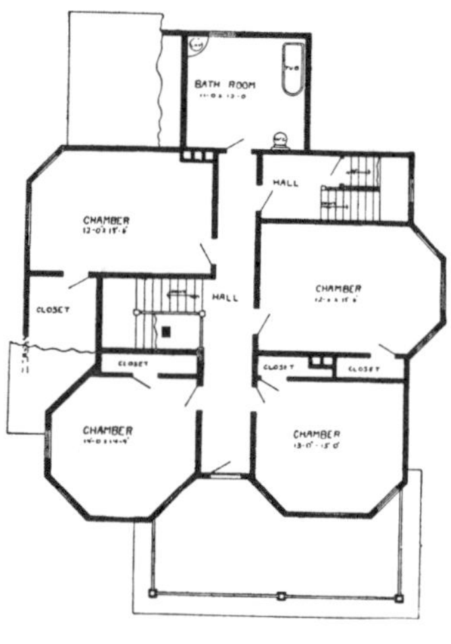

Second Floor Plan

PRICE

of Blue Prints, together with a complete set of typewritten specifications

ONLY FIFTEEN DOLLARS

We mail Plans and Specifications the same day order is received.

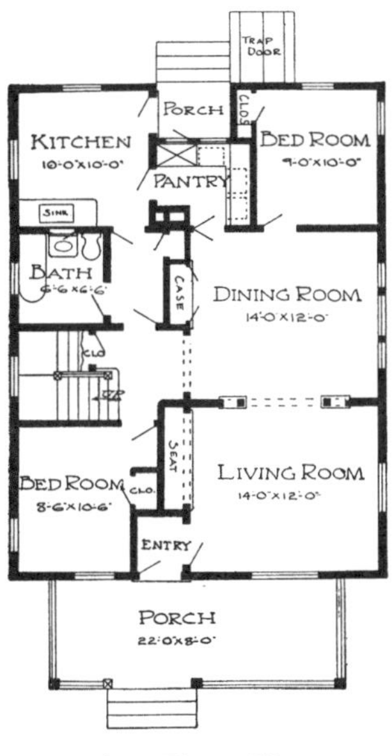

First Floor Plan.

Design No. 9035

The arrangement of this House is as follows:

FIRST FLOOR.

Living Room, 14 feet by 12 feet.
Dining Room, 14 feet by 12 feet.
Kitchen, 10 feet by 10 feet.
Bedroom, 9 feet by 10 feet.
Bedroom, 8 feet 6 inches by 10 feet 6 inches.
Pantry, Front and Rear Porches.

SECOND FLOOR.

Bedroom, 12 feet 6 inches by 8 feet 6 inches.
Bedroom, 14 feet by 13 feet.
Bathroom, 6 feet 6 inches by 6 feet 6 inches.
6 Closets.

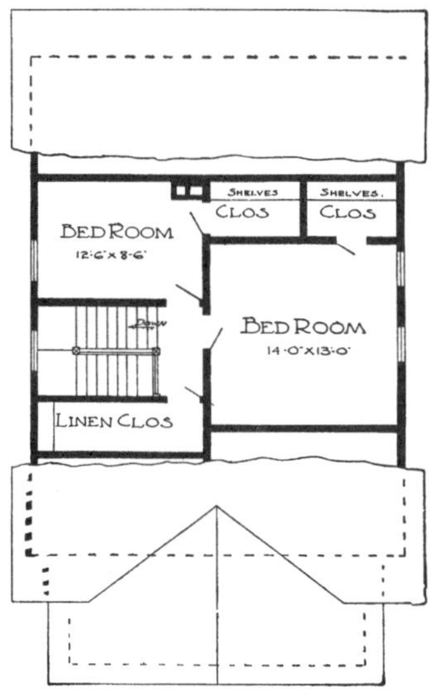

Second Floor Plan.

This Building is 28 feet in width; 36 feet in length.

Price of Complete Working Plans and Specifications.. $10.00

The Blue Printed Working Plans for this House consist of foundation plan; first and second floor plans, front, right, left and rear elevations; wall sections and all necessary details.

The Typewritten Specifications contain all the necessary info mation for the proper construction of the House.

Design No. 9022

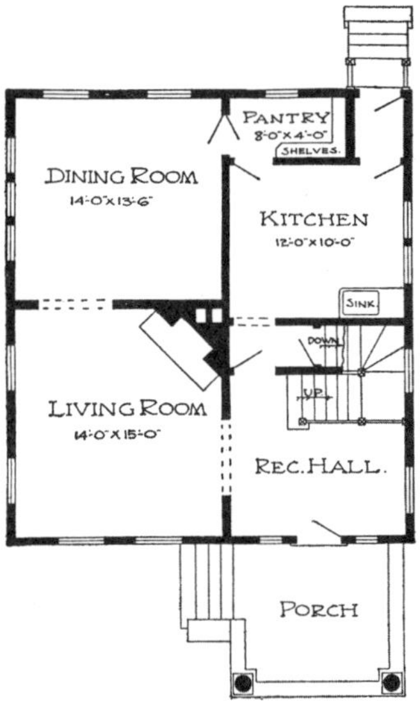

First Floor Plan.

The arrangement of this House is as follows:

FIRST FLOOR.

Reception Hall, 12 feet by 10 feet 6 inches.
Living Room, 14 feet by 15 feet.
Dining Room, 14 feet by 13 feet 6 inches.
Kitchen, 12 feet by 10 feet.
Pantry, Front and Rear Porches.

SECOND FLOOR.

Alcove, 8 feet 6 inches by 7 feet.
Bedroom, 10 feet 6 inches by 10 feet 6 inches.
Bedroom, 11 feet 6 inches by 9 feet.
Bedroom, 19 feet 6 inches by 8 feet 6 inches.
Bathroom, 8 feet 6 inches by 5 feet 6 inches.
5 Closets.

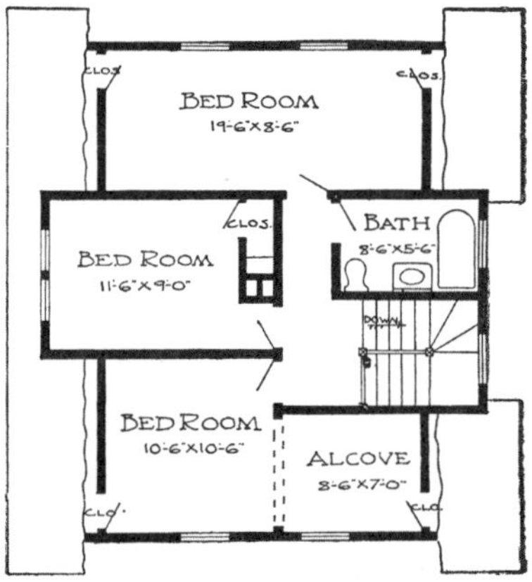

Second Floor Plan.

This building is 27 feet 6 inches in width; 30 feet in length.

Price of Complete Working Plans and Specifications.. $12.00

The Blue Printed Working Plans for this House consist of basement plan; first and second floor plans, front, right, left and rear elevations; wall sections and all necessary details.

The Typewritten Specifications contain all the necessary information for the proper construction of the House.

DESIGN NUMBER 6084

Size: width, 25 feet, 6 inches; length, 45 feet, exclusive of porches

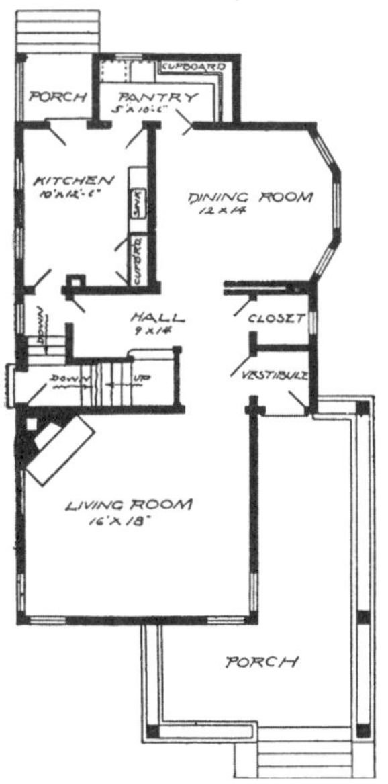

First Floor Plan

BLUE PRINTS consist of basement plan; first and second floor plans; front, rear, two side elevations; wall sections and all necessary interior details. Specifications consist of about twenty pages of typewritten matter.

PRICE

of Blue Prints, together with a complete set of typewritten specifications.

ONLY TWELVE DOLLARS

We mail plans and specifications the same day order is received.

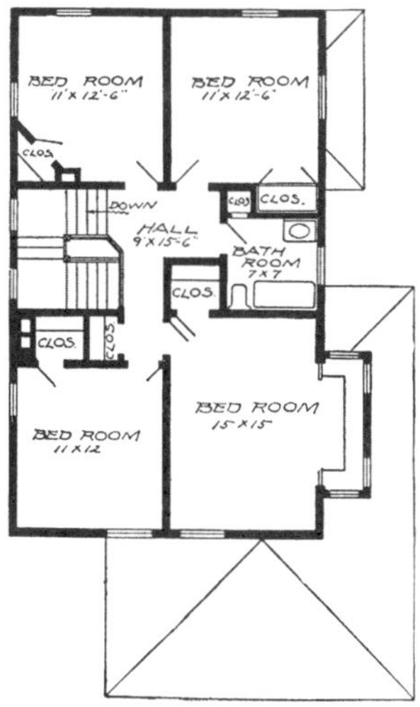

Second Floor Plan

DESIGN NUMBER 6017

Size: width, 22 feet; length, 34 feet, exclusive of porches

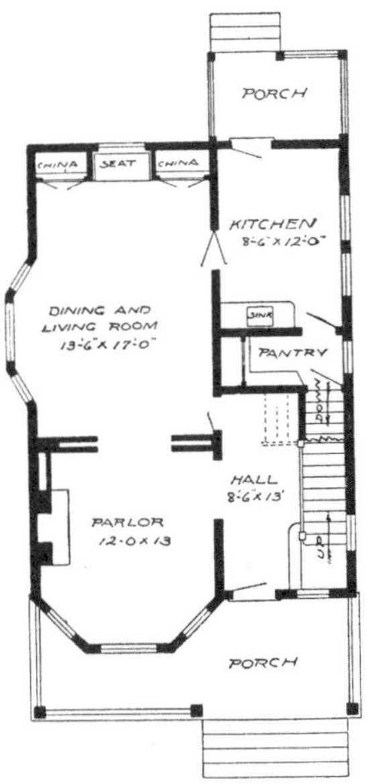

First Floor Plan

BLUE PRINTS consist of basement plan; roof plan; first and second floor plans; front, rear, two side elevations; wall sections and all necessary interior details. Specifications consist of about twenty pages of typewritten matter.

PRICE

of Blue Prints, together with a complete set of typewritten specifications

ONLY TEN DOLLARS

We mail plans and specifications the same day order is received.

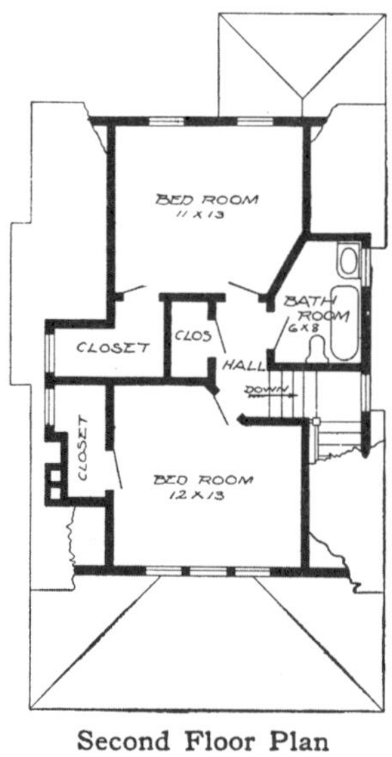

Second Floor Plan

Design No. 7033

Size: Width, 27 feet 6 inches; Length, 32 feet 6 inches, exclusive of porch

PRICE

of Blue Prints, together with a complete set of typewritten specifications

ONLY TWELVE DOLLARS

We mail Plans and Specifications the same day order is received.

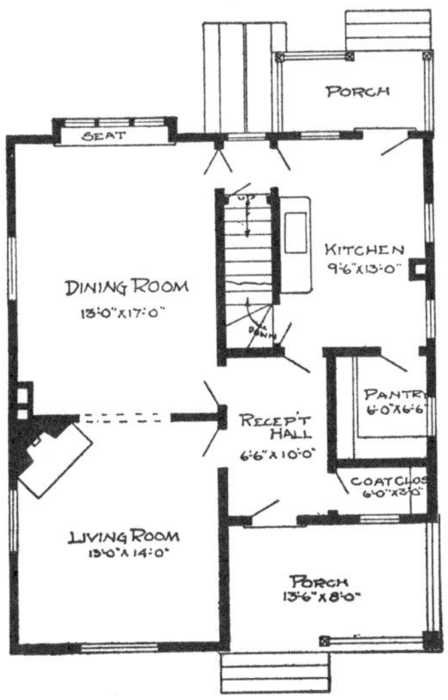

First Floor Plan

Blue prints consist of basement plan; roof plan first and second floor plans; front, rear, two side elevations; wall sections and all necessary interior details. Specifications consist of about twenty pages of typewritten matter.

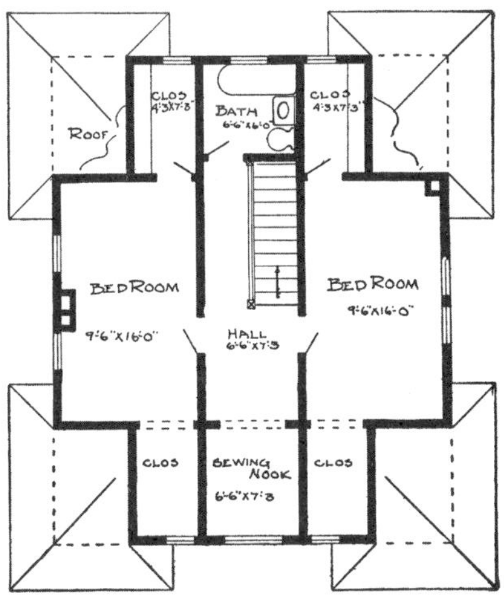

Second Floor Plan

Design No. 7031

Size: Width, 27 feet; Length, 35 feet, exclusive of porches

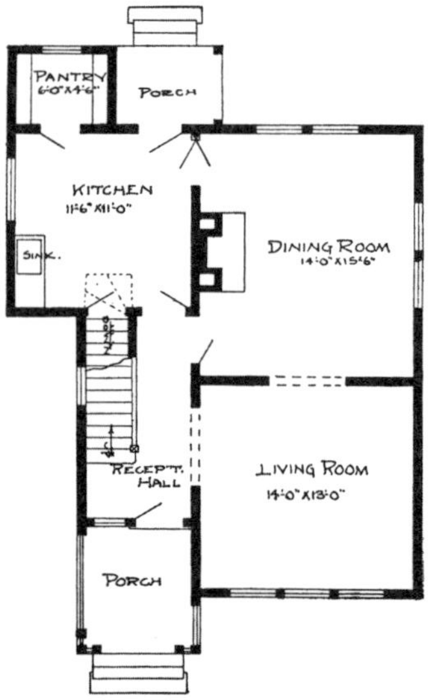

First Floor Plan

Blue prints consist of cellar and foundation plan; roof plan; first and second floor plans; front, rear, two side elevations; wall sections and all necessary interior details. Specifications consist of about twenty pages of typewritten matter.

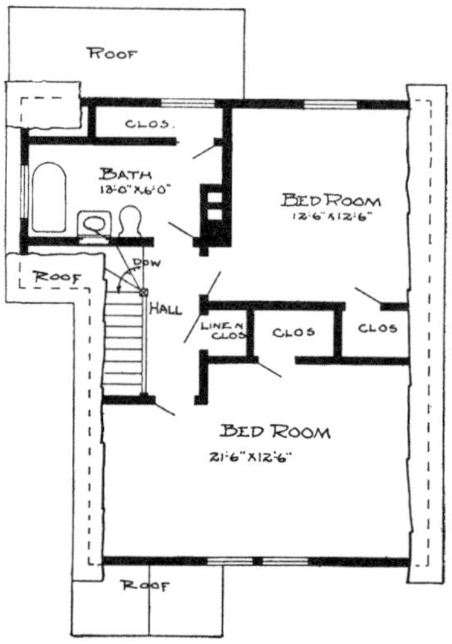

Second Floor Plan

PRICE

of Blue Prints, together with a complete set of typewritten specifications

ONLY TWEL VE DOLLARS

We mail Plans and Specifications the same day order is received.

Design No. 9072

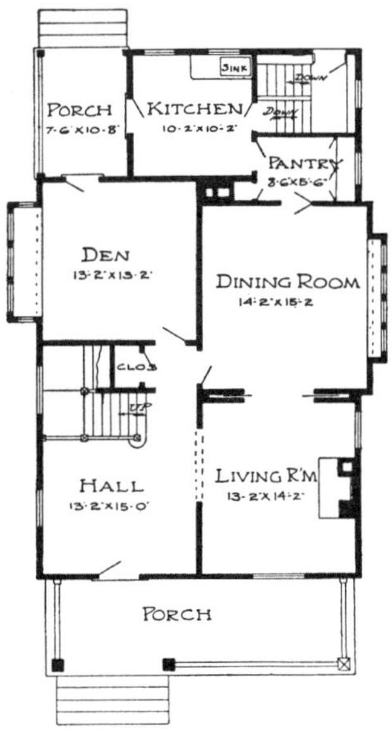

First Floor Plan.

The arrangement of this House is as follows:

FIRST FLOOR.

Reception Hall, 13 feet 2 inches by 15 feet.
Living Room, 13 feet 2 inches by 14 feet 2 inches.
Dining Room, 14 feet 2 inches by 15 feet 2 inches.
Kitchen, 10 feet 2 inches by 10 feet 2 inches.
Den, 13 feet 2 inches by 13 feet 2 inches.
Pantry, Front and Rear Porches.

SECOND FLOOR.

Bedroom, 13 feet 2 inches by 10 feet 10 inches.
Bedroom, 13 feet 2 inches by 14 feet 10 inches.
Bedroom, 13 feet 2 inches by 13 feet 2 inches.
Bathroom, 9 feet 2 inches by 11 feet.
5 Ciosets.

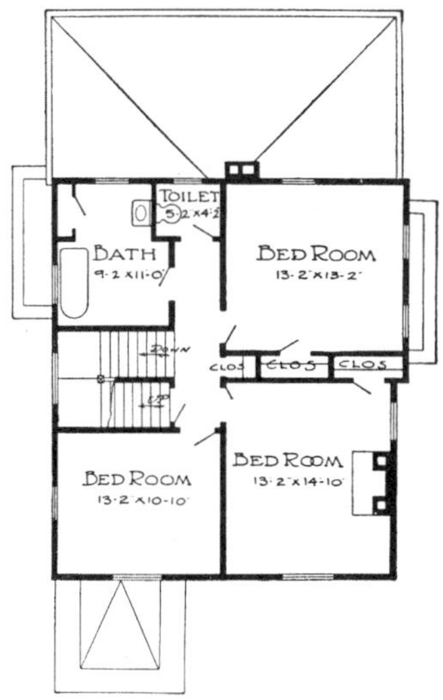

Second Floor Plan.

This Building is 32 feet in width; 43 feet in length.

Price of Complete Working Plans and Specifications **$12.00**

The Blue Printed Working Plans for this House consist of basement plan; roof plan; first and second floor plans; front, right, left and rear elevations; wall sections and all necessary details.

The Typewritten Specifications contain all the necessary information for the proper construction of the House.

Design No. 9071

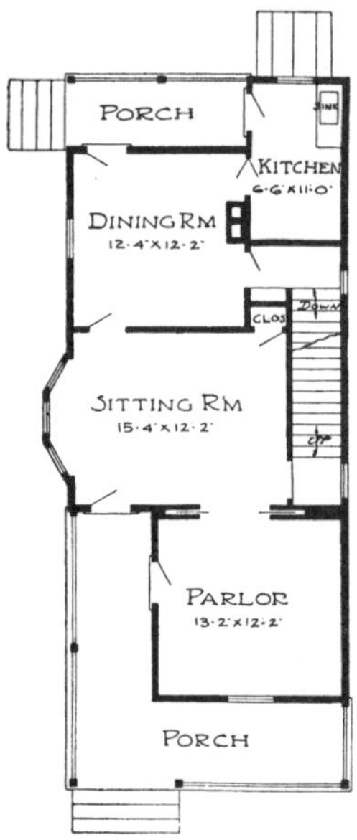

First Floor Plan.

The arrangement of this House is as follows:

FIRST FLOOR.

Parlor, 13 feet 2 inches by 12 feet 2 inches.
Sitting Room, 15 feet 4 inches by 12 feet 2 inches.
Dining Room, 12 feet 4 inches by 12 feet 2 inches.
Kitchen, 6 feet 6 inches by 11 feet.
Front and Rear Porches.

SECOND FLOOR.

Bedroom, 13 feet 2 inches by 11 feet 8 inches.
Bedroom, 11 feet by 10 feet 2 inches.
Bedroom, 11 feet by 7 feet 10 inches.
Bedroom, 11 feet 10 inches by 8 feet 4 inches.
Bathroom, 7 feet by 8 feet 4 inches.
5 Closets.

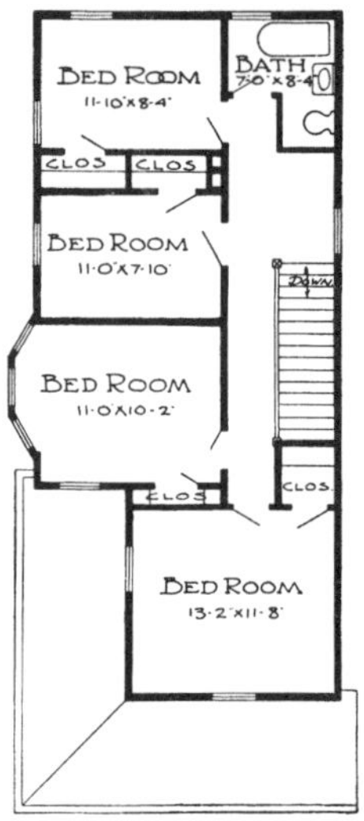

Second Floor Plan.

This Building is 22 feet in width; 43 feet 6 inches in length.

Price of Complete Working Plans and Specifications.. $12.00

The Blue Printed Working Plans for this House consist of basement plan; first and second floor plans, front, right, left and rear elevations; wall sections and all necessary details.

The Typewritten Specifications contain all the necessary information for the proper construction of the House.

DESIGN NUMBER 6004

Size: Width, 26 feet, 5 inches; length, 25 feet, 6 inches exclusive of porches

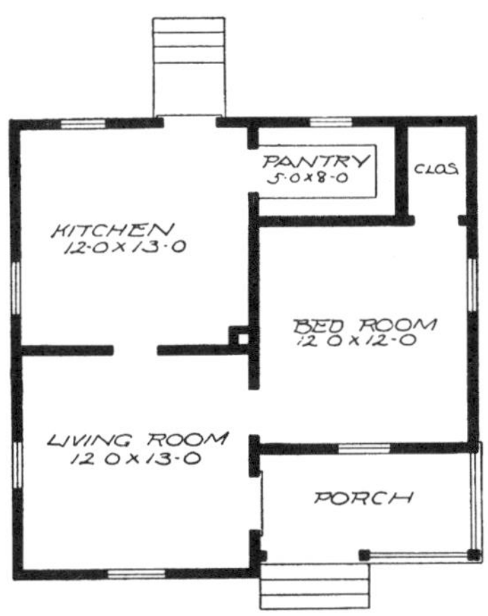

Floor Plan

BLUE PRINTS consist of foundation plan; floor plan; front, rear, two side elevations; wall sections and all necessary interior details. Specifications consist of about fifteen pages of typewritten matter.

PRICE

of Blue Prints, together with a complete set of typewritten specifications

ONLY EIGHT DOLLARS

We mail plans and specifications the same day order is received.

DESIGN NUMBER 6038

Size: width, 36 feet; length, 51 feet 6 inches, exclusive of porches

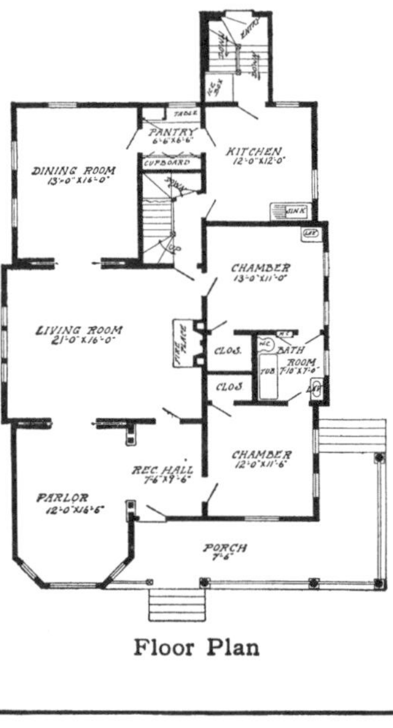

Floor Plan

BLUE PRINTS consist of basement plan; roof plan; floor plan; front, rear, two side elevations; wall sections and all necessary interior details. Specifications consist of about fifteen pages of typewritten matter.

PRICE

of Blue Prints, together with a complete set of typewritten specifications

ONLY TEN DOLLARS

We mail plans and specifications the same day order is received.

Design No. 7082

Size: Width, 29 feet 6 inches; Length, 44 feet, exclusive of porches

PRICE

of Blue Prints, together with a complete set of typewritten specifications

ONLY FIFTEEN DOLLARS

We mail Plan; and Specifications the same day order is received.

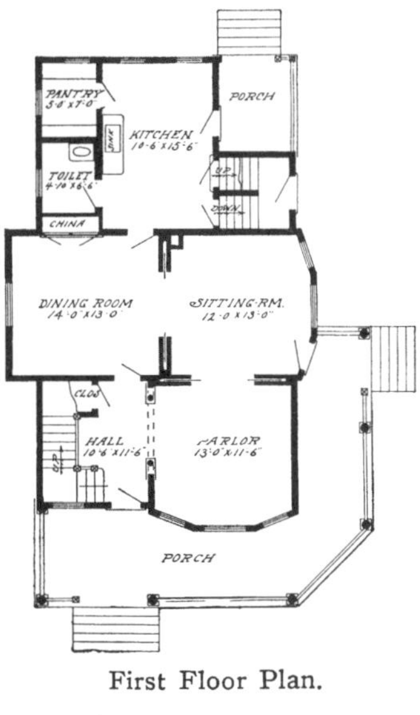

First Floor Plan.

Blue prints consist of basement plan; roof plan; first and second floor plans; front, rear, two side elevations; wall sections and all necessary interior details. Specifications consist of about twenty pages of typewritten matter.

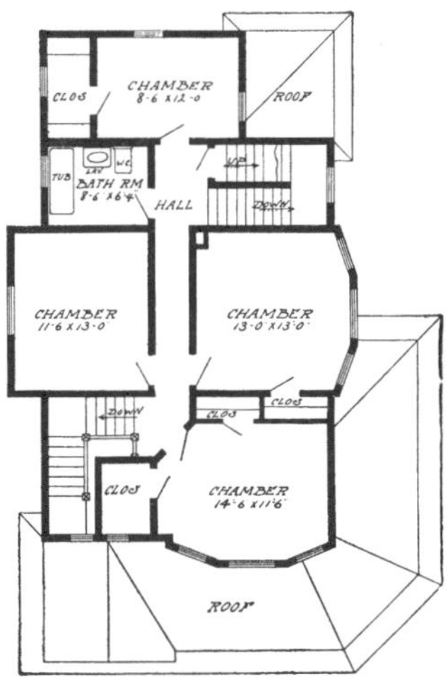

Second Floor Plan

Design No. 7053

Size: Width, 33 feet 6 inches: Length, 47 feet 6 inches, exclusive of porches

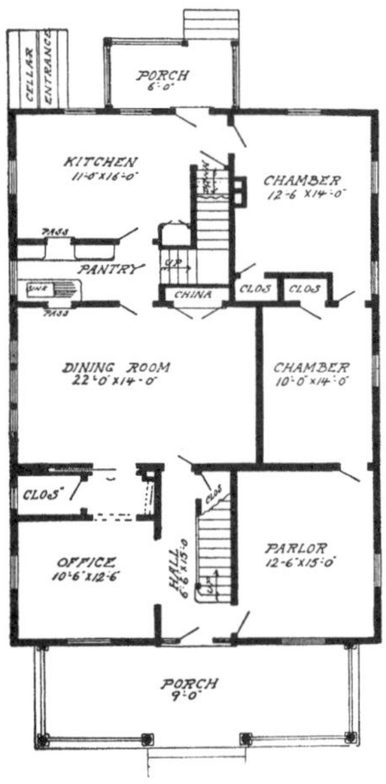

First Floor Plan.

Blue prints consist of basement plan; first and second floor plans; front, rear, two side elevations; wall sections and all necessary interior details. Specifications consist of of about twenty pages of typewritten matter.

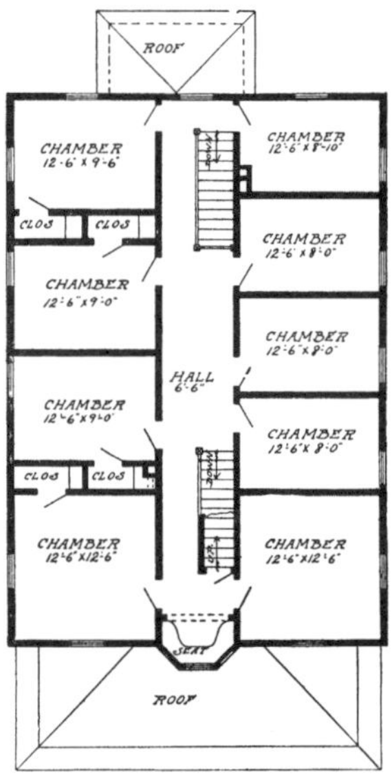

Second Floor Plan

PRICE

of Blue Prints, together with a complete set of typewritten specifications

ONLY FIFTEEN DOLLARS

We mail Plans and Specifications the same day order is received.

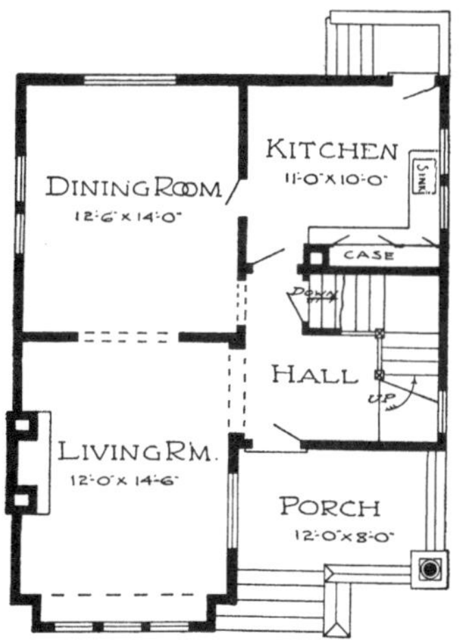

First Floor Plan.

Design No. 9059

The arrangement of this House is as follows:

FIRST FLOOR.

Reception Hall, 11 feet by 6 feet.
Living Room, 12 feet by 14 feet 6 inches.
Dining Room, 12 feet 6 inches by 14 feet.
Kitchen, 11 feet by 10 feet.
Front and Rear Porches.

SECOND FLOOR.

Bedroom, 12 feet by 14 feet 6 inches.
Bedroom, 16 feet by 10 feet 6 inches.
Bathroom, 8 feet by 9 feet 6 inches.
2 Closets.

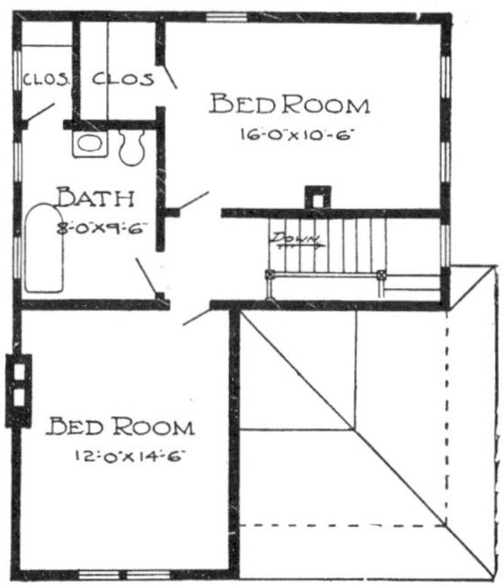

Second Floor Plan.

This Building is 25 feet in width; 31 feet 6 inches in length.

Price of Complete Working Plans and Specifications.. **$12.00**

The Blue Printed Working Plans for this House consist of basement plan; first and second floor plans; front, right, left and rear elevations; wall sections and all necessary details.

The Typewritten Specifications contain all the necessary information for the proper construction of the House,

Design No. 9073

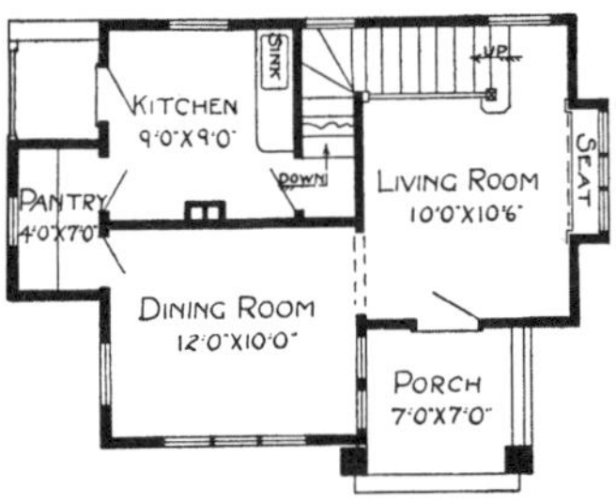

First Floor Plan.

The arrangement of this House is as follows:

FIRST FLOOR.

Living Room, 10 feet by 10 feet 6 inches.
Dining Room, 12 feet by 10 feet.
Kitchen, 9 feet by 9 feet.
Pantry, Front and Rear Porches.

SECOND FLOOR.

Bedroom, 10 feet by 10 feet 6 inches.
Bedroom, 12 feet by 10 feet.
Bathroom, 9 feet by 5 feet 6 inches.
2 Closets.

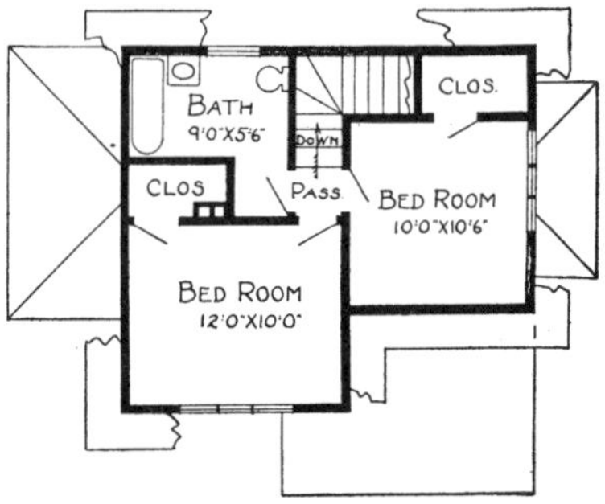

Second Floor Plan.

This Building is 29 feet 6 inches in width; 20 feet 6 inches in length.

Price of Complete Working Plans and Specifications.. **$12.00**

The Blue Printed Working Plans for this House consist of basement plan; first and second floor plans; front, right, left and rear elevations; wall sections and all necessary details.

The Typewritten Specifications contain all the necessary information for the proper construction of the House,

DESIGN NUMBER 6085

Size: width, 26 feet; length, 40 feet, exclusive of porches

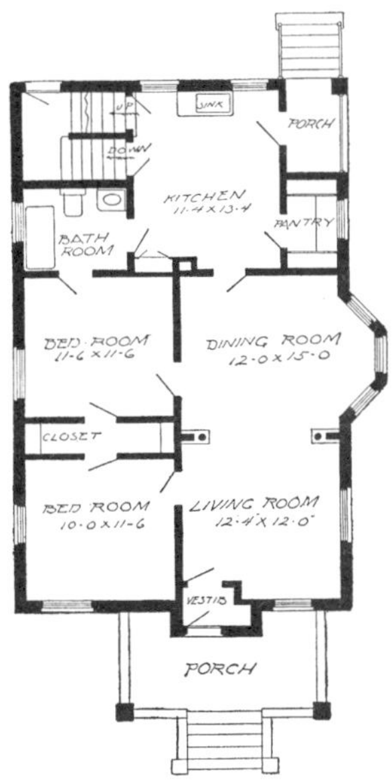

Floor Plan

BLUE PRINTS consist of basement plan; floor plan; front, rear, two side elevations; wall sections and all necessary interior details. Specifications consist of about fifteen pages of typewritten matter.

PRICE

of Blue Prints, together with a complete set of typewritten specifications

ONLY TEN DOLLARS

We mail plans and specifications the same day order is received.

DESIGN NUMBER 6087

Size: width, 29 feet 10 inches; length, 40 feet 10 inches, exclusive of porches

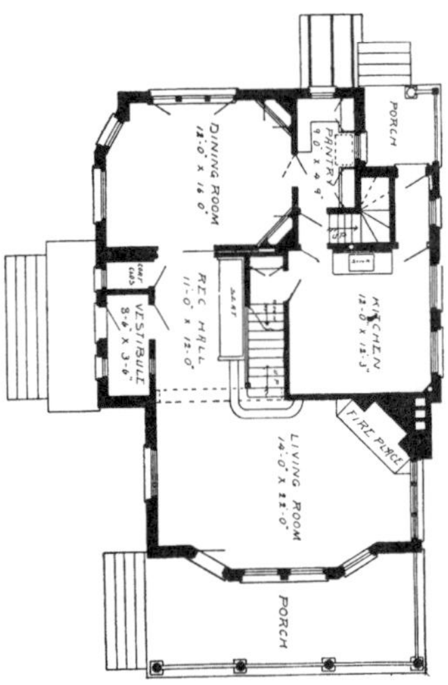

First Floor Plan

BLUE PRINTS consist of cellar and foundation plan; roof plan; first and second floor plans; front, rear, two side elevations; wall sections and all necessary interior details. Specifications consist of about twenty pages of typewritten matter.

PRICE

of Blue Prints, together with a complete set of typewritten specifications

ONLY FIFTEEN DOLLARS

We mail plans and specifications the same day order is received.

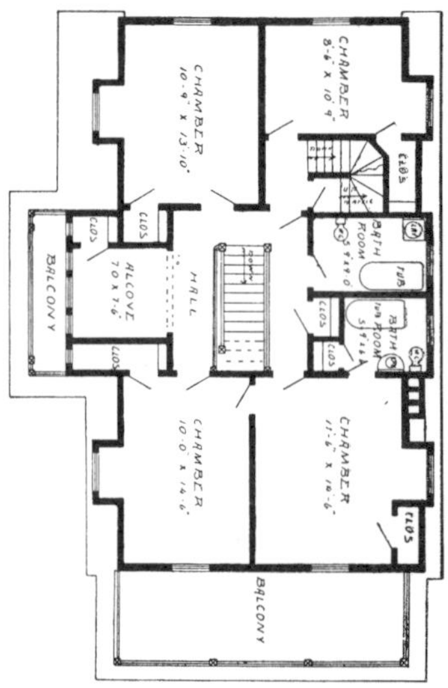

Second Floor Plan

DESIGN NUMBER 6090

Size: width, 32 feet; length, 40 feet 6 inches, exclusive of porches

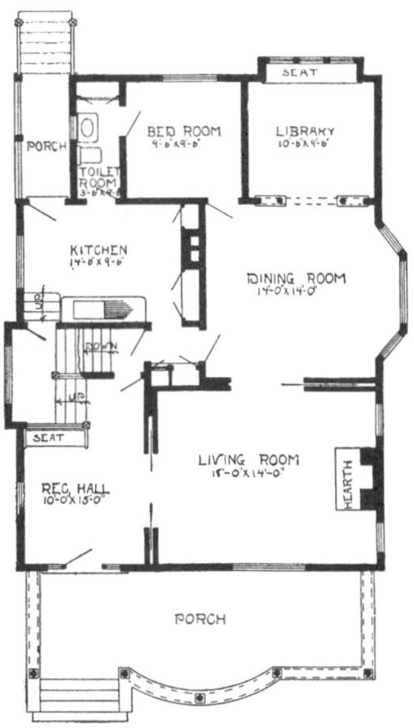

First Floor Plan

BLUE PRINTS consist of cellar and foundation plan; roof plan; first and second floor plans; front, rear, two side elevations; wall sections and all necessary interior details. Specifications consist of about twenty pages of typewritten matter.

PRICE

of Blue Prints, together with a complete set of typewritten specifications

ONLY FIFTEEN DOLLARS

We mail plans and specifications the same day order is received.

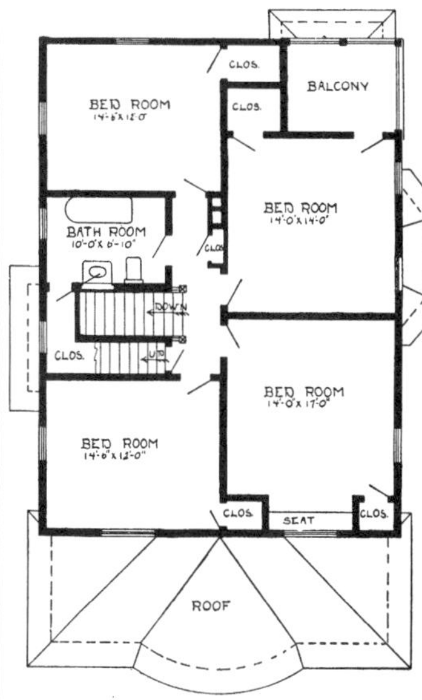

Second Floor Plan

DESIGN NUMBER 6091

Size: width, 35 feet; length, 48 feet, exclusive of porches

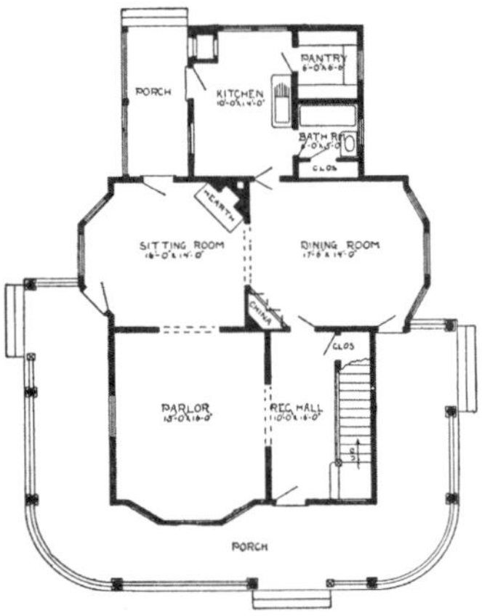

First Floor Plan

BLUE PRINTS consist of cellar and foundation plan; roof plan; first and second floor plans; front, two side elevations; wall sections and all necessary interior details. Specifications consist of about twenty pages of typewritten matter.

PRICE

of Blue Prints, toge r with a complete set of typewritten specifications

ONLY FIFTEEN DOLLARS

We mail plans and specifications the same day order is received.

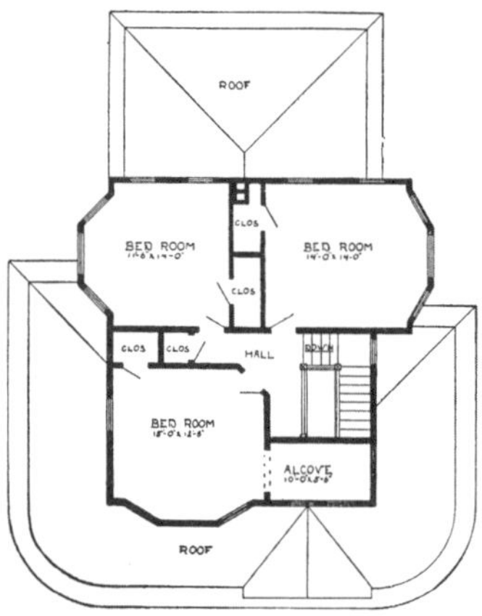

Second Floor Plan

ESTIMATING THE COST

It is impossible for us to make an exact estimate of the cost of any of the houses illustrated in this book and have that price hold good in every section of the country. Should we claim to be able to do so, a child would know that our statement was false. The price of labor and material varies so in the different sections that it is absolutely necessary for us to put a price on these houses that is elastic.

The houses shown on these pages are modern, practical and attractive and are the best that the highest architectural skill was able to produce. Every requirement is taken into consideration. Economy in the use of material also was kept constantly in mind.

If there is any house in this book that is pleasing to you, and which you would like to erect, we would advise consultation with your responsible contractor and material dealer. They will go into the matter thoroughly with you on the price proposition and it will not be necessary for you to run any risk whatever. They will be honest and fair with you as to the estimated cost of the building and the price will depend upon the amount of work to be done, the cost of material and the labor conditions. You are well aware that there are certain seasons of the year when you will be able to build a structure for from ten to fifteen per cent less than at other times. You will also experience a fluctuation in the price of building materials, over which we have no control, and you are no doubt well aware that even the finish in the house will increase or decrease the price considerably.

The subject of estimated cost is one which has been discussed at great length by everyone who has done any building, and we have come to the conclusion that the only way we can estimate the cost of the houses we illustrate is, to put a price on them that is attractive and then advise our customers to consult with their reliable dealers and responsible contractors before beginning the work. They being on the on the ground are familiar with local conditions and the only people in position to make you an absolutely correct price.

Never attempt to build without plans and specifications. They prevent mistakes and settle all disputes which may arise. Our plans and specifications can also be made the basis of contract. Start right, know exactly what you are going to do, and then you will find building a home a very pleasant task.

OUR GUARANTEE

There are many who feel that on account of the very low price at which we sell plans and specifications that the plans are of a cheap variety. We wish to assure you that you run no risk whatever. If, upon receipt of the plans, you do not find them exactly as represented, if you do not think them complete and accurate in every respect, if you do not find them as well prepared as those furnished by any architect in the United States, or any that you have ever seen, we will immediately refund your money upon return of the plans in good condition. All of the plans we furnish have been prepared by licensed architects standing at the head of their profession and the standard of their work is of the very highest.